NEW ENCYCLOPEDIA OF

PAPER-FOLDING DESIGNS

Easy-to-Understand Ways of Folding Printed Matter

≪折り方大全集≫カタログ・DM編

P·I·E BOOKS

NEW ENCYCLOPEDIA OF **PAPER-FOLDING DESIGNS**
Easy-to-Understand Ways of Folding Printed Matter

P·I·E BOOKS
2-32-4, Minami Otsuka, Toshima-ku, Tokyo 170-0005 Japan
Tel : 03-5395-4811 Fax : 03-5395-4812
e-mail : sales division : sales@piebooks.com
: editorial division : editor@piebooks.com
http://www.piebooks.com

ISBN4-89444-271-X
Printed in Japan

はじめに

一枚の紙を『折る』ことによって紙のかたちが変わります。ただ一本の折線を入れて『折る』だけで平面の世界から次元の違う世界へと導いてくれるのです。平面とは違う世界――それは『折る』ことから生まれる奥行の世界。その奥行の幅や深さが数学的論理を超えて驚きや面白さ、美しさを呼び、ひとつの魅力になって私たちを惹きつけるのでしょう。

また、『折り』は物をたたむ、はさむなどの機能を備えることもできます。これを発展させると物を入れる、保護する、運ぶなど複合的機能を持つ立体となります。

このようにデザインの表現方法のひとつとして『折り』は重要な役割を持っています。日本古来の折形、例えば花や墨を贈る時に使われた折りのかたちや折り紙など、様式化された折りから、封筒のような特定のサイズに納めるためのたたむ折り、ポップアップ絵本などの飛び出すかたちをつくる折りまで、折りの範囲はかなり広いものです。

本書は好評の前作『折り方デザイン集』に続き、日頃、なにげなく目にしているDMやカードなど身近なデザインの中に表現されている『折り』から、企業の広告物、商品のカタログの『折り』まで、幅広い作例を紹介しています。『折り』の機能を活かし、さらに美しくビジュアル表現されたこれらの作品は、相乗効果を得て、より強く人の意識の中に入りこんできます。技巧的に先走らないバランス感覚が完成度を高くしているのです。本書では、『折り』の構造をわかりやすくするために、折りの分類と展開図（CD-ROM付）をつけました。日頃の創作作業に活用され、表現の幅を広くしていただけたら幸いです。

最後に、本書への作品を出品していただいた皆様に心よりお礼を申し上げます。

ピエ・ブックス編集部

Foreword

Fold a sheet of paper and it transforms — a mere single fold takes it from the second to the third dimension. That dimensional shift signifies the depth of the world of paper-folding, a depth and breadth that transcends the logic of mathematics, that inspires surprise, interest, and beauty, and has universal allure.

Folding also has a functional side. Folding up for storing, containing, protecting, transporting — it creates multi-function dimensional objects.

As such, folding performs critical roles both as expressive and functional components of design. Stylized forms of traditional Japanese paper-folding like the forms and types of paper used for wrapping flowers or ink sticks as gifts, folding to fit standardized sizes such as in envelopes, folding to create pop-up pictures for cards and books — the folded realm is wide ranging.

This volume presents examples of folding in common design applications such as direct-mail and cards. Works that function optimally and make visually aesthetic statements have synergetic effects that make them more interesting, and command greater attention. These are works that not only communicate information but have a power that expands their image upon receipt. They balance aesthetics and craftsmanship to create a high level of finish. And to make the structure of folding more readily understandable, we have classified the folds and included folding diagrams. We hope that this book will inspire future creative work in a wide range of applications.

Lastly, we would like to thank all those who contributed, and granted us permission to publish, the works in this book.

The P·I·E Books Editorial staff

9-FOLDING DESIGNS WORKS

DM & Card ダイレクト・メール＆カード作品

Christmas & New Year Card クリスマス・新年挨拶状

10,13,14,18,21,29,30,60,61,72,73,100,108,120,132,133,136,137,144,145,147,148,165,169,
187,198,210-212,229,232

Greeting Card 挨拶・お祝い状

22,46,81,116,119,126,128,129,138,142,143,164,182,188,189,206

Promotion & Gift Card プロモーション＆ギフト カード

26,75,86,146,152,161,202,230

Invitation Card & DM 招待状＆ダイレクト・メール

12,16,17,27,38,45,48,53,54,56,78-80, 82,84,87,94,96,98,99,
102,104,105,114,115,117,134,135,141,159,160,162,163,166,168,176,185,
186,191,192,196,203,208,214,215,221,224,228

Catalog カタログ類型作品

Catalog/Pamphelt カタログ/パンフレット

15,32,43,45,49,50-52,57,64-70, 76,85,88-90, 95,97,110,111,113,118,121-123,
125,172-175,177,184,194,195,226

Folder 書類・物入れフォルダー

28,44

Book 書籍

33,36,58,62,63,107,140,190,197

Others その他の作品

Visiting Card 名刺

34,35

Others その他

40,41,54,83,92,101,112,124,130,131,155,156,158,170,178,180,201,209,213,
216-218,220,222,223,227

PAPER-FOLDING DESIGNS INDEX

FOLD OVER 重ねる

The paper is scored and folded over.
紙に折り線を入れ、折り重ねる。

FOLD UP たたむ

WRAP 包む

The paper edges are folded in toward the center.
紙の中央に向けて折り寄せる。

LIFT 起こす

The paper edges are folded in toward the center.
紙に切り込みを入れ、その部分を折り返す。

COMPRESS 縮める

Parallel diagonal folds are added to a V-fold to create a step-like compression of the overall form.
紙を二つ折りにする折り線から始まる対の斜めの折り線をいくつか入れ、それらを折り縮める。

PAPER-FOLDING DESIGNS INDEX

INSERT 差し込む
Slits are inserted into one sheet of paper into which a second sheet of paper is inserted allowing it to slide.
紙にスリットを入れ、そこに別紙を差し込み、スライドさせる。

ASSEMBLE 組む
Slits are inserted into multiple sheets of paper and they are assembled into a dimensional form.
紙にスリットを入れ、複数の紙を組んで立体にする。

WARP たわめる
Cuts and holes inserted in a sheet of paper are pulled and twisted to create warping and distortion.
切り込みや穴を空けた紙を、引っ張ったり、ひねったりすることで歪ませたり、たわませたりする。

PROJECT 出っ張る
Perpendicular cuts are inserted in a V-fold, and the portion between the cuts forms an opposing V-fold.
紙を二つ折りにする谷折り線に、切り込み線を入れ、その部分を山折りにして手前に出張らせる。

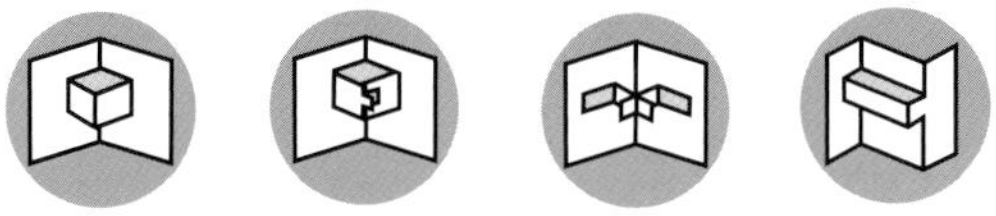

POP UP せり出す
Diagonal folds are added to a V-fold (radiating from the center fold) and the triangle formed projects forward.
紙を二つ折りにする折り線から始まる対の斜めの折り線を折ってできる三角形を手前に迫り出させる。

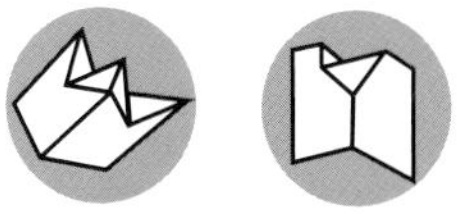

OPEN UP 空ける
The paper opens up into tubular form
紙を筒状にし、立体にする。

PARTICULAR 特殊な折り
Particular fold design that does not fit into one of the above.
上記に分類される折りの種類に属さない特殊な折りの方法。

EDITORIAL NOTES

Ways of Folding
折り方の種類

Credit Format
クレジットフォーマット

The Purpose of the Artwork
作品名 または 作品の使用目的

COUNTRY from which submitted
出品者国名

Year of Completion
制作年度

Creative Staff
制作スタッフ
CL: Client クライアント
CD: Creative Director クリエイティブ ディレクター
AD: Art Director アートディレクター
D: Designer デザイナー
P: Photographer フォトグラファー
I: Illustrator イラスレーター
CW: Copywriter コピーライター
DF: Design Firm デザイン事務所

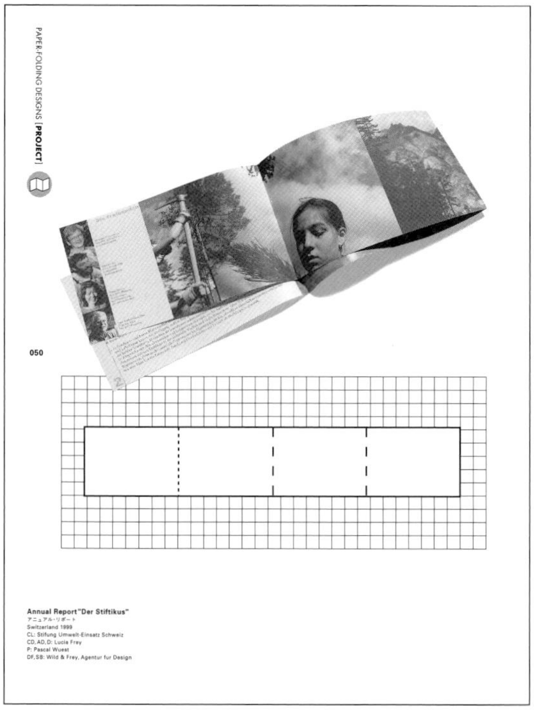

Please note that some credit data has been omitted at the request of the submittor.
提供者の意向によりクレジットデータの一部を記載していないものがあります。

Photos and flat diagrams are provided for reference only, and therefore differ from the actual piece and/or mechanical art.
写真や図版は、あくまでも展開図に対する参考例として掲載しています。
したがって、作品と展開図は実際は異なる場合があります。

Some of the Development Design introduced in the book and CD-ROM are protected by submittor's own copyright and can not be used in any form or by any means, graphic, electronic or mechanical, including photocopying and recording by an information storage and retrieval system, without permission in writting from the submittor.
出品者自身が展開図の著作権を保有しており、使用する場合に使用許可を必要とする作品に関しては、その旨を明記しております。
展開図を営利目的の使用に活用される場合には、出品者に許可をお取りください。

Flat diagrams are based on a 5mm grid.
展開図の方眼は 1マスが 5ミリです。

- - - - - - - - - - - - - -
V-fold line
谷折り

— — — — —
Inverted V-fold line
山折り

———————
Cut-out line
切り取り線

PAPER-FOLDING DESIGNS **FOLDS**

PAPER-FOLDING DESIGNS **FOLDS**

PAPER-FOLDING DESIGNS **FOLDS**

Christmas Card
クリスマス・カード
USA 1998
CL: Aspen Traders
CD, AD, D, I: Bill Gardner
D: Brian Miller
DF, SB: Gardner Design

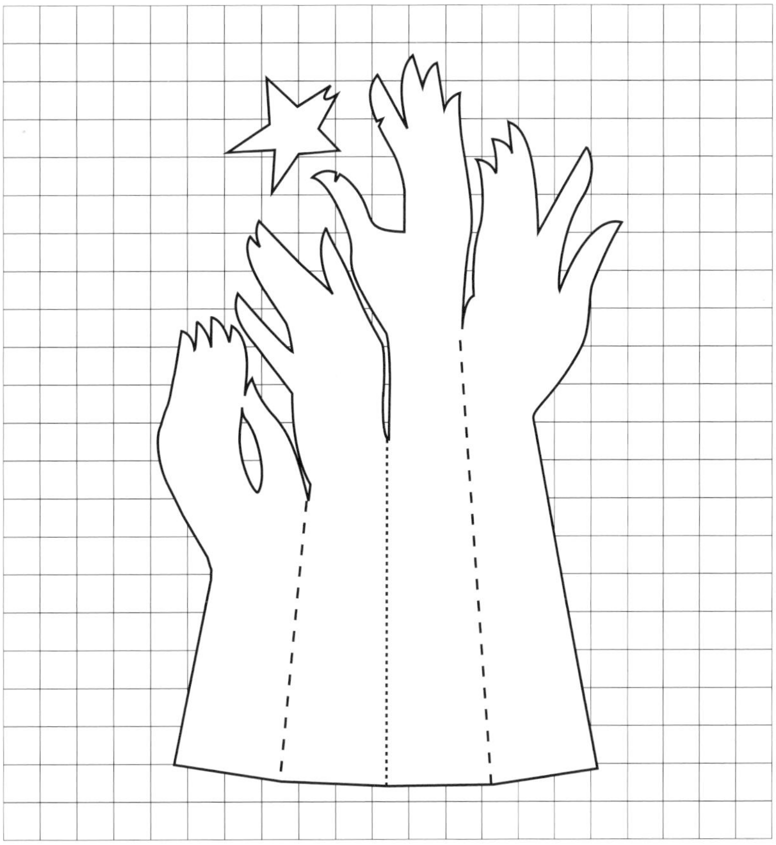

ASPEN
TRADERS

Nienkämper is turning 30.

012

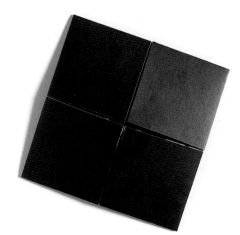

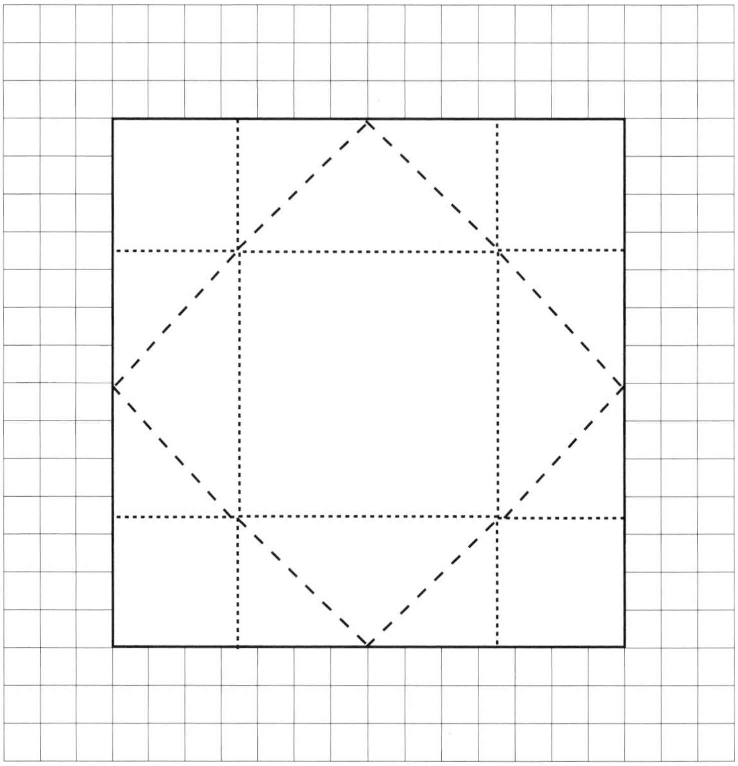

Party Invitation Card
家具会社30周年パーティー案内状
Canada 1998
CL: Nienkamper "Nienkamper 1968-1998"
CD: Claudia Neri
DF, SB: Teikna Design Inc.

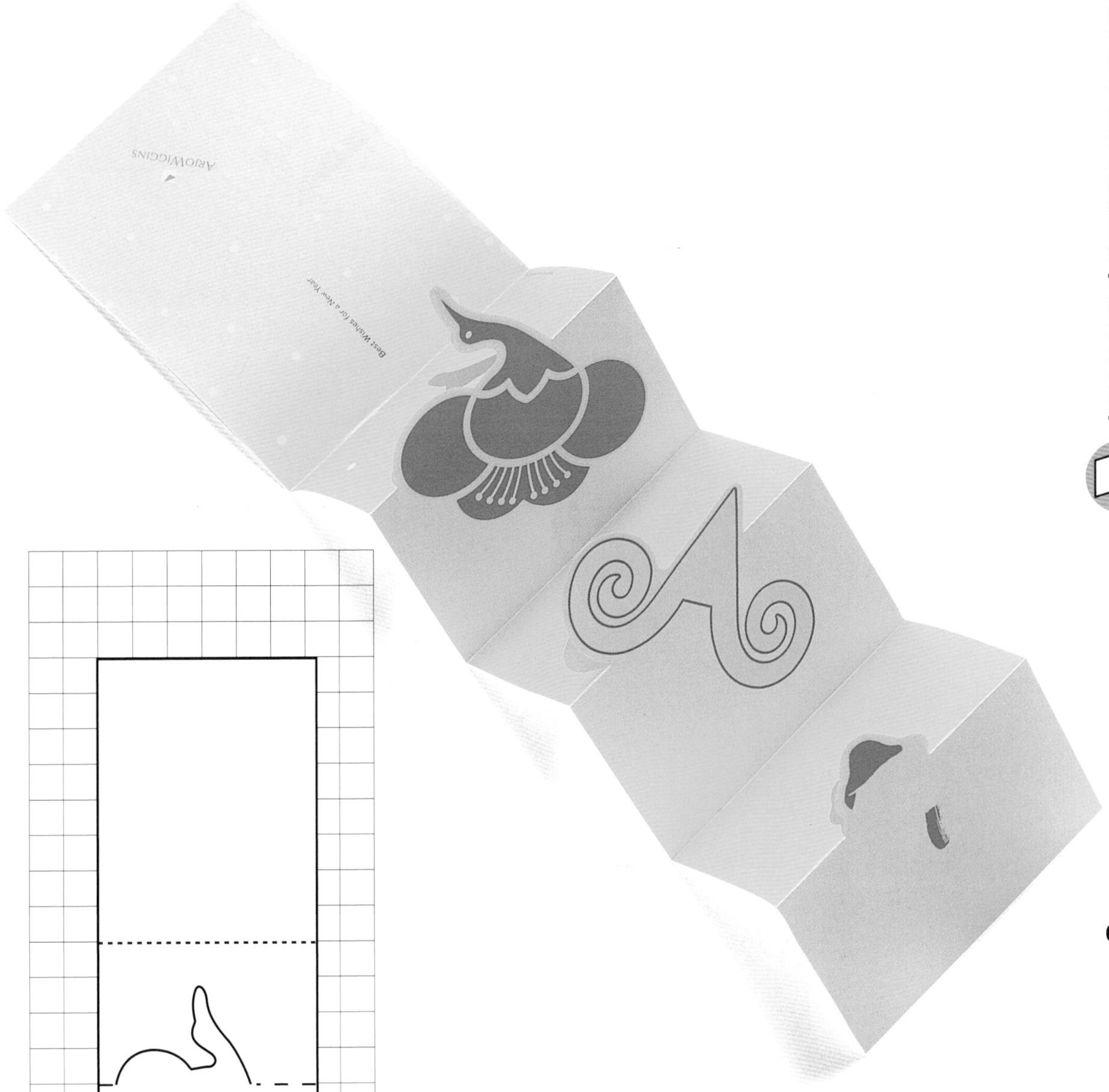

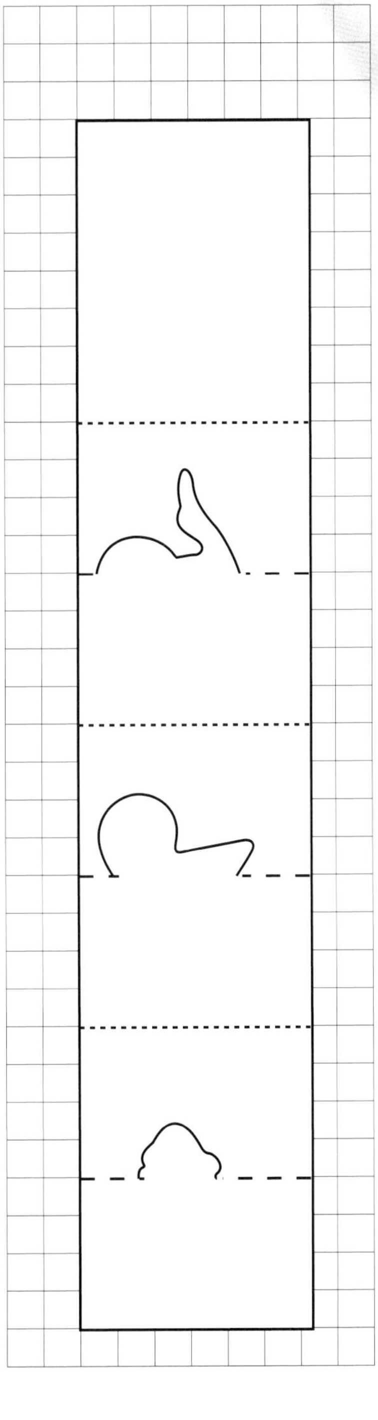

Christmas & New Year Card

クリスマス・新年挨拶状

Japan 2002

CL: Arjo Wiggins Canson KK

AD, D: Akihiko Tsukamoto

I: Frank Viva

DF, SB: Design Club

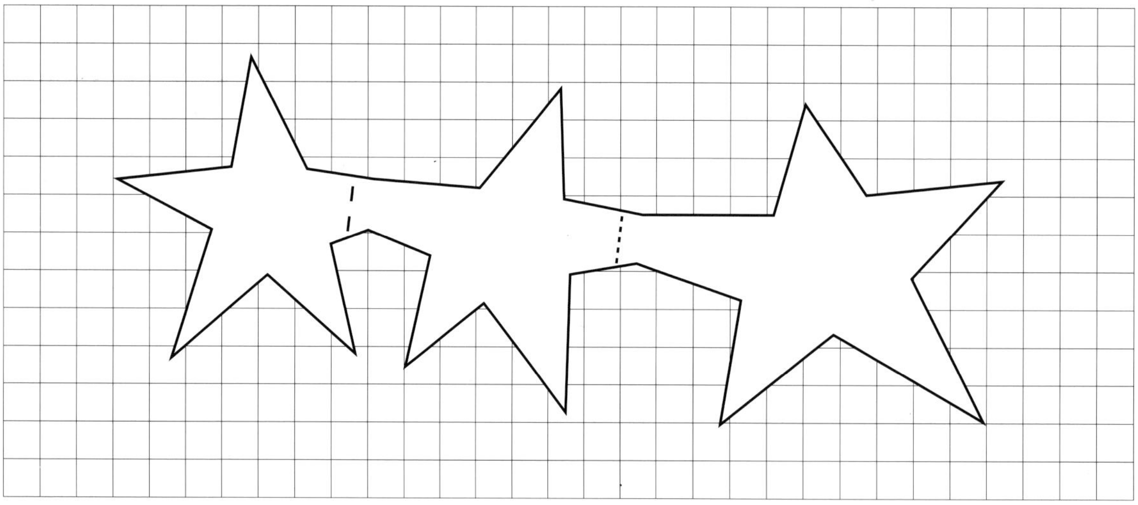

Christmas & New Year Card
クリスマス・新年挨拶状
Japan 1993
CL: Be International Corporation
D: Akihiko Tsukamoto
DF, SB: Design Club

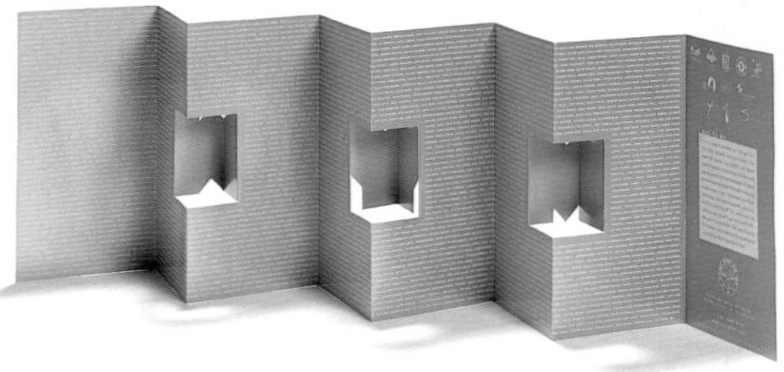

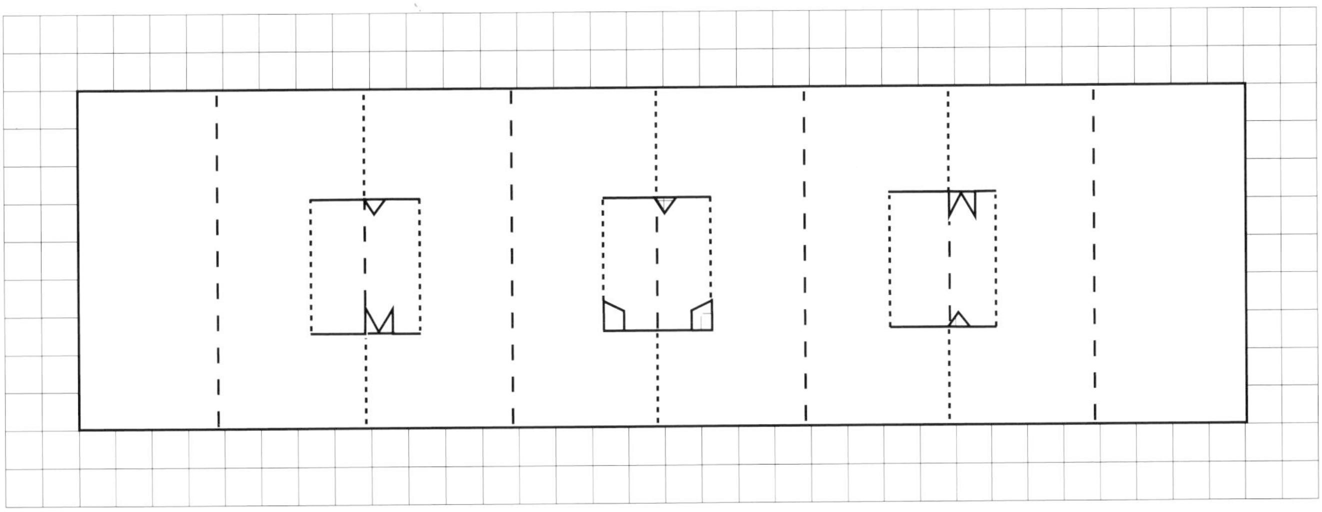

Mini Yo We Camp Brochure

キャンプ場プロモーション用ブローシャー

Canada 2000

CL: Camp Mini Yo We

CD: Dan Wheaton

AD: Ric Riordon

D: Amy Montgomery

P: Steve Grimes

DF, SB: The Riordon Design Group

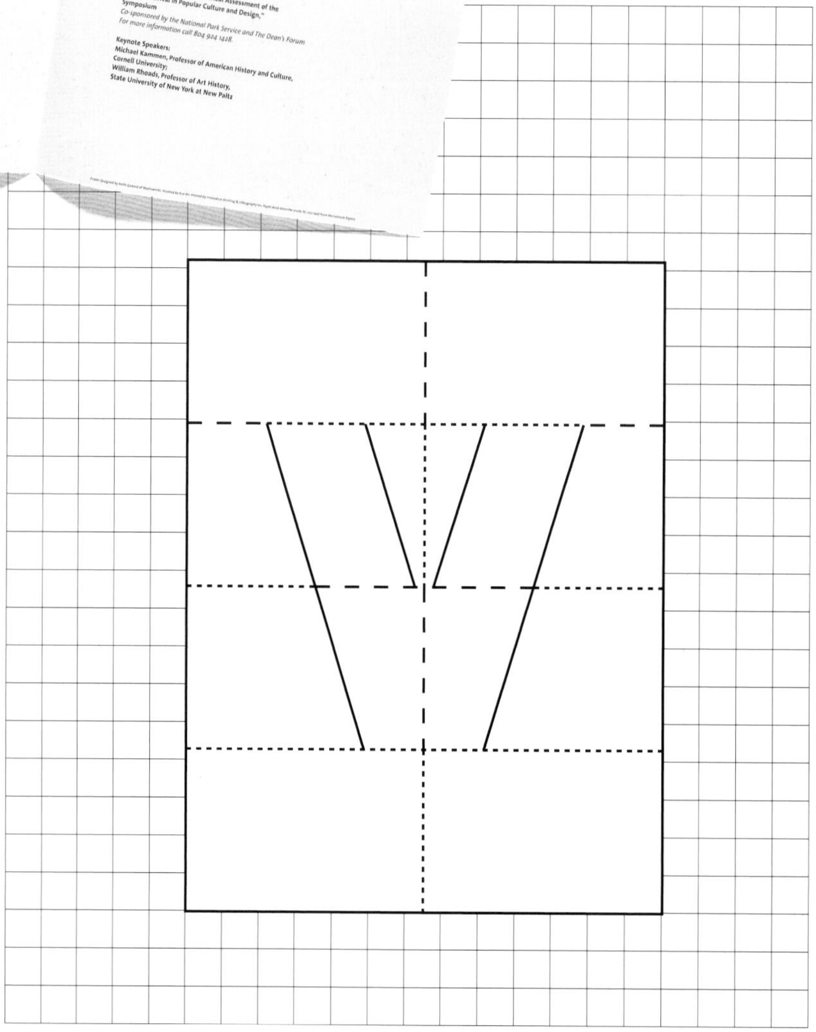

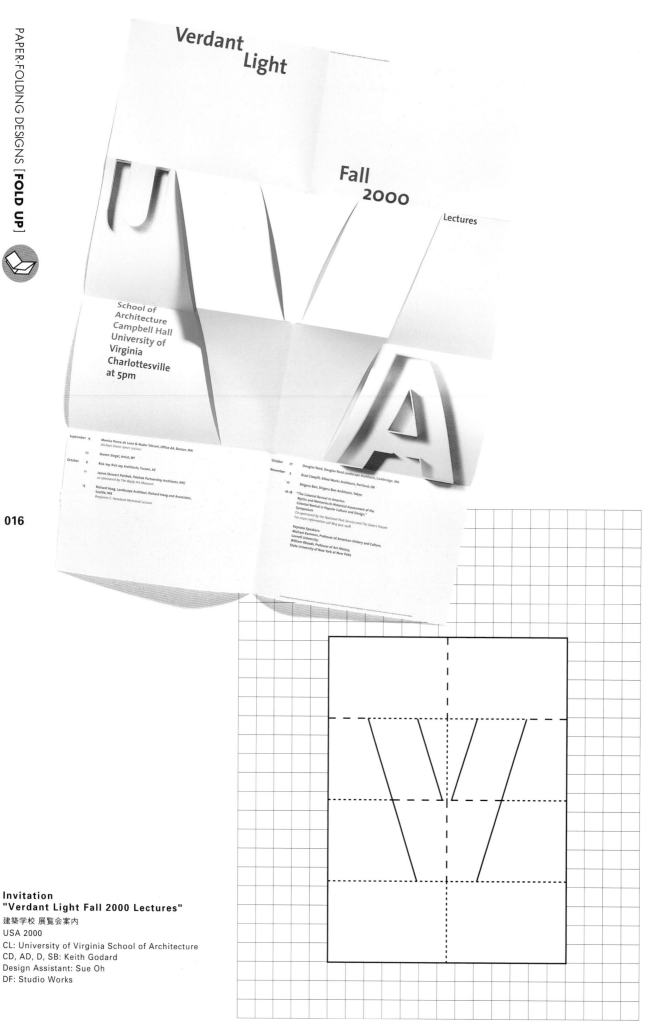

Invitation
"Verdant Light Fall 2000 Lectures"
建築学校 展覧会案内
USA 2000
CL: University of Virginia School of Architecture
CD, AD, D, SB: Keith Godard
Design Assistant: Sue Oh
DF: Studio Works

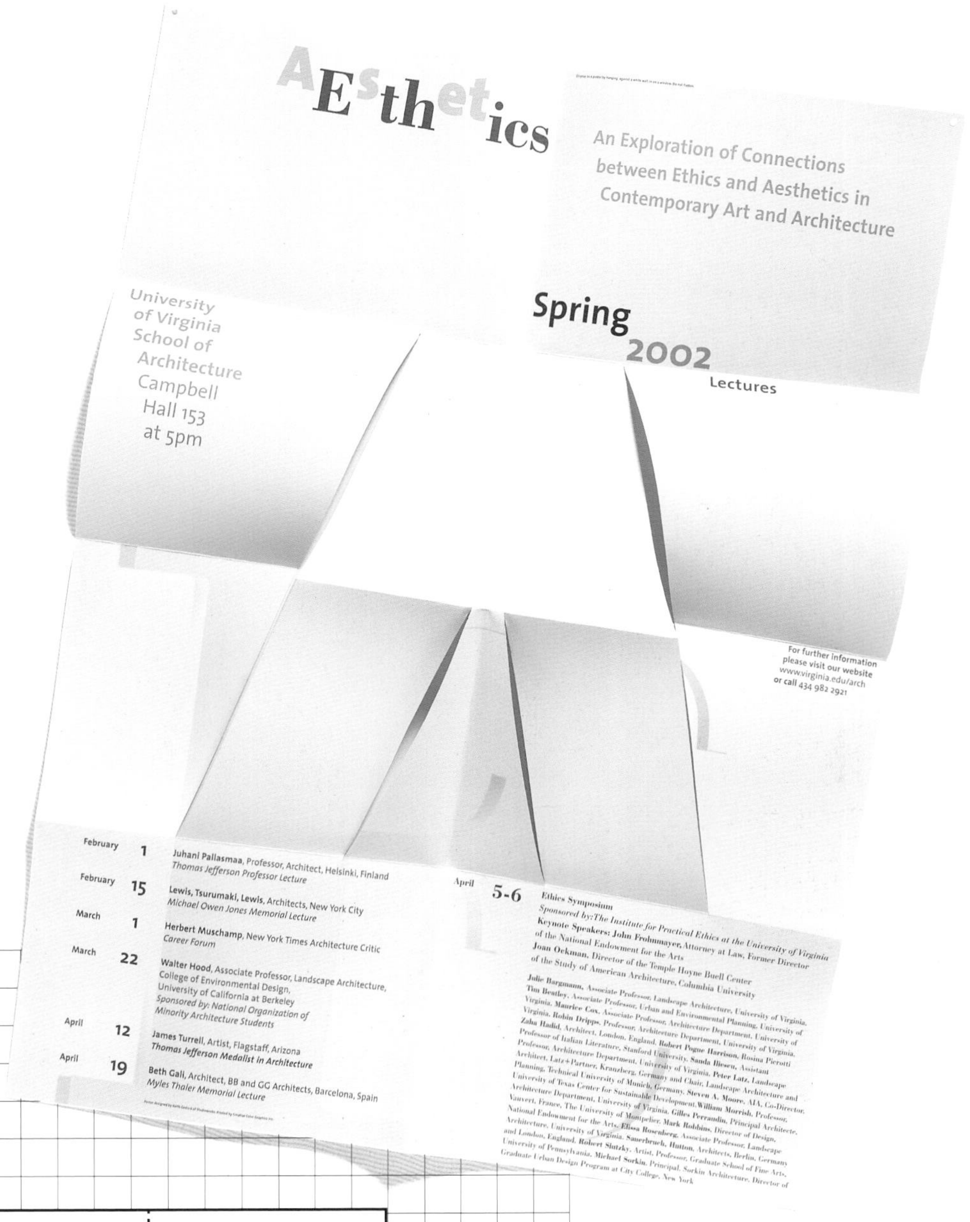
AEsthetics
An Exploration of Connections between Ethics and Aesthetics in Contemporary Art and Architecture
University of Virginia School of Architecture Campbell Hall 153 at 5pm
Spring 2002 Lectures
For further information please visit our website www.virginia.edu/arch or call 434 982 2921
February 1 Juhani Pallasmaa, Professor, Architect, Helsinki, Finland
Thomas Jefferson Professor Lecture
February 15 Lewis, Tsurumaki, Lewis, Architects, New York City
Michael Owen Jones Memorial Lecture
March 1 Herbert Muschamp, New York Times Architecture Critic
Career Forum
March 22 Walter Hood, Associate Professor, Landscape Architecture, College of Environmental Design, University of California at Berkeley
Sponsored by: National Organization of Minority Architecture Students
April 12 James Turrell, Artist, Flagstaff, Arizona
Thomas Jefferson Medalist in Architecture
April 19 Beth Gali, Architect, BB and GG Architects, Barcelona, Spain
Myles Thaler Memorial Lecture
April 5-6 Ethics Symposium
Sponsored by: The Institute for Practical Ethics at the University of Virginia
Keynote Speakers: John Frohnmayer, Attorney at Law, Former Director of the National Endowment for the Arts
Joan Ockman, Director of the Temple Hoyne Buell Center of the Study of American Architecture, Columbia University
Julie Bargmann, Associate Professor, Landscape Architecture, University of Virginia. Tim Beatley, Associate Professor, Urban and Environmental Planning, University of Virginia. Maurice Cox, Associate Professor, Architecture Department, University of Virginia. Robin Dripps, Professor, Architecture Department, University of Virginia. Zaha Hadid, Architect, London, England. Robert Pogue Harrison, Rosina Pierotti Professor of Italian Literature, Stanford University. Sanda Iliescu, Assistant Professor, Architecture Department, University of Virginia. Peter Latz, Landscape Architect, Latz+Partner, Kranzberg, Germany and Chair, Landscape Architecture and Planning, Technical University of Munich, Germany. Steven A. Moore, AIA, Co-Director, University of Texas Center for Sustainable Development. William Morrish, Professor, Architecture Department, University of Virginia. Gilles Perraudin, Principal Architecte, Vauvert, France, The University of Montpelier. Mark Robbins, Director of Design, National Endowment for the Arts. Elissa Rosenberg, Associate Professor, Landscape Architecture, University of Virginia. Sauerbruch, Hutton, Architects, Berlin, Germany and London, England. Robert Slutzky, Artist, Professor, Graduate School of Fine Arts, University of Pennsylvania. Michael Sorkin, Principal, Sorkin Architecture, Director of Graduate Urban Design Program at City College, New York

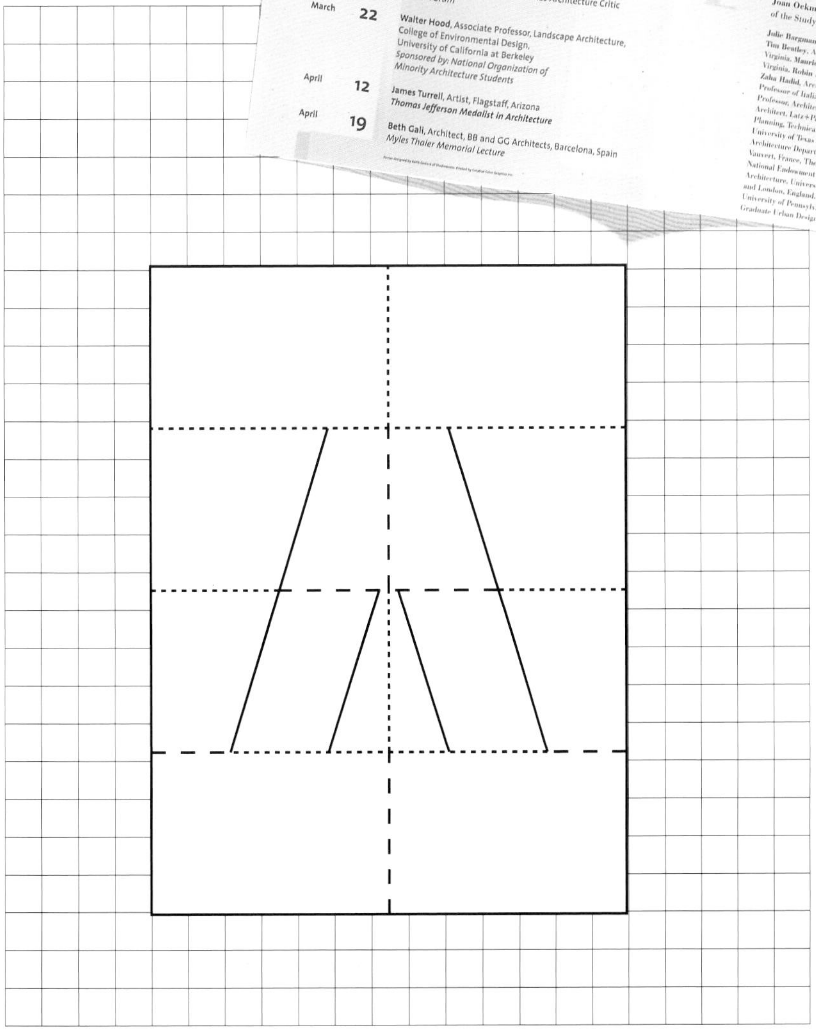

Invitation
"Ethics and Aesthetics Spring 2002 Lectures"

建築学校 展覧会案内

USA 2002

CL: University of Virginia School of Architecture

CD, AD, D, SB: Keith Godard

DF: Studio Works

Christmas Card
クリスマス・カード
USA 2000
CL: Aspen Traders
CD, D: Bill Gardner
AD, D, I: Brian Miller
DF, SB: Gardner Design

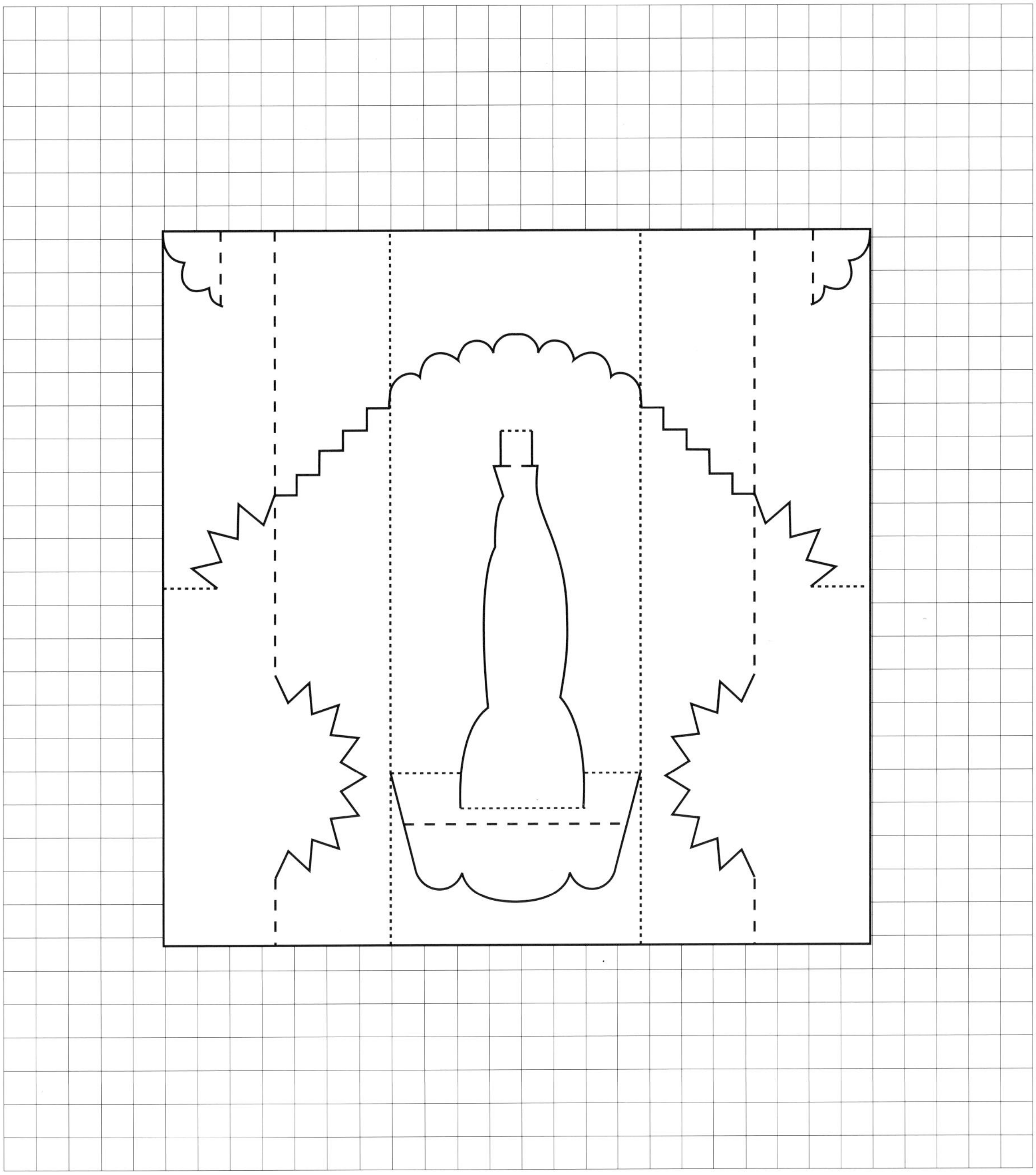

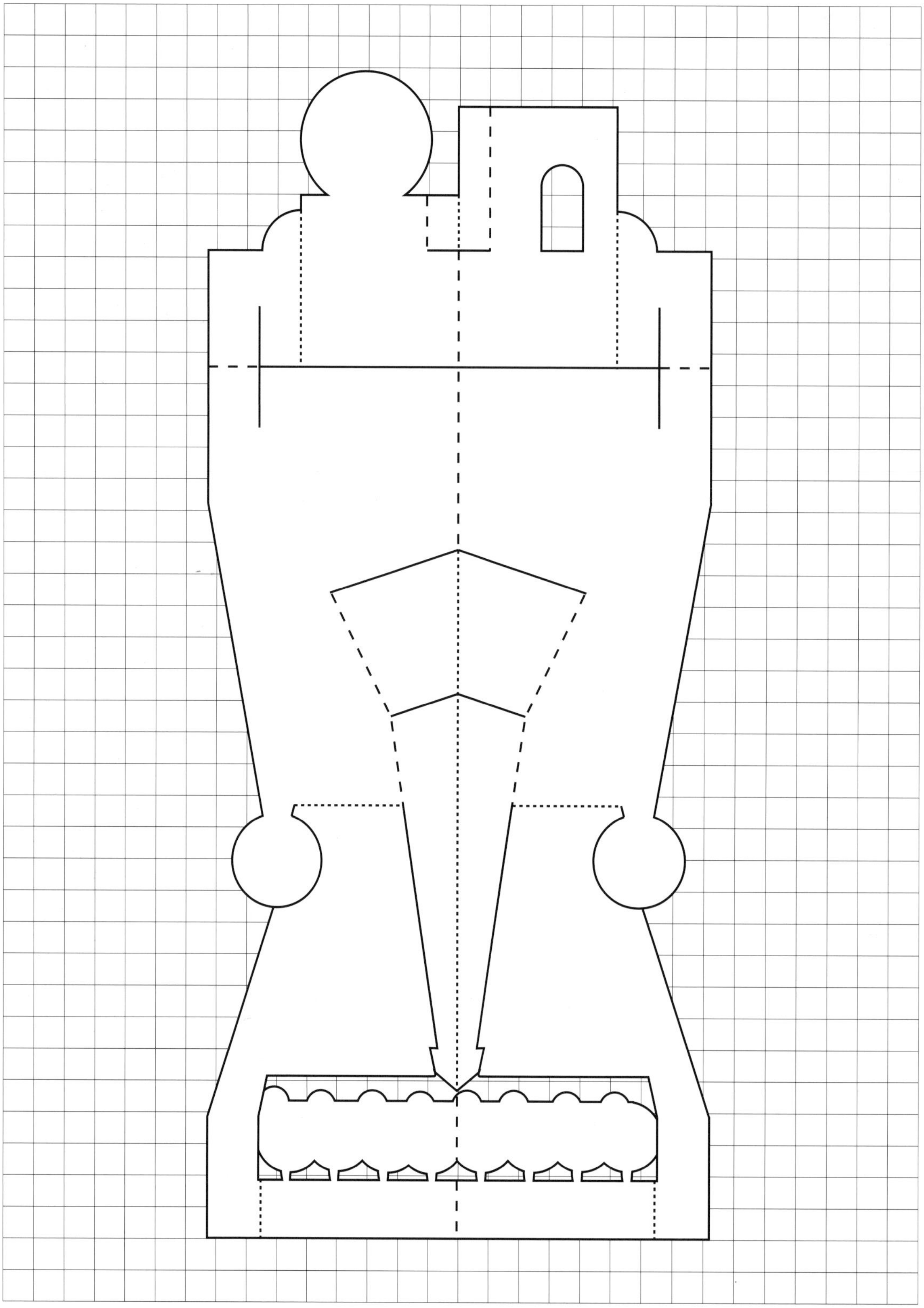

Christmas Card
クリスマス・カード
USA 2001
CL: Aspen Traders
CD: Bill Gardner
AD, D, I: Brian Miller
DF, SB: Gardner Design

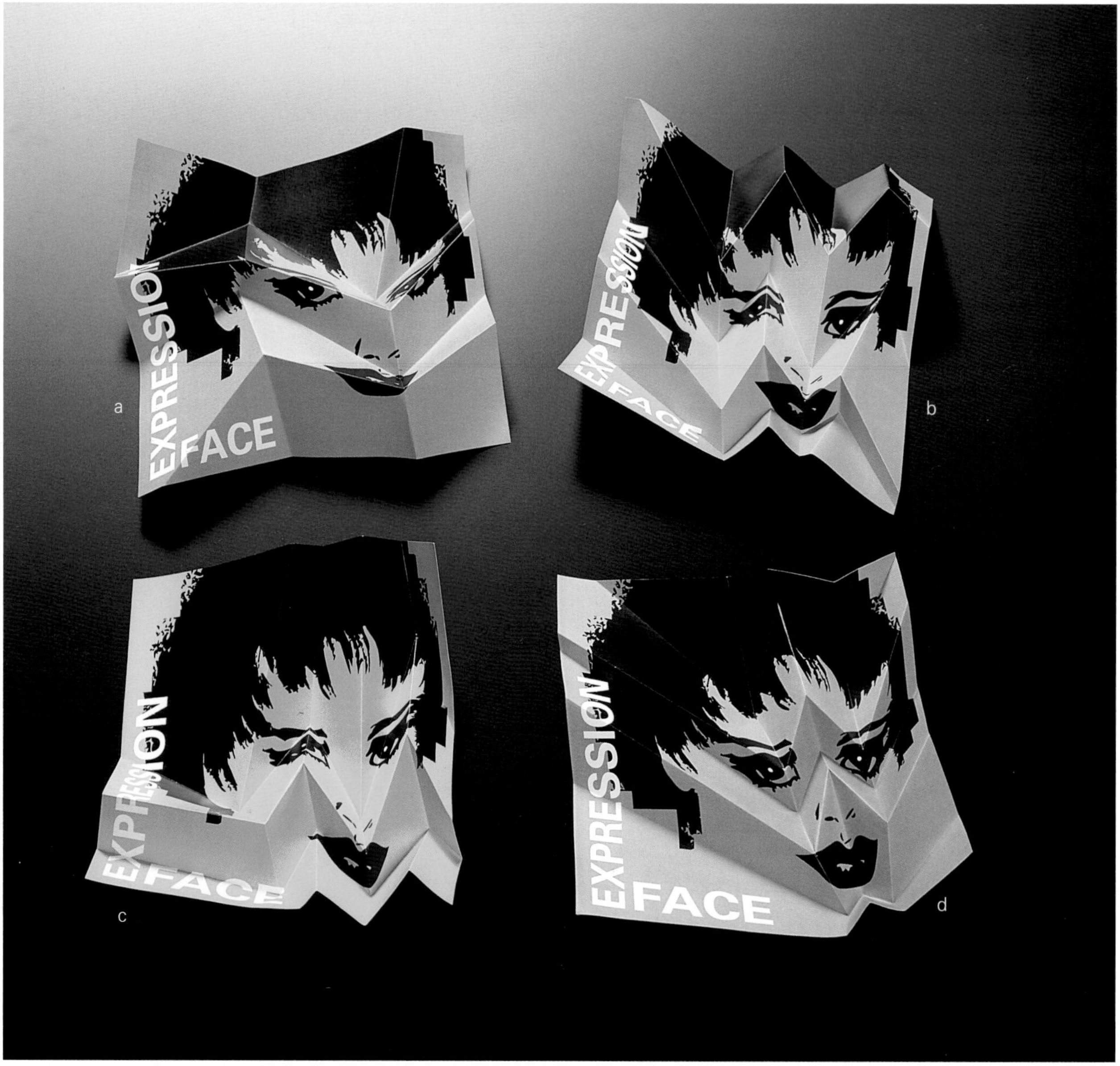

Greeting Card (FACE)
グリーティング・カード（フェイス）
Japan 2002
CL: PLAN Y
AD, D, SB: Miyuki Yoshida
I: Fumiyo Hoshizaki

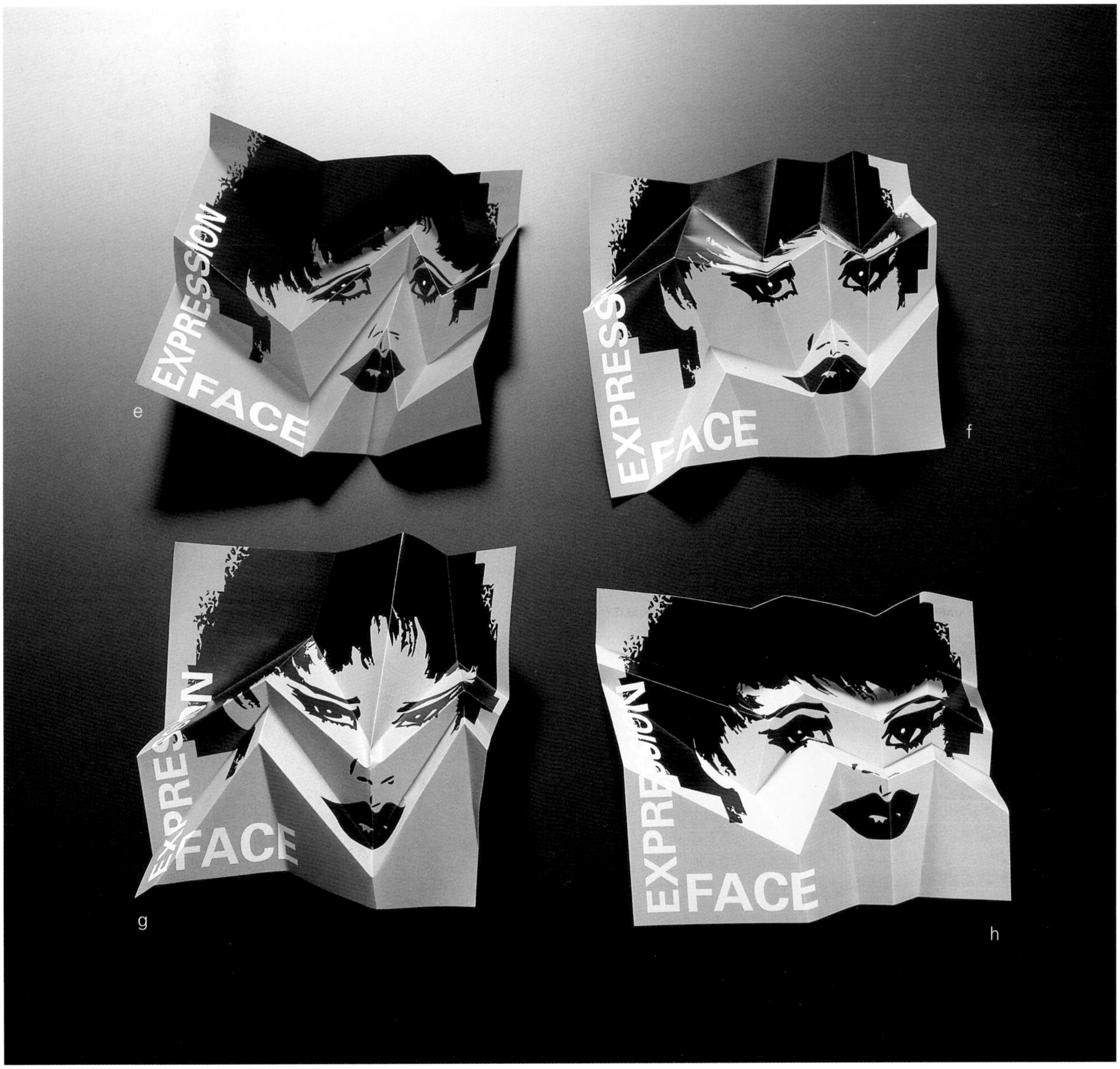
EXPRESSION
FACE
e
EXPRESS
FACE
f
EXPRESSION
FACE
g
EXPRESSION
FACE
h

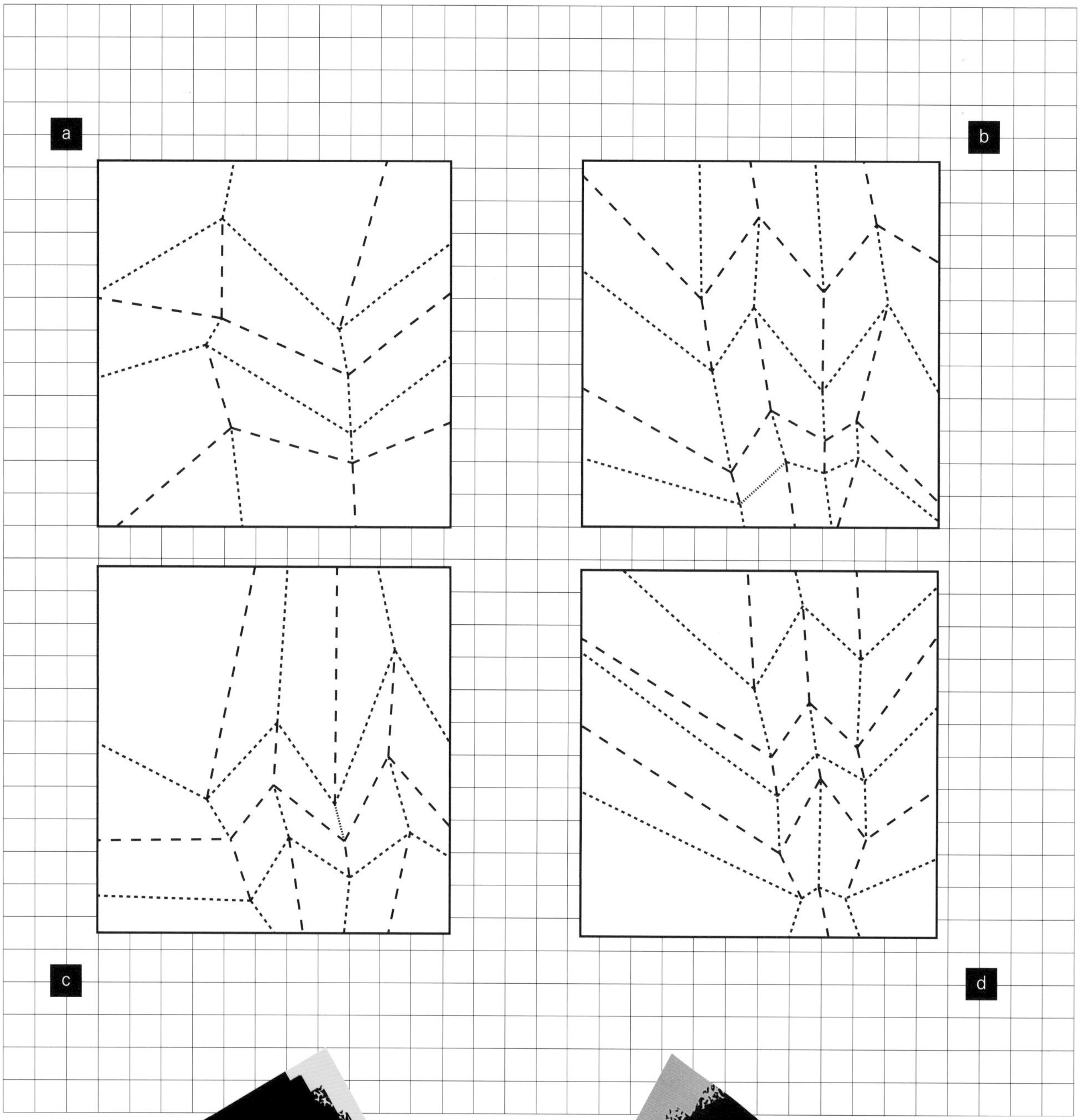
a
b
c
d

EXPRESSION
FACE

EXPRESSIO
FACE

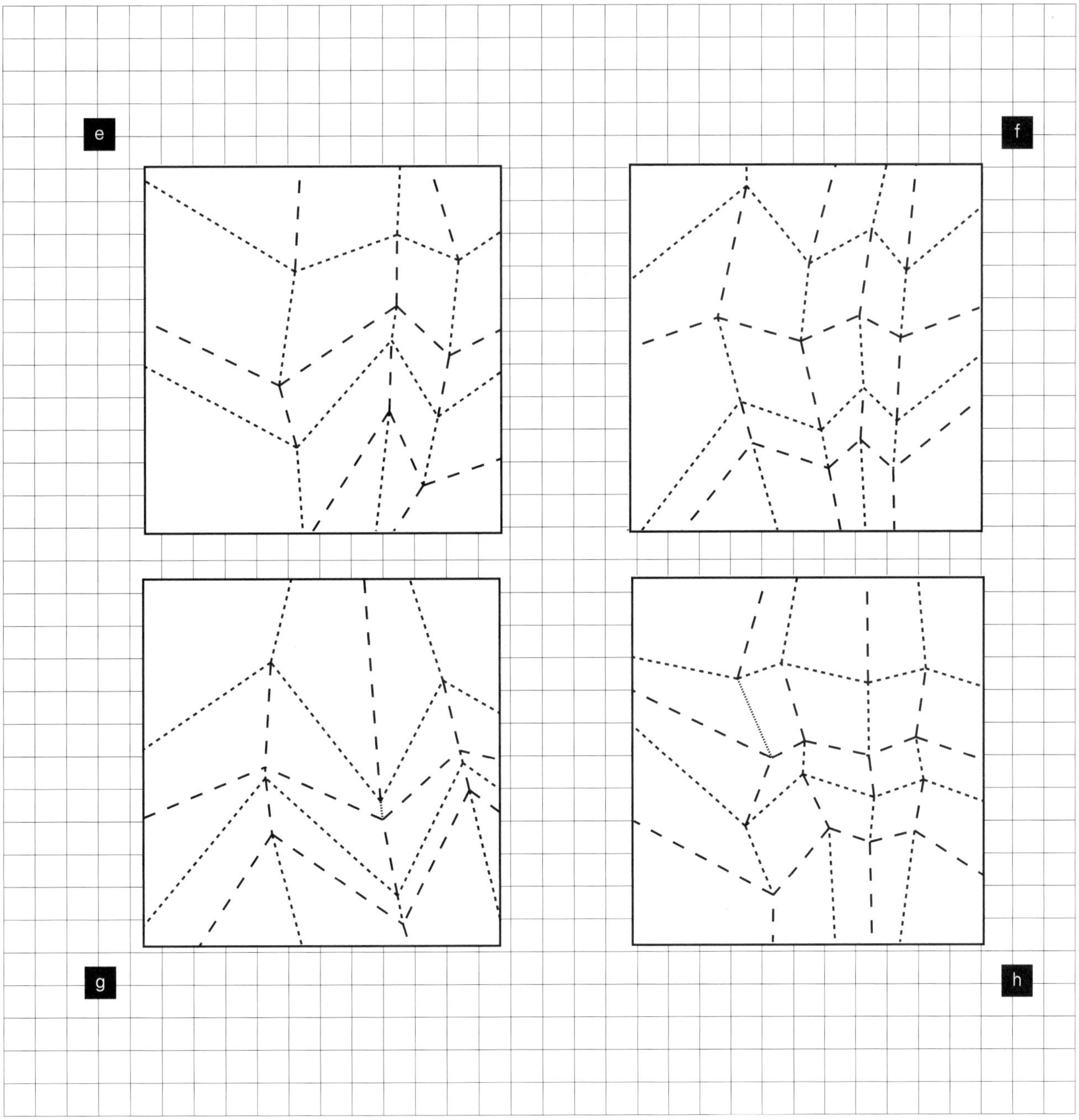
e
f
g
h

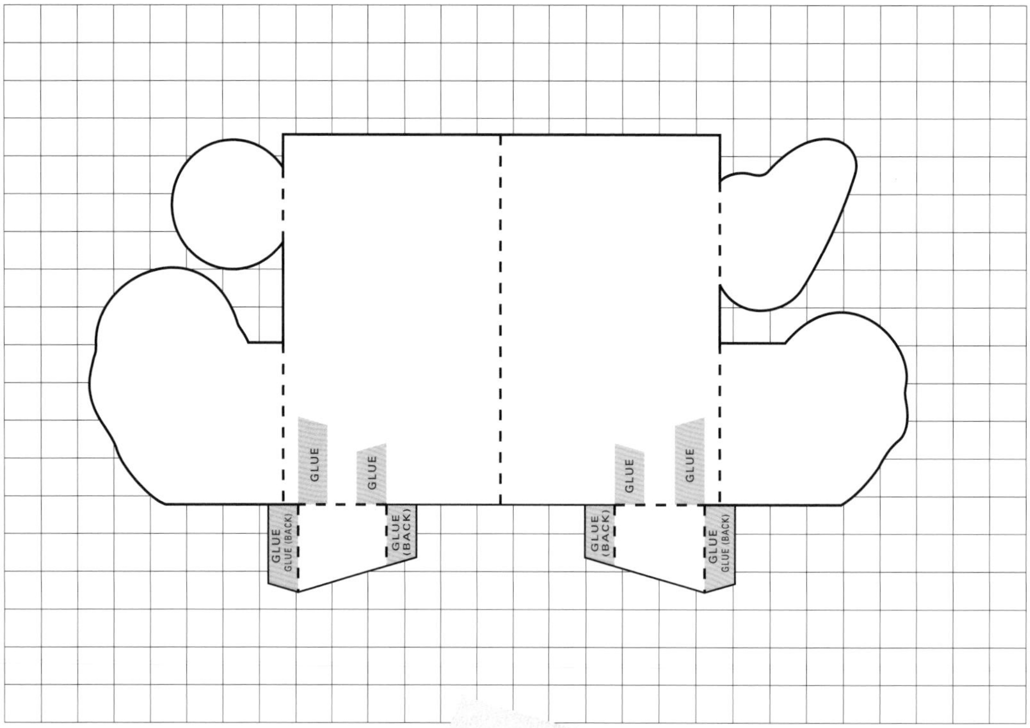

026

Arjo Wiggins
Curious Collection DM

新紙シリーズの紹介DM

Japan 2002

CL: Arjo Wiggins Canson KK

C: Hiromi Ouchi

AD, D: Akihiko Tsukamoto

I: Yukari Miyagi

CW: Haruki Nagumo

DF, SB: Design Club

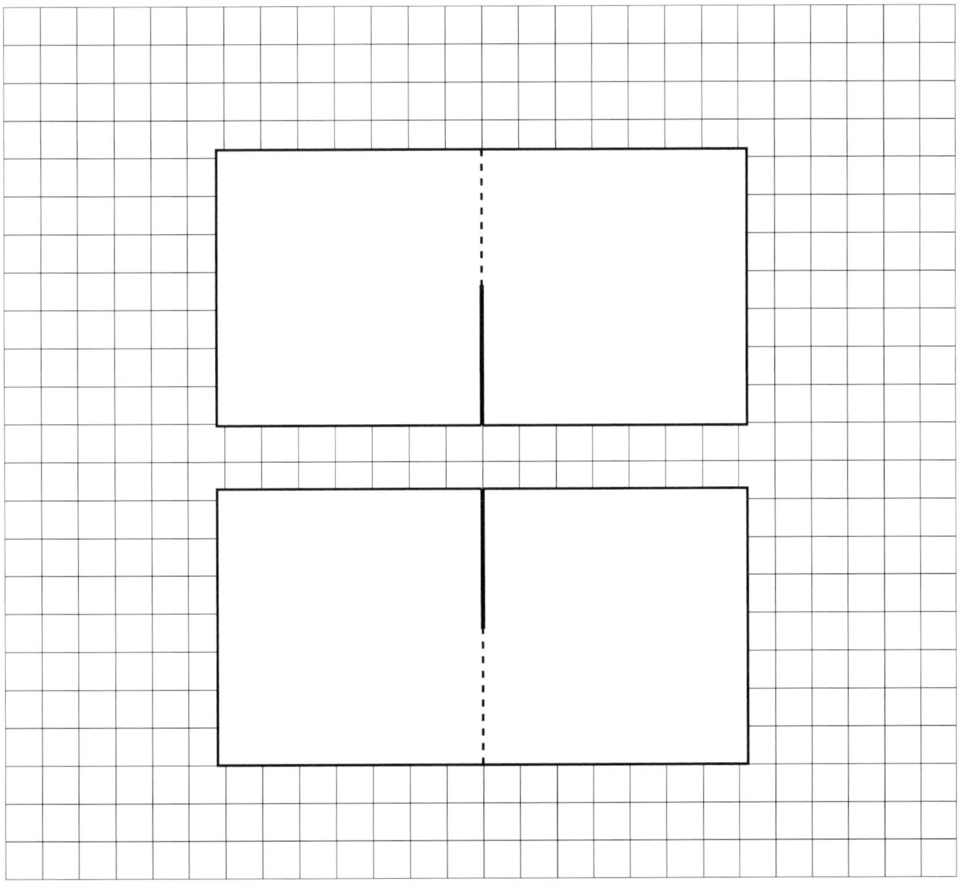

DM "Bend Your Knee"

製紙会社 DM

UK 2001

CL: The Very Interesting Paper Company

CD: Lynn Trickett, Brian Webb

D: Matt Lowe

DF, SB: Trickett & Webb Ltd.

028

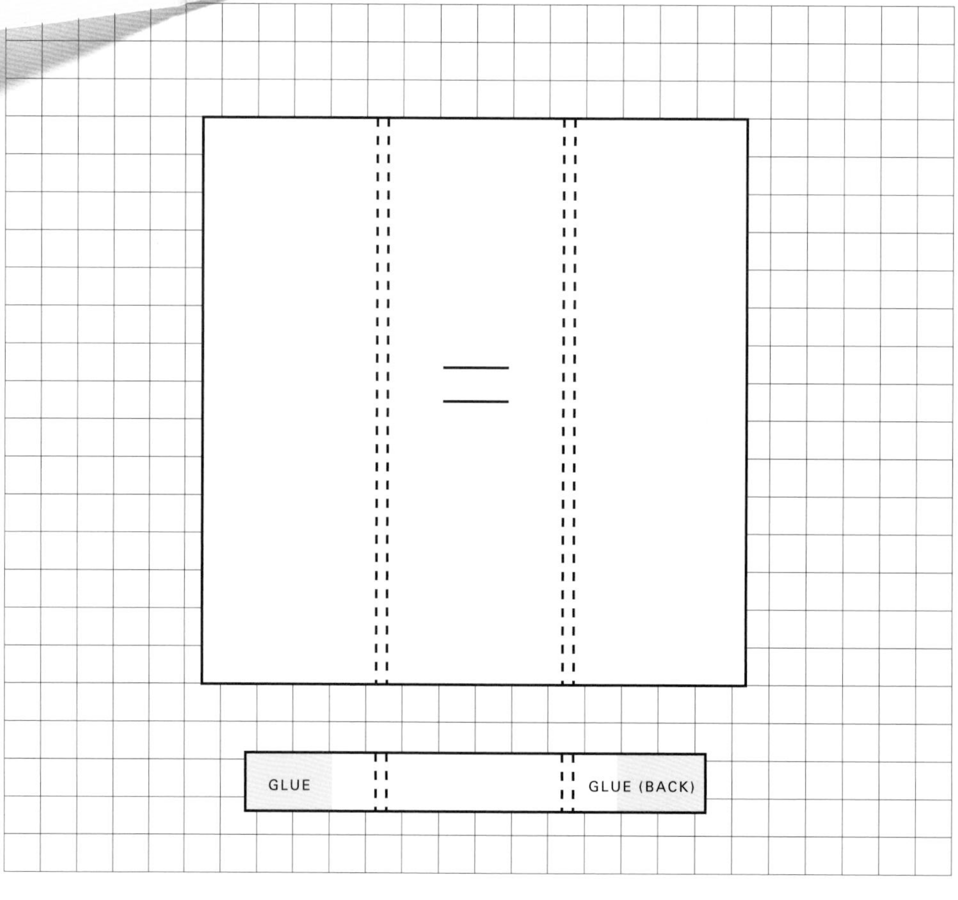

Chopstick Folder
飛行食割り箸入れ「和」
Thailand
CL, SB:Thai Airlines

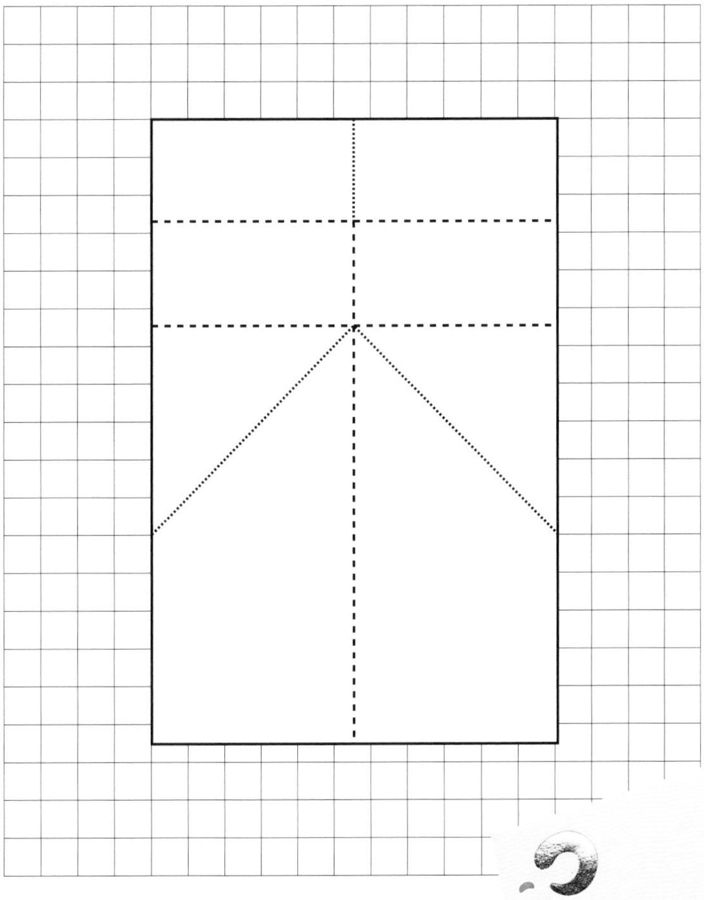

New Year's Card
年賀状
Japan 1991
CL: Packaging Create
AD, D, SB: Akio Okumura

Design Firm New Year Greeting Card
"Cricket"

デザイン事務所年賀状

Argentina 1991

CL: Victor Garcia & Adriana Ellinger

CD, AD, D, SB: Victor Garcia

DF: Victor Garcia & Adriana Ellinger

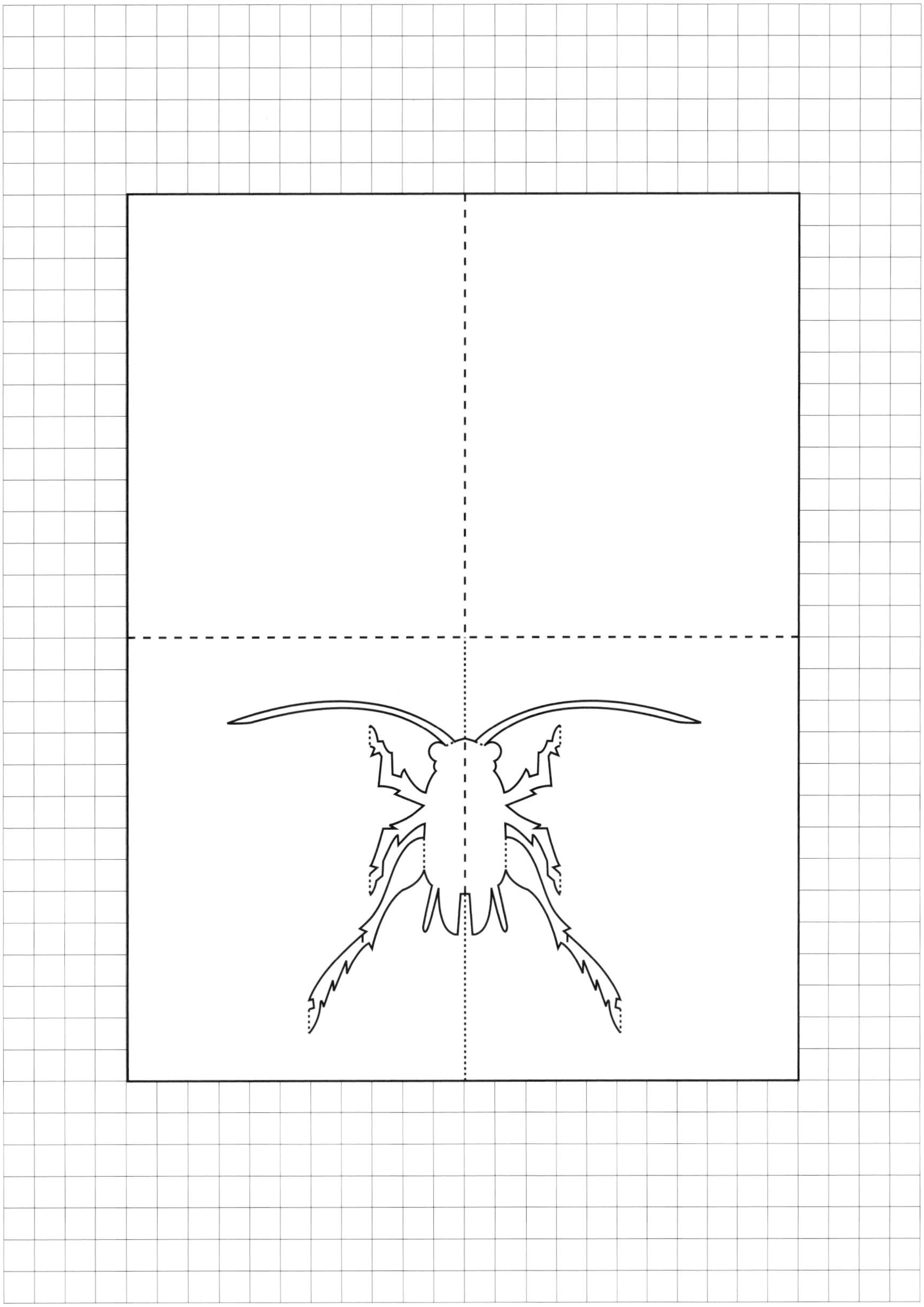

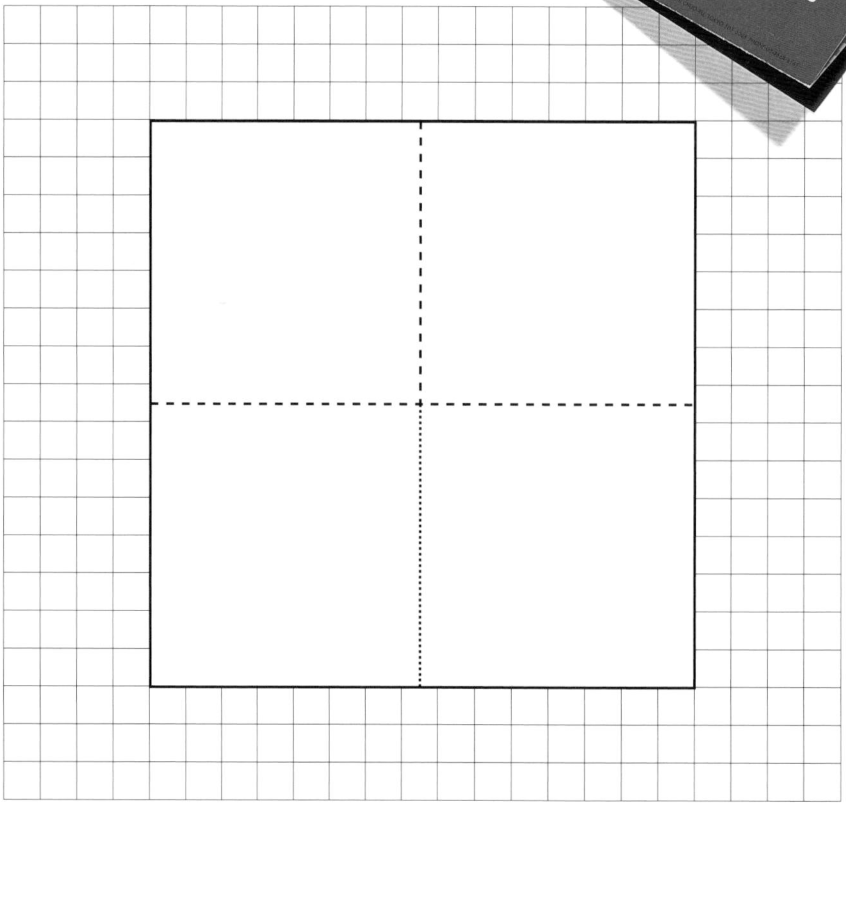

Atsuki Onishi Sleeping Gift Catalog

ギフト・カタログ

Japan 1998

CL: Nishikawa Sangyo Co., Ltd.

AD: Katsunori Hironaka

D: Sho Sawada

P: Mototsugu Abe

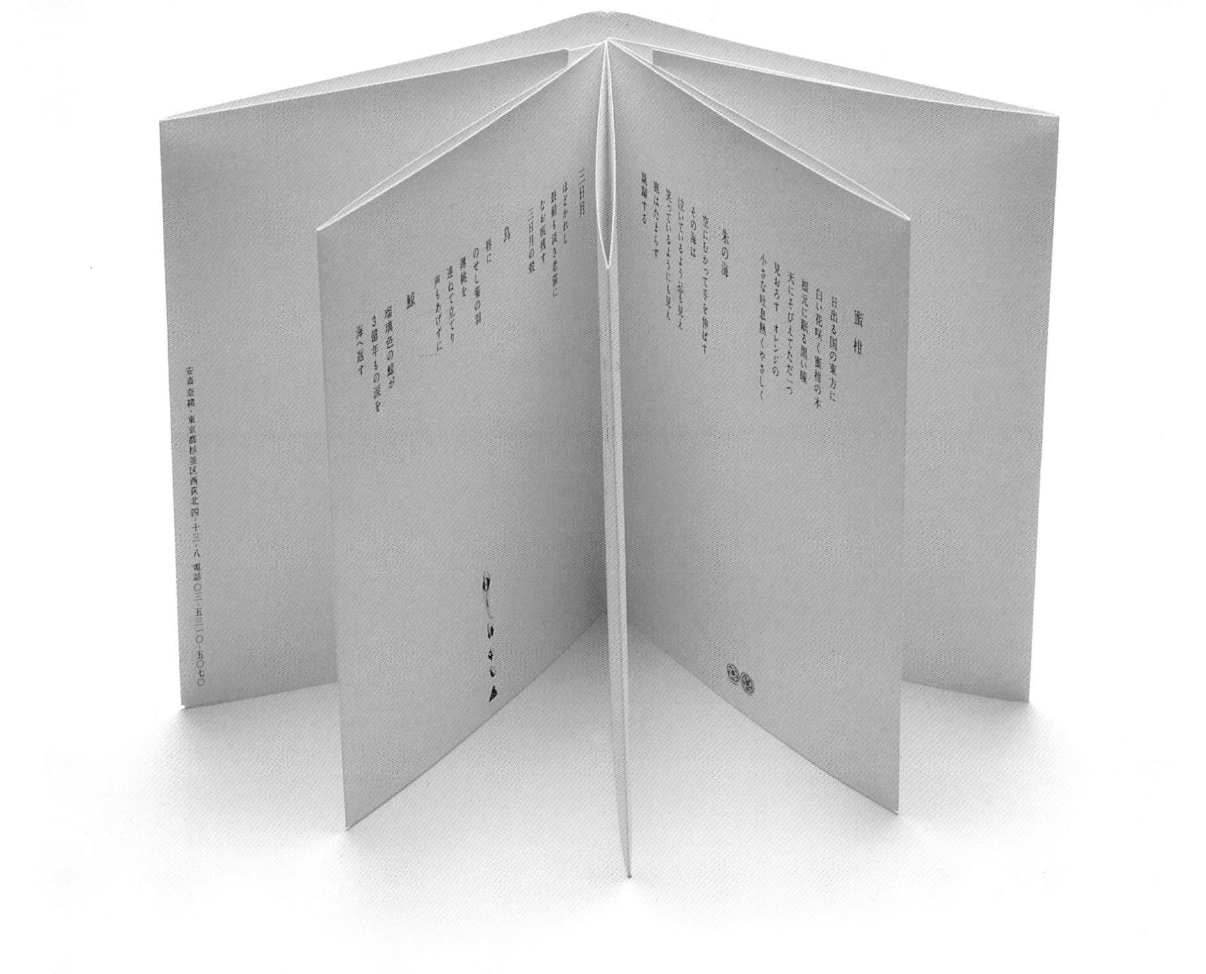

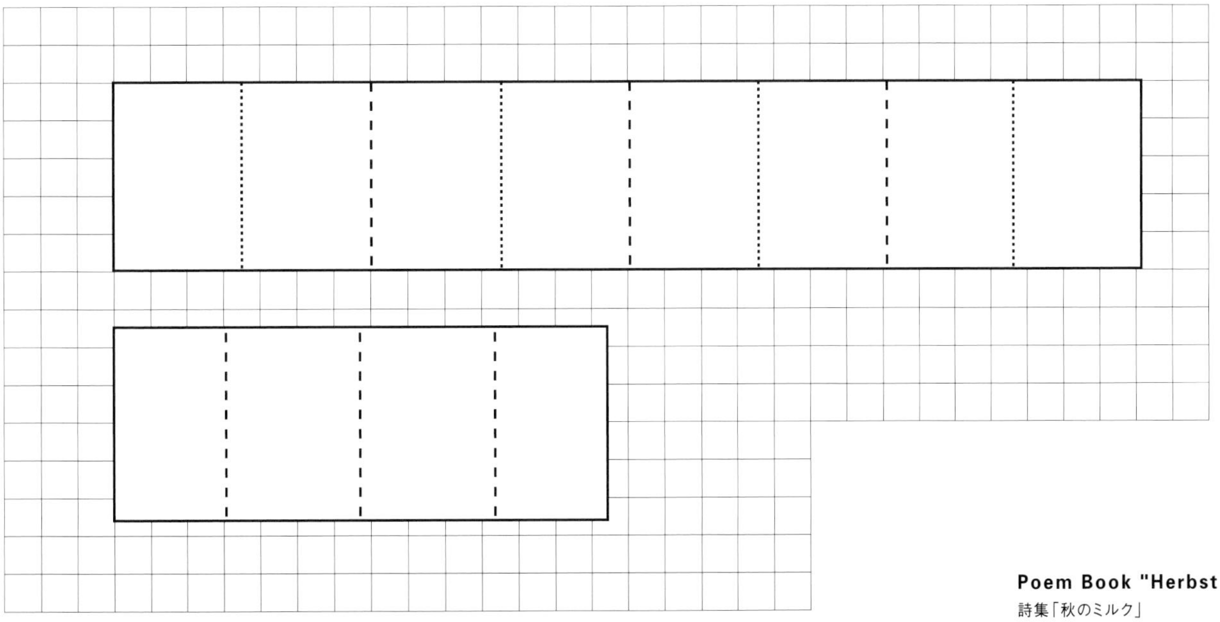

Poem Book "Herbst Milch"
詩集「秋のミルク」
Japan
CL, SB:Nao Anzai

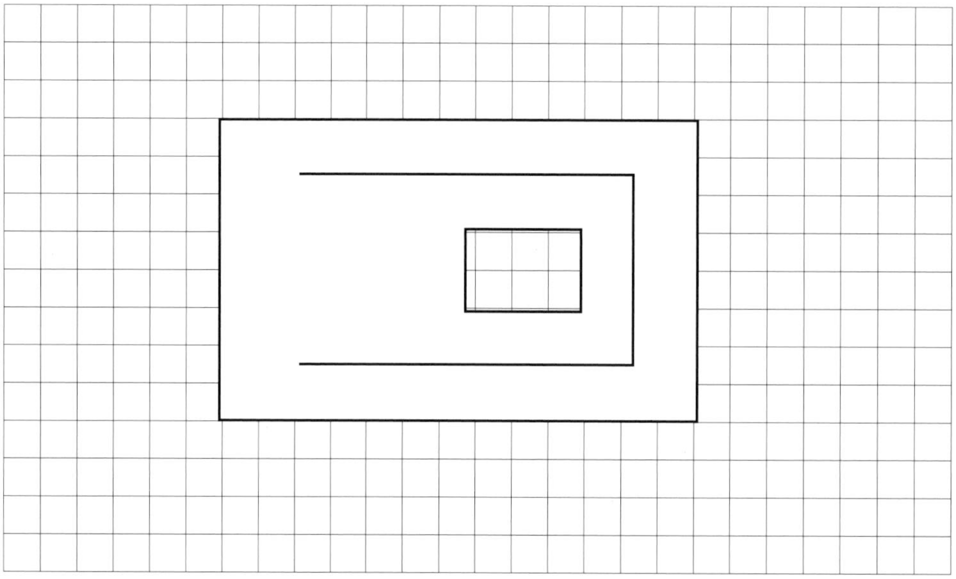

Visting Card
名刺
Japan 2001
CL, SB:Masami Design
AD, D: Masami Takahashi
I: Kahori Maki , Masami Design

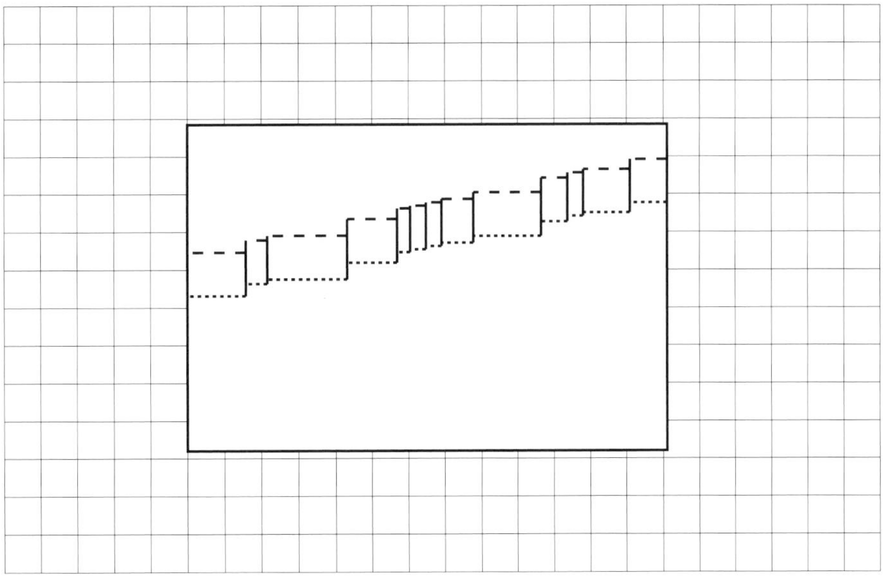

Visiting Card
名刺
Japan 1996
CL: PLAN Y
AD, D, SB: Miyuki Yoshida

Calender Book "Minutes"
デザイン事務所プロモーション用書籍
UK
D, DF, SB: Strukturr Design

And A aoyama
Opening Reception DM

アンド エー オープニング案内DM
Japan 2001
CL: And A
AD, D: Tadashi Kitagawa

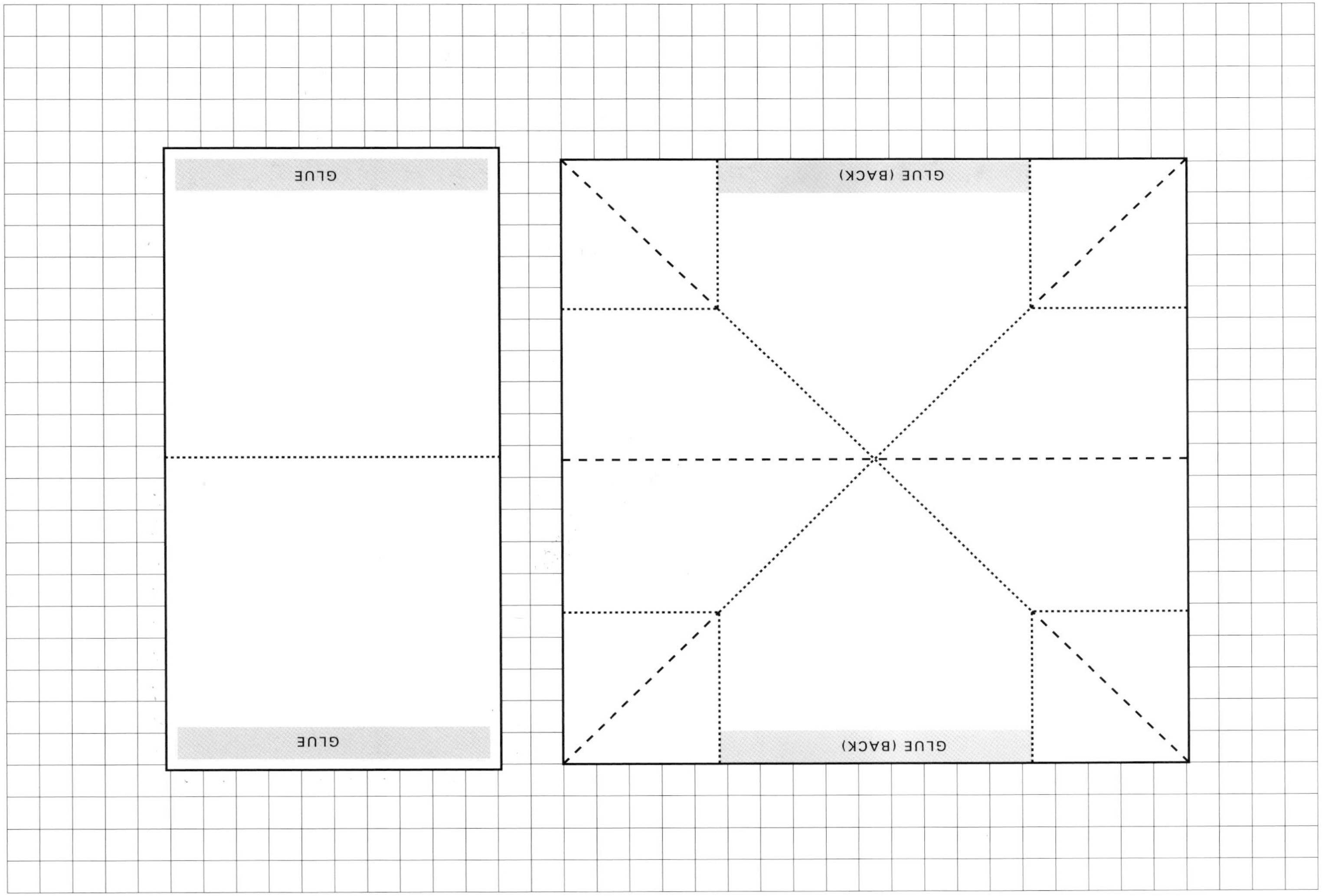
GLUE
GLUE
GLUE (BACK)
GLUE (BACK)

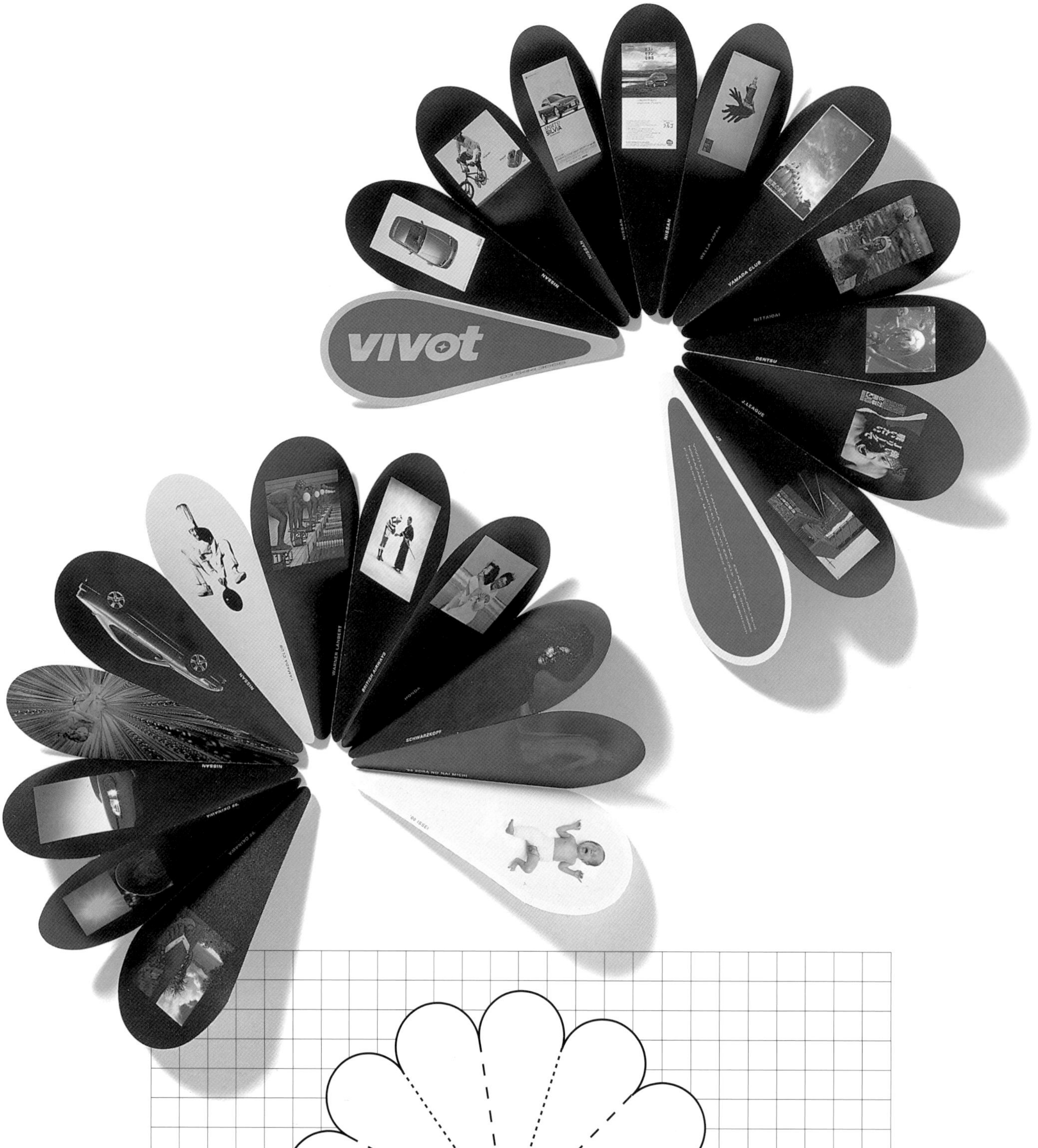

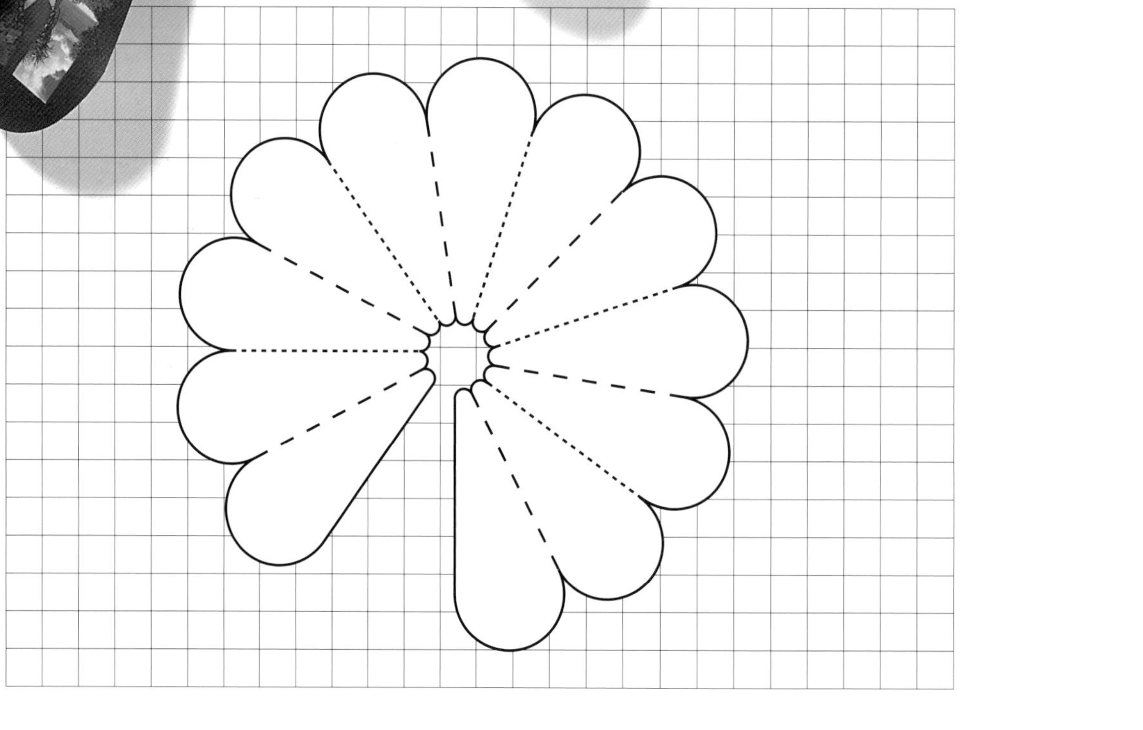

Company Establishment
会社設立
Japan 2000
CL: Vivot
AD: Michihiro Ishizaki
D: Ryo Sakamoto
P: Yoshitomo Tanaka
DF, SB: DRAFT Co., Ltd.

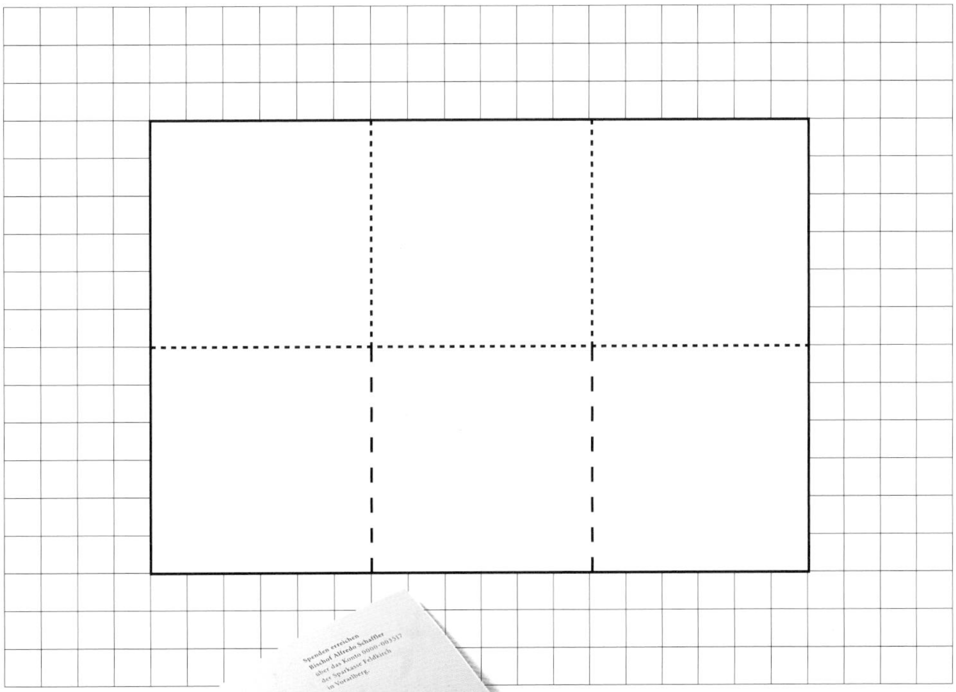

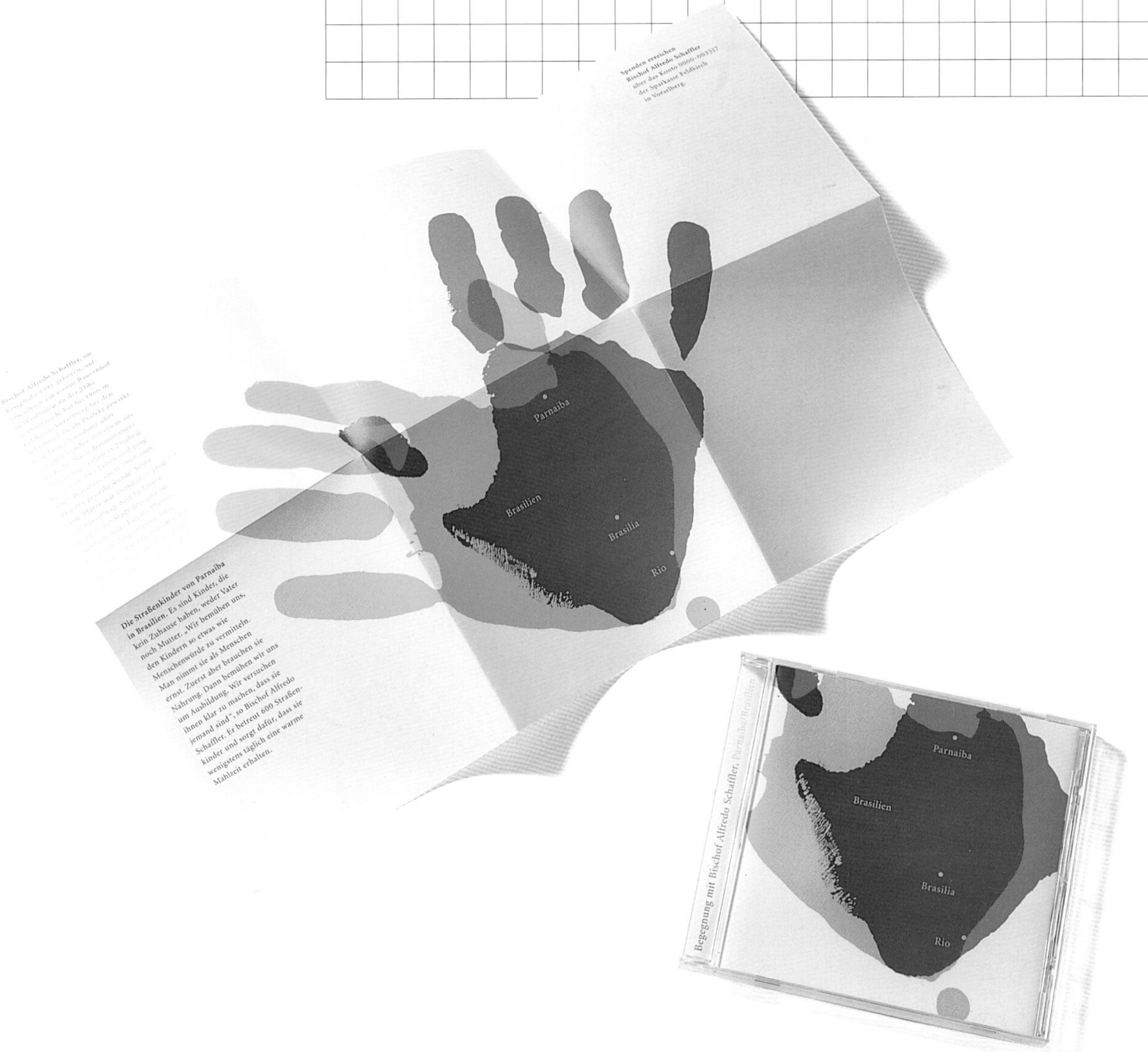

CD Pamphlet
CDパッケージ・パンフレット
Austria 2002
CL: Alfredo Schaffler, Brazil
AD, D: Peter Felder
DF, SB: Peter Felder Grafikdesign

July 31 - Aug. 5
Aug. 7 - 19
Aug. 21 - Sept. 2
Sept. 25 - Oct. 20
DSM Subscription Performances Sept. 25 - Oct. 7
2001
Here's The Scoop For Our 61st Summer Season!

Broadway Shows Ticket Sales
"Here's the Scoop for
Our 61st Summer Season "

劇団チケット案内

USA 2001

CL: Dallas Summer Musicals

CD: Jack Evans

AD: Bonnie Evans

D: Clay McClure

Photographix: Tom Welch

DF, SB: Unigraphics, Inc.

Advertising Folder
"Les Ateliers de Chassingrimont"

広告用フォルダー

Belgium 2001

CL: Les Ateliers de Chassingrimont

CD, AD, D: Nathalie Wathelet, Oliver Vandervliet

CD, AD, D, P: Anne Franssen

DF, SB: Reflex Design / Pop X Studio

Product Pamphlet

和イスキー膳 小冊子こんばん和

Japan 2000

CL: Suntory Ltd.

CD: Hiroshi Sasaki

AD: Hiroaki Nagai

D: Hisaki Otake

I: Sanpei Sato

CW: Jun Maki

DF, SB: N.G. Inc.

Invitation Card "Holzwasser"
家具展招待状
Austria 2001
CL: Luise + Bruno Schweizer
CD, AD, D, SB: Sigi Ramoser
DF: Sagenvier Design Kommunikation

Paul Smith Watch Catalog
ポール スミス ウォッチ店頭用カタログ
Japan 1999
CL: Citizen Trading Co., Ltd.
AD: Hideaki Muto
D: Chikako Ogawa
P: Makoto Yokokawa
DF, SB: Muto Office Inc.

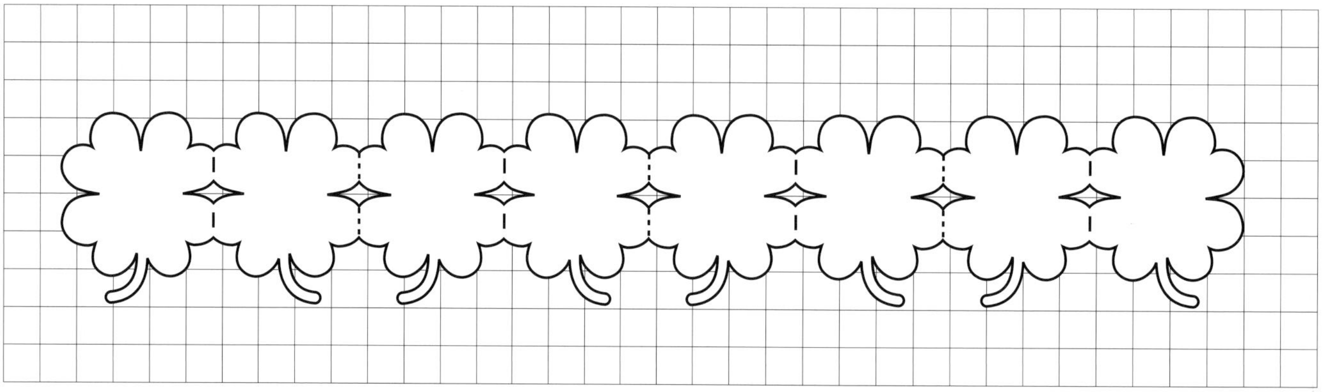

Birthday Greeting
Decoration Card Clover & Dove

バースディカード

Japan 2001

AD: Etsuko Yago

D: Aiko Maenaka

Invitation
"A Society of Rooms"
建築学校案内状
Belgium 2000
CL: Provinciale Hoge School Limburg
CD, AD, D, P: Jo Klaps
DF, SB: Brussels Lof

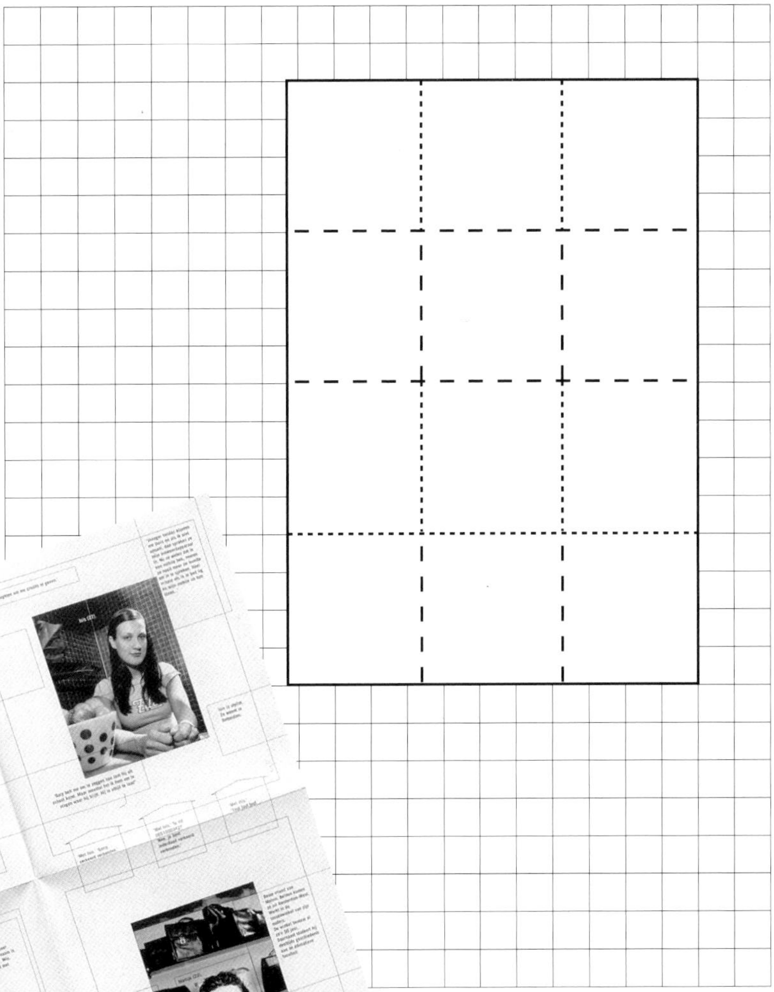

Brochure
"The Network of Malvin"

携帯電話会社ブローシャー

The Netherlands 2001

CL: Ben

CD: Johan Kramer, Erik Kessels

AD, D: Karen Heliter

P: Mourad Bouchakour

DF, SB: Kessels Kramer

050

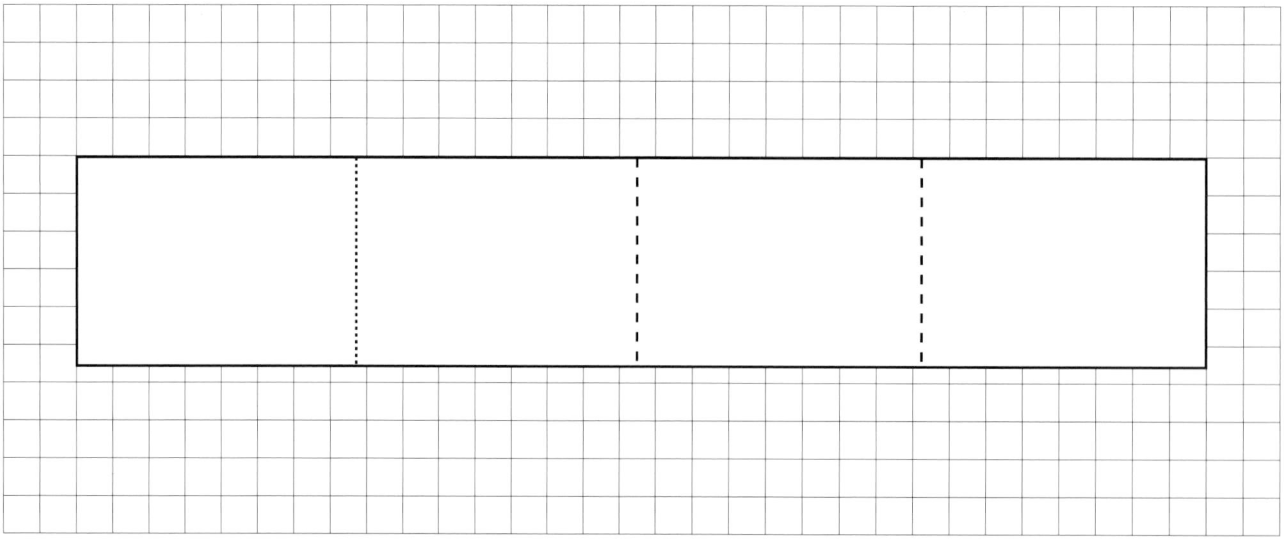

Annual Report "Der Stiftikus"

アニュアル・レポート

Switzerland 1999

CL: Stifung Umwelt-Einsatz Schweiz

CD, AD, D: Lucia Frey

P: Pascal Wuest

DF, SB: Wild & Frey, Agentur fur Design

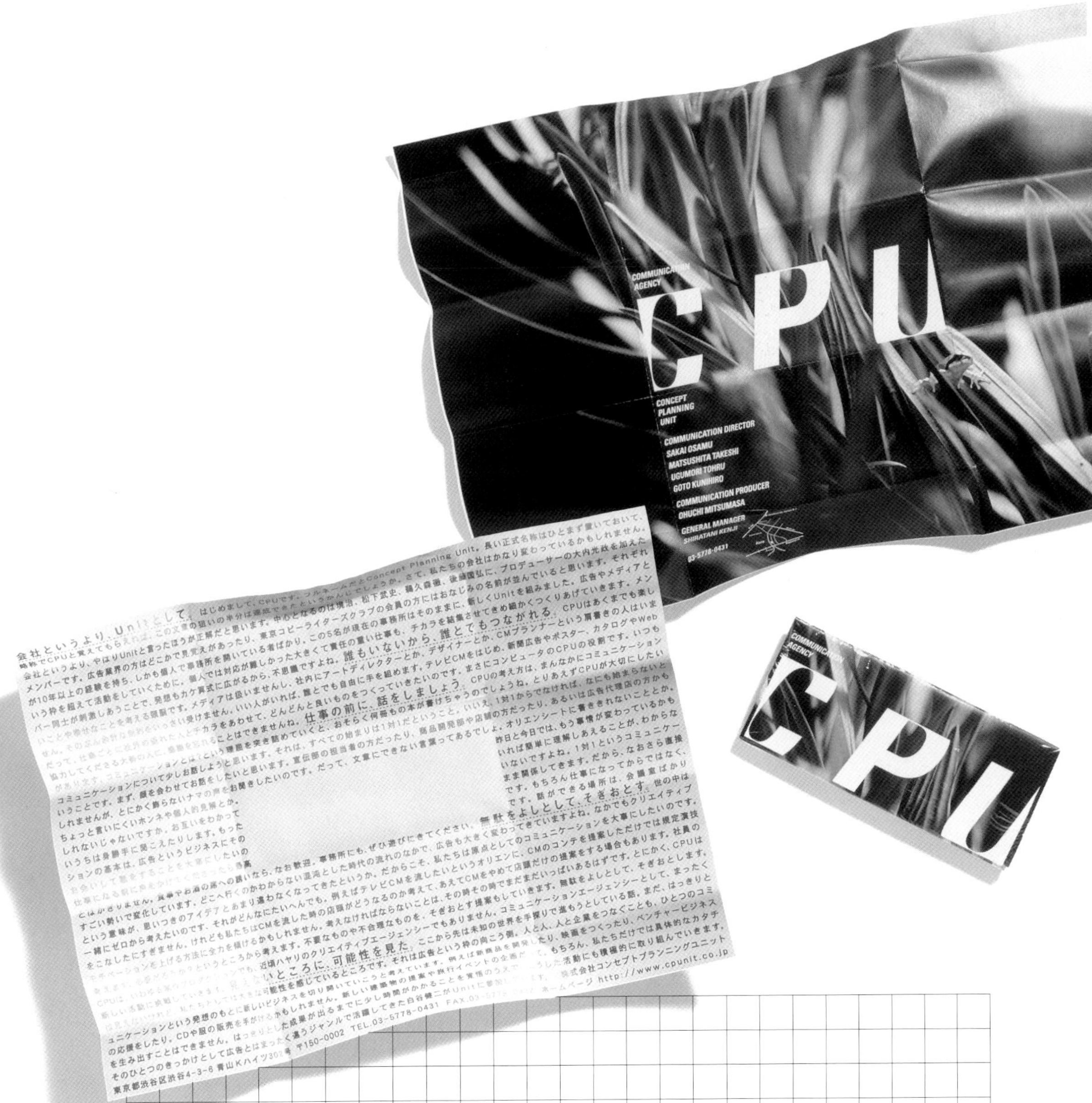

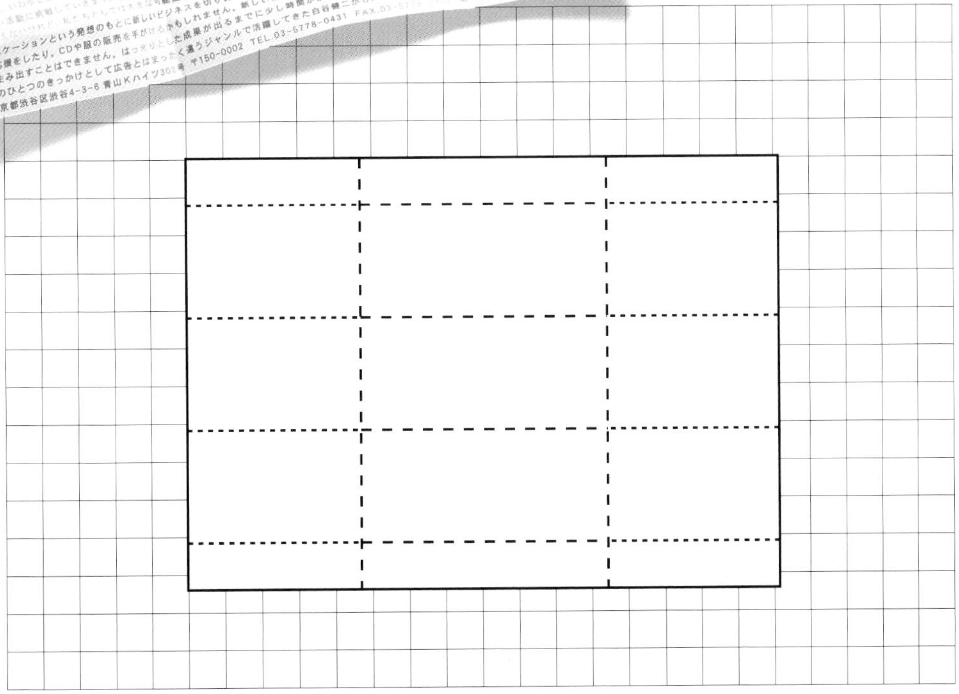

Promotion Leaflet

プロモーション用リーフレット

Japan

CL: Communication Agency
Concept Planning Unit

DF, SB: DRAFT Co., Ltd.

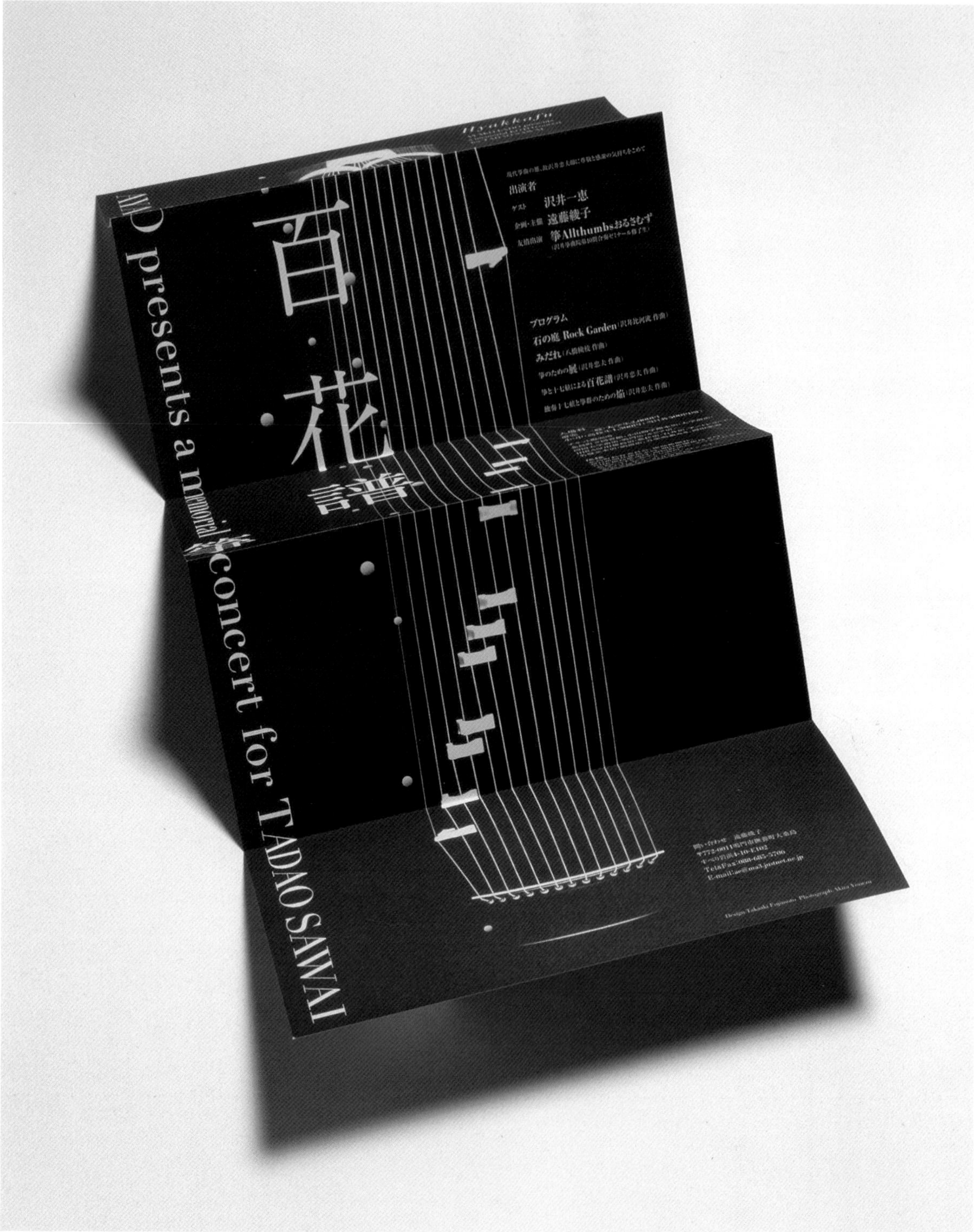

Photo Exhibition Pamphlet
米津光NYC写真展パンフレット
Japan 2001
CL: Akira Yonezu
AD, D, SB: Takaaki Fujimoto
P: Akira Yonezu
DF: Kisaragisha

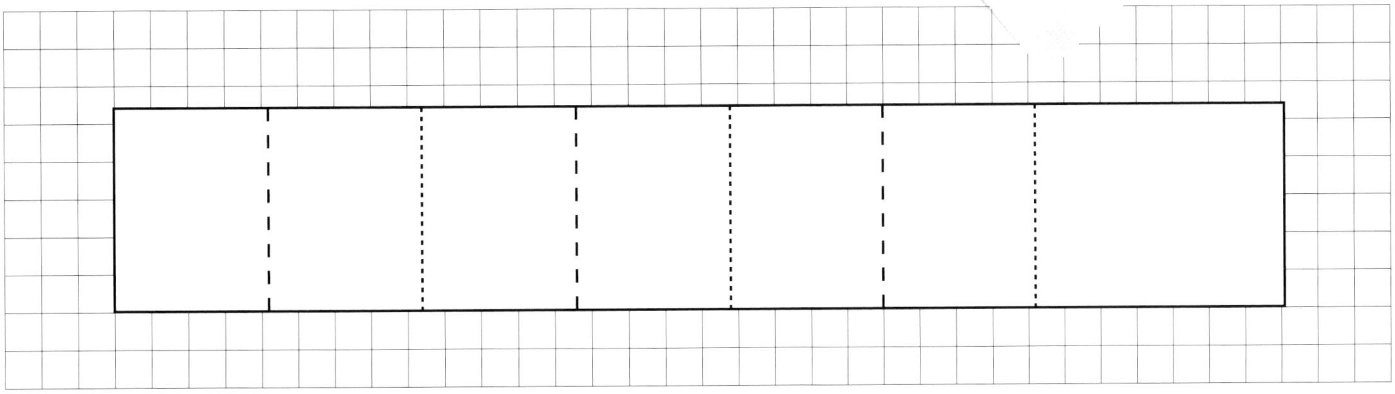

40th Anniversary Announcement

パーティー案内状

USA

CL: Ruth Bannon

CD, AD, D, I: Trudy Cole - Zielanski

DF, SB: Trudy Cole - Zielanski Design

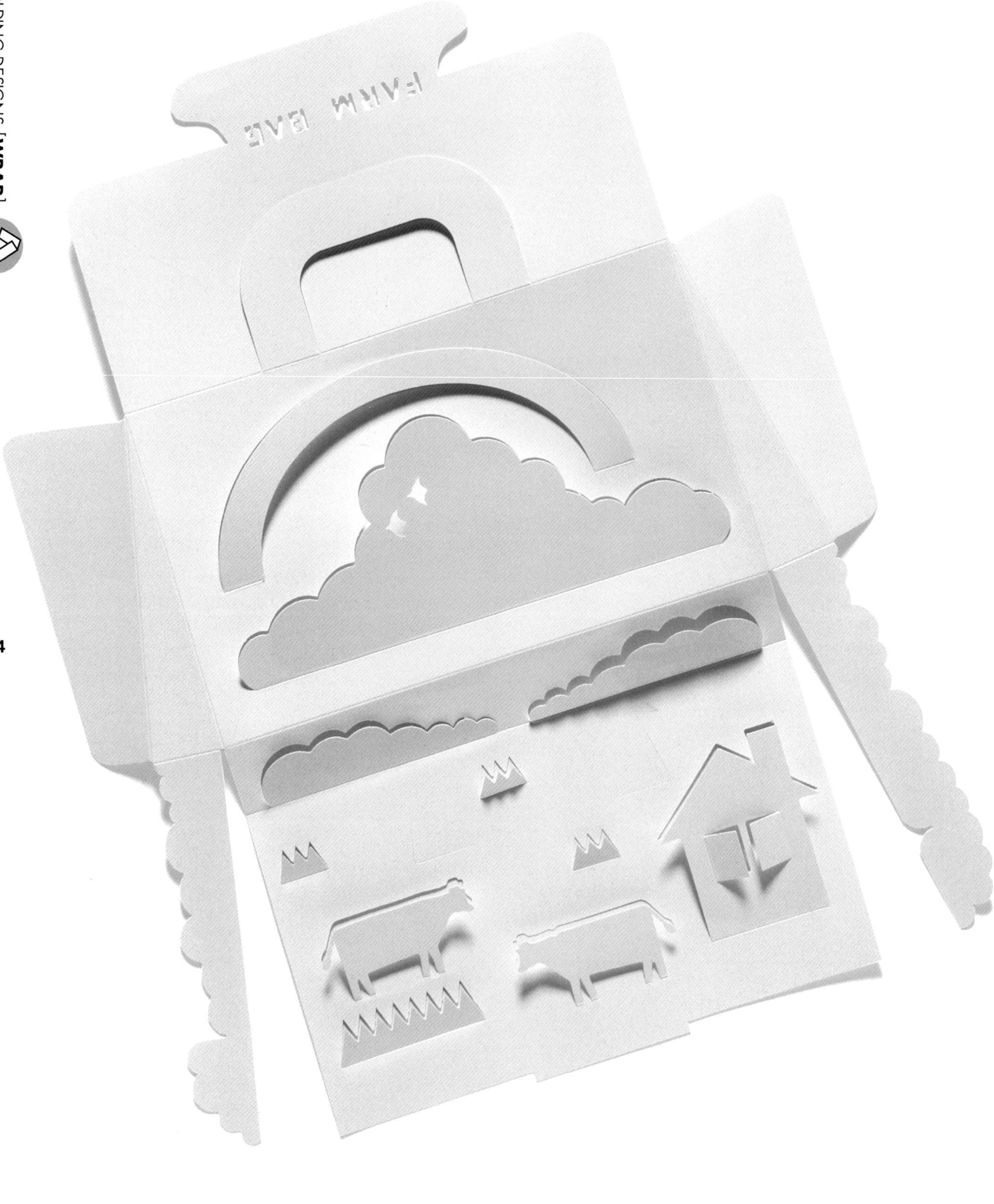

Farm Bag
ファームバッグ
Japan 2002
CL: Bijutsu Shuppan Design Center Co., Ltd.
AD, D: Masami Takahashi
DF, SB: Masami Design

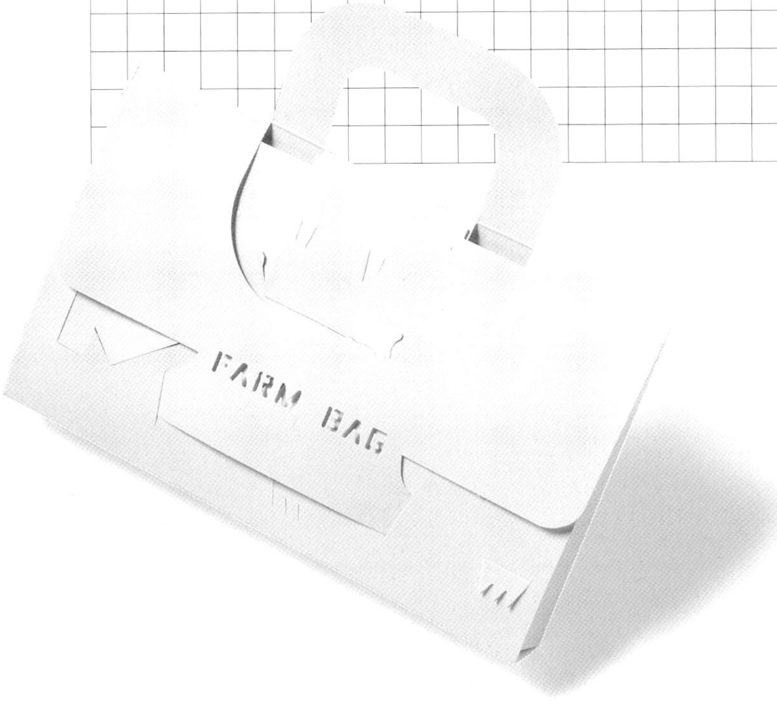
FARM BAG

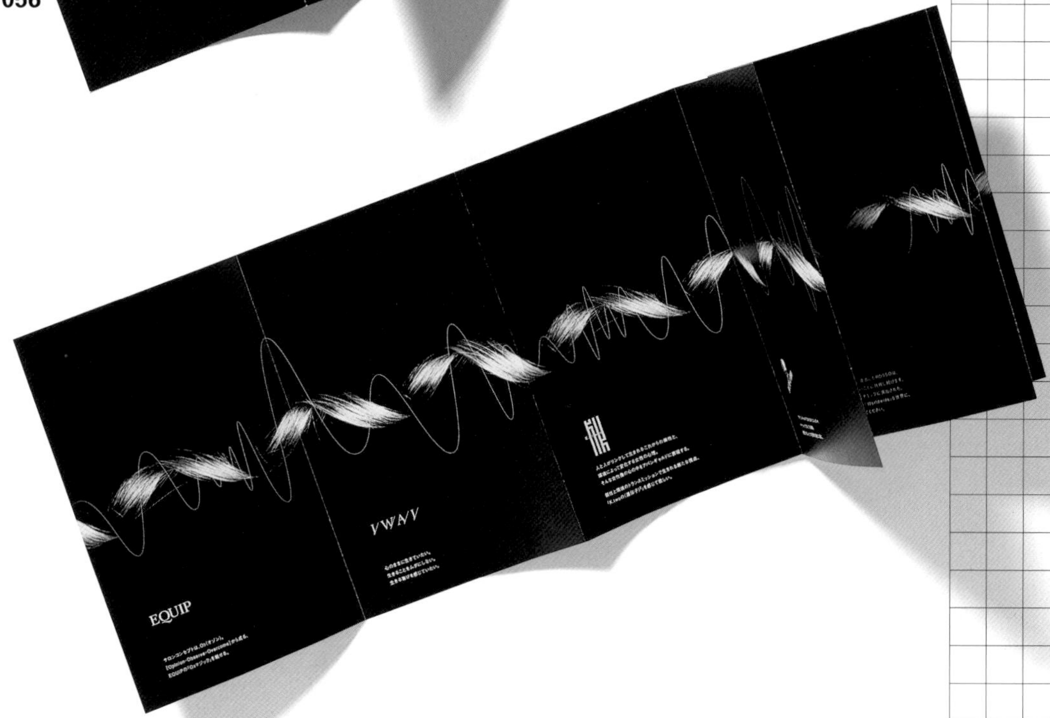

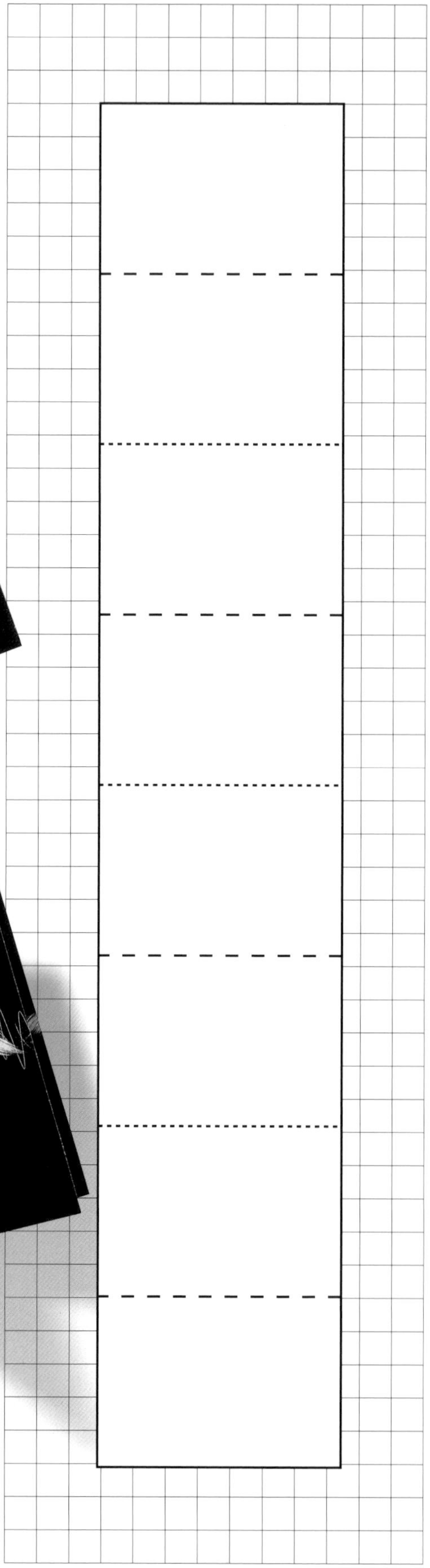

Event Announcement
イベント案内
Japan 2000
CL: Schwarzkopf K.K
AD: Michihiro Ishizaki
D: Ryo Sakamoto
P: Yoshitomo Tanaka
DF, SB: DRAFT Co., Ltd.

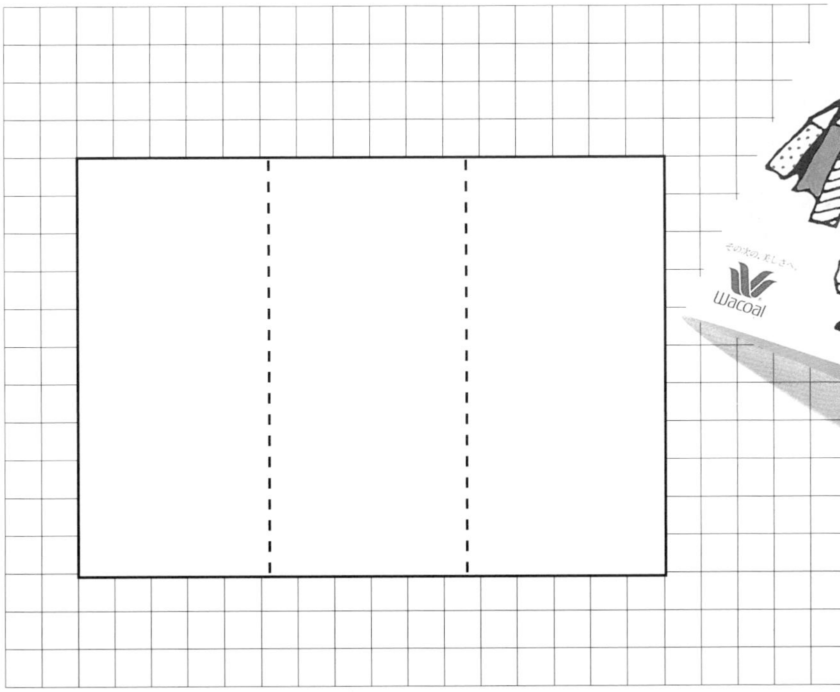

Promotional Leaflet "Essence Check"

販促用リーフレット「エッセンス・チェック」

Japan

CL, SB:Wacoal Co., Ltd.

AD, D: Kiyomi Imanishi

I: Mari Oono

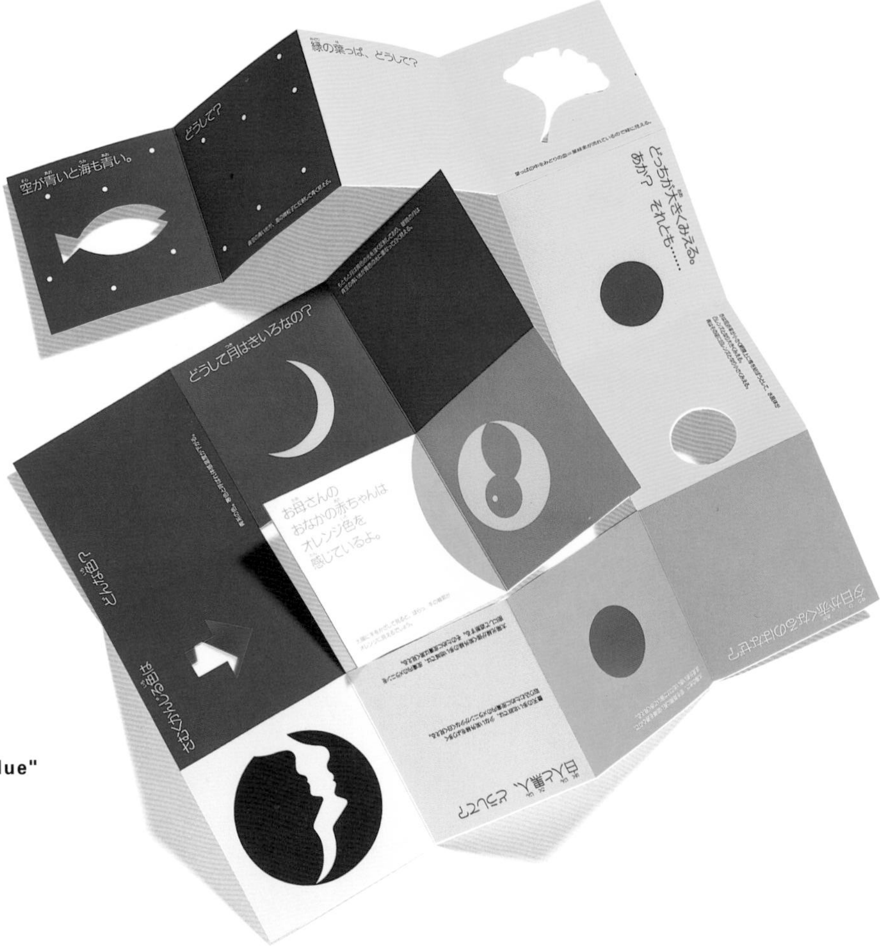

Mini Book
"Sea is blue when Sky is blue"
書籍「空が青いと海も青い」
Japan 1995
CL, SB:One Stroke Co., Ltd.
AD, D, I: Katsumi Komagata
DF, SB: One Stroke Co., Ltd.

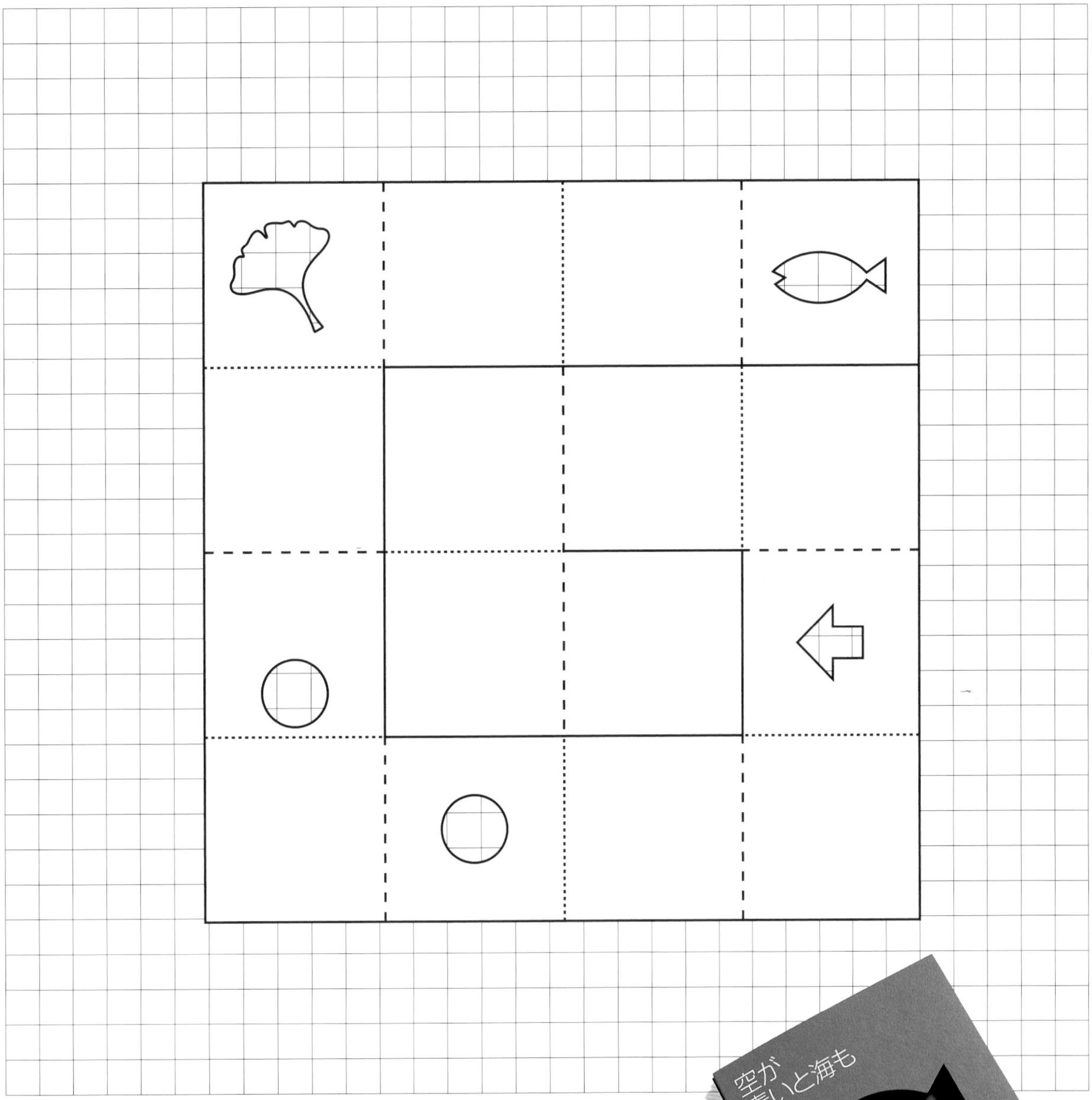

空が青いと海も青い。
どうして?
葉っぱの中をみどりの血＝葉緑素が流れているので緑に見える。
空が
青いと海も
青い。
駒形克己

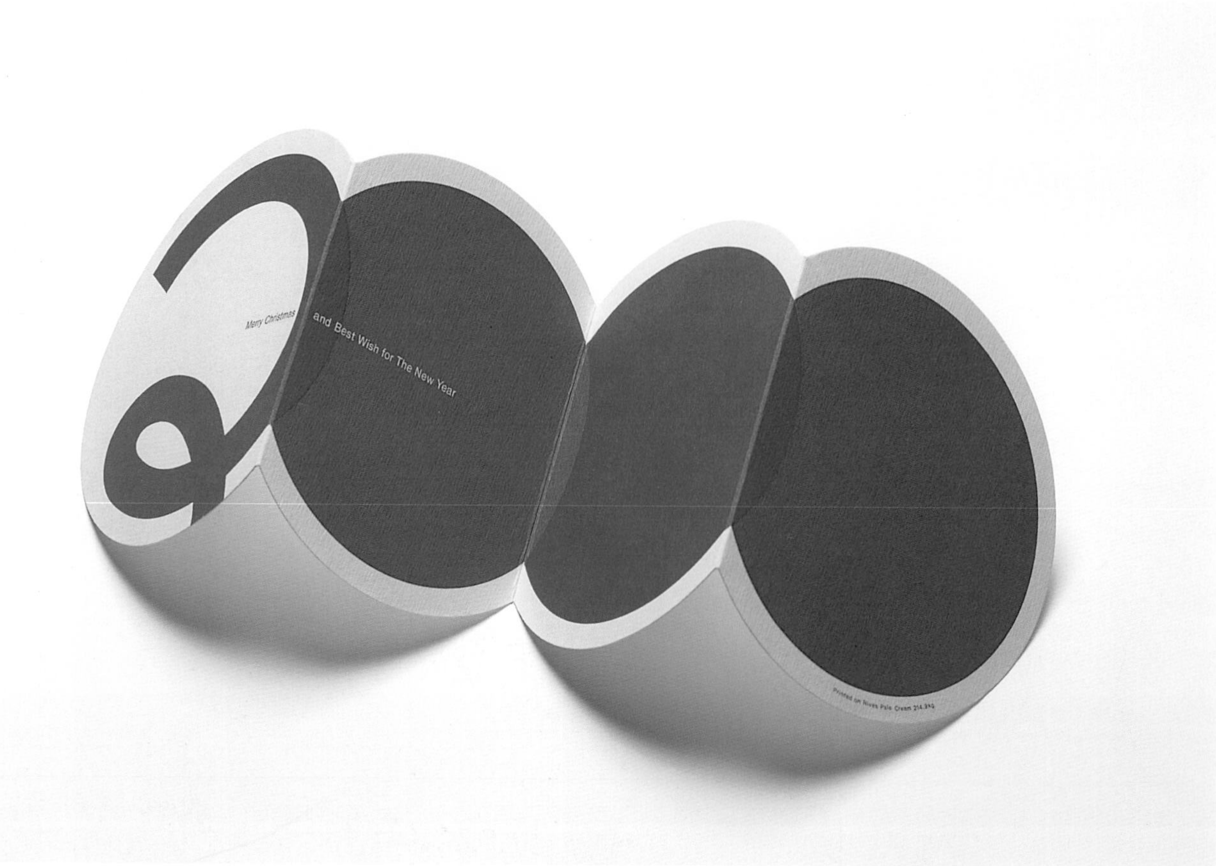

060

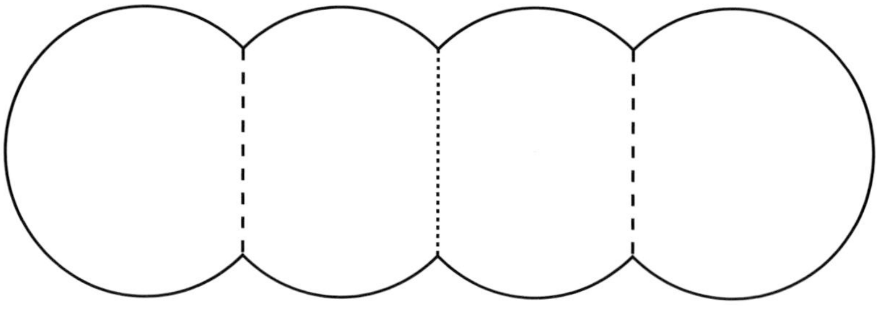

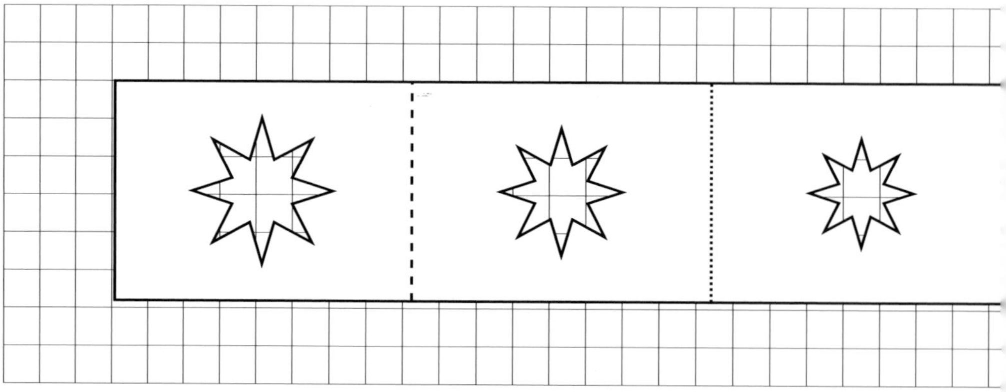

Christmas & New Year Card
クリスマス・新年挨拶カード
Japan 1999
AD, D: Akihiko Tsukamoto
DF, SB: Design Club

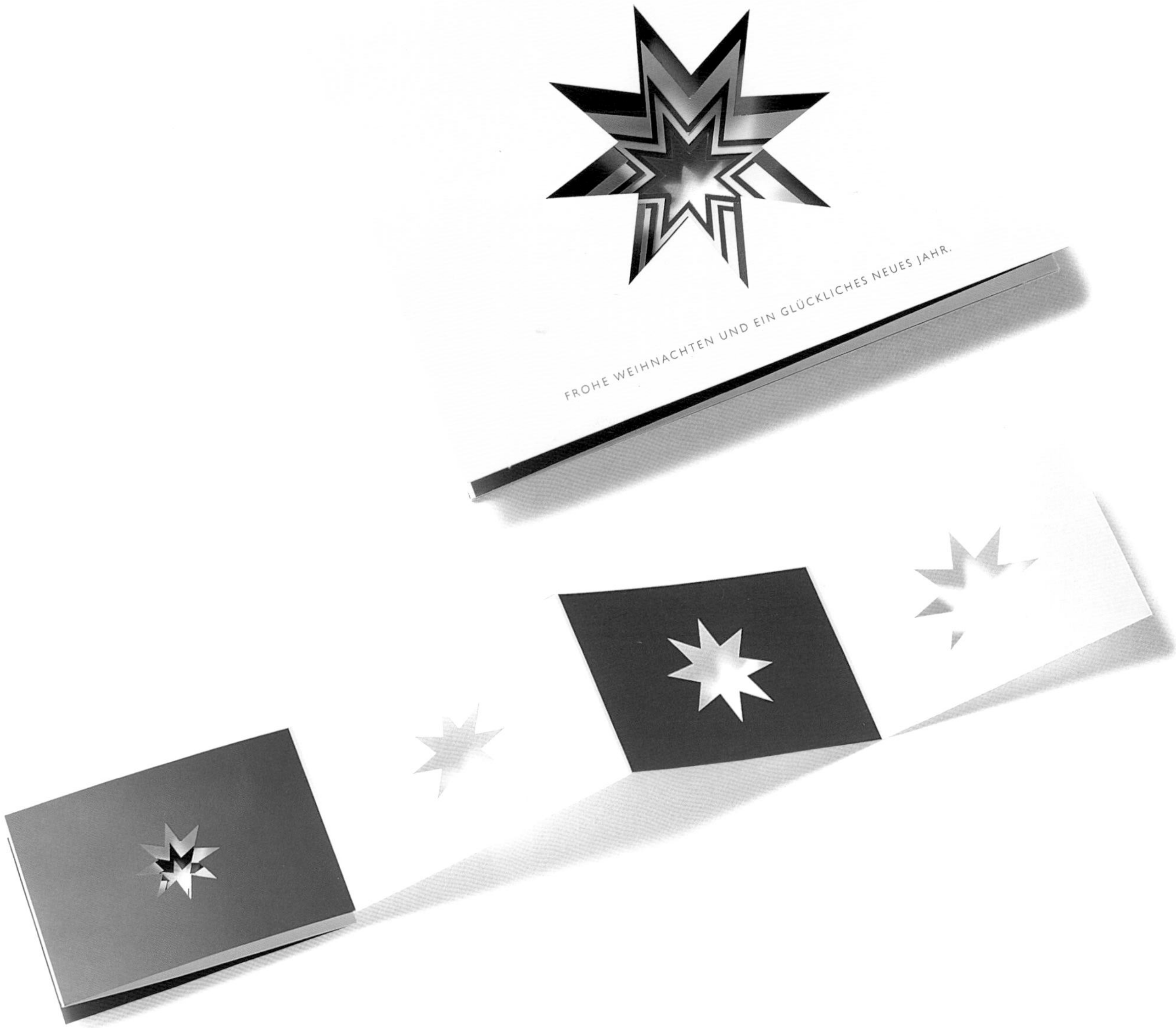
FROHE WEIHNACHTEN UND EIN GLÜCKLICHES NEUES JAHR.

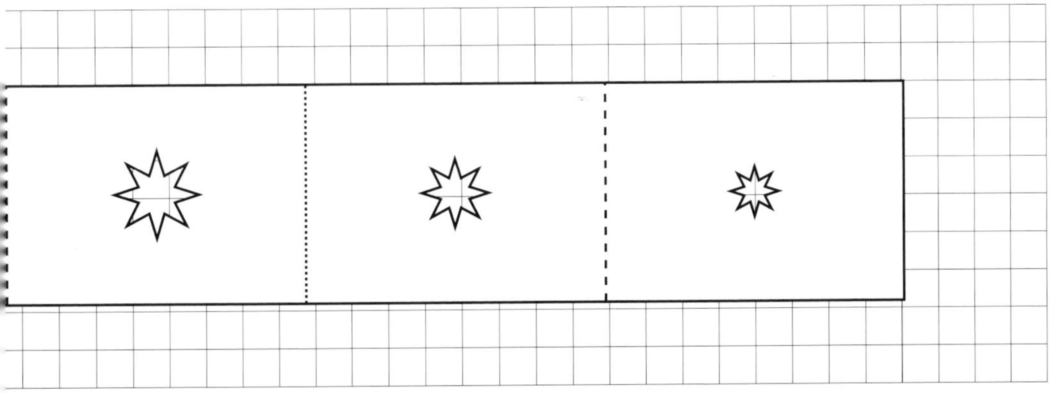

New Year Greetings

年賀状

Switzerland 1999

CL: Cd Cartondruck AG

CD, AD, D: Heinz Wild

DF, SB: Wild & Frey, Agentur fur Design

062

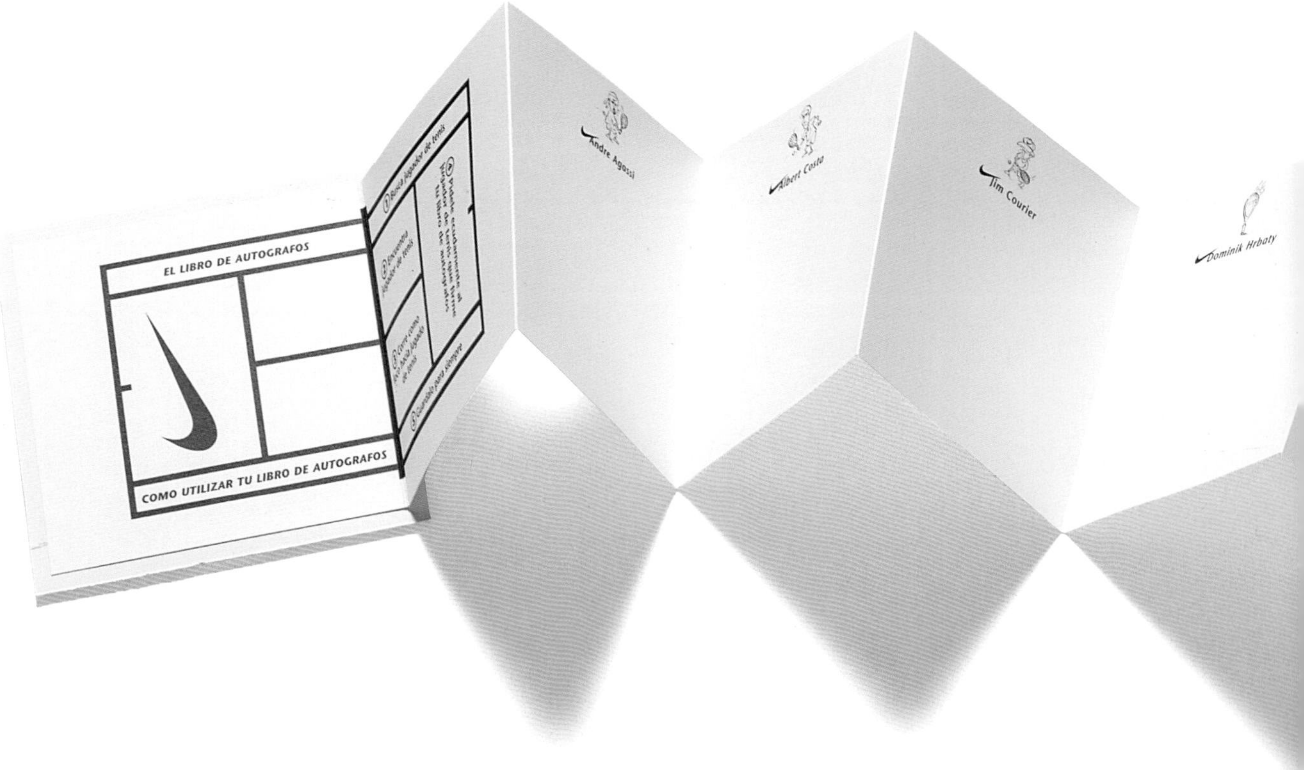

Nike Autograph Book
ナイキ・サイン用ブック
The Netherlands 1998
CL: Nike
CD: Johan Kramer
CD, AD, D: Erik Kessels
DF, SB: Kessels Kramer

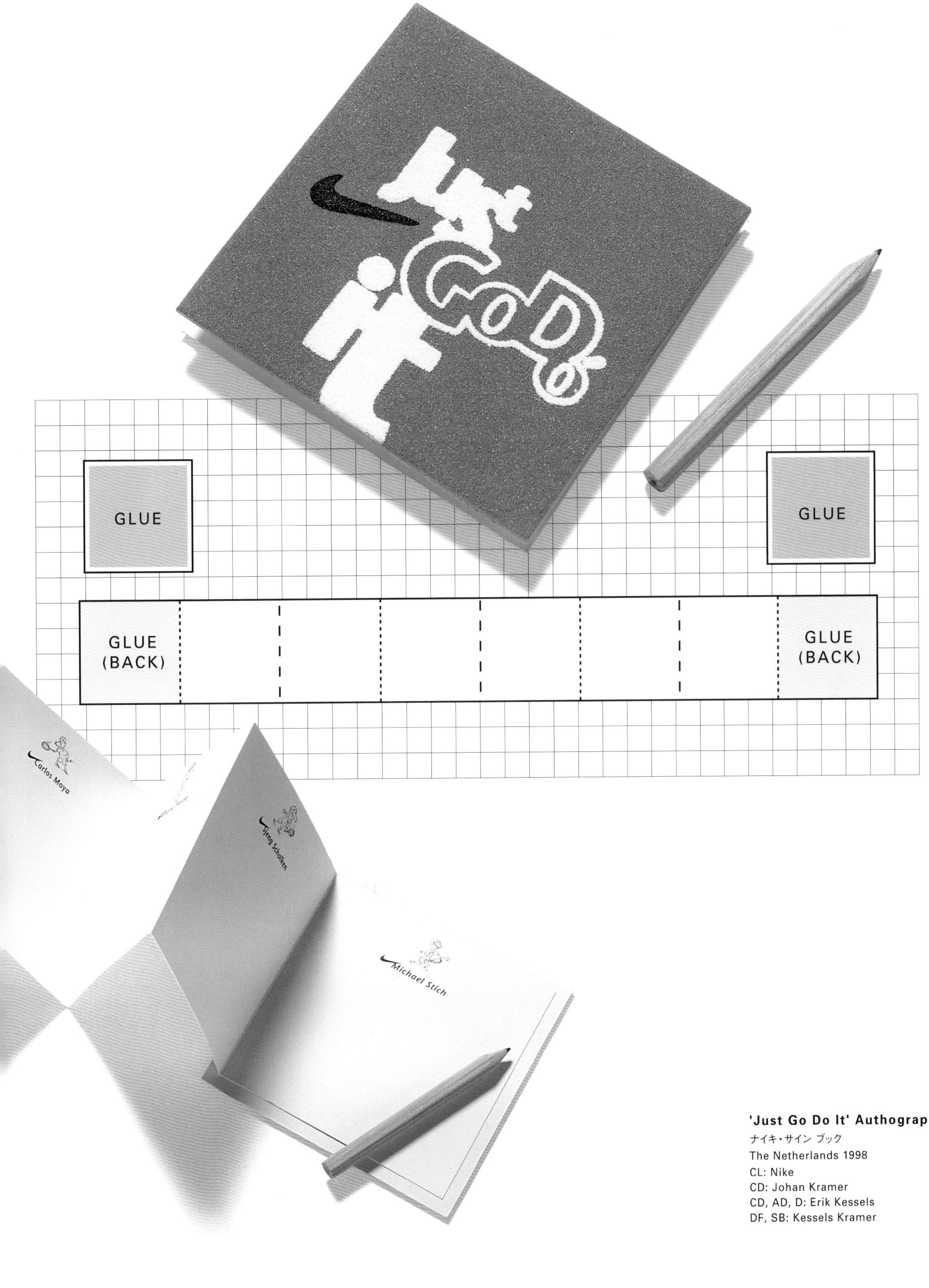

'Just Go Do It' Authograph Book

ナイキ・サイン ブック

The Netherlands 1998

CL: Nike

CD: Johan Kramer

CD, AD, D: Erik Kessels

DF, SB: Kessels Kramer

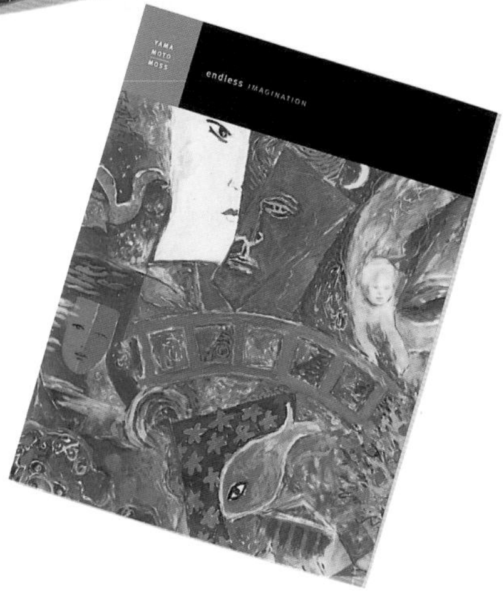

Promotion Leaflet "Endless Imagination" "Digital Brand Experiences" "Corporate and Brand Identity"

広告代理店プロモーション用リーフレット

USA 20002002

CL, SB:Yamamoto Moss

CD, P: Hideki Yamamoto

AD, D: Kasey Hatzung

I: Miranda Moss

DF, SB: Yamamoto Moss

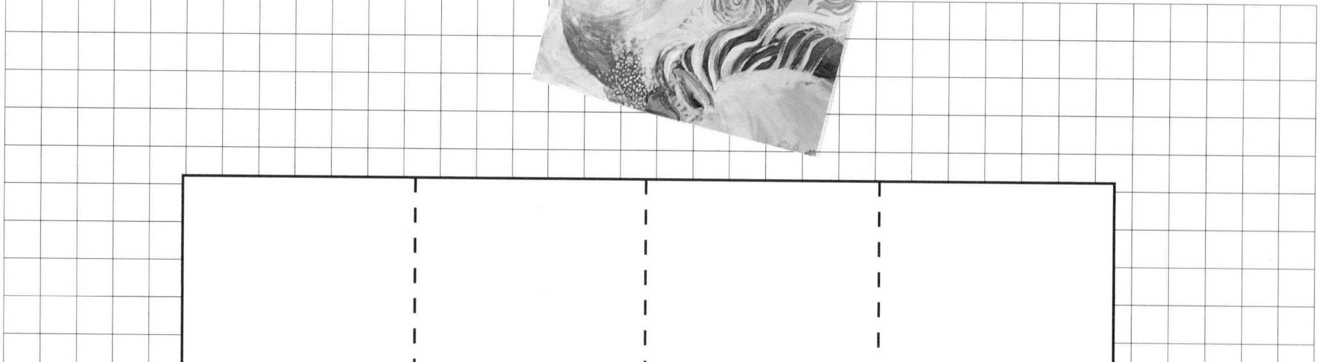

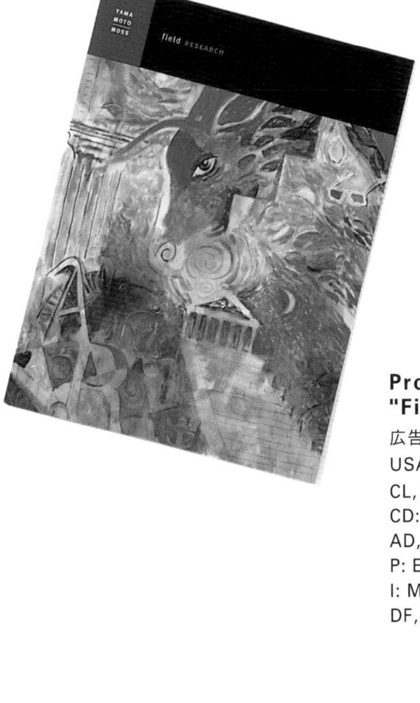

Promotion Leaflet "Field Research"

広告代理店プロモーション用リーフレット

USA 2001

CL, SB:Yamamoto Moss

CD: Hideki Yamamoto

AD, D: Kasey Hatzung

P: Ellie Kingsbury

I: Miranda Moss

DF, SB: Yamamoto Moss

Infromation Pamphlet
案内パンフレット
Japan 1999
CL: Umitsubaki Hayama
CD: Daisaku Fujiwara
AD: Hiroaki Nagai
D: Hisaki Otake
P: Mikiya Takimoto

Ishikawa Ongakudo Guide Pamphlet

石川県立音楽堂案内パンフレット

Japan 2001

CL: Yoshida Printing Inc.

AD: Toshio Gobou

D: Masashi Yanagiyachi

P: Yoshihiro Shinano

DF, SB: Val Design Group Co., Ltd.

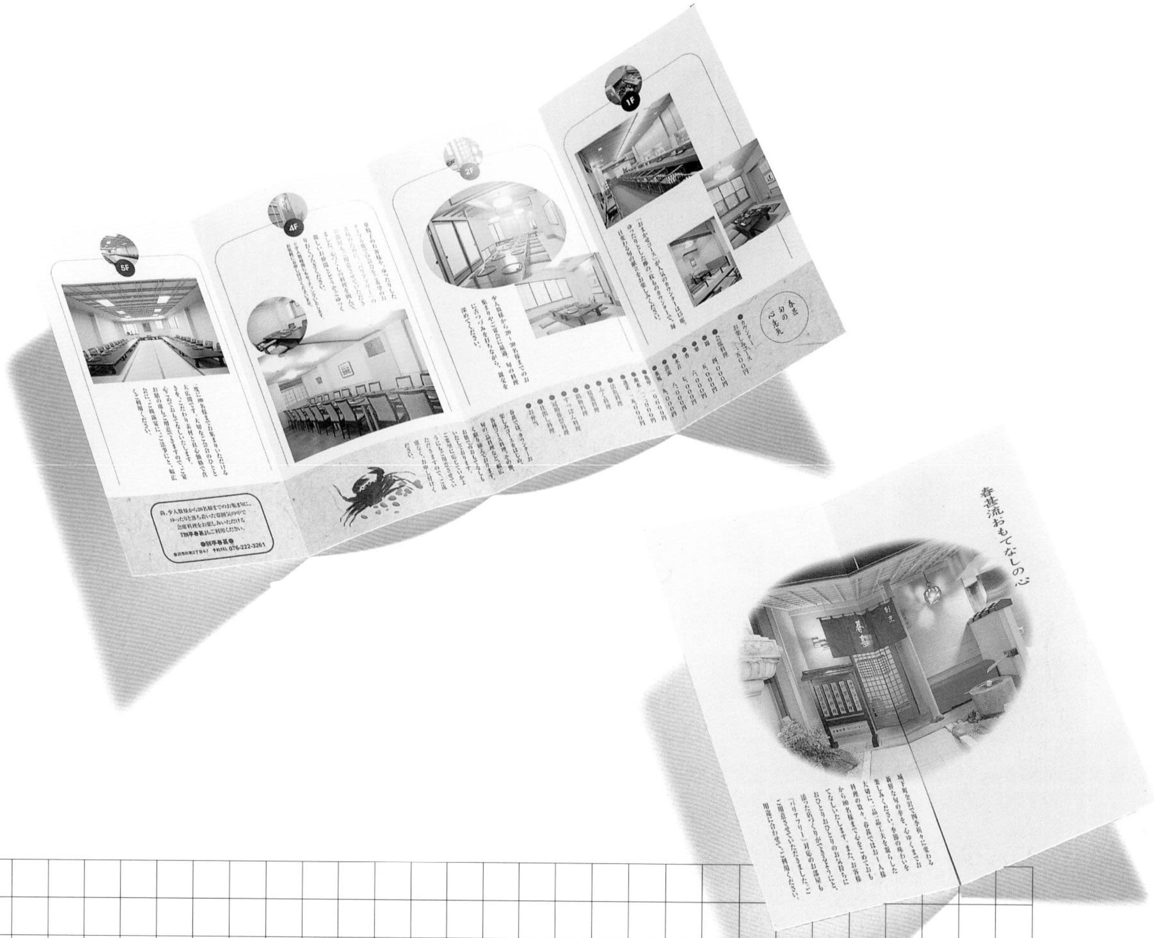

068

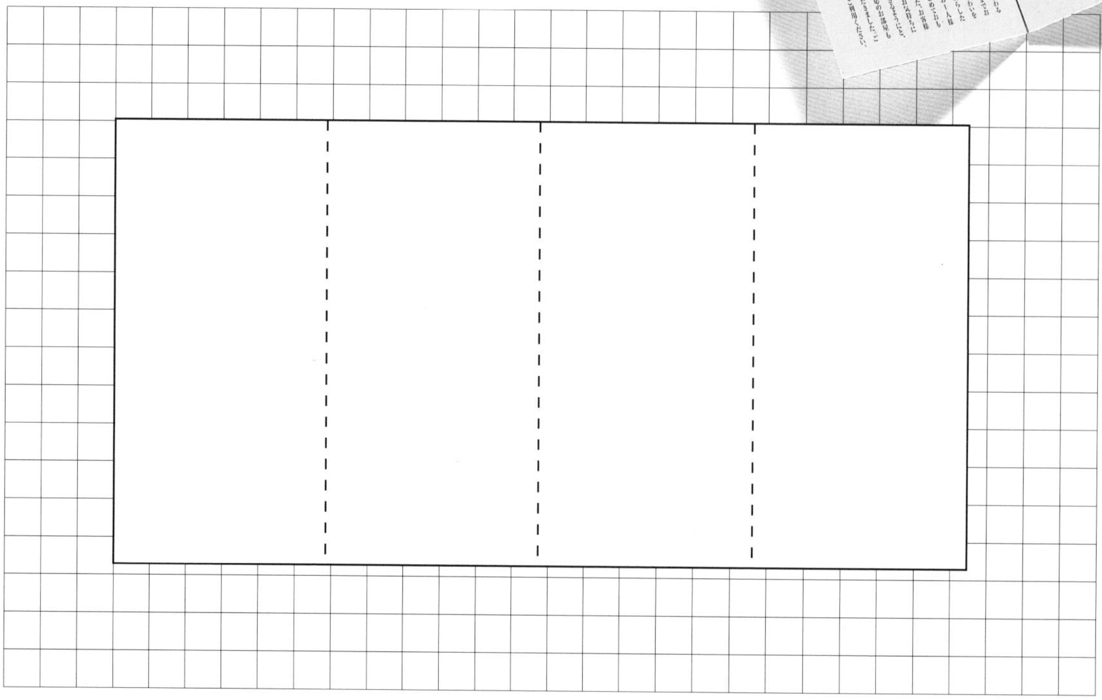

Restaurant Pamphlet

割烹案内パンフレット

Japan

AD: Toshio Gobou

DF, SB: Val Design Group Co., Ltd.

Product Pamphlet
小田原鈴廣パンフレット
Japan
CL, SB: Odawara Suzuhiro

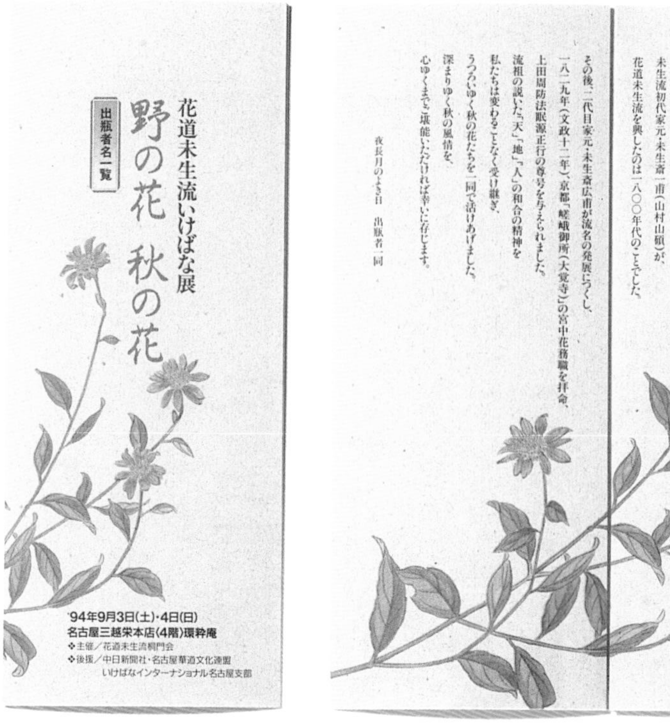

070

花道未生流いけばな展
野の花 秋の花
夏の花だより
出瓶者名一覧
'93年7月3日(土)・4日(日)
名古屋三越栄本店〈4階〉環粋庵
❖主催／花道未生流
❖後援／中日新聞社・名古屋華道文化連盟
七夕月のよき日
出瓶者一同
未生流初代家元・未生斎一甫(山村山碩)が、
花道未生流を興したのは、千八百年代のことでした。
その後、二代目家元・未生斎広甫が流名の発展につくし、
一八二九年(文政十二年)、京都「嵯峨御所(大覚寺)」の宮中花務職を拝命、
上田周防法眼源正行の尊号を与えられました。
うつろいゆく秋の花たちを一同で活けあげました。
以来、星霜をかさね、歴代を経て、今代の未生斎一甫で第九世を数えました。
時を経ても、
流祖の説いた〈天・地・人の和合〉の精神は変わることなく、
一輪の花に人生を託して今に息づいています。
花で、季節の移ろいを知り、歓びを知る……
夏のひとときを心おもむくままに、
山野の草木やさまざまな花たちとともに、
ゆっくりとお過ごしいただければ望外のよろこびでございます。

Ikebana Exhibition Announcement Leaflet
いけばな展告知リーフレット
Japan 19931997
CL: Kadou Mishouryu Toumonkai
CD: Chizue Katou
AD, D: Eiko Holy
I: Chihiro Usui
DF, SB: Studio Thanatos

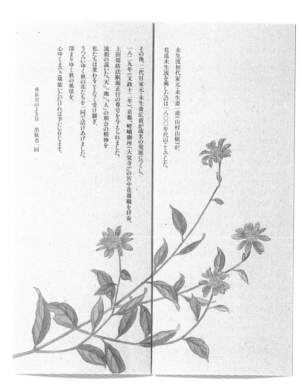

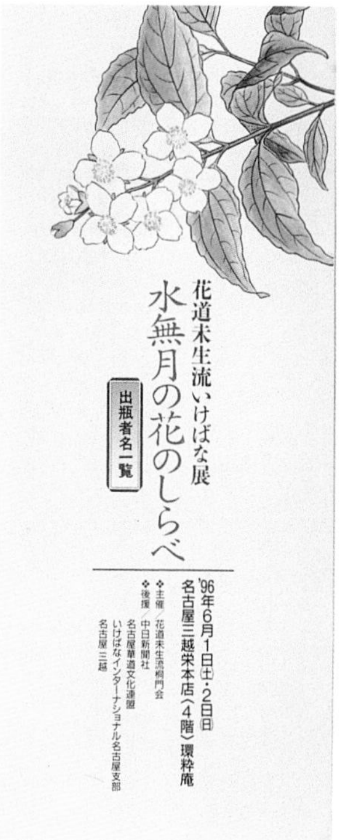
花道未生流いけばな展
水無月の花のしらべ
出瓶者名一覧
'96年6月1日(土)・2日(日)
名古屋三越栄本店〈4階〉環粋庵
❖主催／花道未生流桐門会
❖後援／中日新聞社
名古屋華道文化連盟
いけばなインターナショナル名古屋支部
名古屋三越

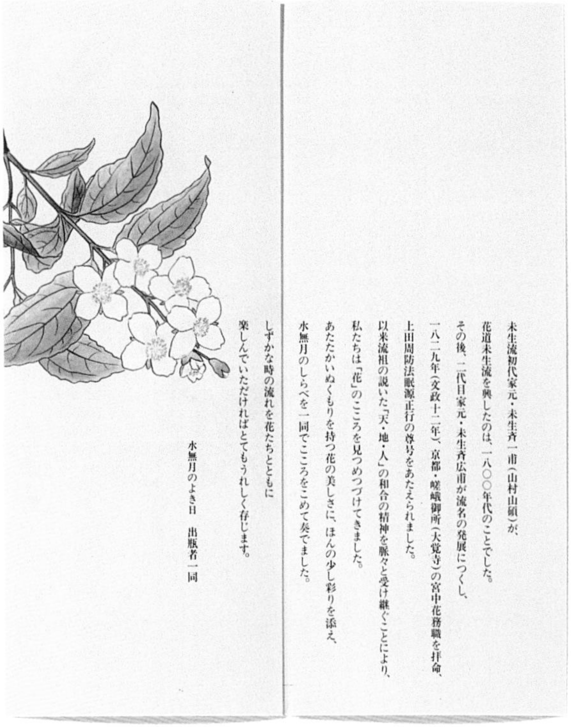
未生流初代家元・未生斉一甫(山村山碩)が、
花道未生流を興したのは、一八〇〇年代のことでした。
その後、二代目家元・未生斉広甫が流名の発展につくし、
一八二九年(文政十二年)、京都・嵯峨御所(大覚寺)の宮中花務職を拝命、
上田周防法眼源正行の尊号をあたえられました。
以来流祖の説いた「天・地・人」の和合の精神を脈々と受け継ぐことにより、
私たちは「花」のこころを見つめつづけてきました。
あたたかいぬくもりを持つ花の美しさに、ほんの少し彩りを添え、
水無月のしらべを一同でこころをこめて奏でました。
しずかな時の流れを花たちとともに
楽しんでいただければとてもうれしく存じます。
水無月のよき日　出瓶者一同

花道未生流いけばな展
秋の花、秋の彩。
出瓶者名一覧
'97年10月25日(土)・26日(日)
名古屋三越栄本店〈4階〉環粋庵
(最終日は午後5時まで)
◆主催／花道未生流桐門会
◆後援／中日新聞社
名古屋華道文化連盟
いけばなインターナショナル名古屋支部
名古屋三越

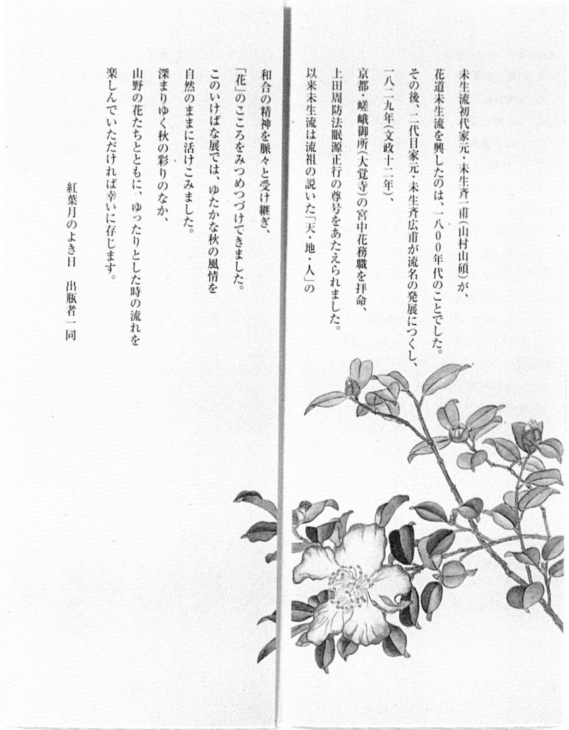
未生流初代家元・未生斉一甫(山村山碩)が、
花道未生流を興したのは、一八00年代のことでした。
その後、二代目家元・未生斉広甫が流名の発展につくし、
一八二九年(文政十二年)、
京都・嵯峨御所(大覚寺)の宮中花務職を拝命、
上田周防法眼源正行の尊号をあたえられました。
以来未生流は流祖の説いた「天・地・人」の
和合の精神を脈々と受け継ぎ、
「花」のこころをみつめつづけてきました。
このいけばな展では、ゆたかな秋の風情を
自然のままに活けこみました。
深まりゆく秋の彩りのなか、
山野の花たちとともに、ゆったりとした時の流れを
楽しんでいただければ幸いに存じます。
紅葉月のよき日　出瓶者一同

Christmas Card "Taugram"
クリスマス・カード
Luxemburg 2001
CL, SB:Made by Sams
CD, AD, D: Camilo Matiz
DF, SB: Made by Sams

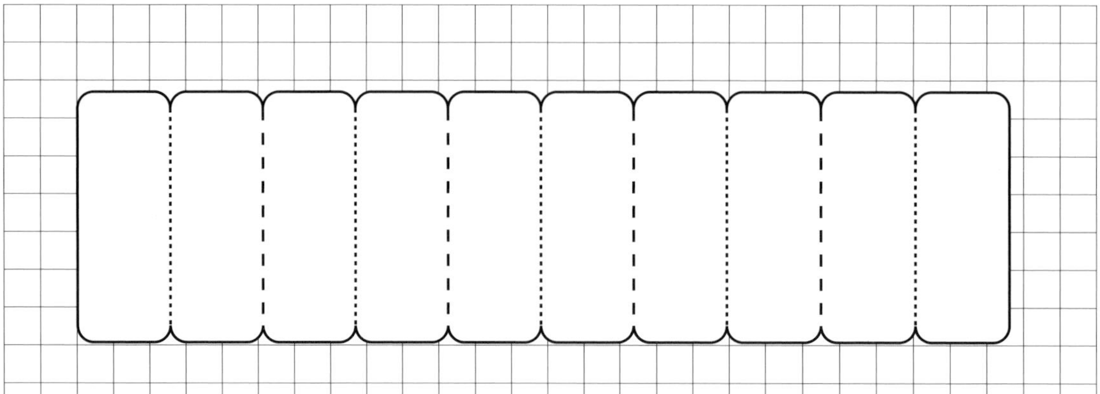

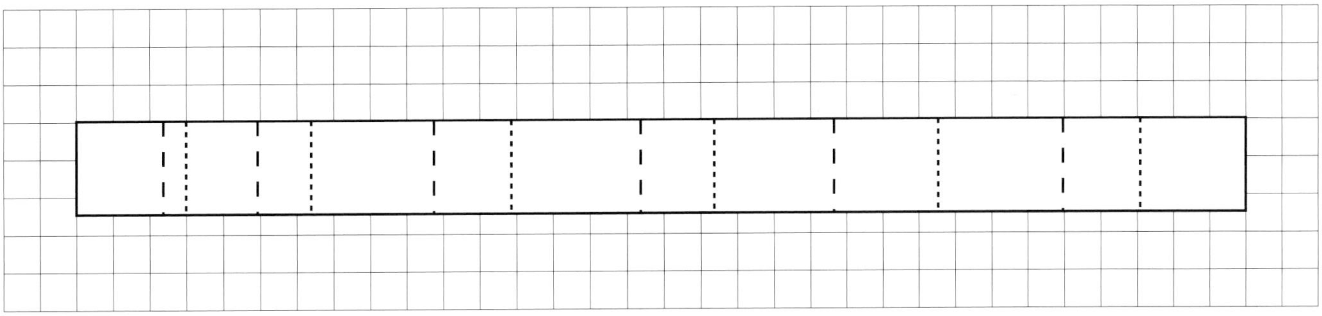

Design Firm
New Year Greeting Card
"MCMXCI (1991)"

デザイン事務所年賀状

Argentina 1990

CL: Victor Garcia & Adriana Ellinger

CD, AD, D, SB: Victor Garcia

DF: Victor Garcia & Adriana Ellinger

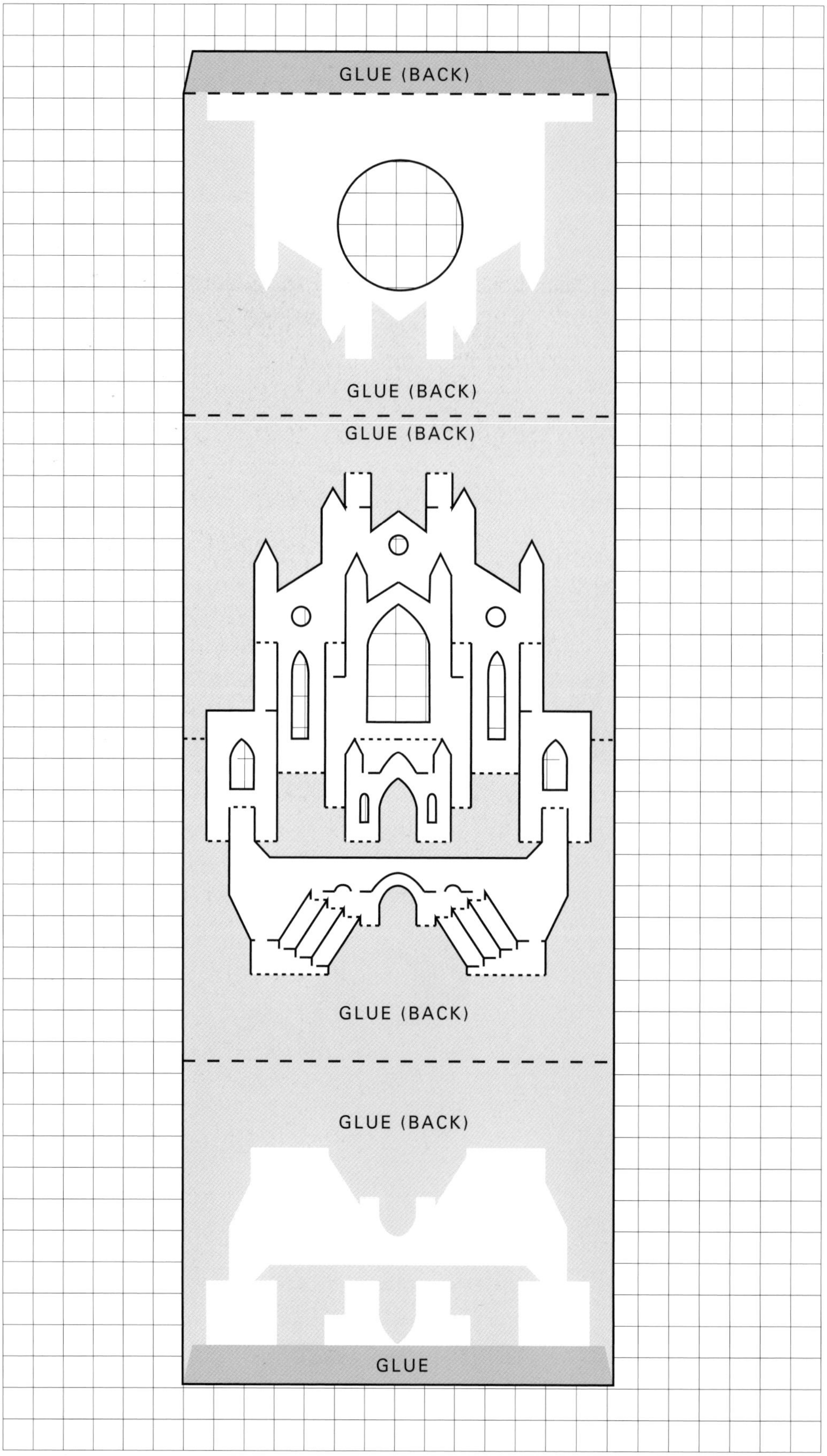
GLUE (BACK)
GLUE (BACK)
GLUE (BACK)
GLUE (BACK)
GLUE (BACK)
GLUE

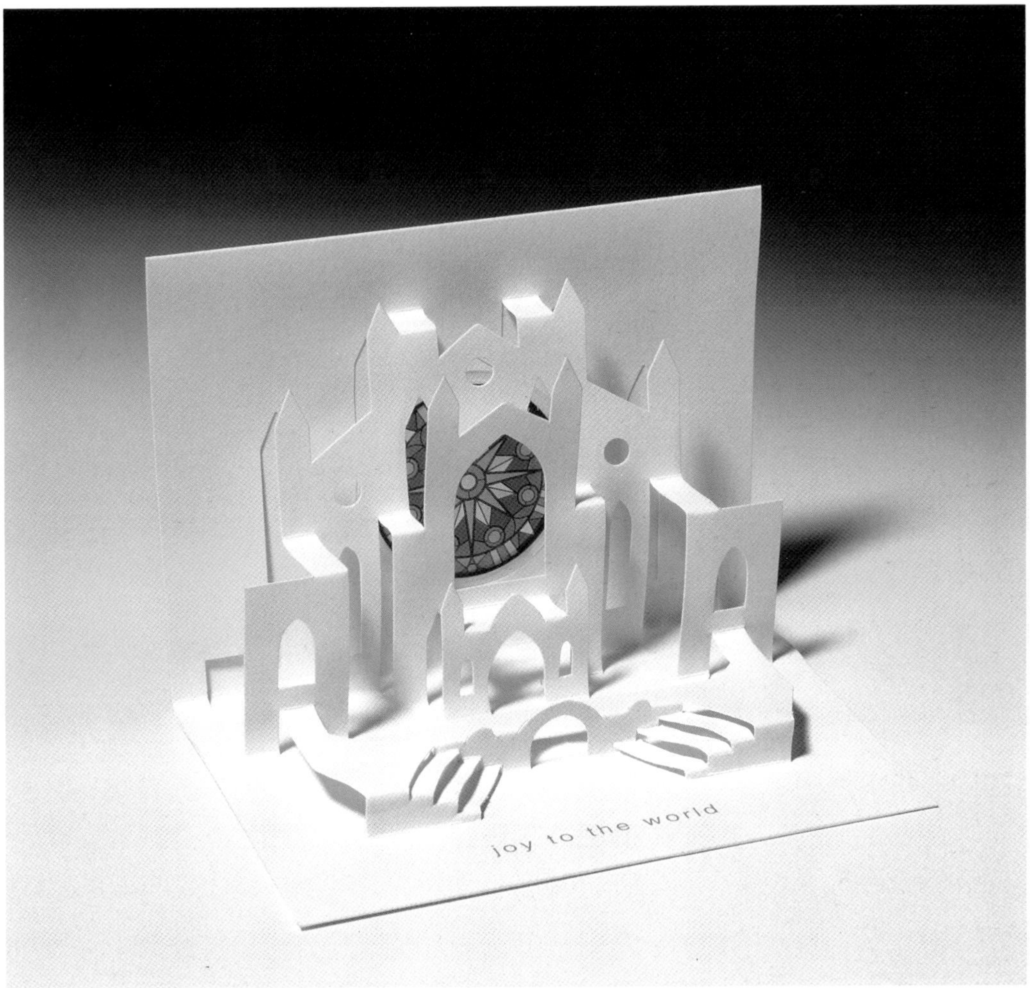

Pop-Up Cathedral
美術館ギフトカード
USA 2002
CL: Museum of Modern Art, New York City
CD: Ashley White
D, I, SB: Robert Sabuda

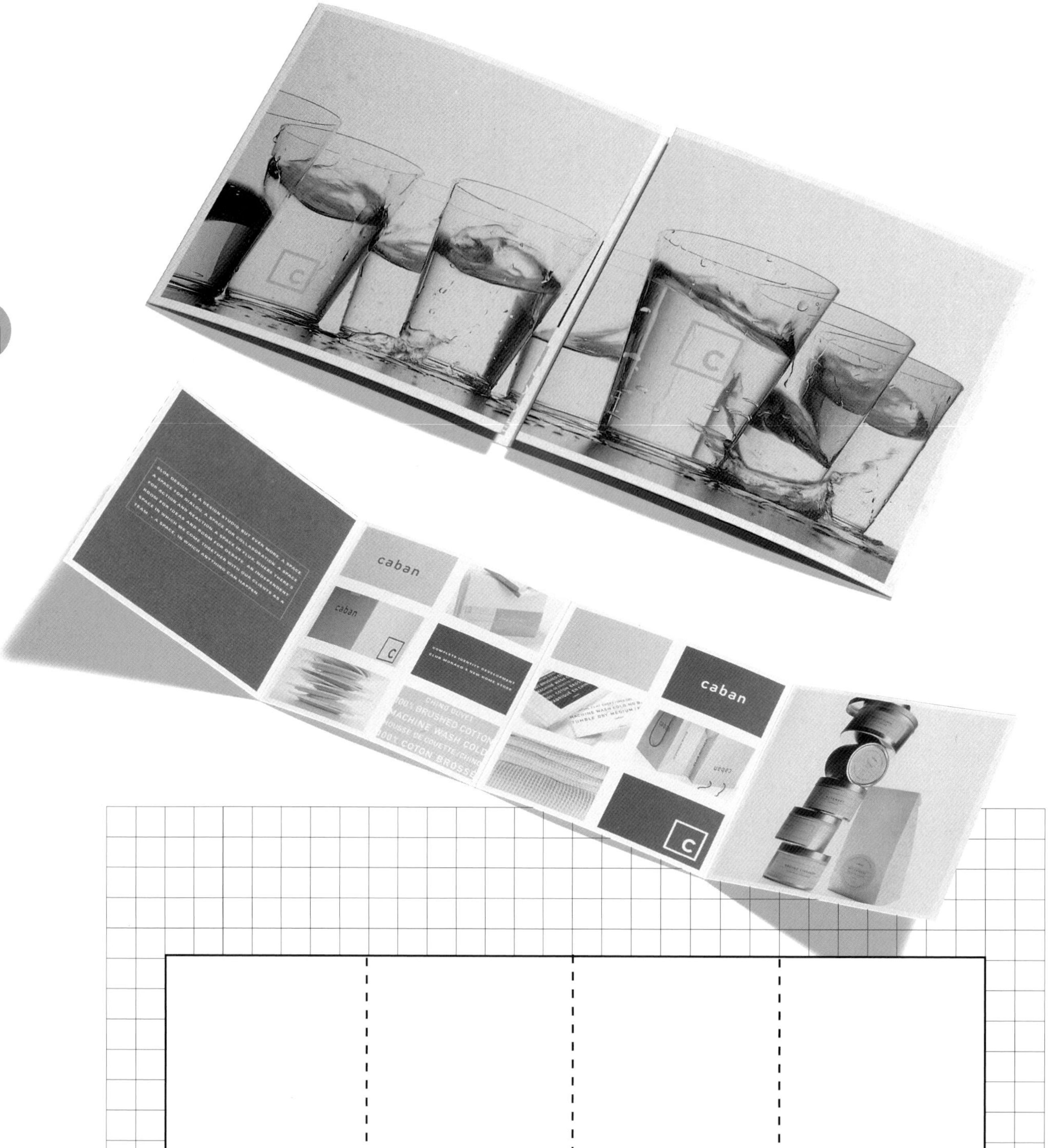

Blok Promo Pamphlet

デザイン事務所 プロモーション用

Canada 2001

CL, SB:Blok Design

CD, AD, D: Vanessa Eckstein

DF, SB: Blok Design

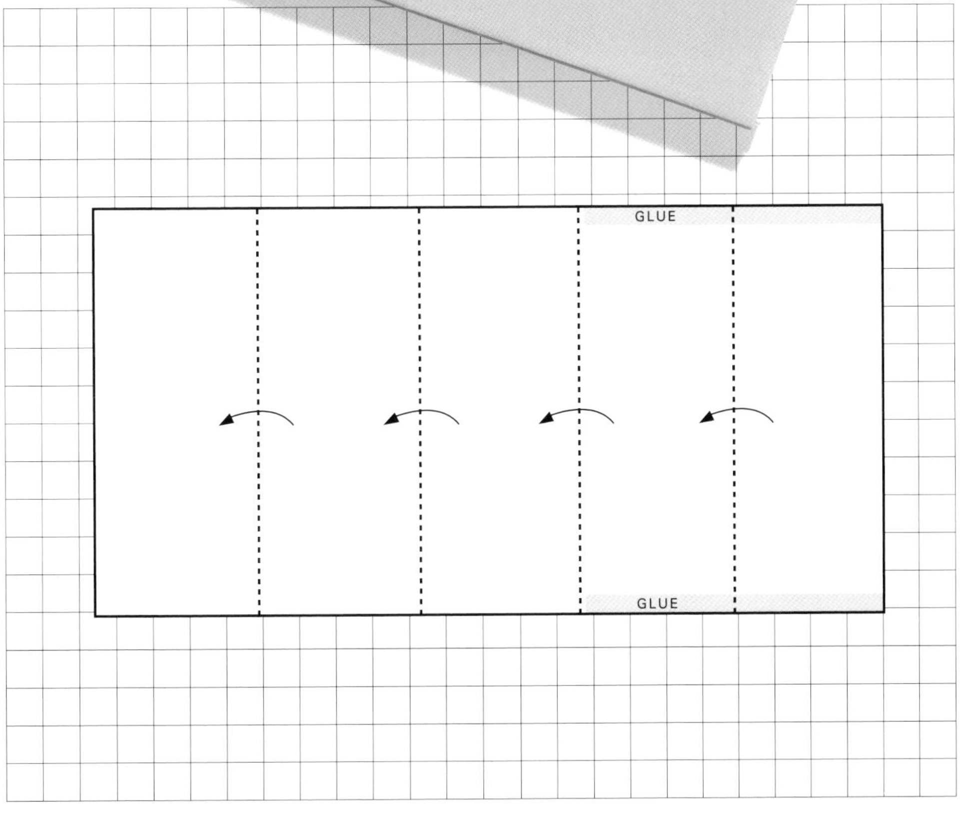

Donations DM "St. Francis School Annual Brochure"

募金活動DM

USA 1991

CL: Association for Portland Progress

CD: Sue Fisher / TriAd

AD, D, I: Jeff Fisher

DF, SB: Jeff Fisher LogoMotives

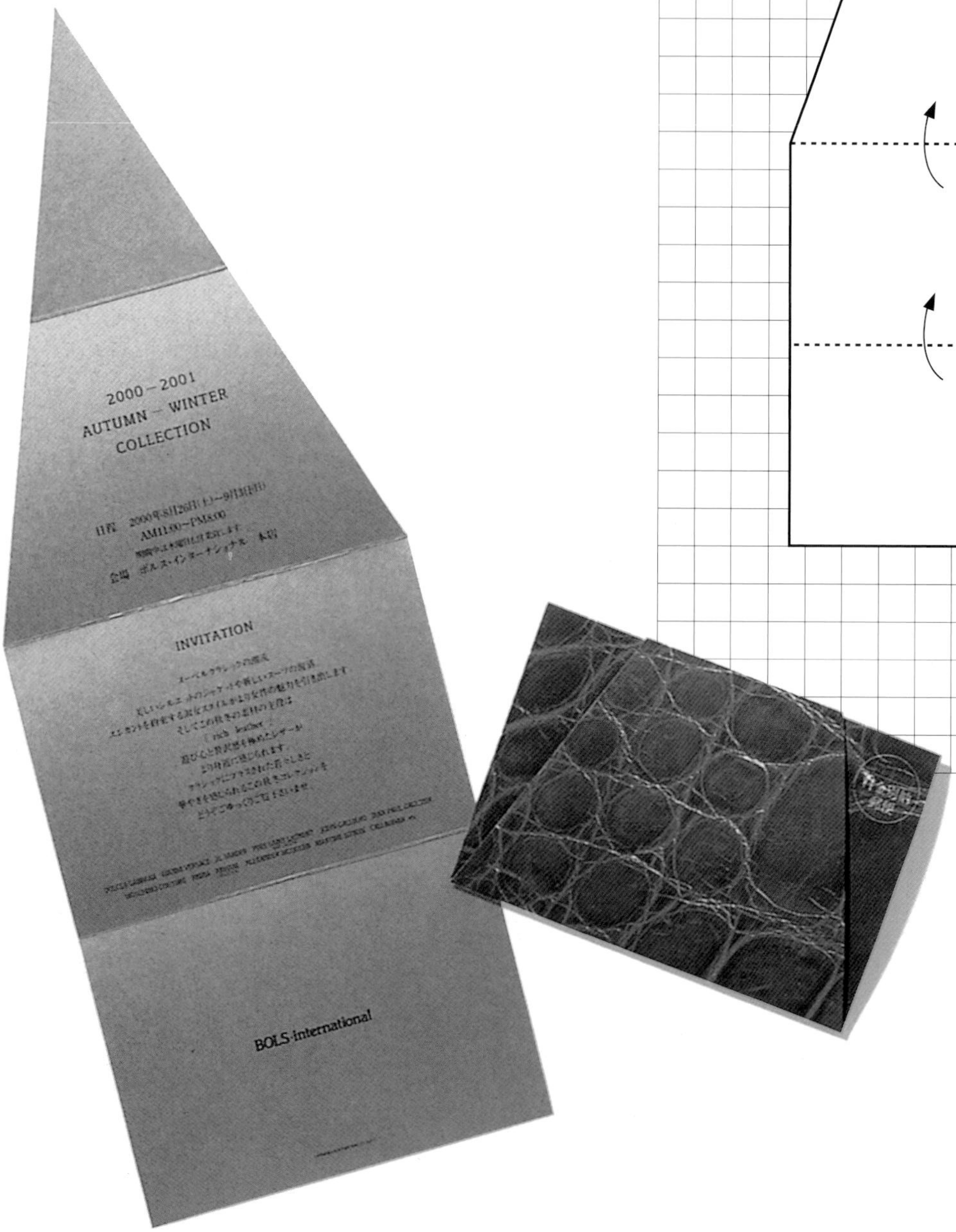

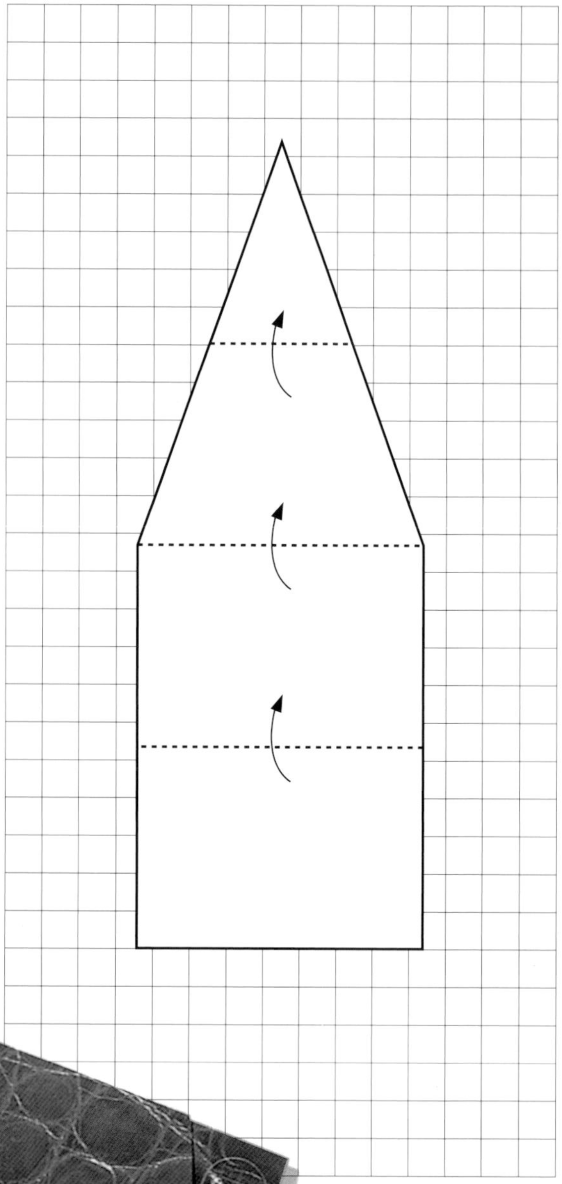

Boutique Collection Invitation Card

ブティック コレクション 招待状

Japan 2000

CL: BOLS International Co., Ltd.

AD, D: Katsunori Watanabe

DF, SB: Bauhaus Inc.

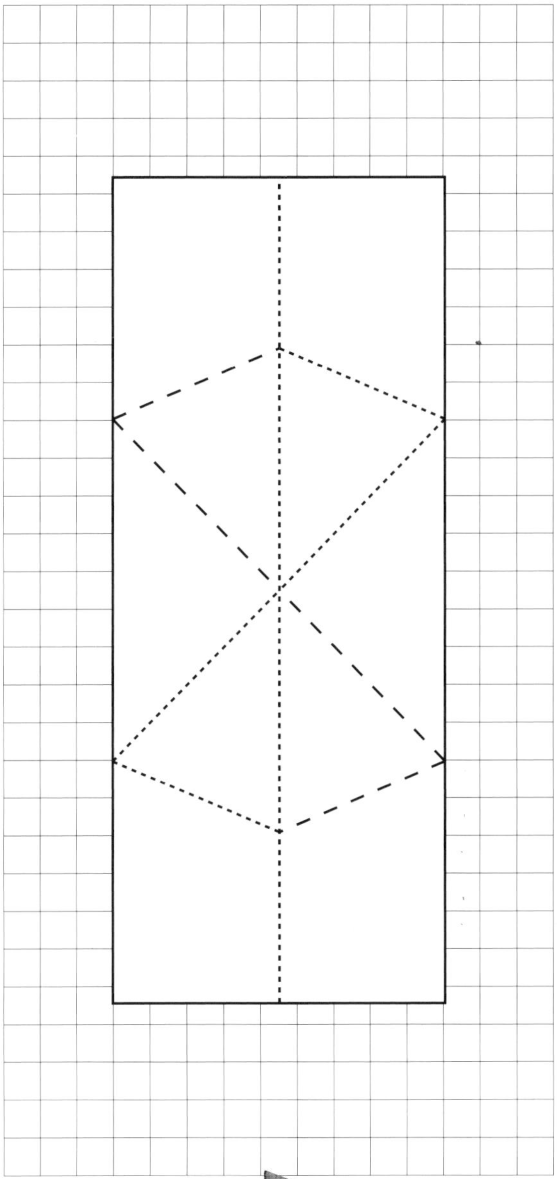

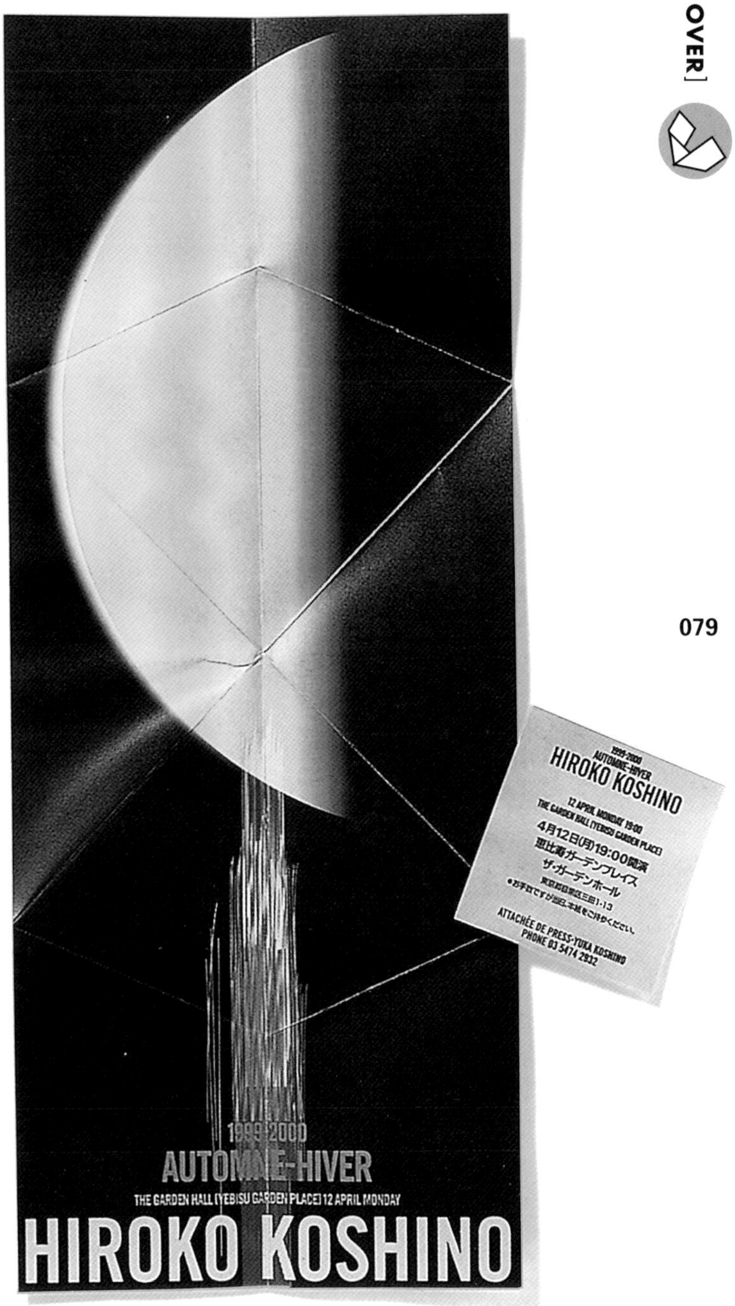

Interior Design
Sales Promotion Tool

インテリア プロモーション ツール

Germany 2000

CL: Uorzicius Interiors

CD: Marius Fahrner

P: Franu Stoecki

DF, SB: Marius Fahrner Design

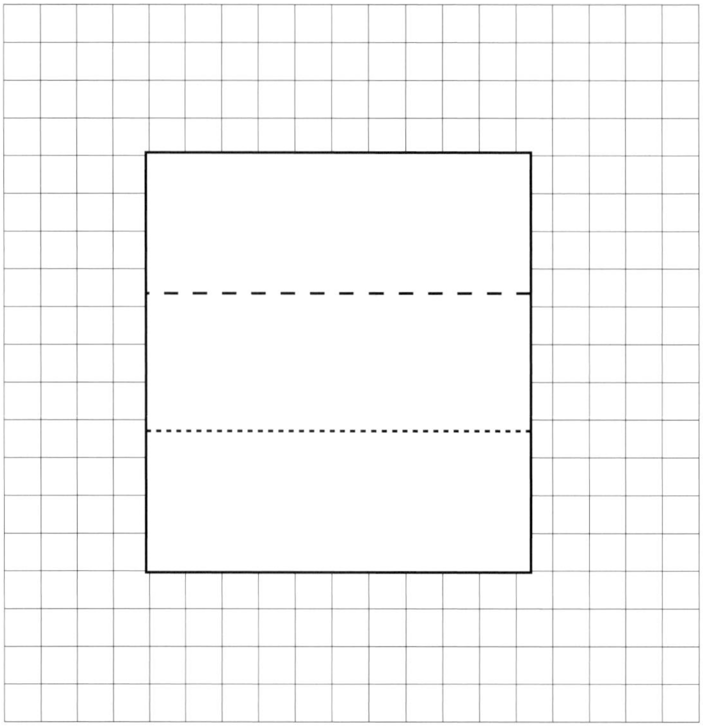

080

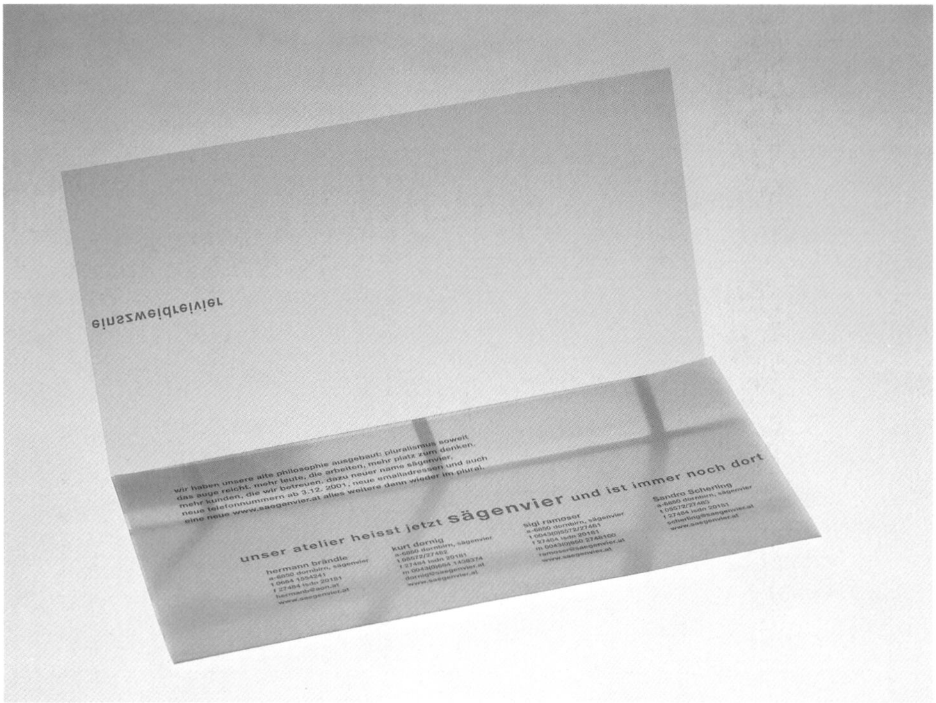

Invitation Card
"Sagenvier Design Kommunication"

デザイン事務所案内状

Austria 2002

CL: Sagenvier

CD, AD, D, P, SB: Sigi Ramoser

DF: Sagenvier Design Kommunikation

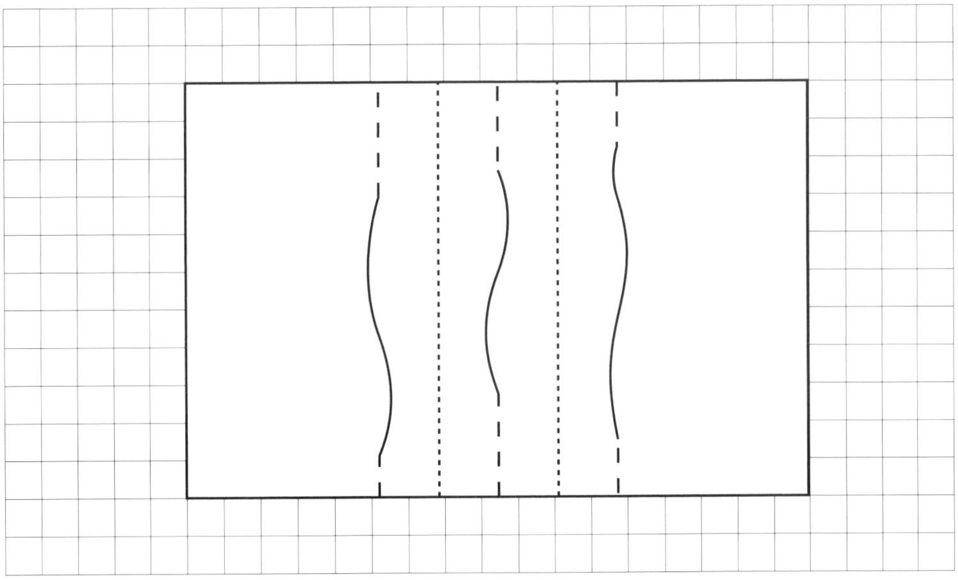

Greeting Card (Spring Breeze)
グリーティング・カード（春のかぜ）
Japan 2001
CL: PLAN Y
AD, D, SB: Miyuki Yoshida

Event Announcement DM
イベント告知DM
Japan 2001
CL: Cassina IXC. Ltd.
AD, D: Katsunori Hironaka
D: Sho Sawada

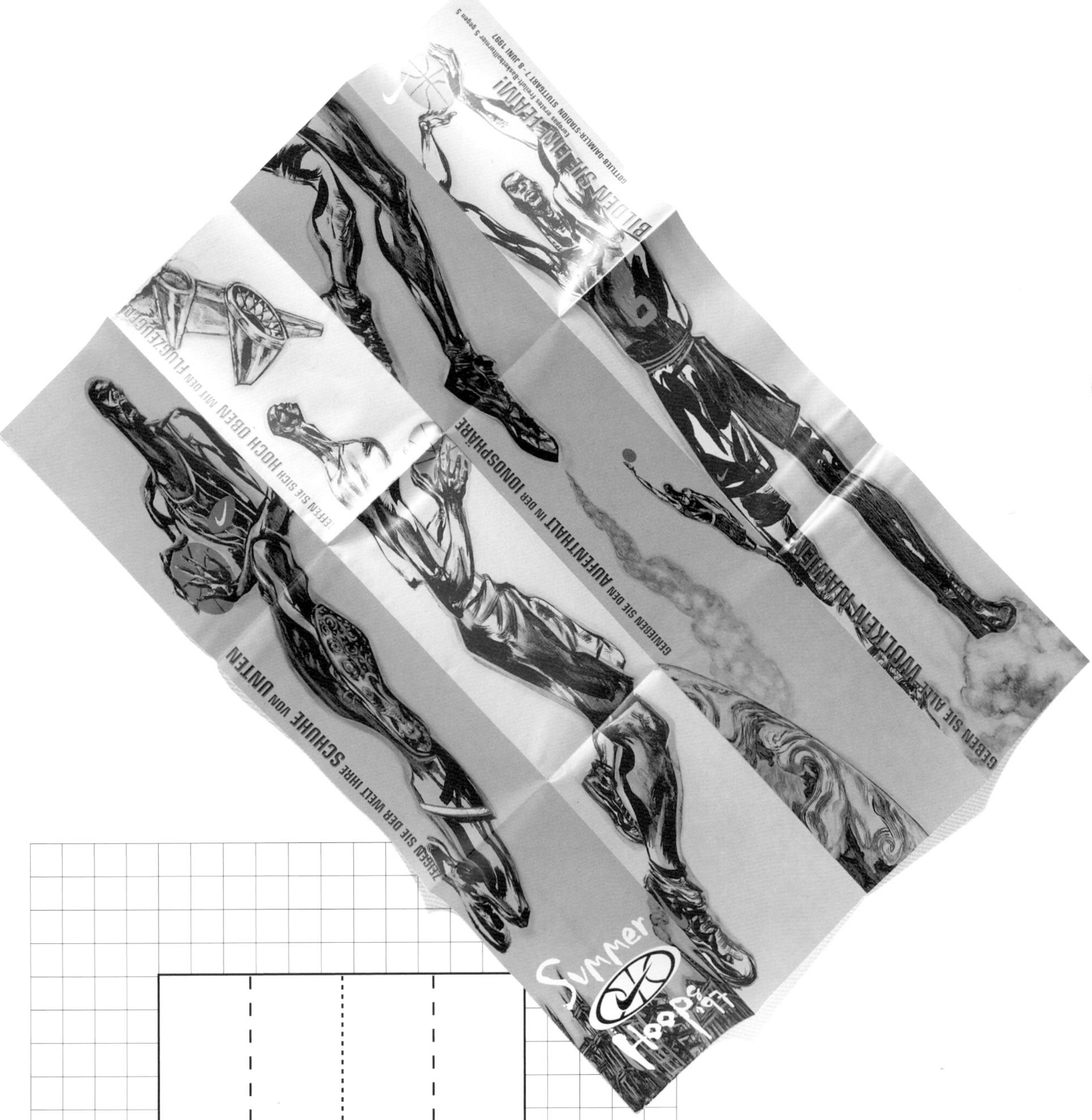

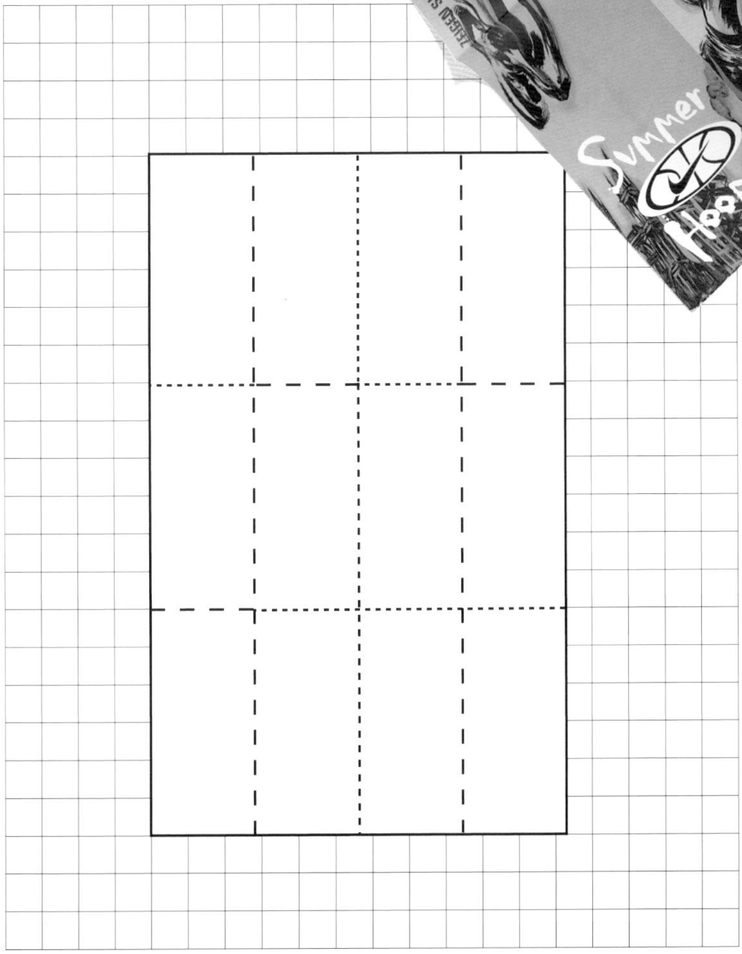

Flyer "Summer Hoops '97"

スポーツメイカー・フライヤー

The Netherlands 1997

CL: Nike

CD: Johan Kramer

CD, AD, D, DF: Erik Kessels

I: Joe Morse

DF, SB: Kessels Kramer

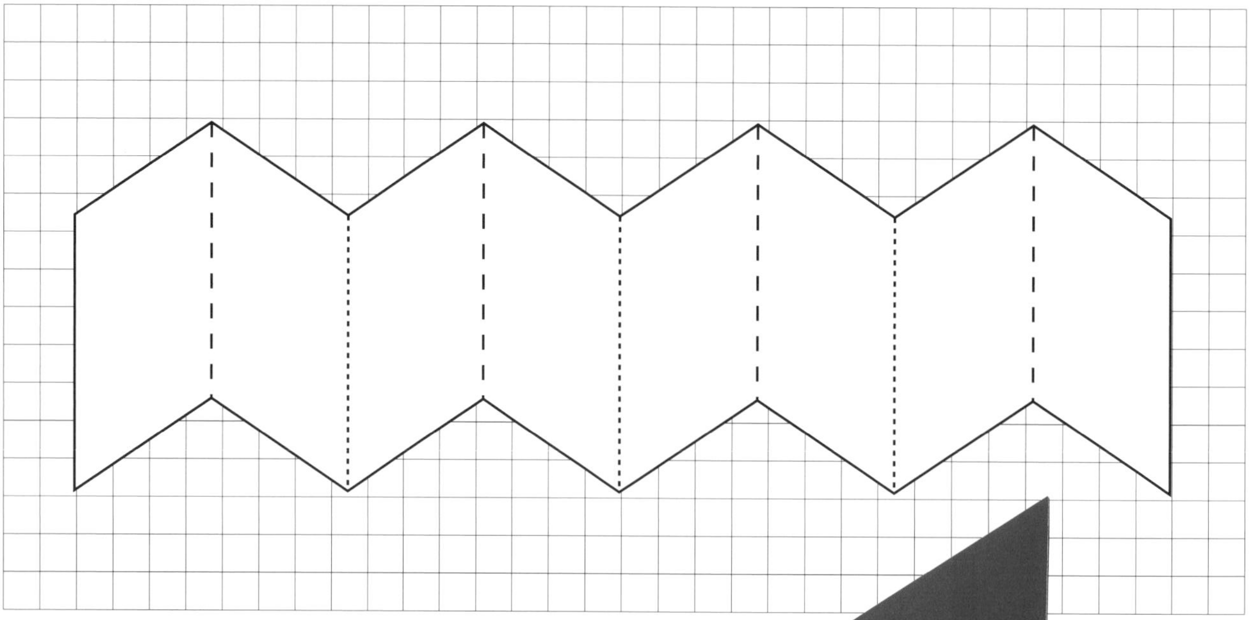

Originate
オリジネイト
Japan 2002
CL: Kuwasawa Design School
AD, D: Masami Takahashi
DF, SB: Masami Design

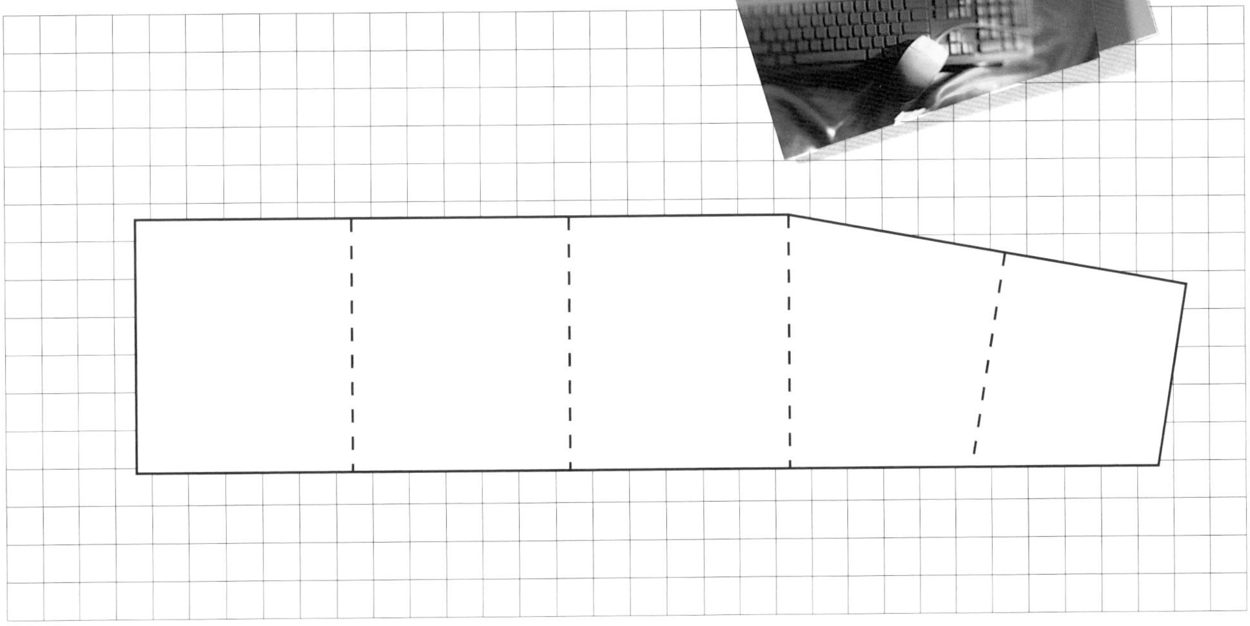

Promotional Leaflet
"Hey! Brochure"

eコマースプロモーション リーフレット

USA 2000

CL: Net Perceptions

AD: Alan Tse

D: Gretchen Blase

P: Ellie Kingsbury

DF, SB: Yamamoto Moss

086

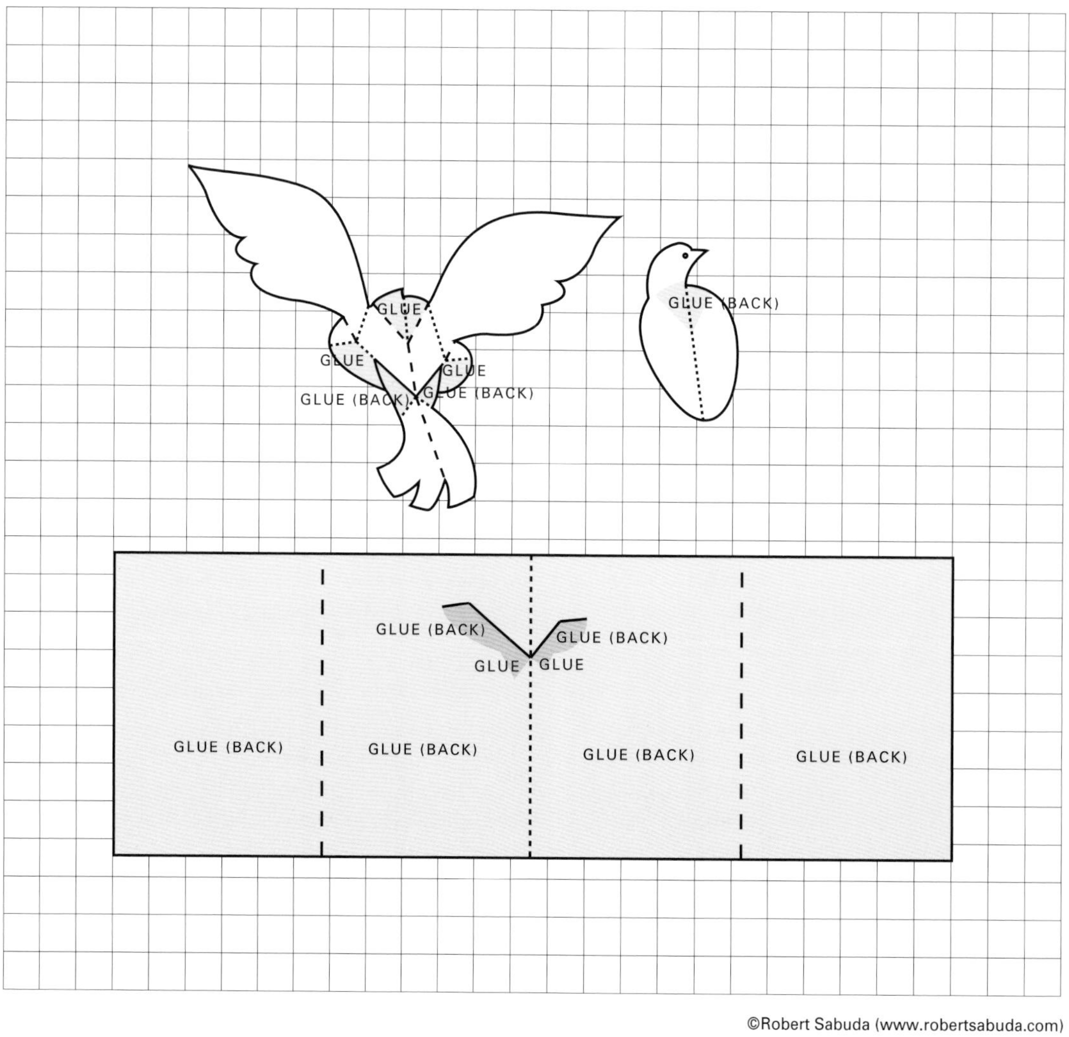

Pop-Up Dove
美術館ギフトカード
USA 2002
CL: Museum of Modern Art, New York City
CD: Ashley White
D, I, SB: Robert Sabuda

P'parco 2002
Christmas Campaign DM

P'parco 2002 クリスマスキャンペーンDM
Japan 2002
CL: Parco Co., Ltd.
AD, D: Masami Takahashi
DF, SB: Masami Design

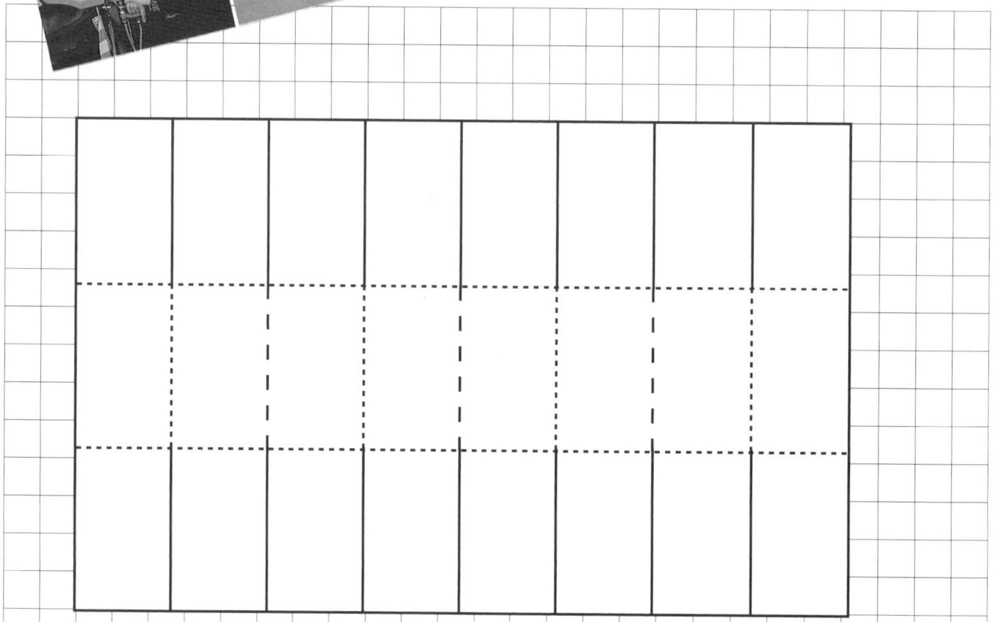

"Zuidwaarts"
Art Galery Guide
アートギャラリー案内
Belgium 1998
CL: Galerie Zuidwaarts
CD, AD, D, I: Jo Klaps
P: Tessa Verder
DF, SB: Brussels Lof

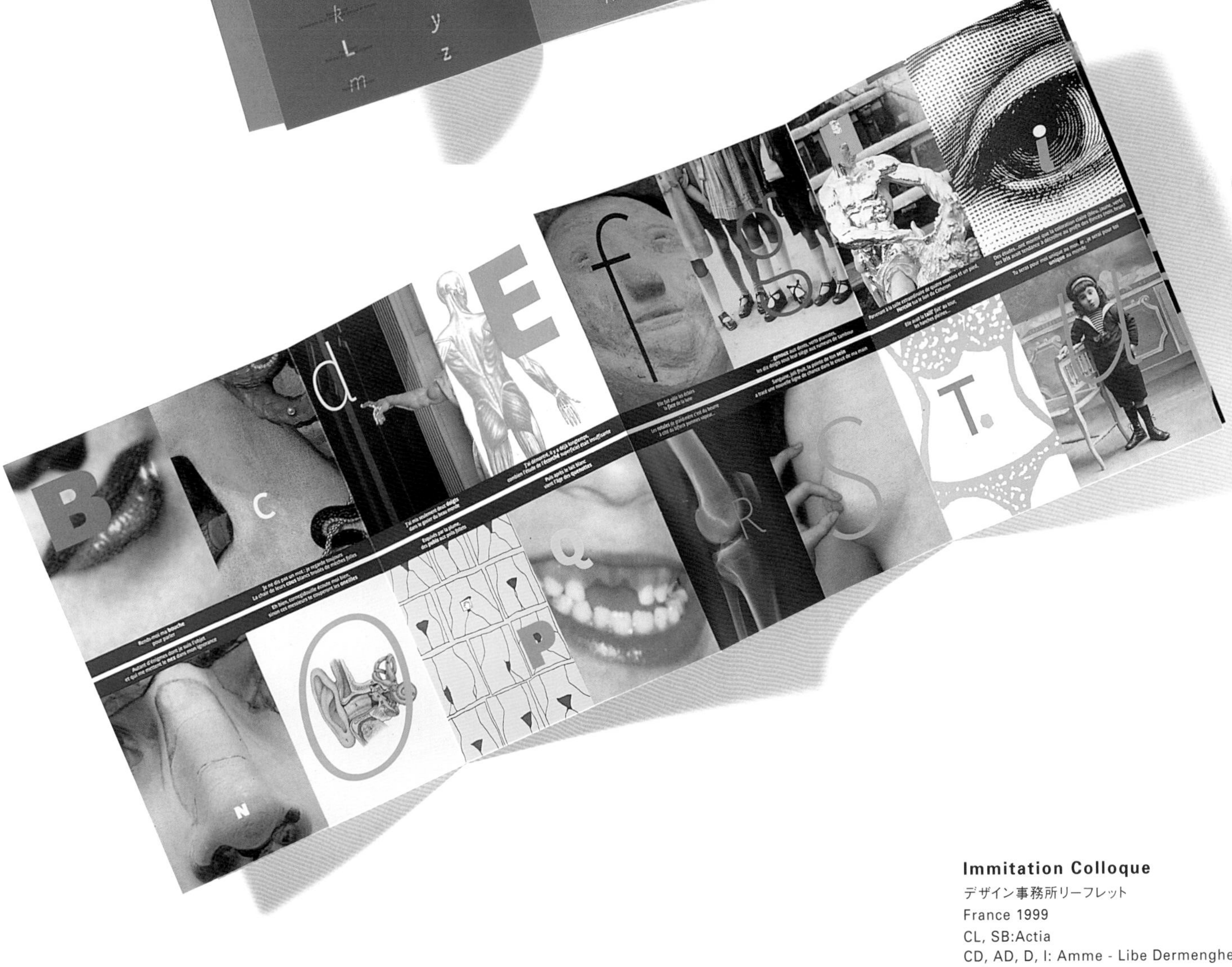

Immitation Colloque
デザイン事務所リーフレット
France 1999
CL, SB:Actia
CD, AD, D, I: Amme - Libe Dermenghem

Soccer Shoes Catalog
サッカーシューズ・カタログ
Japan
CL, SB:Nike Japan Co., Ltd.

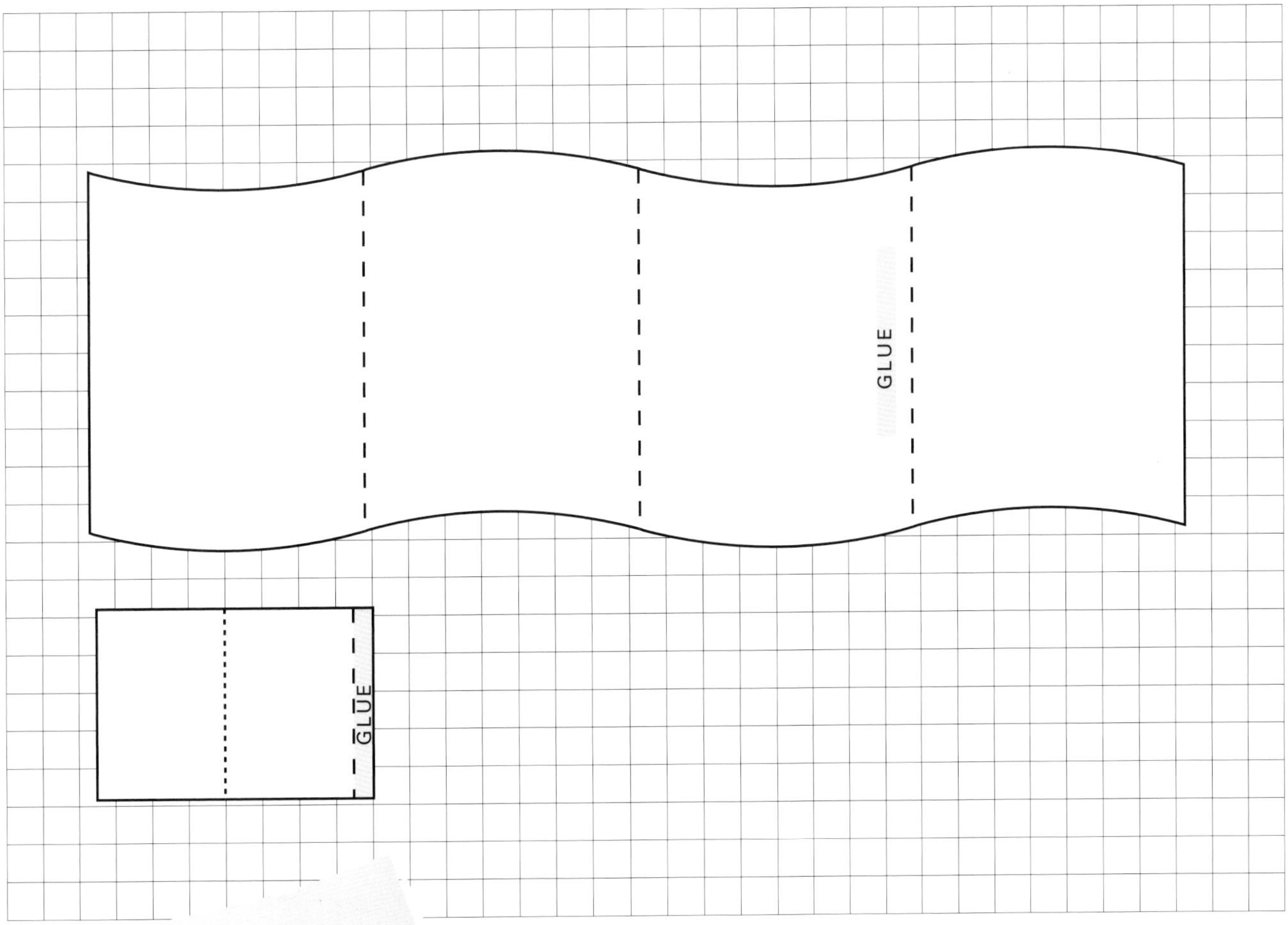
GLUE
GLUE

NIKE BRAZIL APPAREL TECHNOLOGY
ゲームウエア。
ZIL APPAREL
140-8636
株式会社ナイキジャパン
マーケティング部
ブランドコミュニケーション チーム行
NIKE QUESTIONNAIRE
NIKE EQUIPS
ボールを限りな
BRAZIL

092

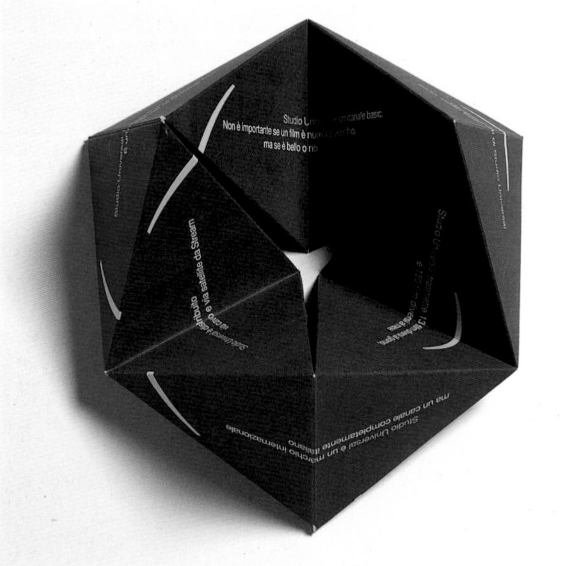

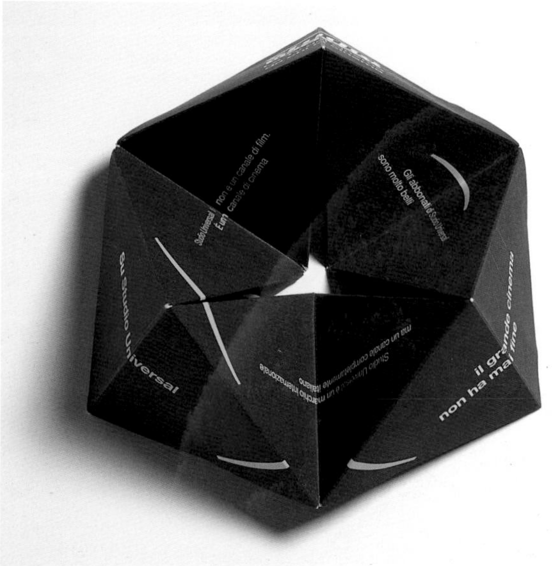

Promotion Kit
プロモーション用キット
Italy 2001
CL: Studio Universal

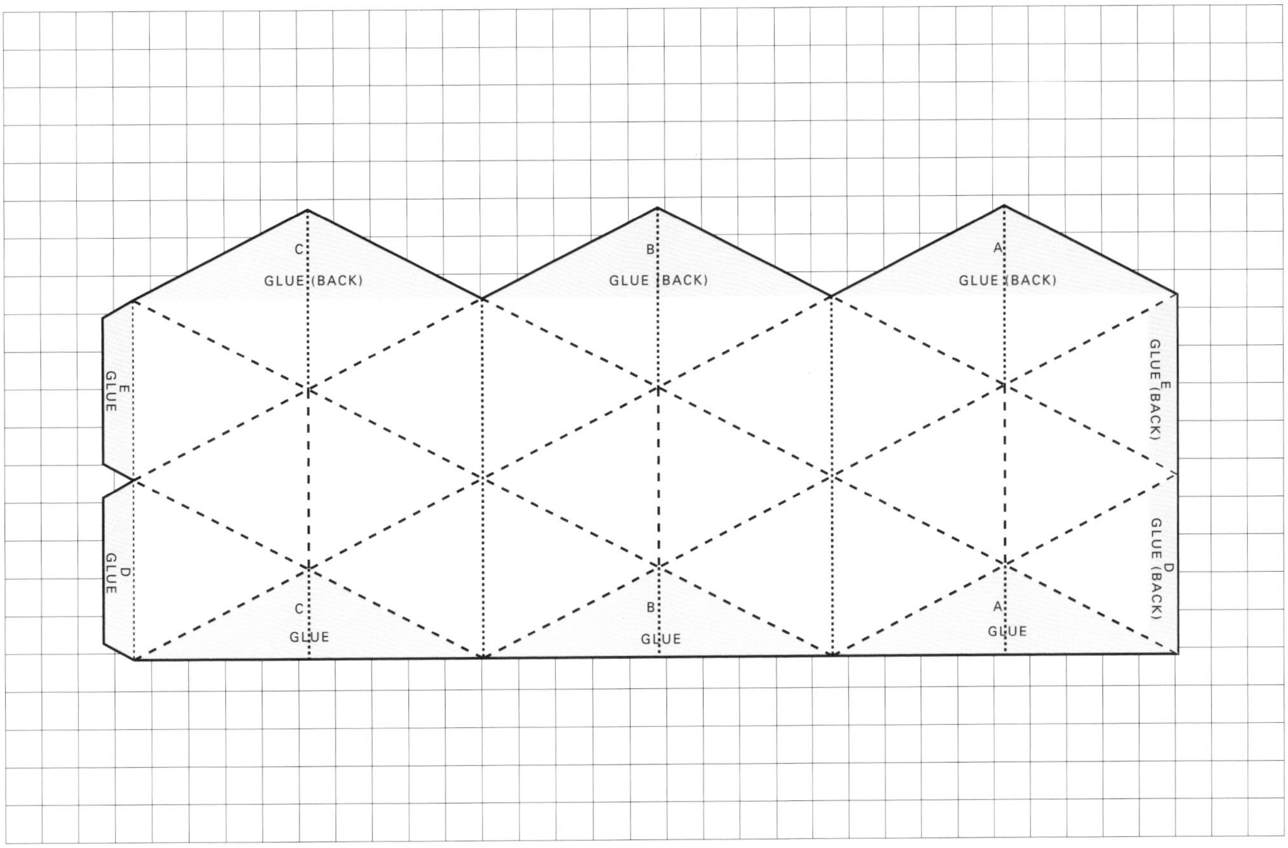
C
GLUE (BACK)
B
GLUE (BACK)
A
GLUE (BACK)
E
GLUE
E
GLUE (BACK)
D
GLUE
D
GLUE (BACK)
C
GLUE
B
GLUE
A
GLUE

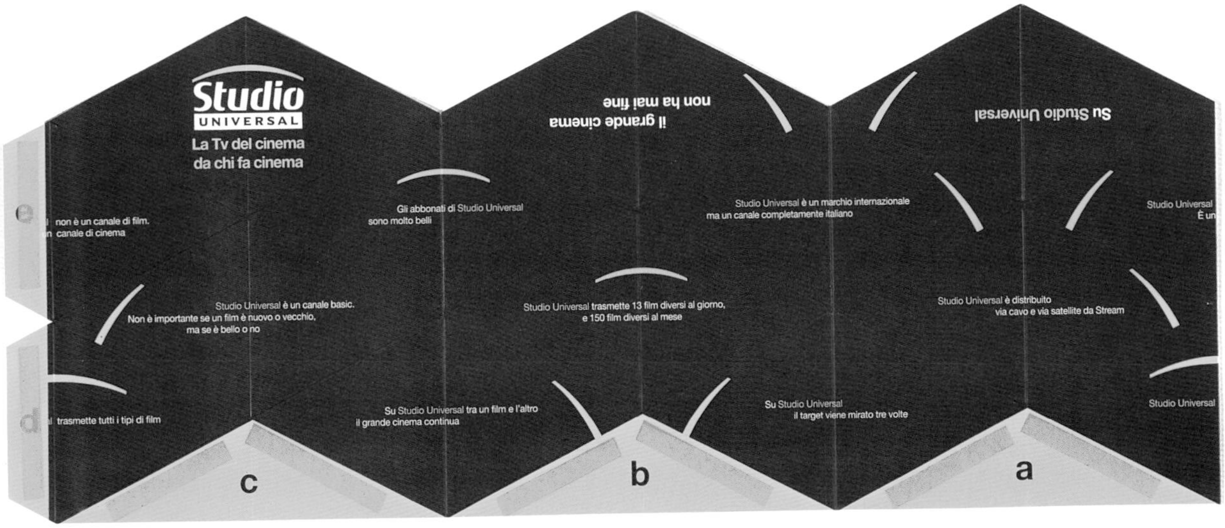
Studio
UNIVERSAL
La Tv del cinema
da chi fa cinema
il grande cinema
non ha mai fine
Su Studio Universal
non è un canale di film.
canale di cinema
Gli abbonati di Studio Universal
sono molto belli
Studio Universal è un marchio internazionale
ma un canale completamente italiano
Studio Universal
È un
Studio Universal è un canale basic.
Non è importante se un film è nuovo o vecchio,
ma se è bello o no
Studio Universal trasmette 13 film diversi al giorno,
e 150 film diversi al mese
Studio Universal è distribuito
via cavo e via satellite da Stream
trasmette tutti i tipi di film
Su Studio Universal tra un film e l'altro
il grande cinema continua
Su Studio Universal
il target viene mirato tre volte
Studio Universal
e
d
c
b
a

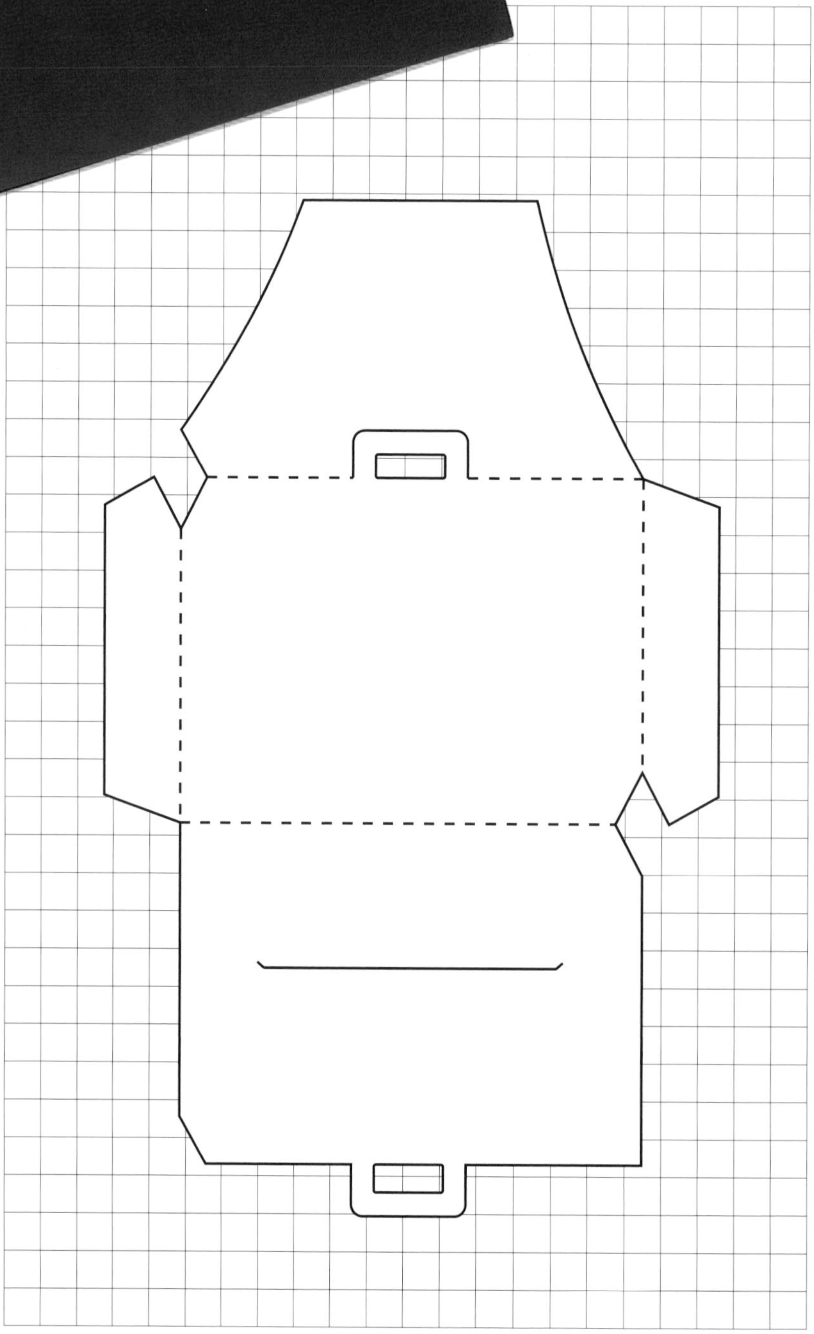

Disco "BUZZ"
Opening Anouncemnt & Invitation

オープニング記念告知&招待状

Japan 1989

CL: A-project, Inc.

CD: Nobuo Inoue

AD, D: Akihiko Tsukamoto

DF, SB: Design Club, NID Inc.

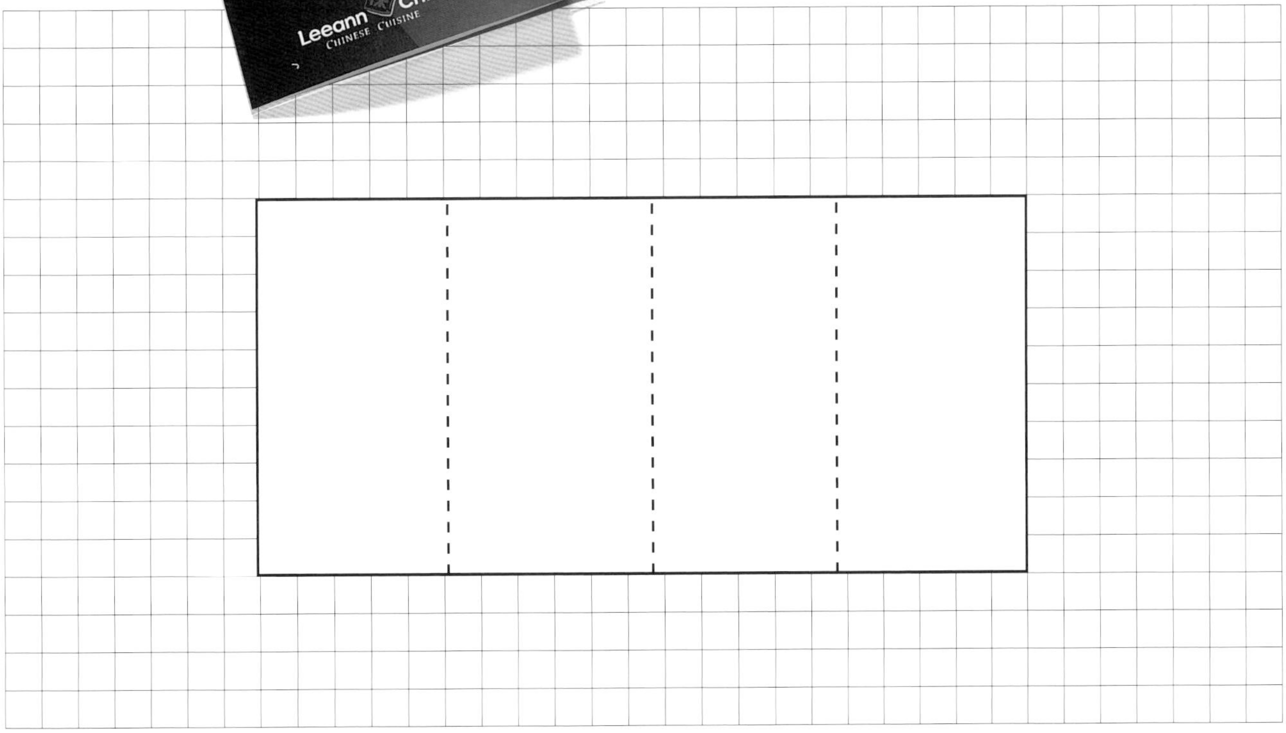

Dine In or Take Home Menu

中華料理メニュー

USA 2001

CL: Leeann Chin

AD: Alan Tse

D, I: Keiko Takahashi

DF, SB: Yamamoto Moss

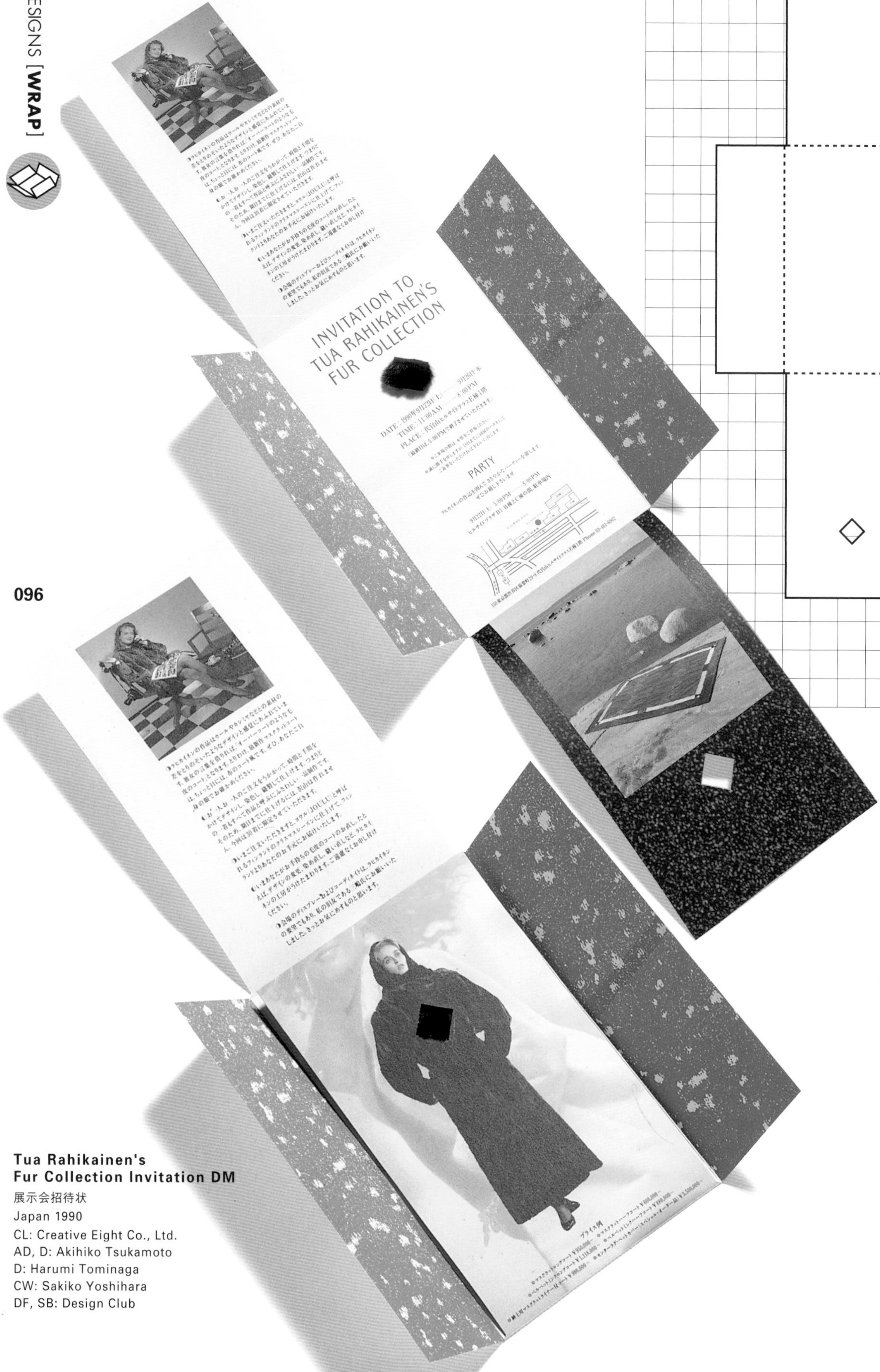

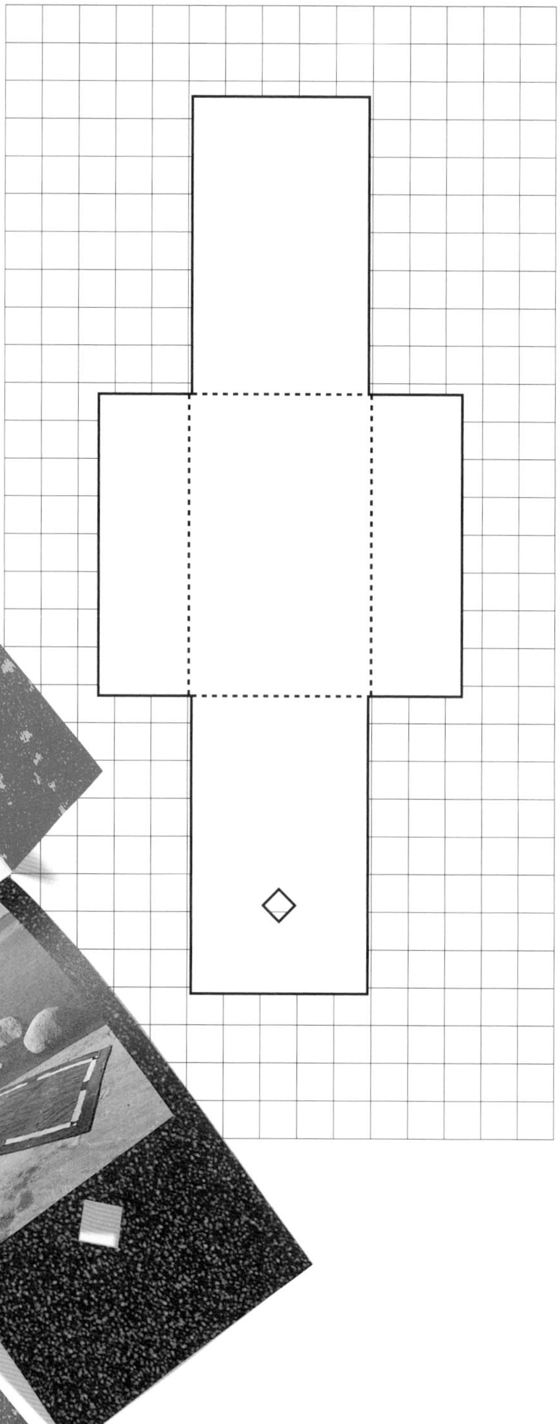

Tua Rahikainen's
Fur Collection Invitation DM

展示会招待状

Japan 1990

CL: Creative Eight Co., Ltd.

AD, D: Akihiko Tsukamoto

D: Harumi Tominaga

CW: Sakiko Yoshihara

DF, SB: Design Club

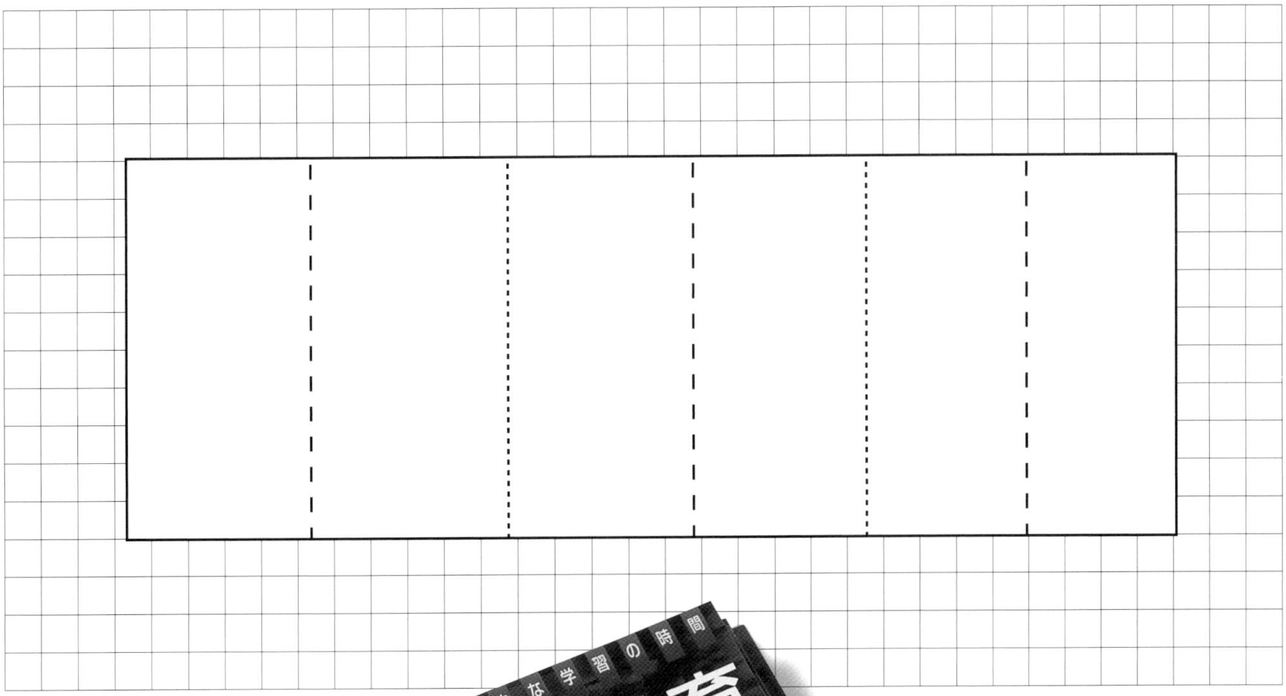

Guidance Pamphlet of Environmental Education

環境教育の案内パンフレット

Japan 2002

CL: National Noto Youth House

CD: Toshio Gobou

AD, D, I: Yasuhiro Azuma

I: Tsuyoshi Murai

DF, SB: Val Design Group Co., Ltd.

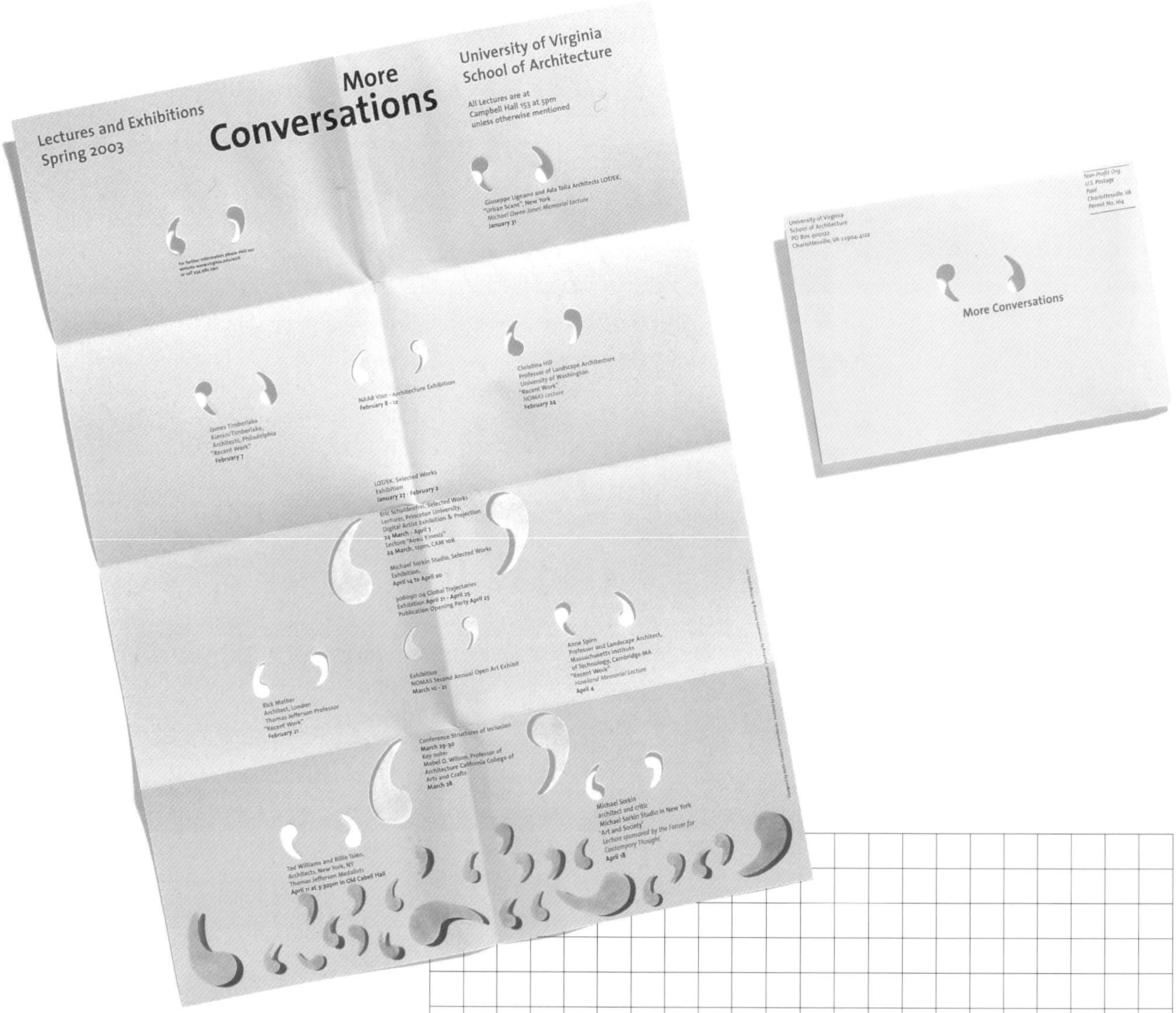

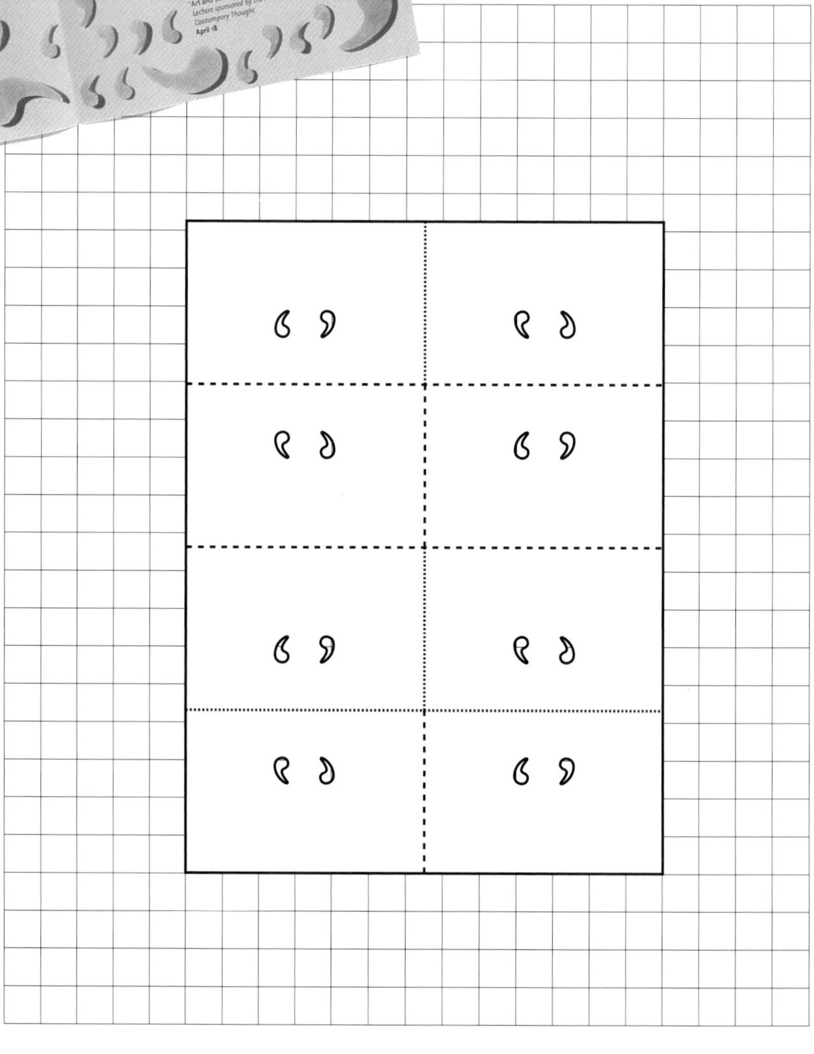

Invitation
"More Conversations Lectures and Exhibitions Spring 2003"
建築学校 展覧会案内
USA 2003
CL: University of Virginia School of Architecture
CD, AD, D, SB: Keith Godard
Design Assistant: Curtis Eberhardt
DF: Studio Works

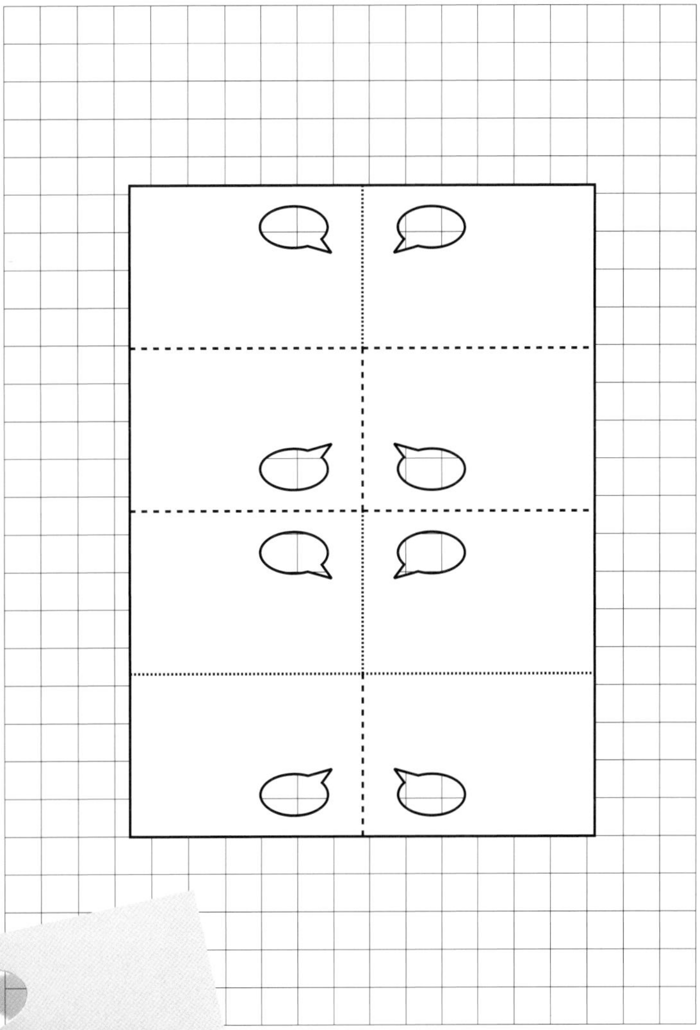

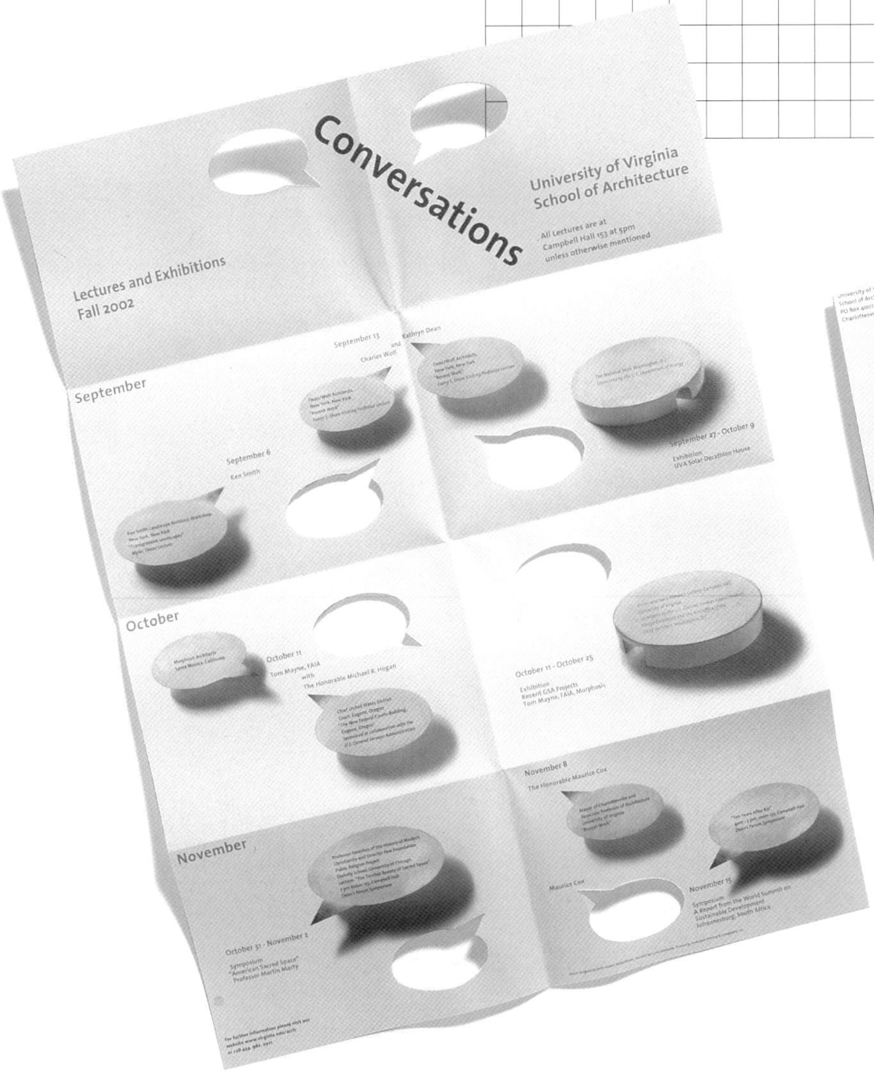

Invitation
"Conversations Lectures and Exhibitions Fall 2002"

建築学校 展覧会案内

USA 2002

CL: University of Virginia School of Architecture

CD, AD, D, SB: Keith Godard

Design Assistant: Curtis Eberhardt

DF: Studio Works

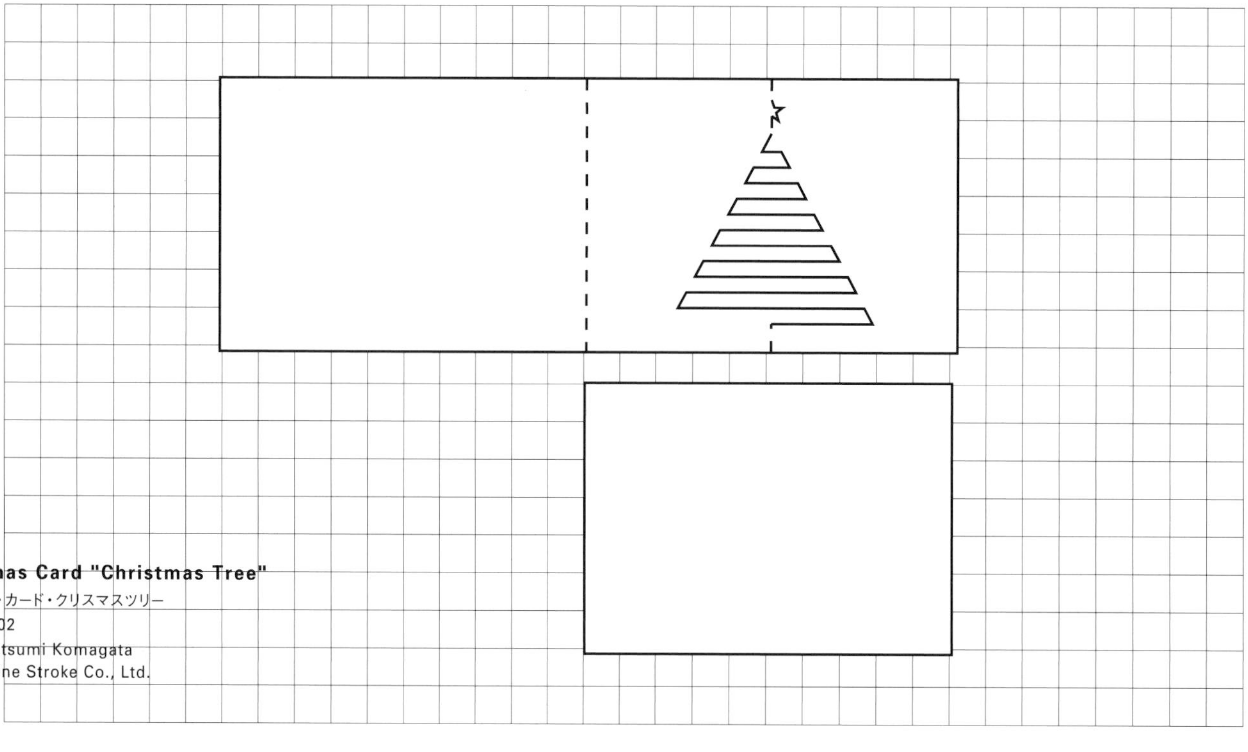

Christmas Card "Christmas Tree"
クリスマス・カード・クリスマスツリー
Japan 2002
AD, D: Katsumi Komagata
DF, SB: One Stroke Co., Ltd.

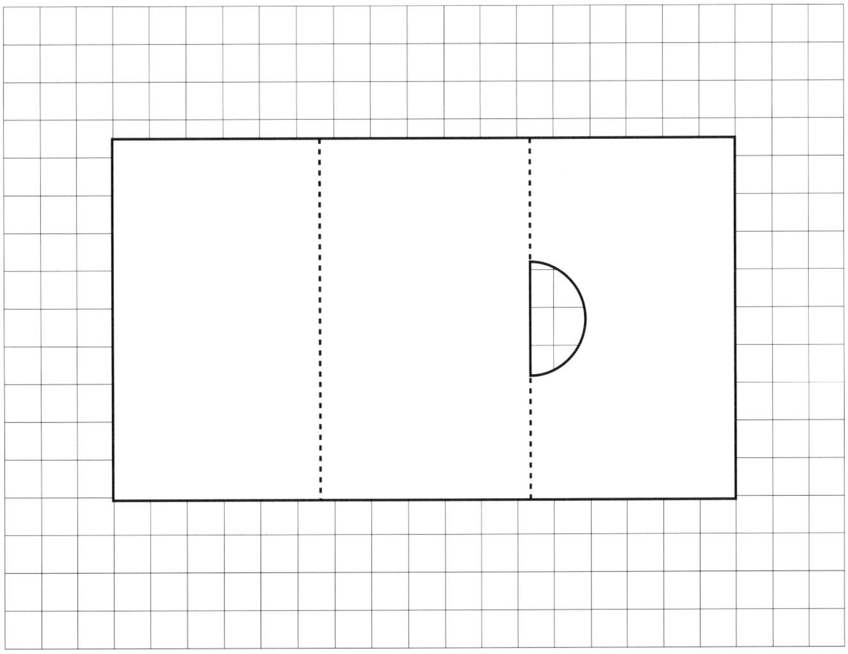

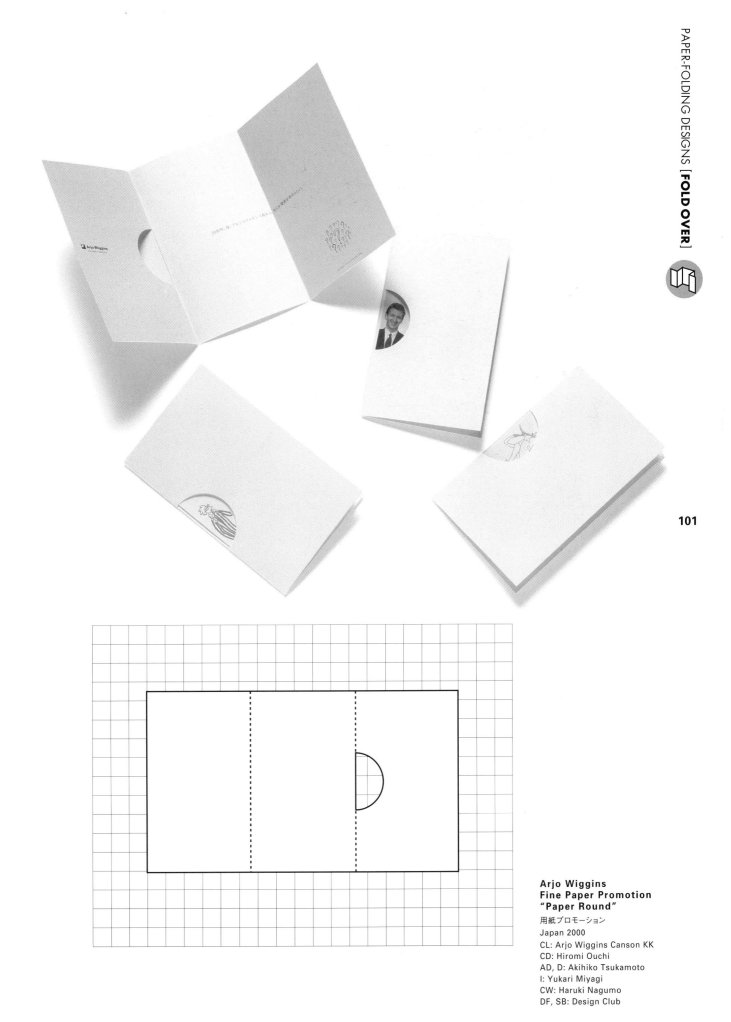

Arjo Wiggins
Fine Paper Promotion
"Paper Round"

用紙プロモーション

Japan 2000

CL: Arjo Wiggins Canson KK
CD: Hiromi Ouchi
AD, D: Akihiko Tsukamoto
I: Yukari Miyagi
CW: Haruki Nagumo
DF, SB: Design Club

Annual Report Workshop Invitation
報告会案内状DM
USA 1992
CL: Sloan Paper Company
AD, D: Marie Weaver
DF, SB: Weaver Design

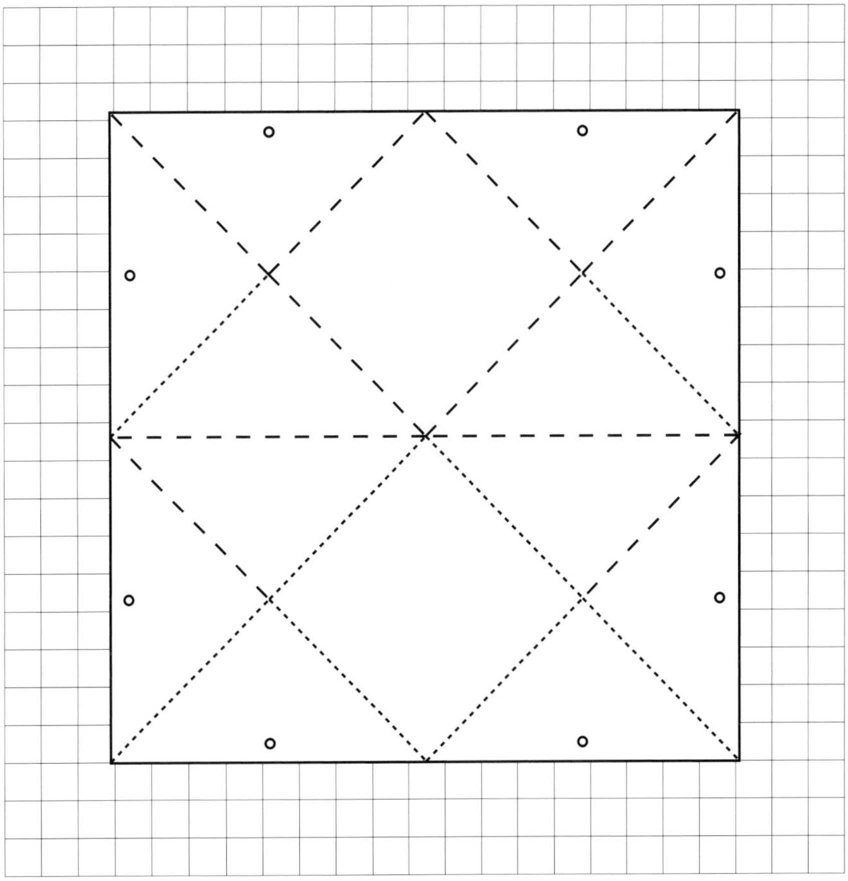

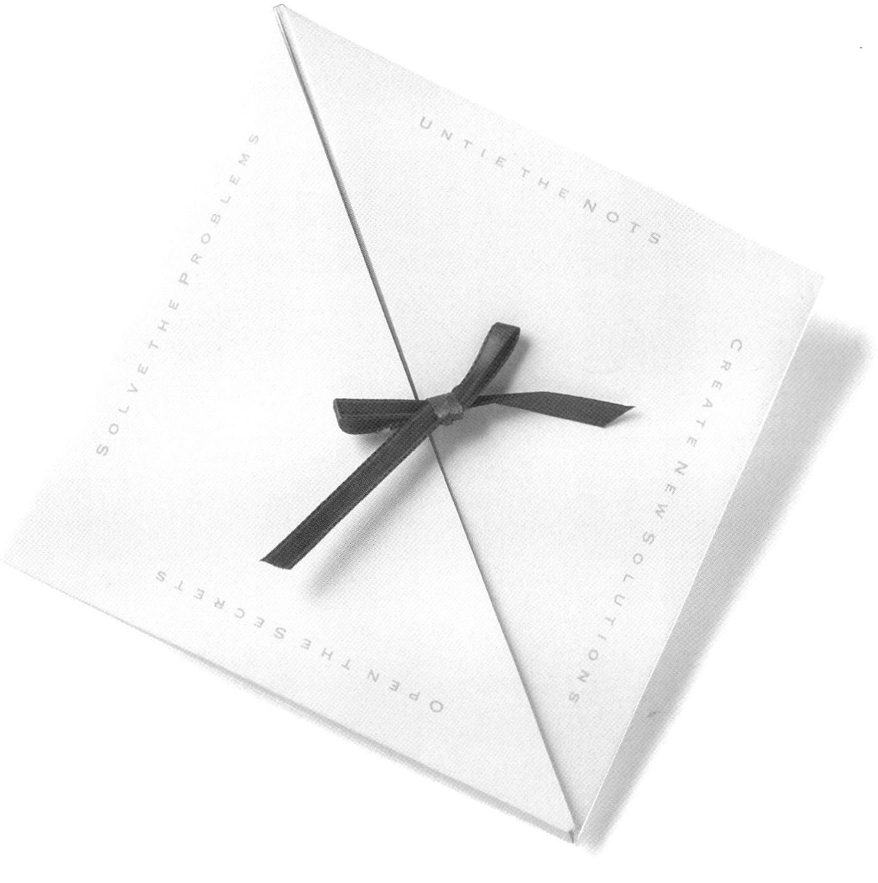
UNTIE THE NOTS
CREATE NEW SOLUTIONS
OPEN THE SECRETS
SOLVE THE PROBLEMS

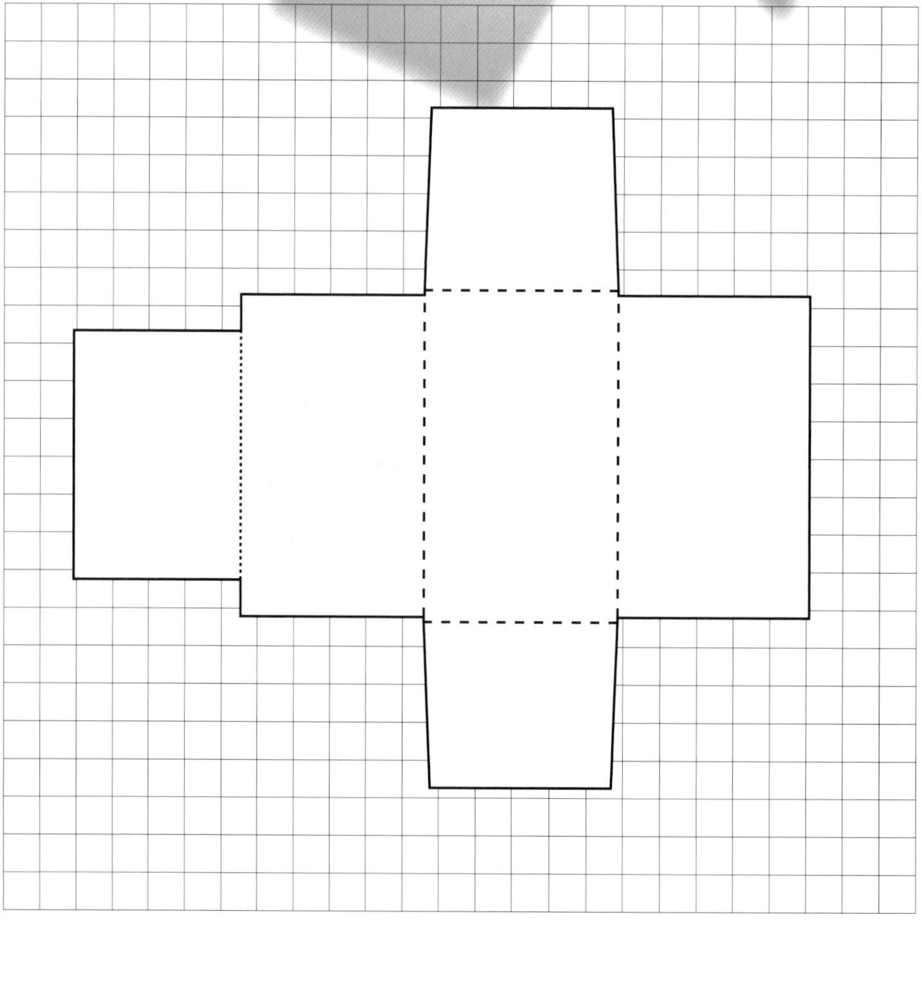

Party Invitation DM

五周年記念パーティー案内DM
Japan 1998
CL: Toku Aguri (Artist)
AD: Toku Aguri
D: Akihiko Tsukamoto
P: Takao Nakamura
DF, SB: Design Club

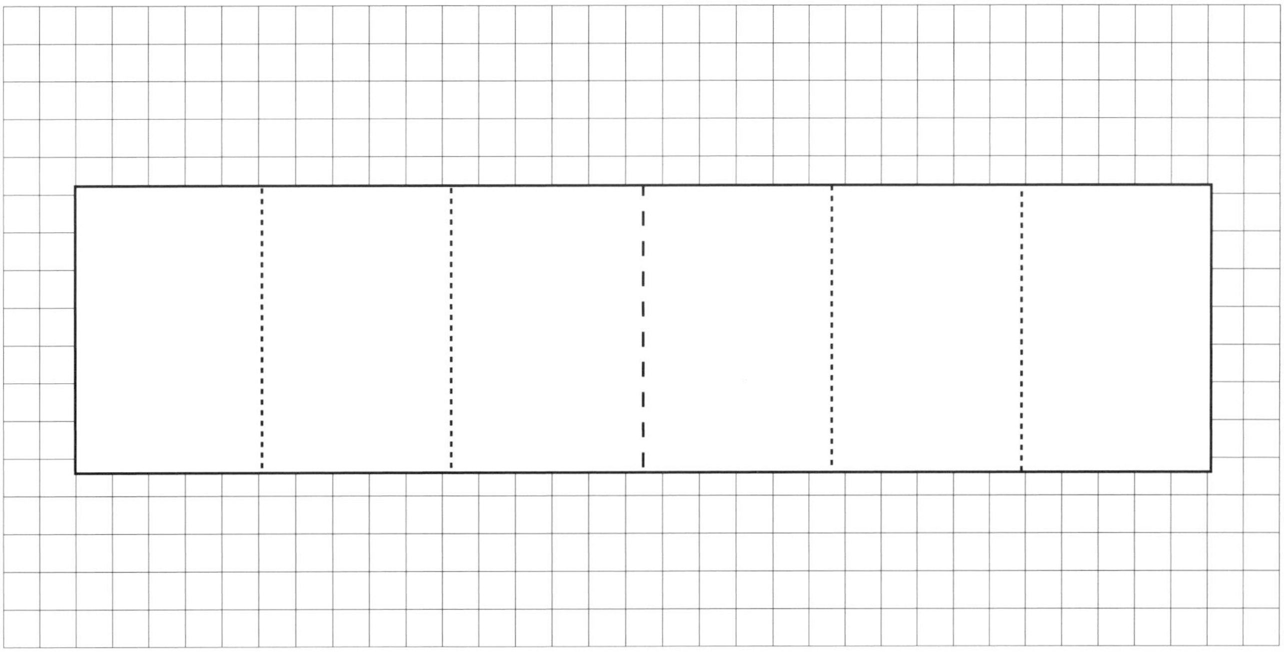

Design Firm Catalog
デザイン事務所カタログ
Belgium
CL: Vizo
CD, AD, D: Jo Klaps
CD: Patrick Reuvis
P: Paul Croes, Eddy Fliers, Bart Van Leuven
CW: Francis Smets
DF, SB: Brussels Lof

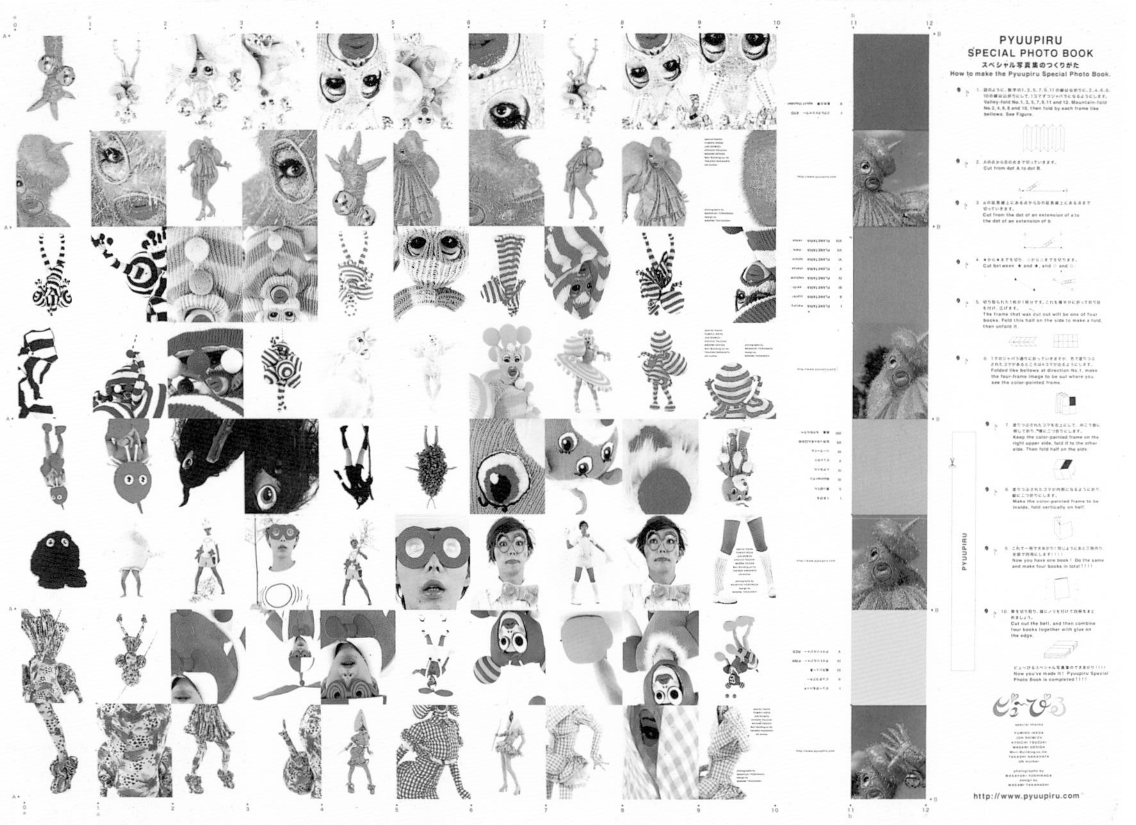
PYUUPIRU
SPECIAL PHOTO BOOK
スペシャル写真集のつくりかた
How to make the Pyuupiru Special Photo Book.
http://www.pyuupiru.com

PYUUPIRU

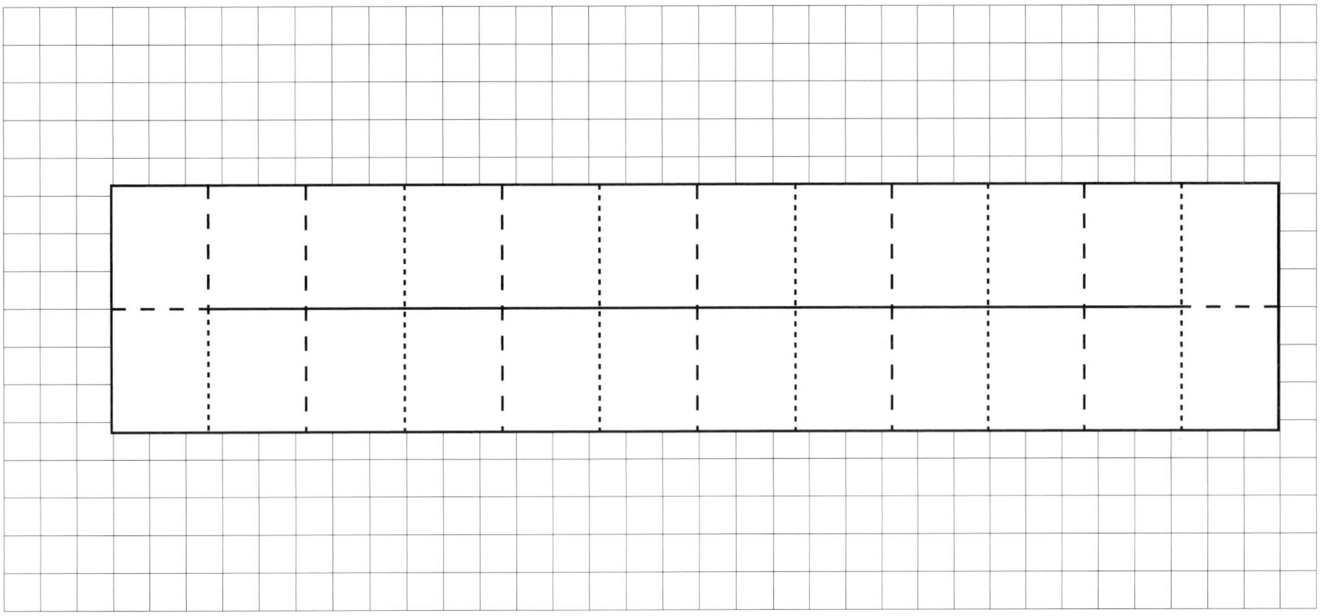

Pyuupiru Special Photo Book

ぴゅ〜ぴるスペシャルフォトブック

Japan 2003

CL: Pyuupiru

AD, D: Masami Takahashi

DF, SB: Masami Design

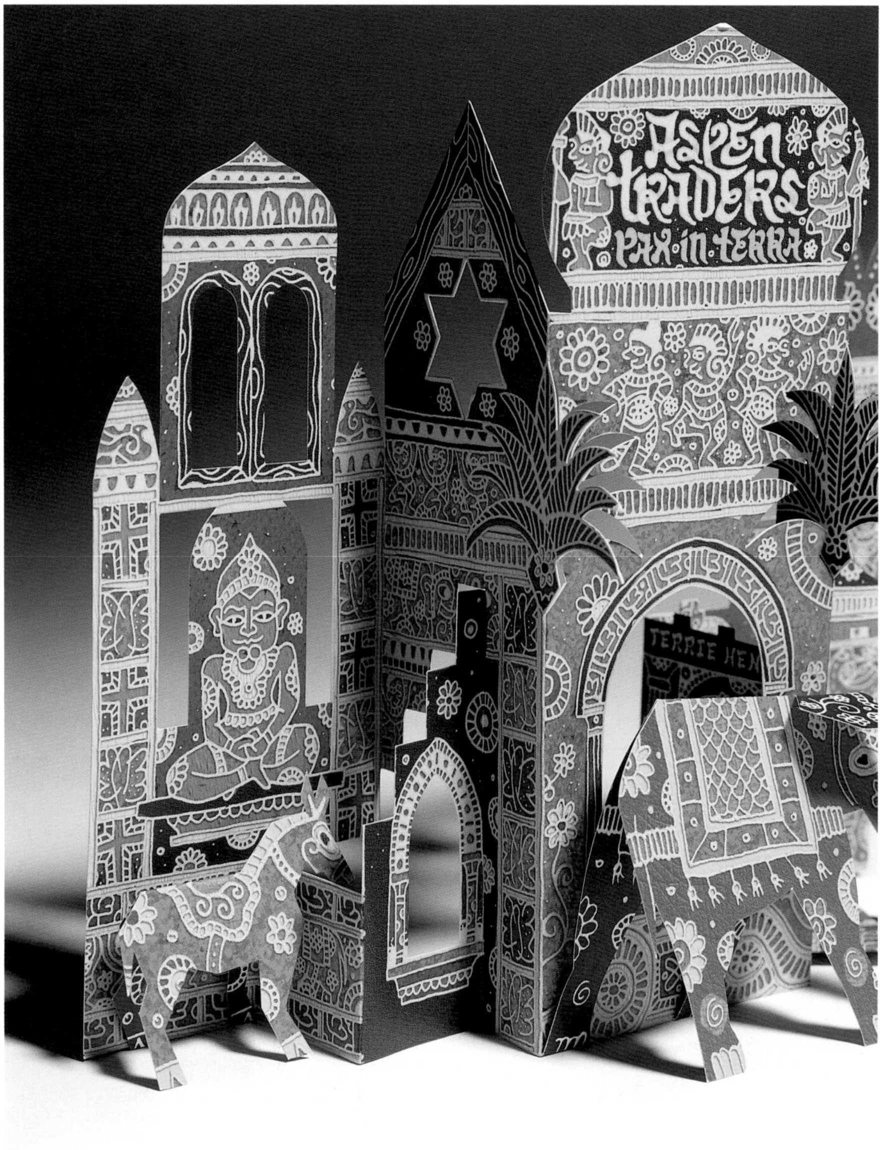

Christmas Card
クリスマス・カード
USA 1999
CL: Aspen Traders
CD, AD, Structure :Bill Gardner
AD, D, I: Chris Parks
DF, SB: Gardner Design

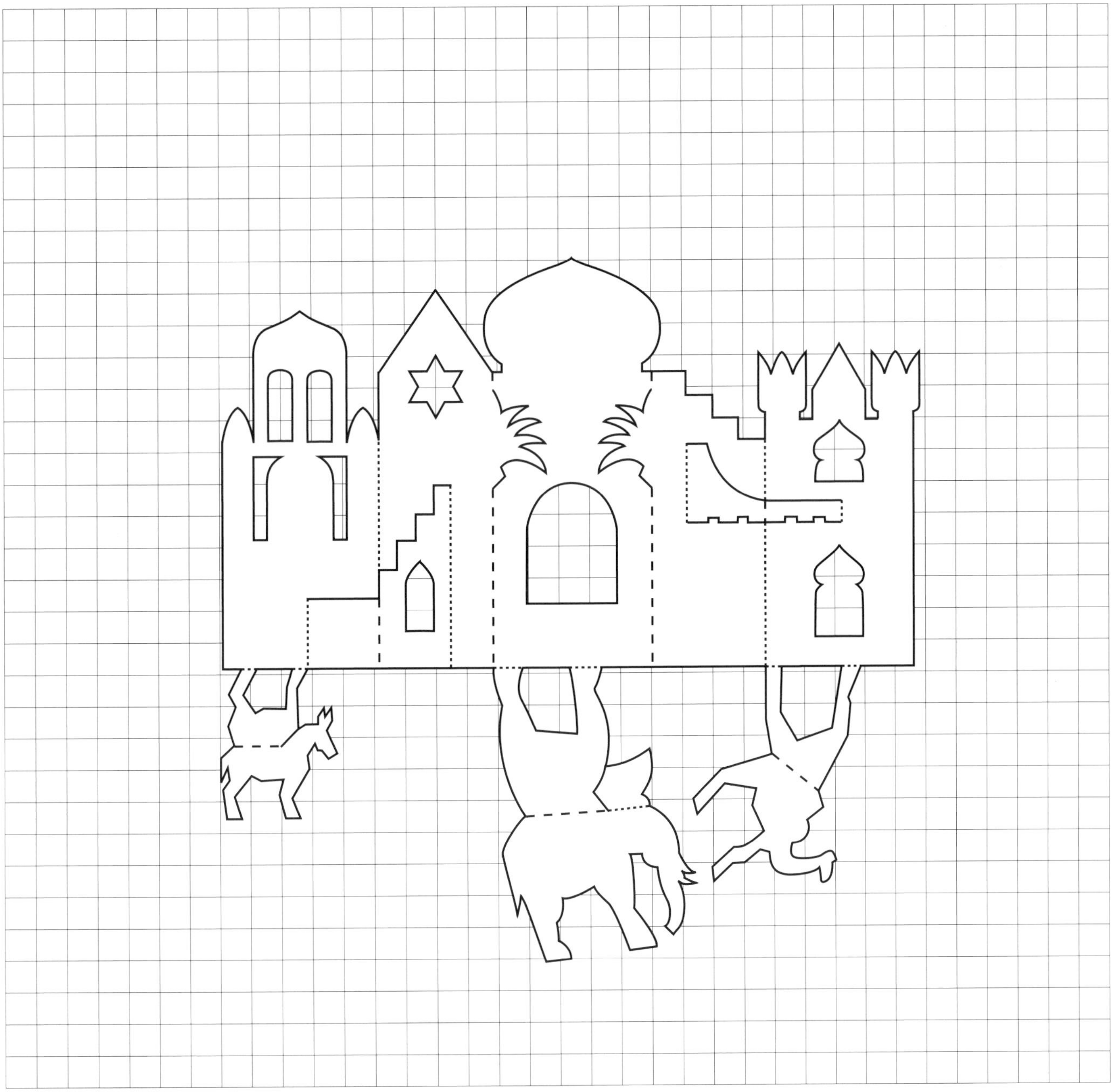

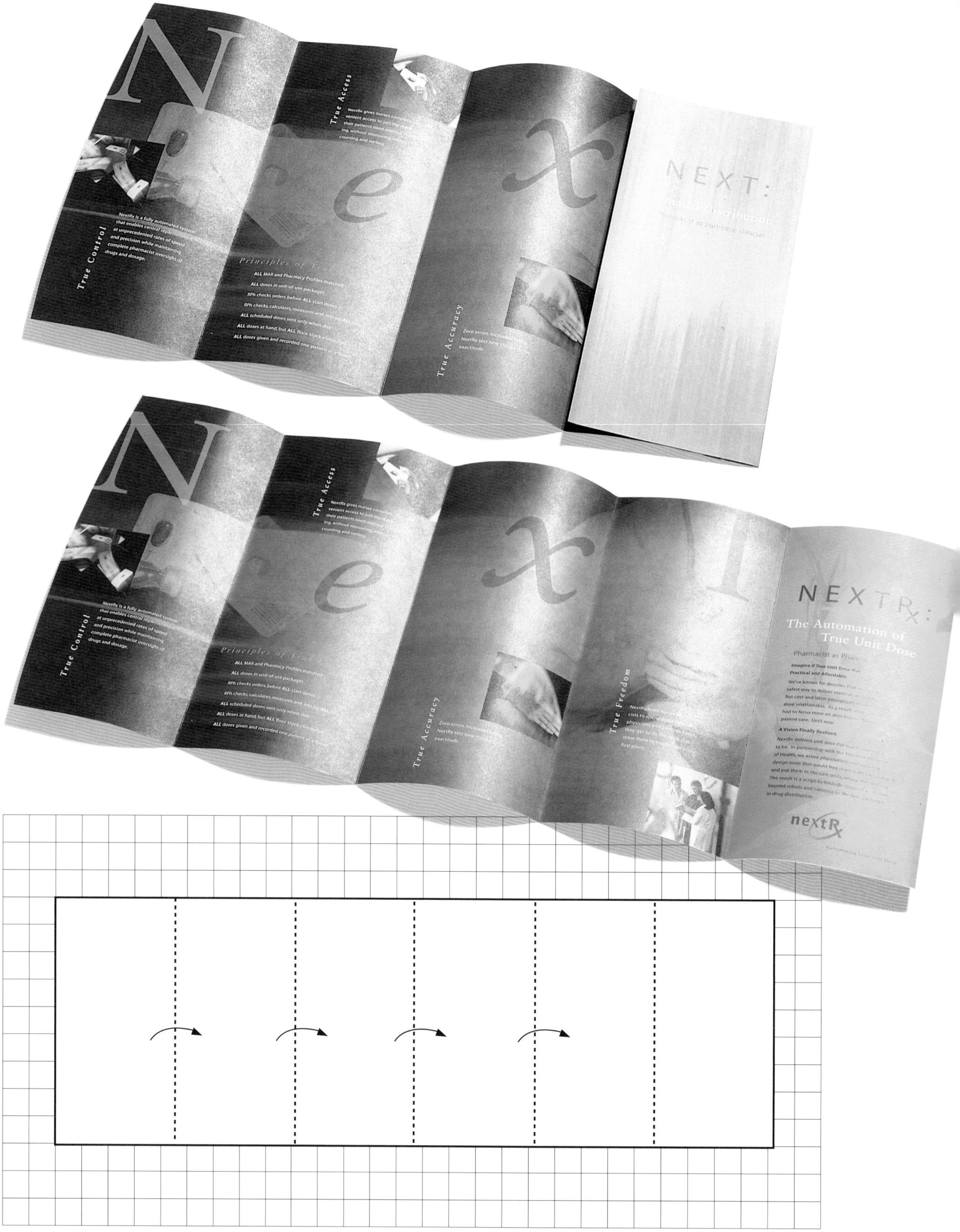

Web Promotion Leaflet

プロモーション用リーフレット

USA 1999

CL: NextRx Corporation

AD: Jon Hornall, John Anicker

D: Julie Lock, Mary Chin Hutchinson

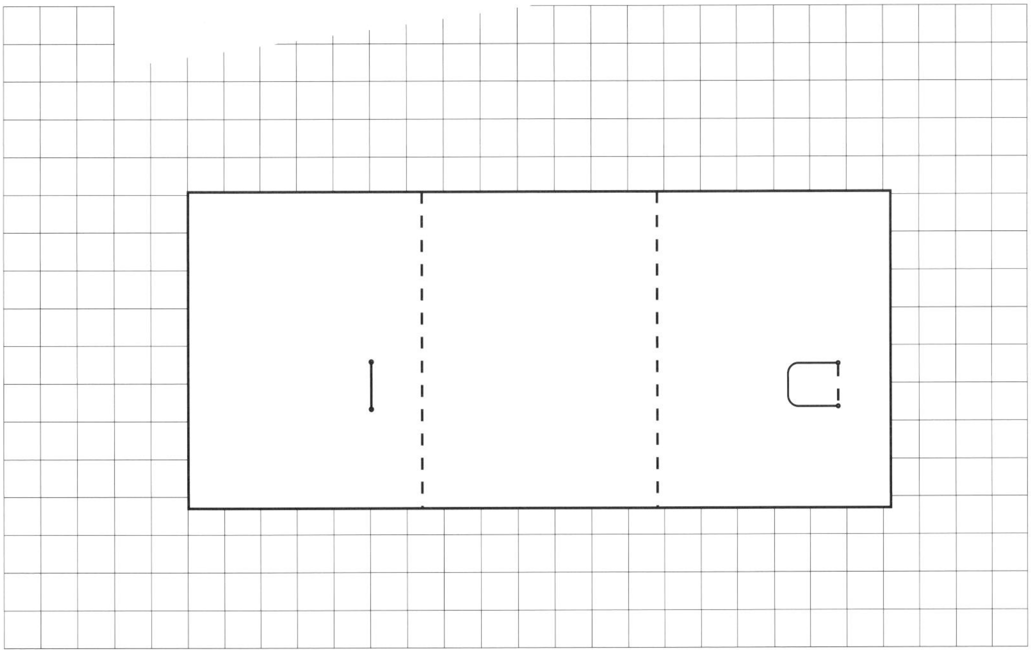

Kahori Maki Exhibition DM
牧かほり個展DM
Japan 2003
CL: Kahori Maki
AD, D: Masami Takahashi
I: Kahori Maki , Masami Design

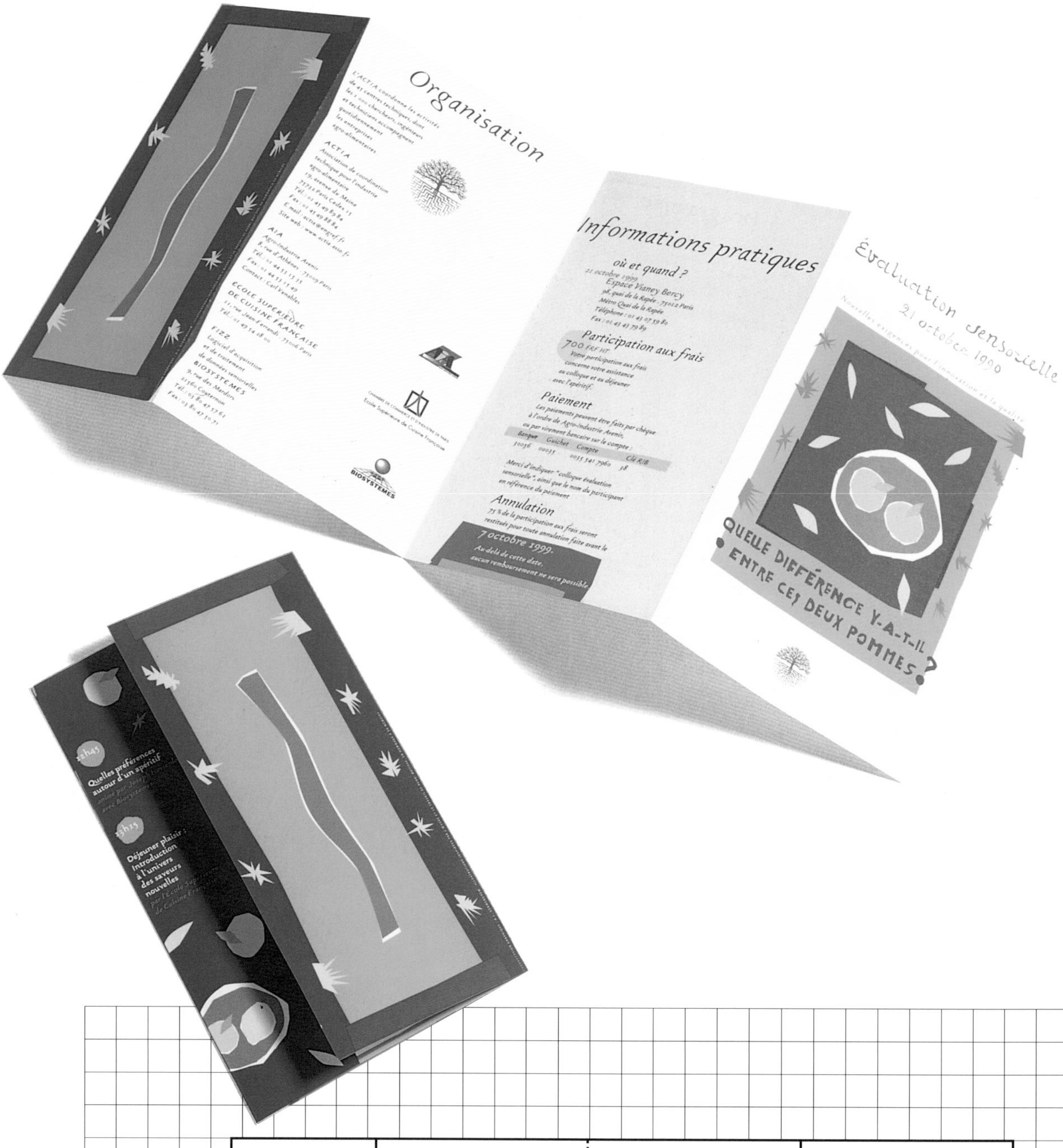

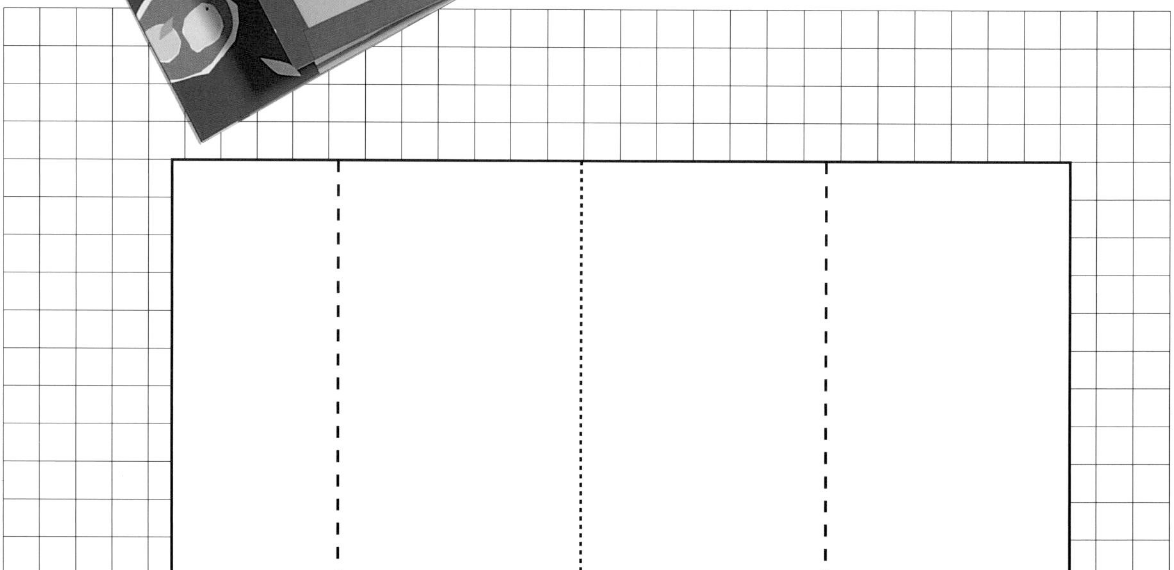

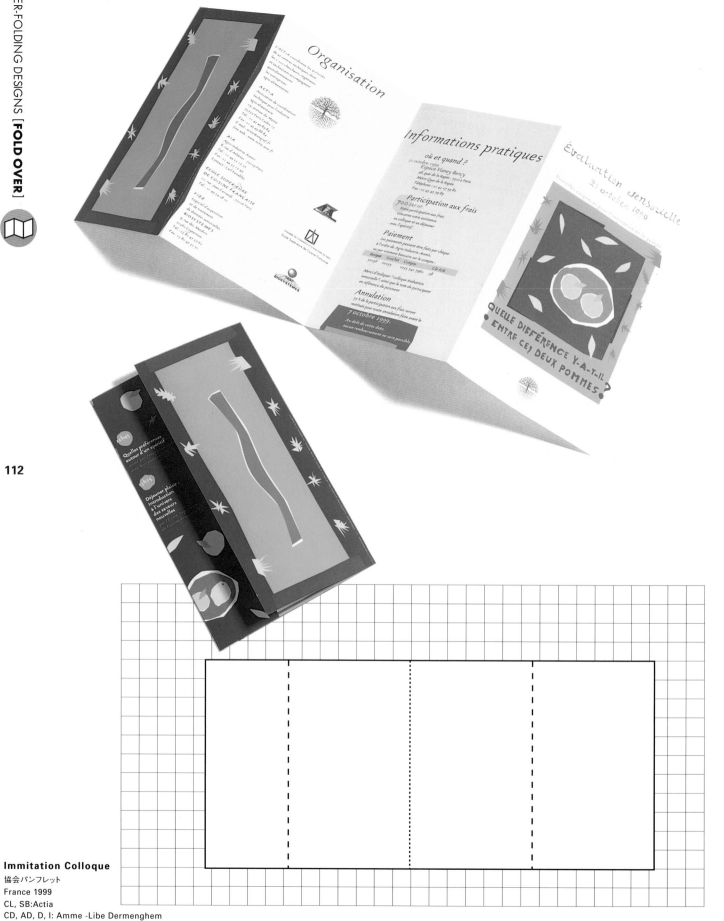

Immitation Colloque
協会パンフレット
France 1999
CL, SB:Actia
CD, AD, D, I: Amme -Libe Dermenghem

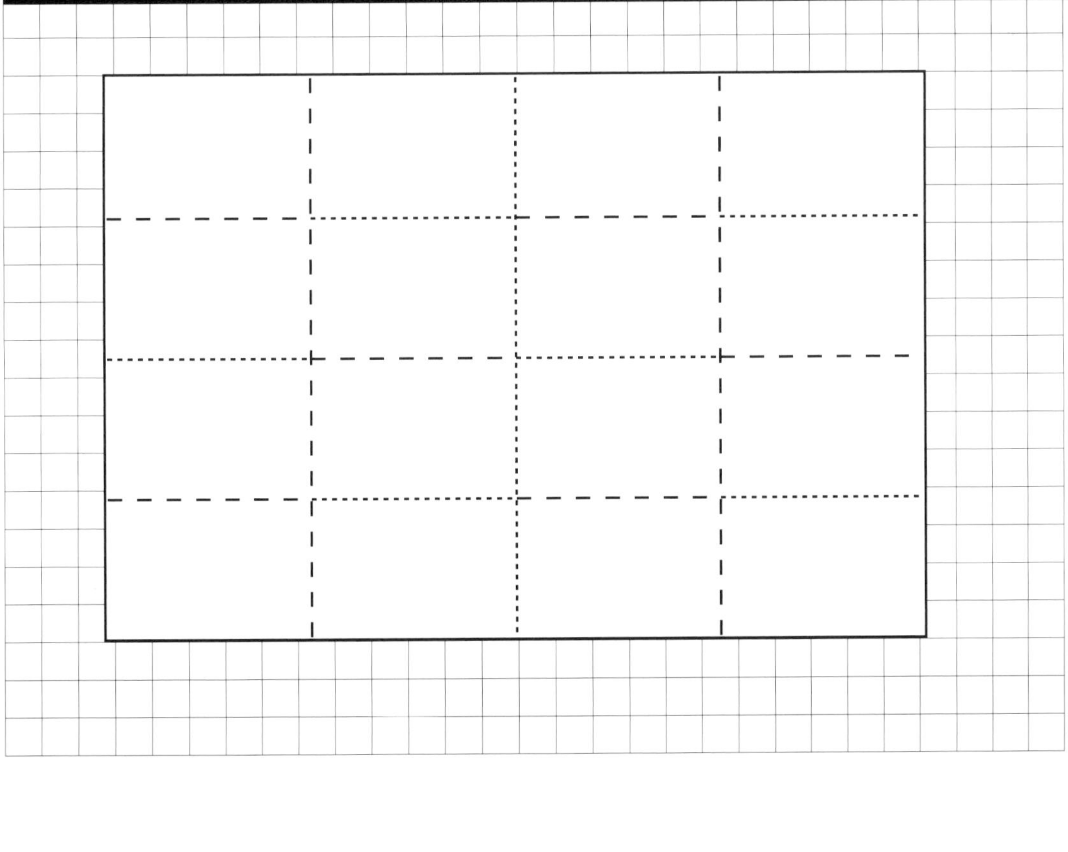

Photo Exhibition Leaflet

米津光NYC写真展リーフレット

Japan 2001

CL: Akira Yonezu

AD, D, SB: Takaaki Fujimoto

P: Akira Yonezu

DF: Kisaragisha

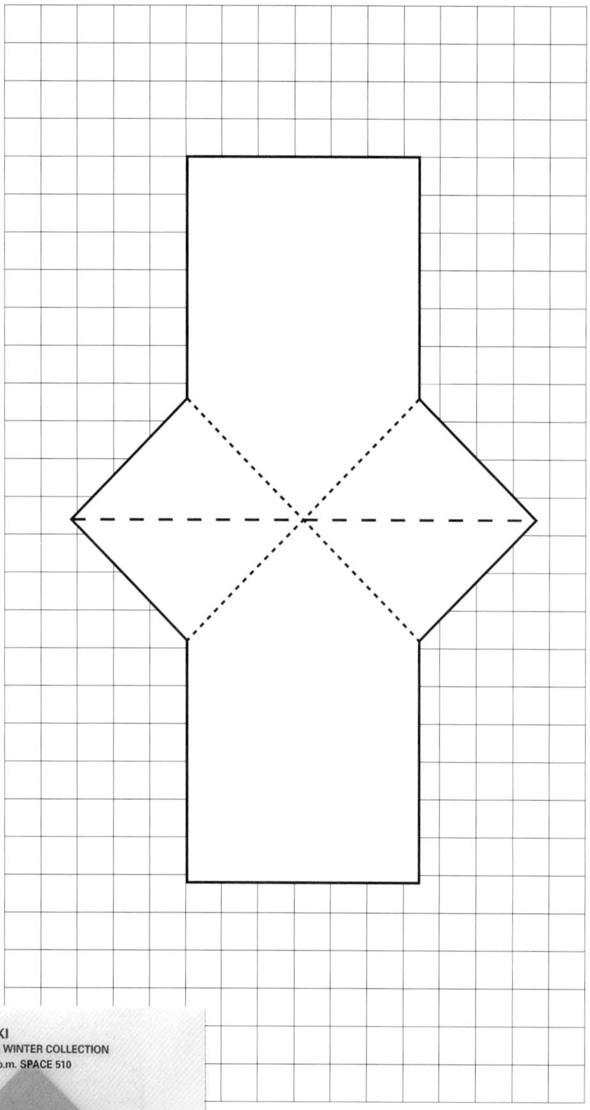

Apparel Exhibit Invitation
アパレルメーカー展示会招待状
Japan 1997
CL: Gunze Ltd.
D: Ryoko Kobayashi
DF, SB: Yes Factory Co., Ltd.

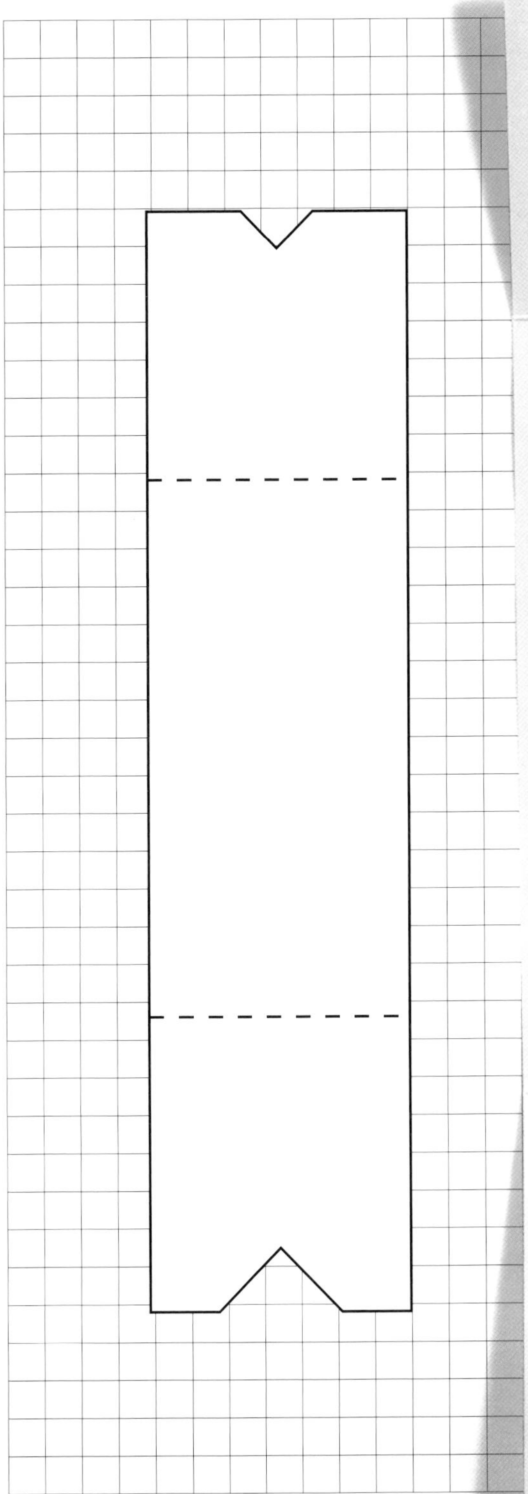

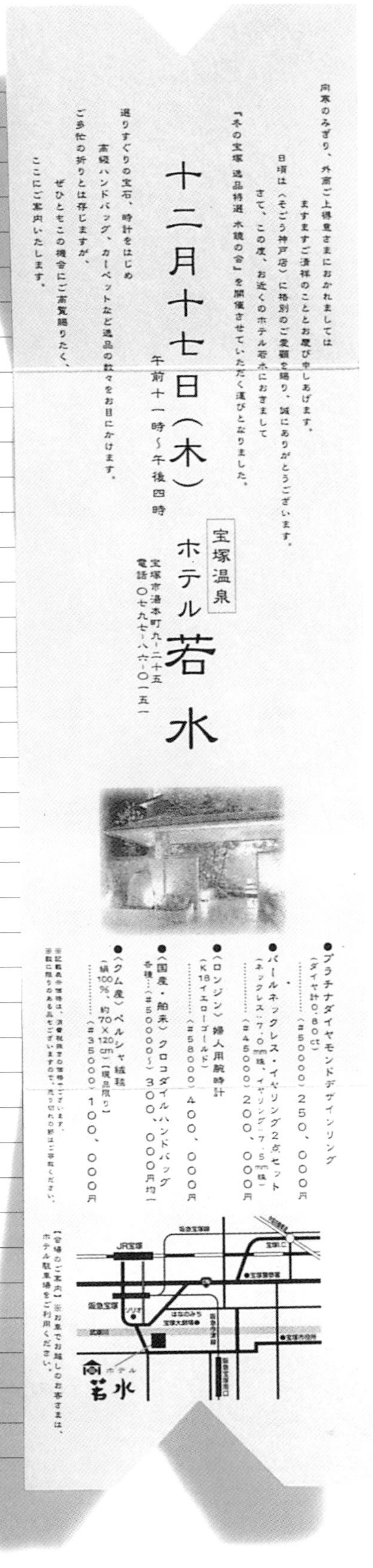

115

Sales Announcement DM
販売会案内状
Japan 1998
CL: Sogo Dept. Store Co., Ltd. Kobe
AD, D: Yuji Yamamoto
DF, SB: Sogo Creative Associates

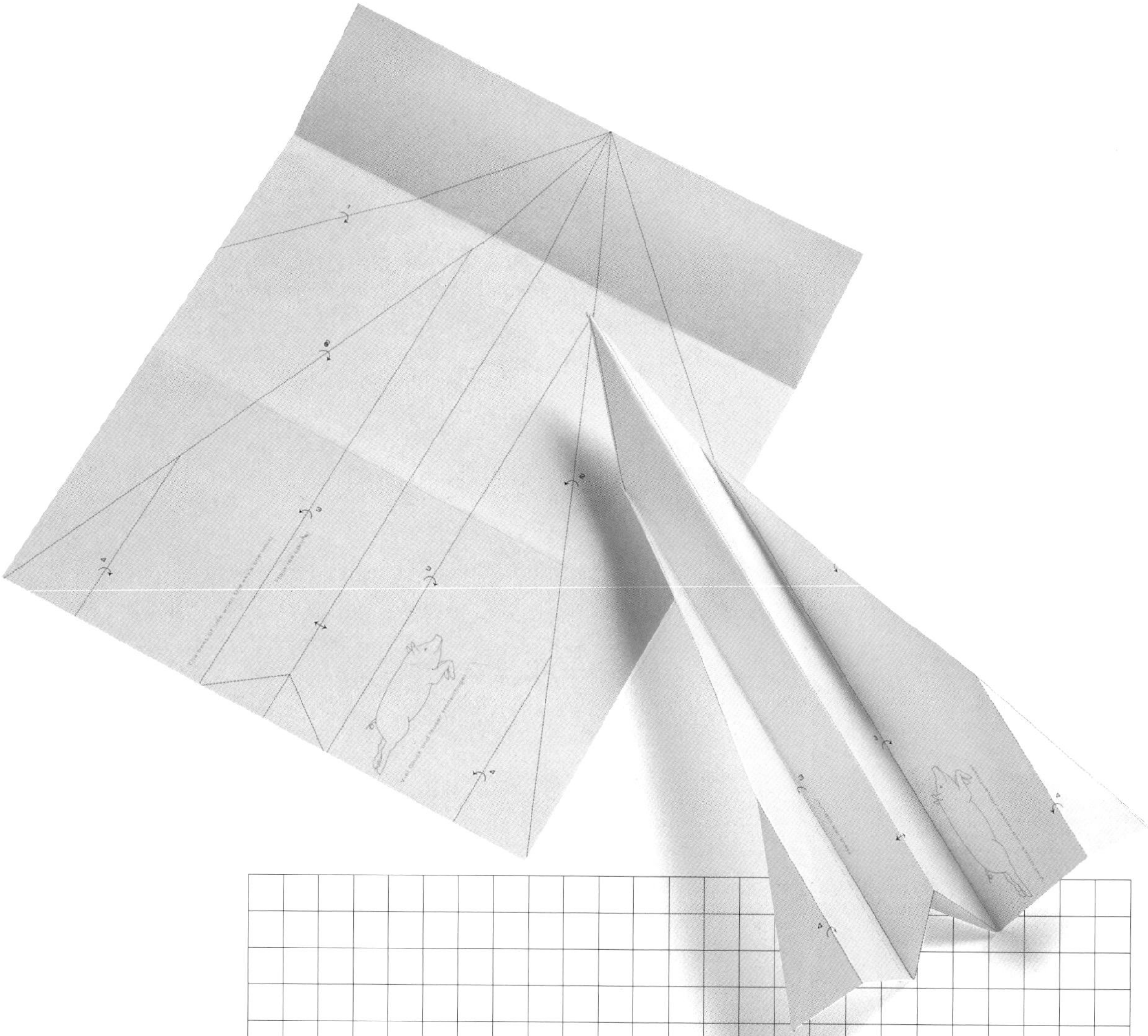

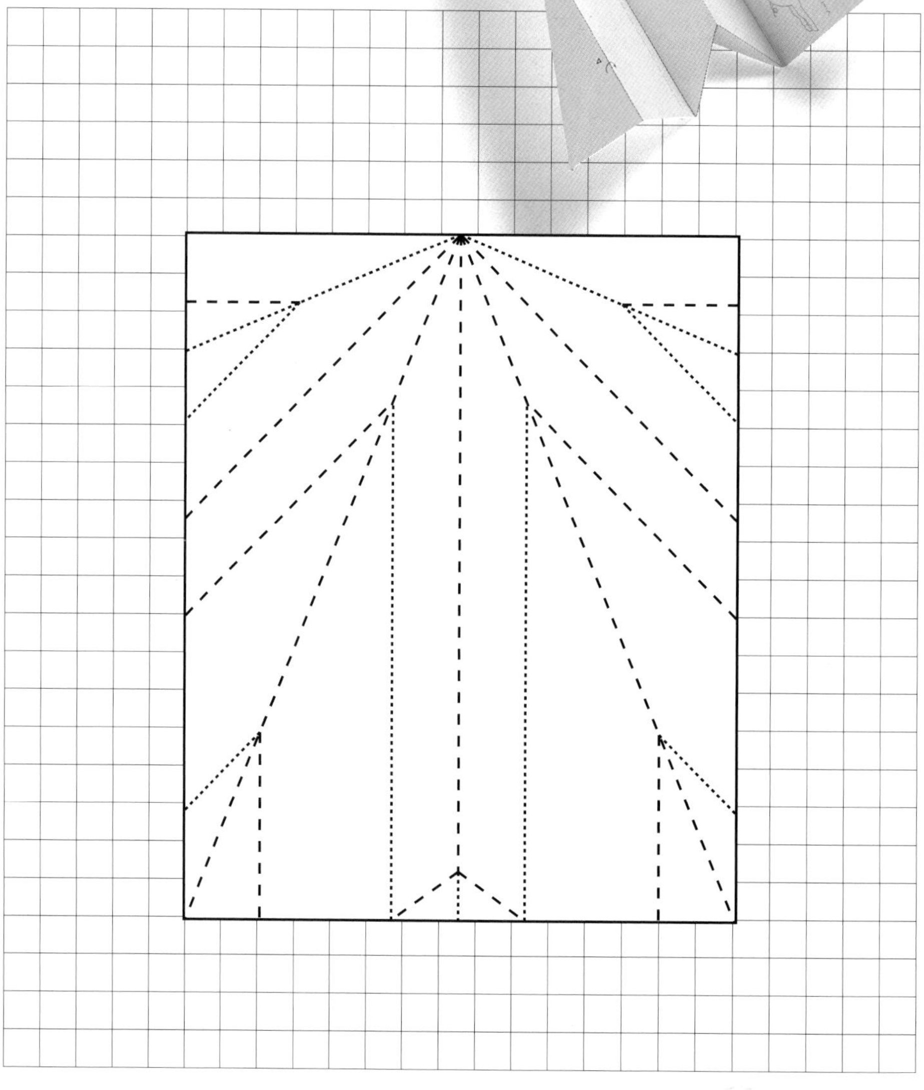

Greeting Card
祭日用カード
Switzerland 1999
CL: Buttenpapierfabrik Gmund
CD, AD, D, I: Lucia Frey, Heinz Wild
DF, SB: Wild & Frey,
Agentur fur Design

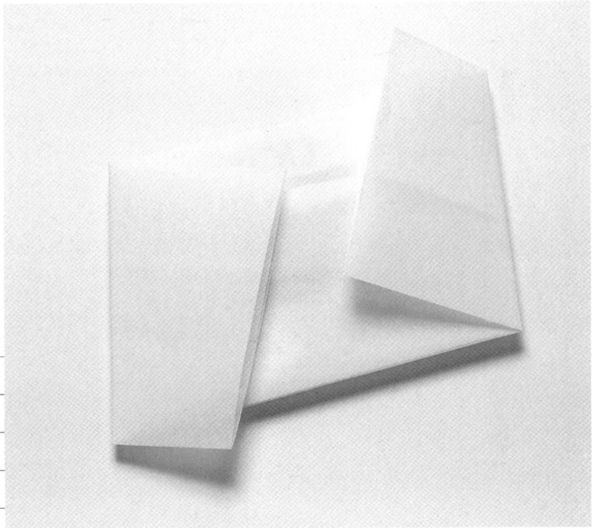

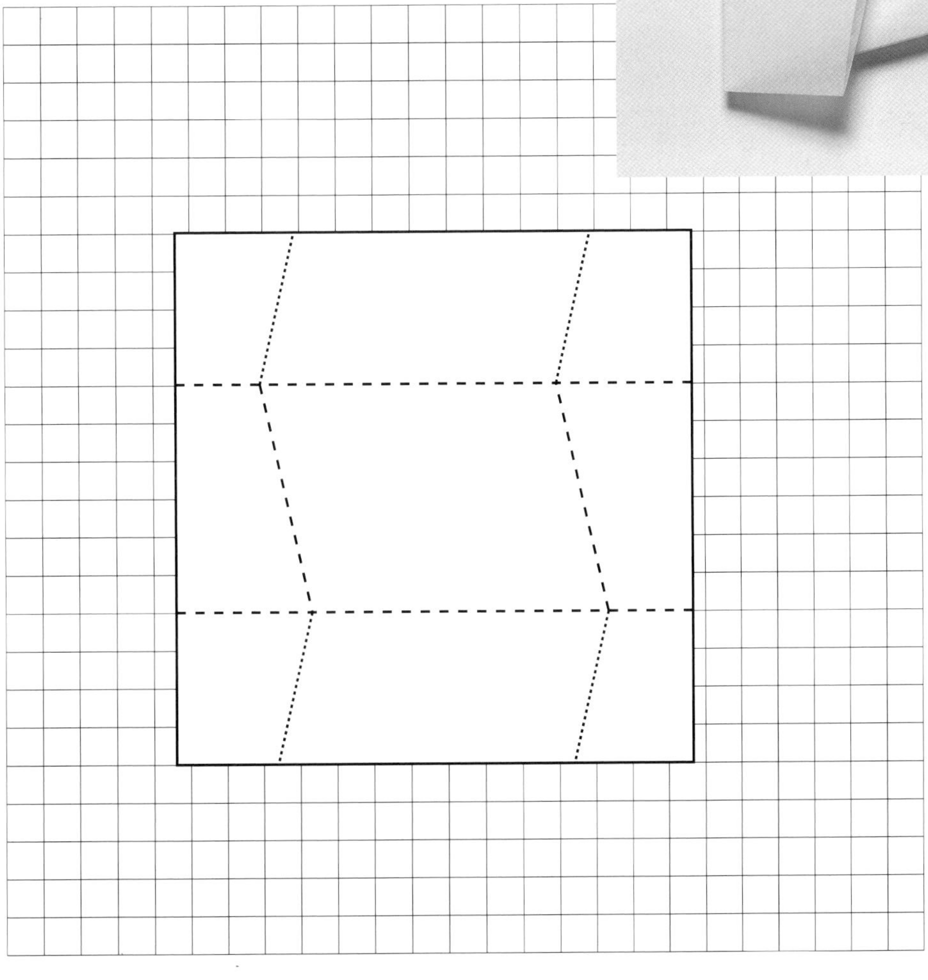

1999 Gallery Gala Invitation
イベント案内状
USA 1999
CL: Department of Art,
University of Northern Iowa
AD, D, SB: Philip Fass

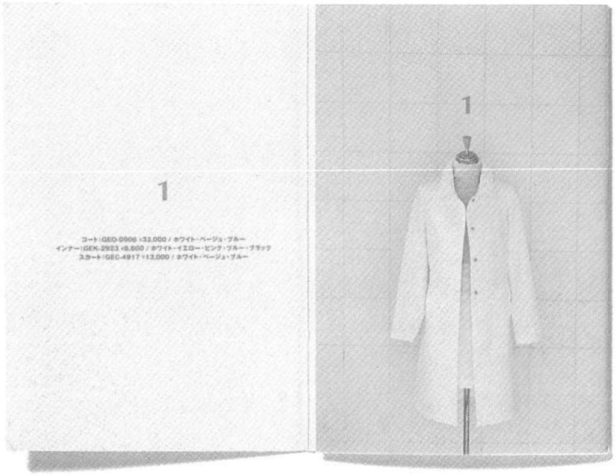

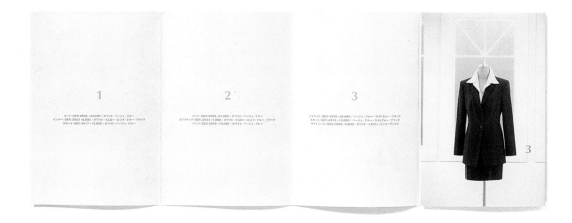

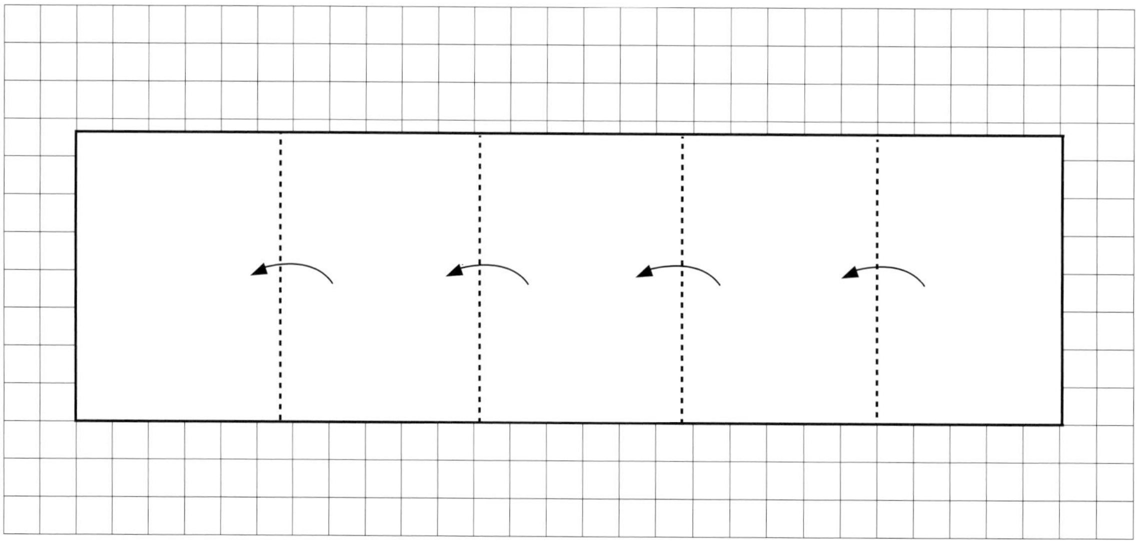

Ladies Fashion Catalog
レディーズ ファッション カタログ
Japan 1999
CL, SB: JUN Co., Ltd.
CD: Junko NIshitani
AD: Akira Miyake
D: Ryouko Iguchi
P: Masataka Kiuchi
CW: Hiroaki Suzuki

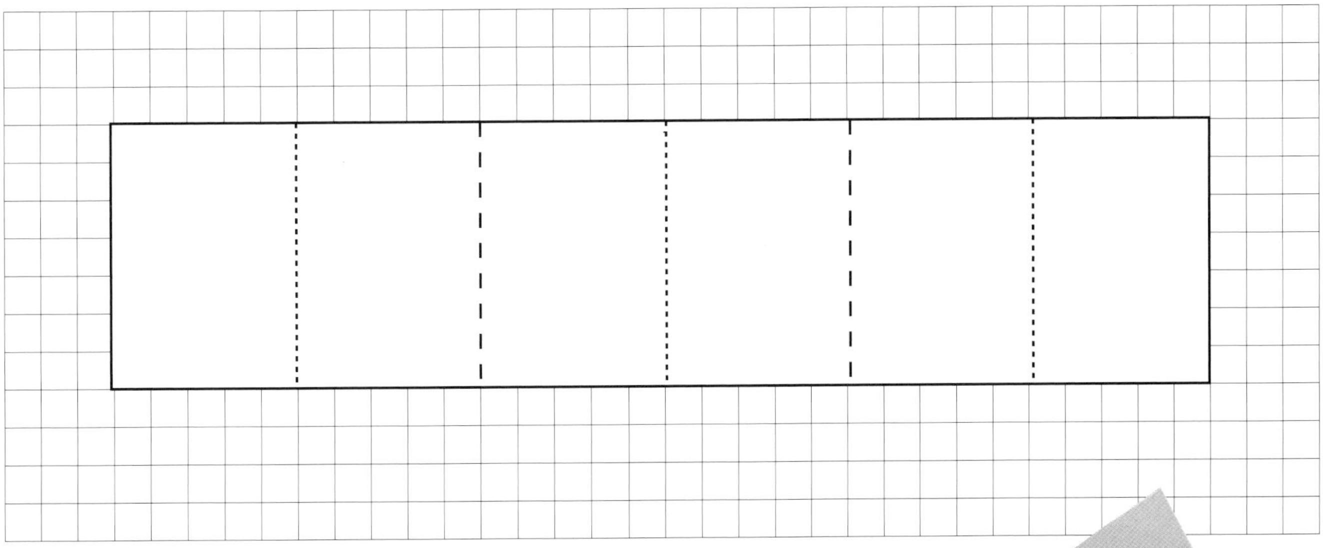

Mail
"Just for fun / about sheep"
デザイナー関係者宛手紙
Switzerland 2000
CL: Heinz Wild
CD, AD, D: Heinz Wild
DF, SB: Wild & Frey, Agentur fur Design

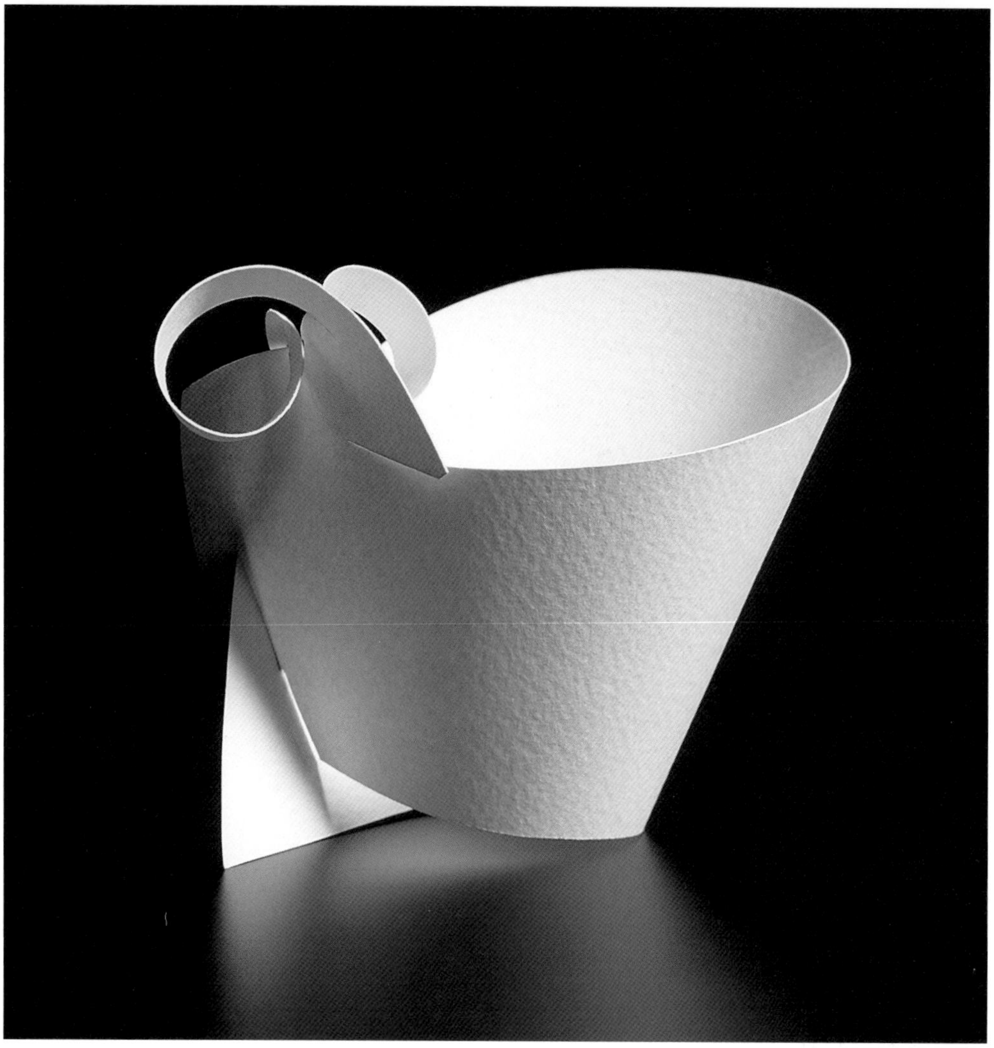

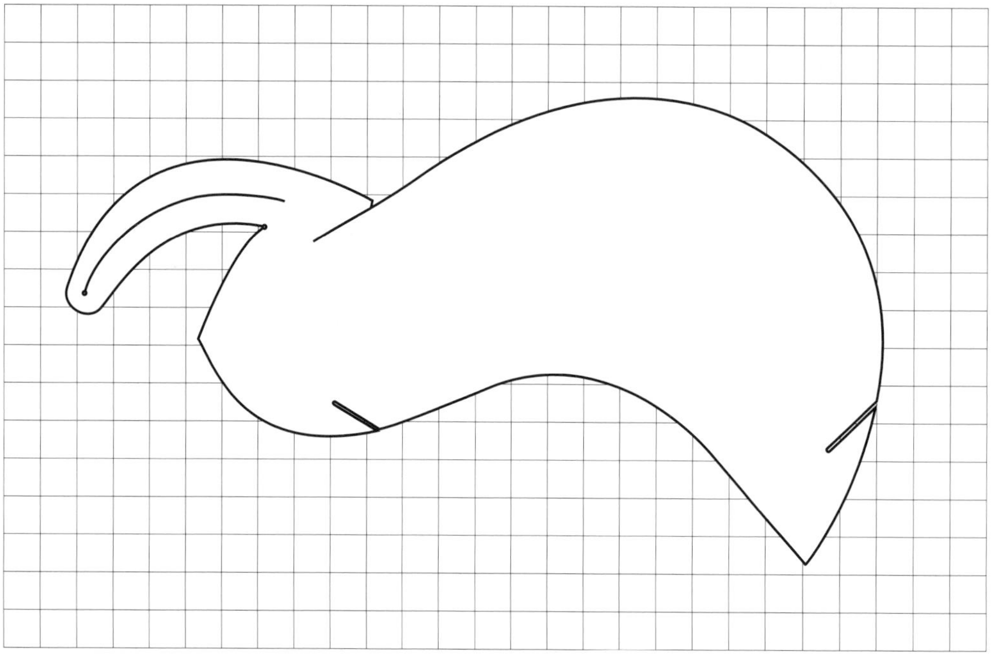

New Year Card (Sheep)
年賀状（ひつじ）
Japan 2002
CL: PLAN Y
AD, D, SB: Miyuki Yoshida

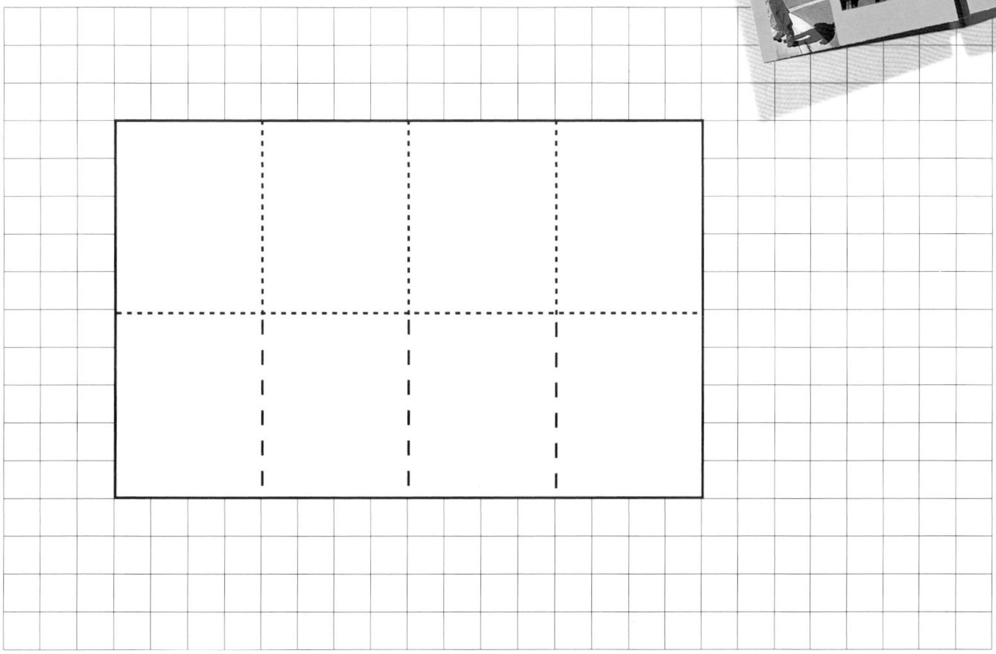

Phenix Sports Catalog

フェニックス スポーツ カタログ

Japan 2001

CL: Phenix Co., Ltd.

CD, AD: Tetsuo Fujiwara

D: Emi Shiratori

P: Dave Norehad, Manabu Nakagawa

DF, SB: Stereo Studio Inc.

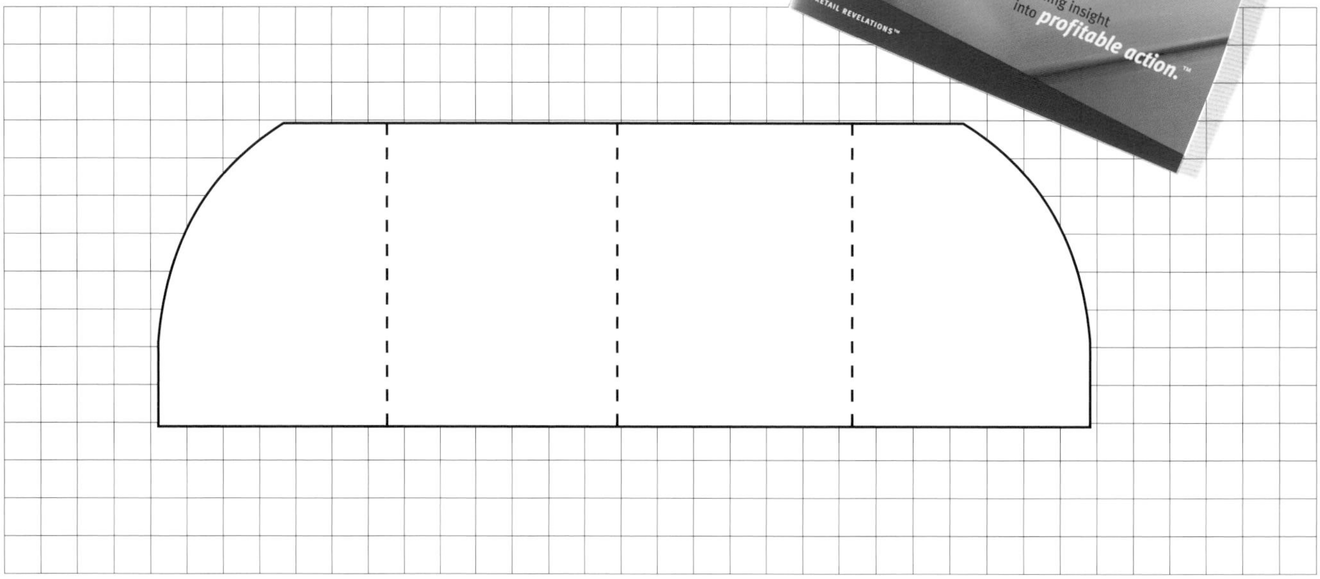

Promotional Leaflet "Retail Revelations"

eコマースプロモーション リーフレット

USA 2001

CL: Net-Perceptions

AD: Alan Tse

D: Kim Welter

P: Ellie Kingsbury

DF, SB: Yamamoto Moss

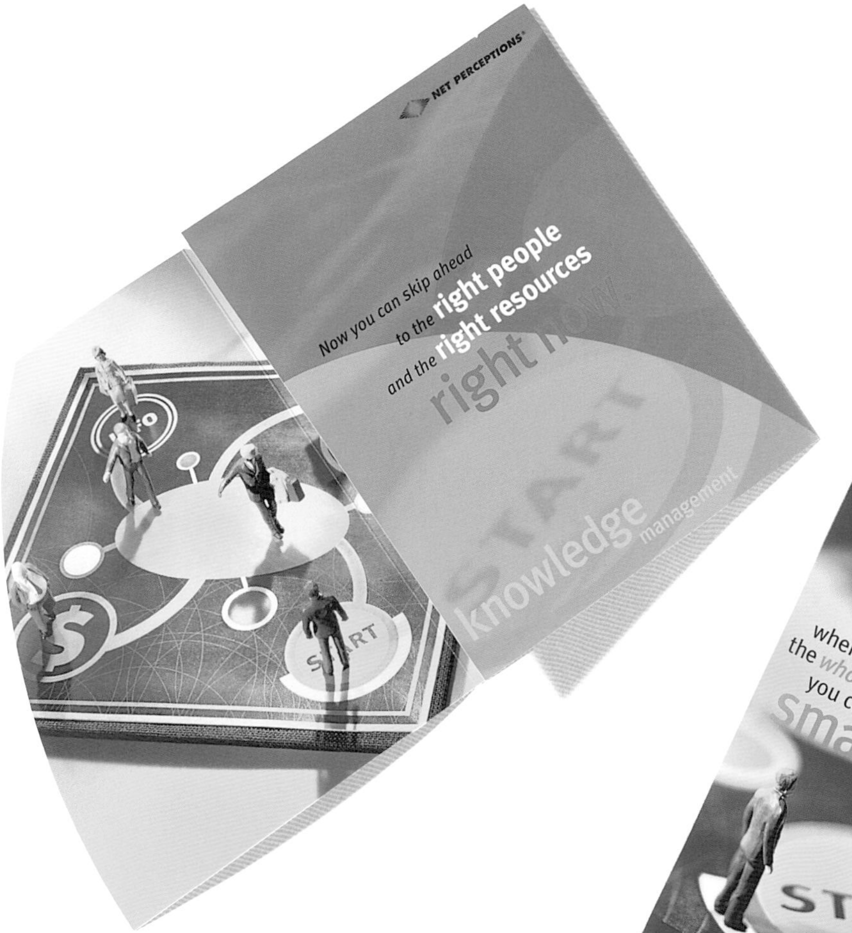

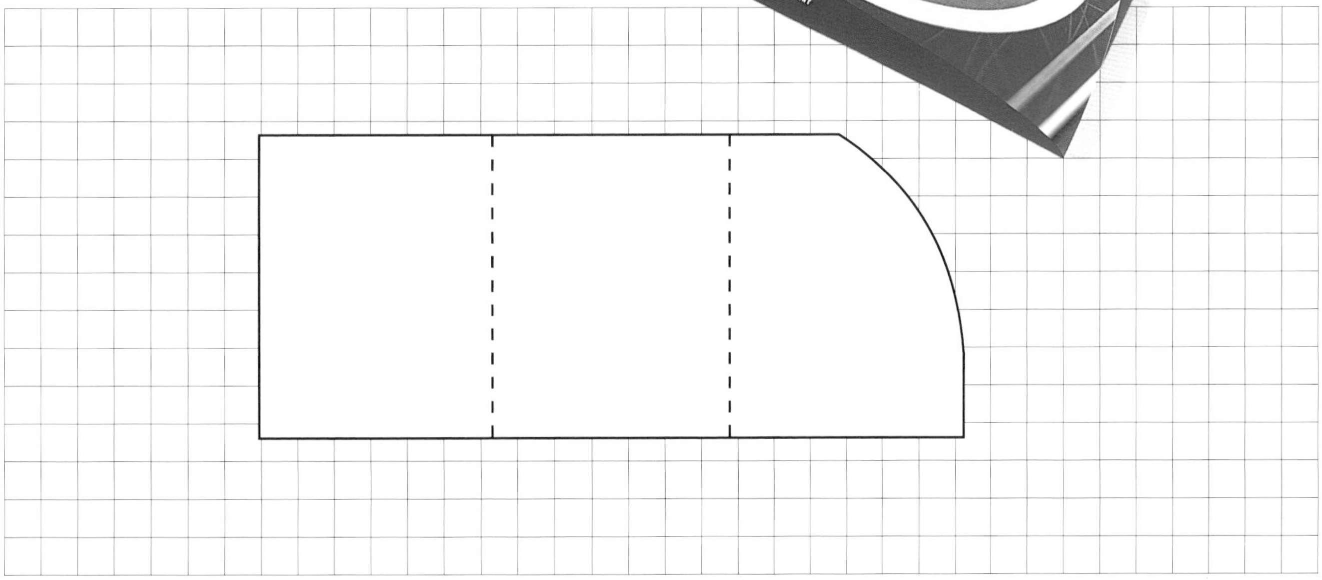

Promotional Leaflet
"Knowledge Management Brochure"

eコマースプロモーション リーフレット

USA 2000

CL: Net Perceptions

AD, D: Alan Tse

D: Kim Welter

P: Ellie Kingsbury

DF, SB: Yamamoto Moss

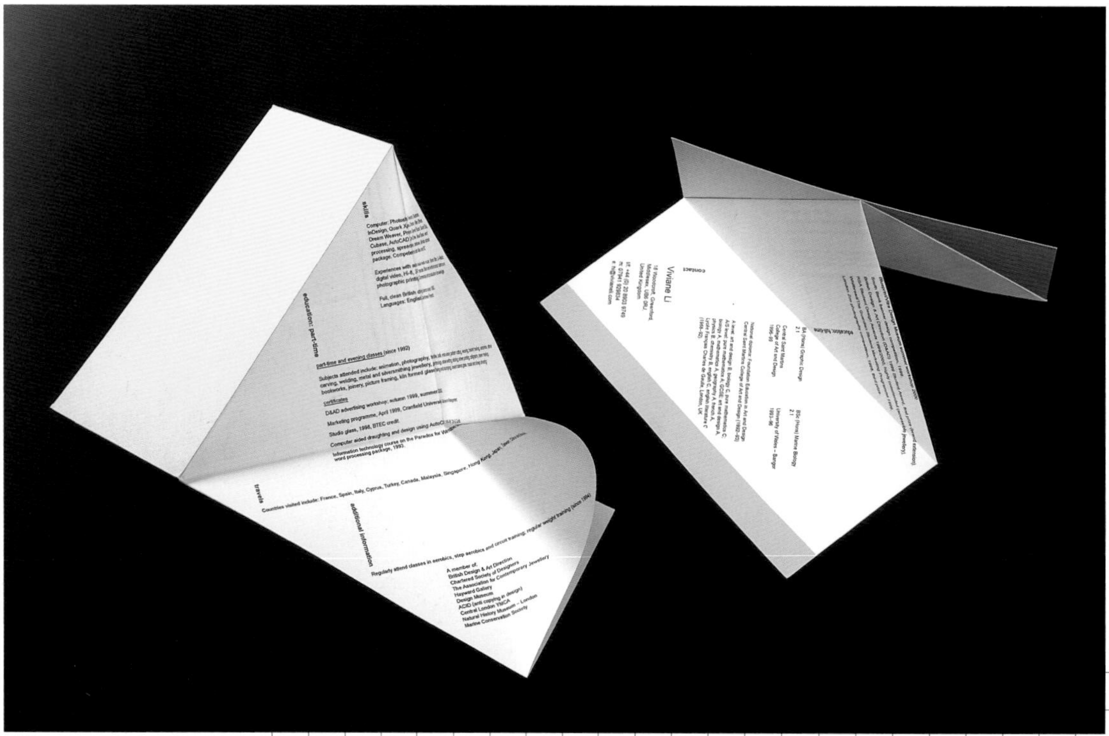

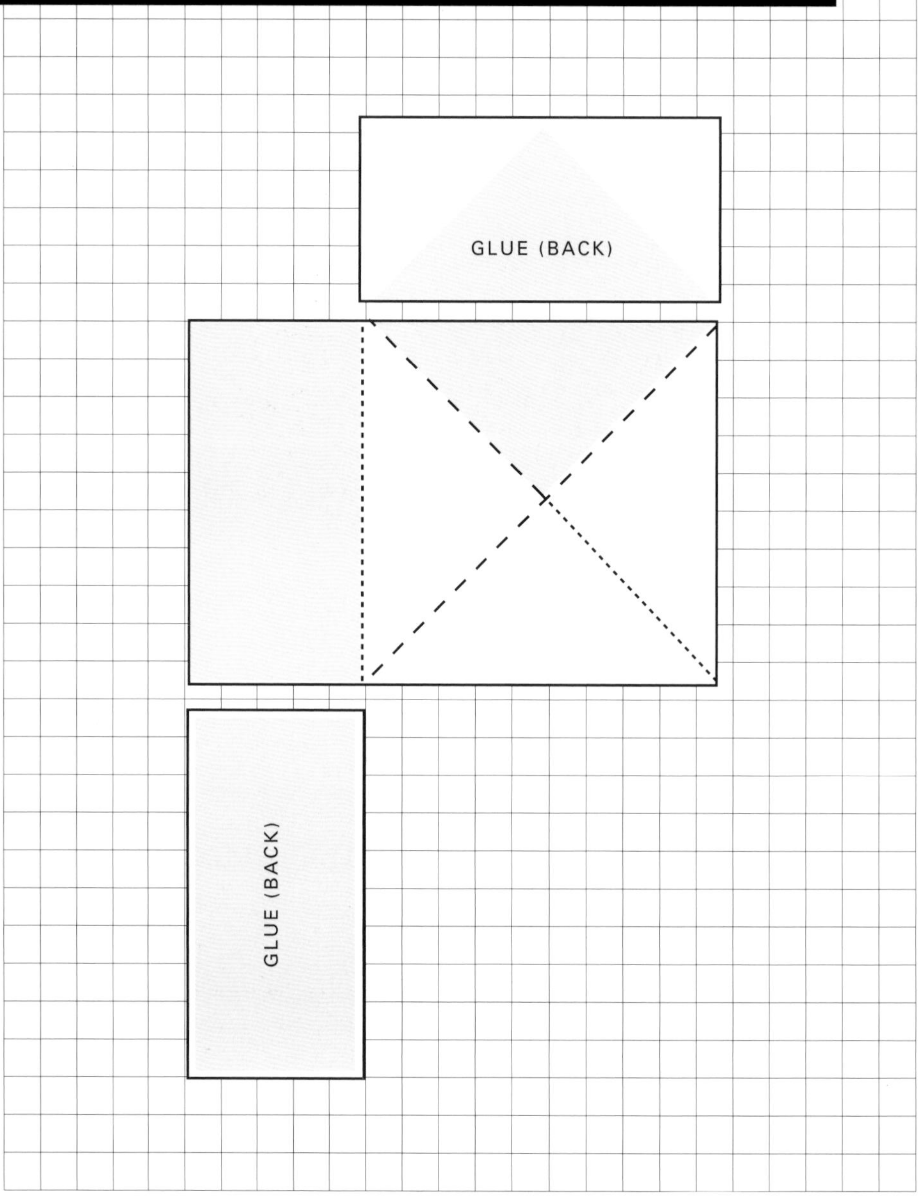

Curriculm Vitae "To Let"
デザイナー プロモーション用
UK 2000
CL, SB:Viviane Li
CD, AD, D, P, I, DF, SB: Viviane Li

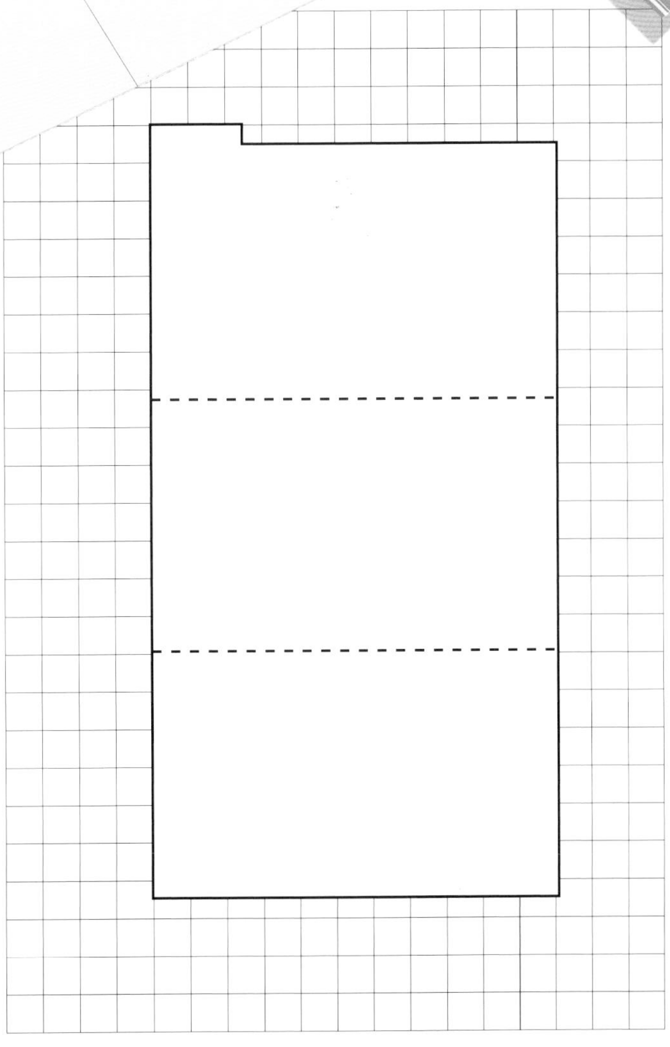

Corporate Profile Brochure
市場調査会社 会社案内
Germany 2000
CL: Performaxx AG
CD, AD, D: Christopher Wiehl
P: Richard Unger
DF, SB: Paarpiloten

Greeting Card (Flower)
グリーティング・カード(花)
Japan 1996
CL: PLAN Y
AD, D, SB: Miyuki Yoshida

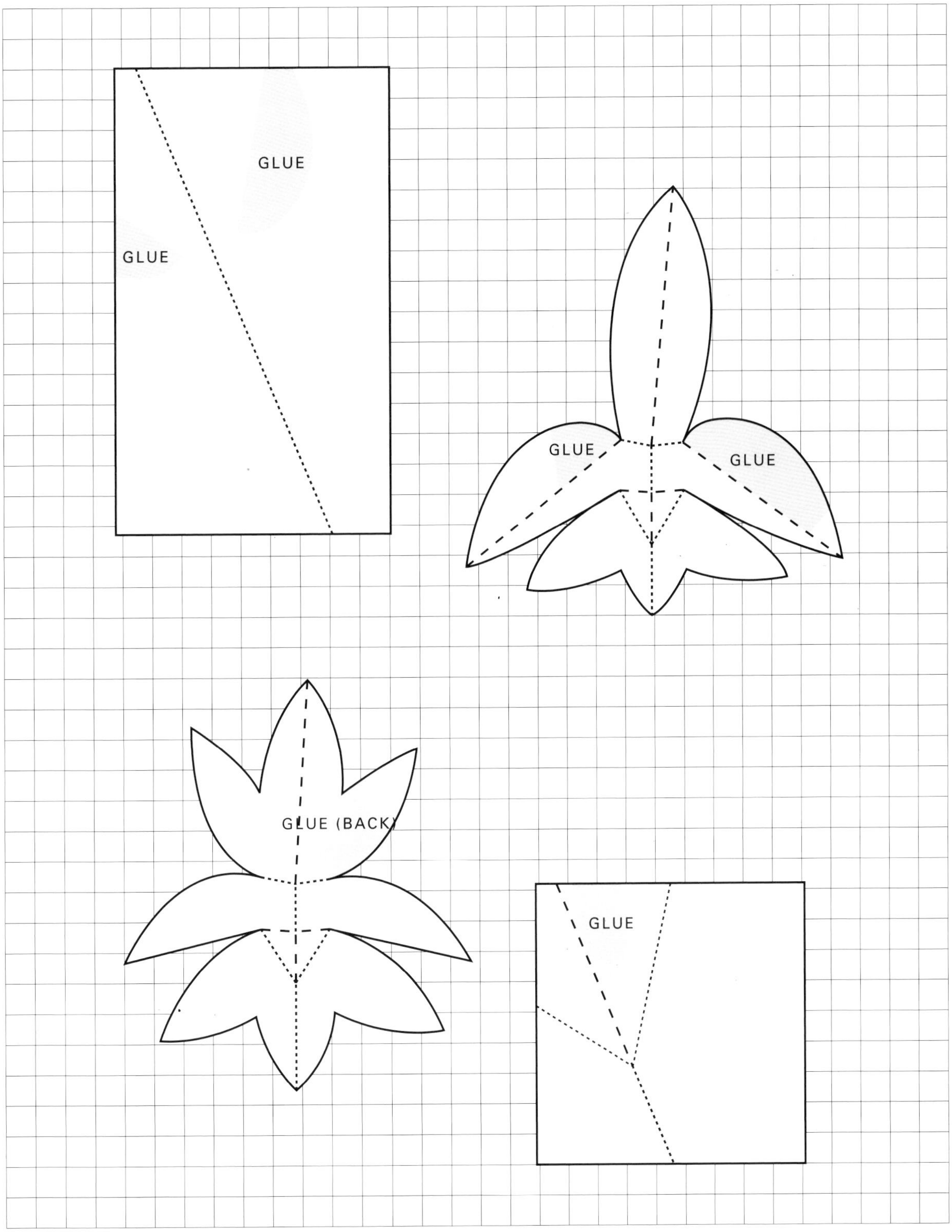
GLUE
GLUE
GLUE
GLUE
GLUE (BACK)
GLUE

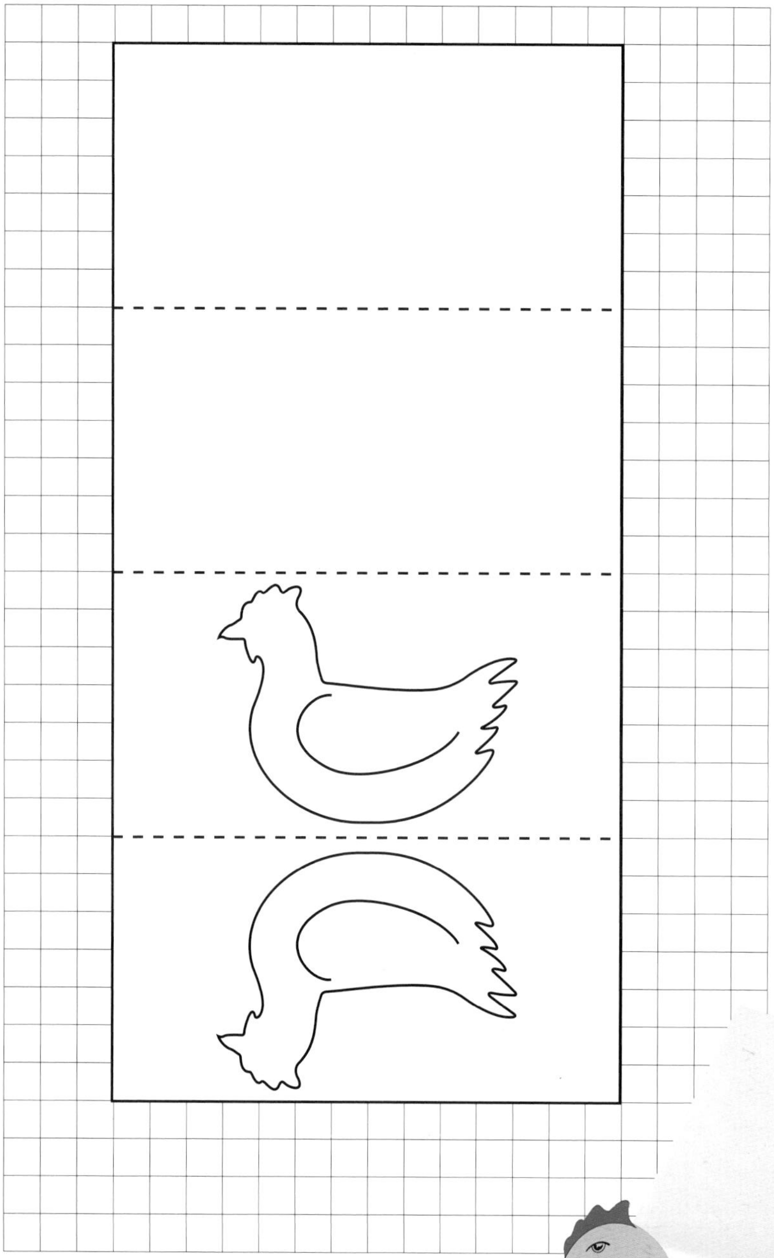

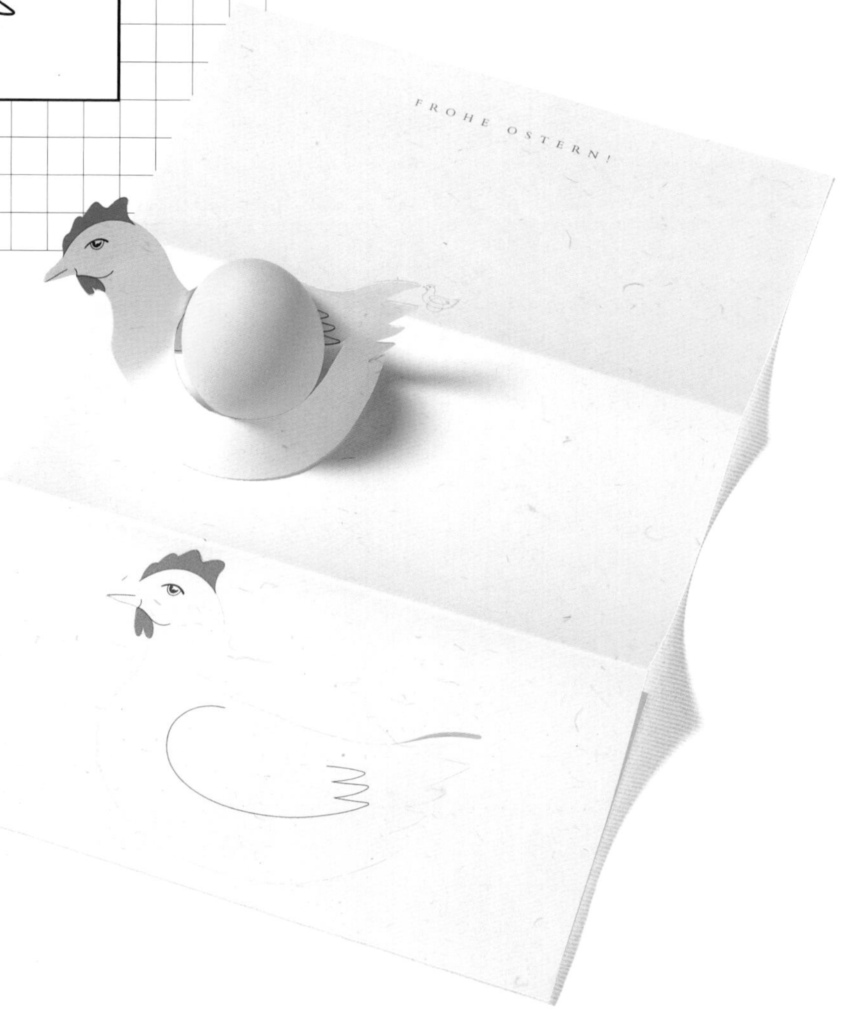

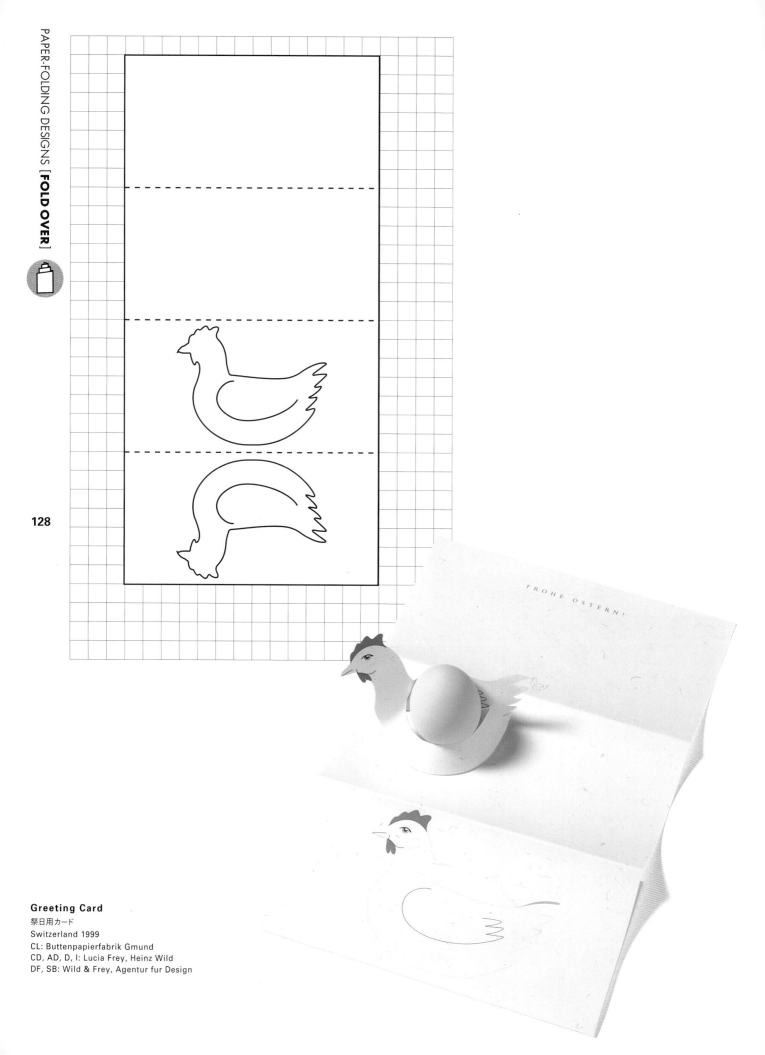

Greeting Card
祭日用カード
Switzerland 1999
CL: Buttenpapierfabrik Gmund
CD, AD, D, I: Lucia Frey, Heinz Wild
DF, SB: Wild & Frey, Agentur fur Design

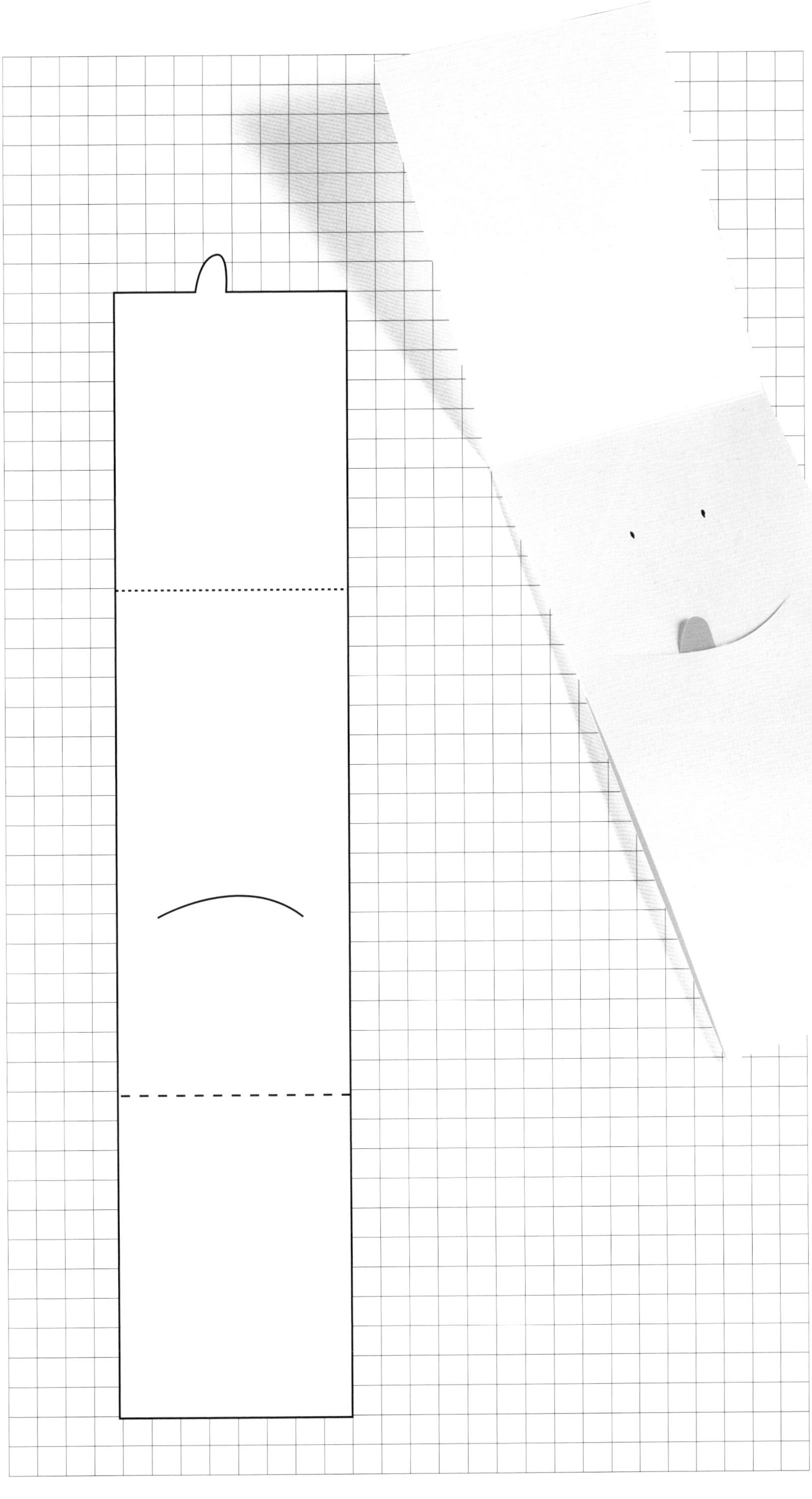

Greeting Card
祭日用カード
Switzerland 1999
CL: Wild & Frey
CD, AD, D, I: Lucia Frey, Heinz Wild
DF, SB: Wild & Frey, Agentur fur Design

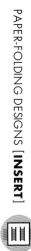

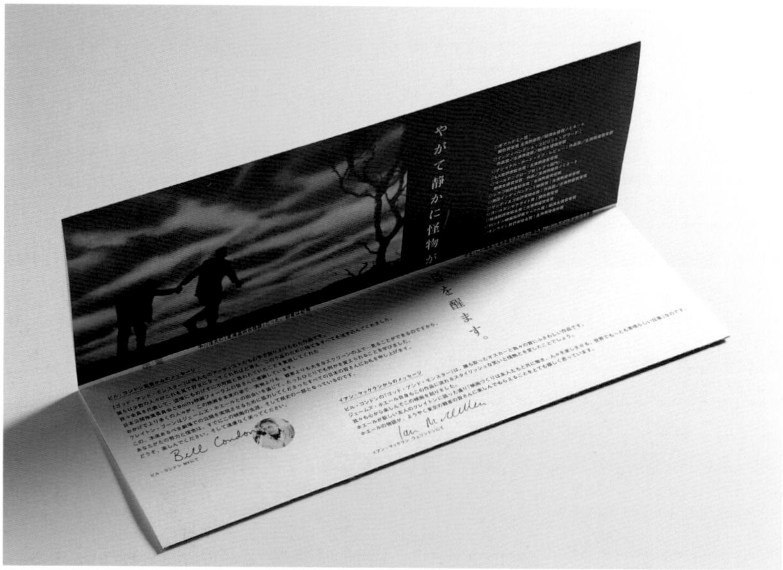

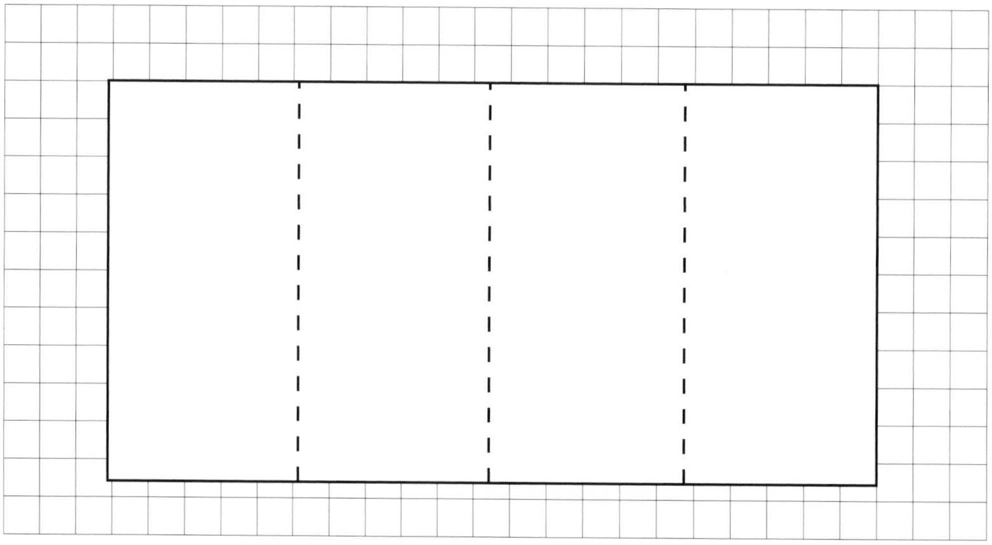

Introducing "Gods and Monsters"

ゴッド＆モンスター（劇場販売用）

Japan 1998

CL: Gods and Monsters Japan Committee

AD, D: Hideaki Muto

DF, SB: Muto Office Inc.

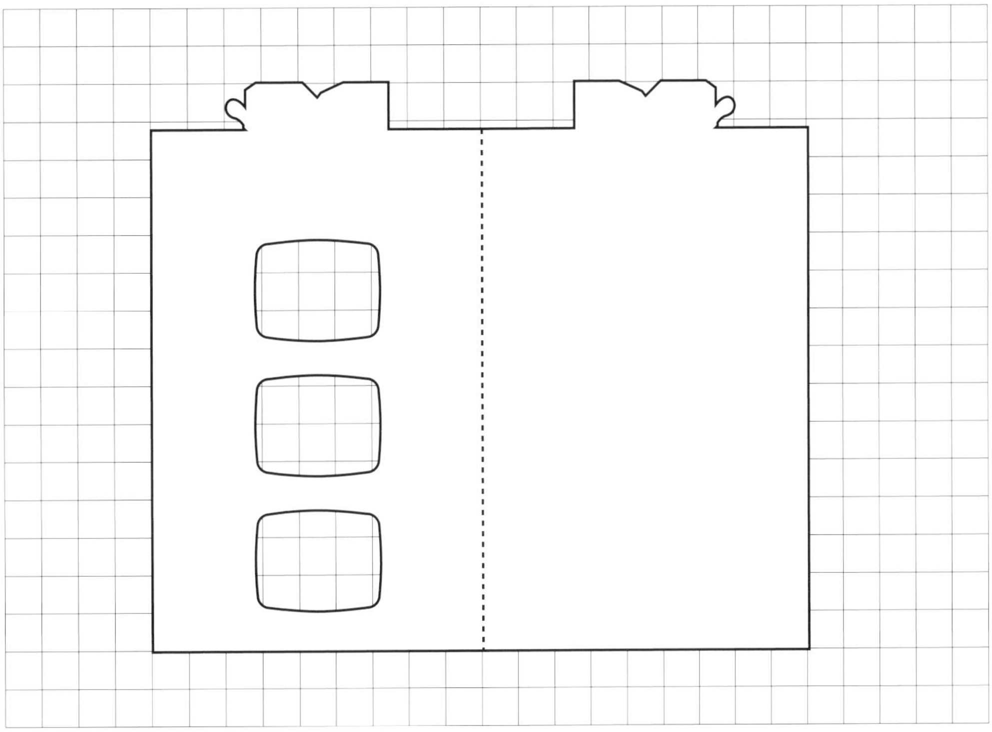

TV Program Guide

MTV 番組ガイド

Japan 1993

CL: Music Channel Co., Ltd.

AD, D, SB: Akihiko Tsukamoto

DF: Tokyu Agency, Inc.

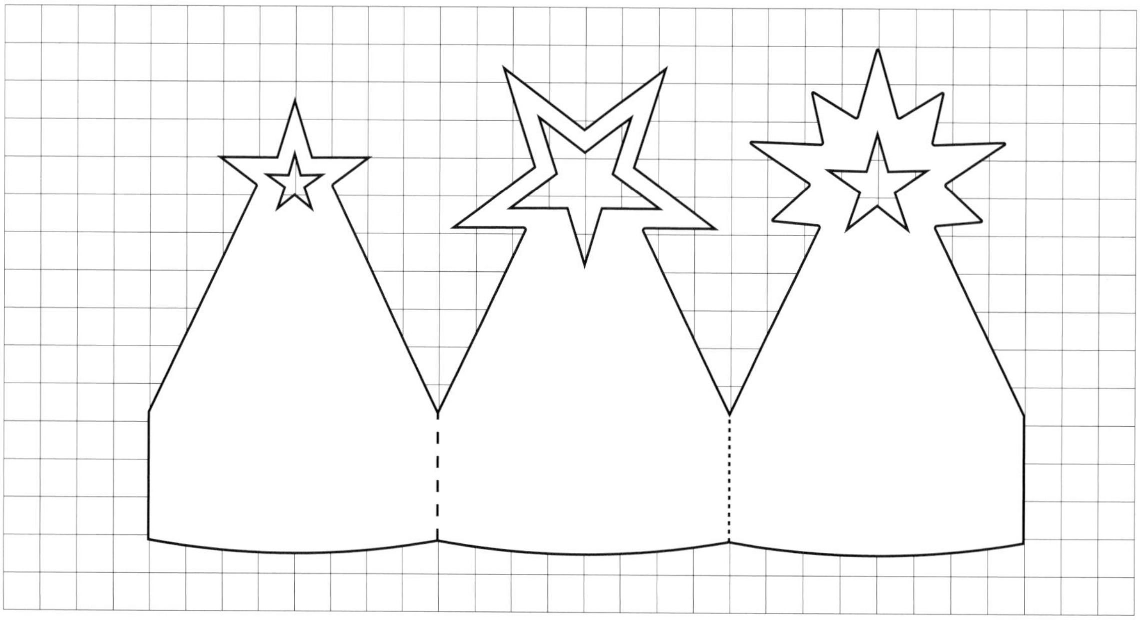

Christmas & New Year Card
クリスマス・新年挨拶状
Japan 1995
CL: Be International Corporation
D: Akihiko Tsukamoto
DF, SB: Design Club

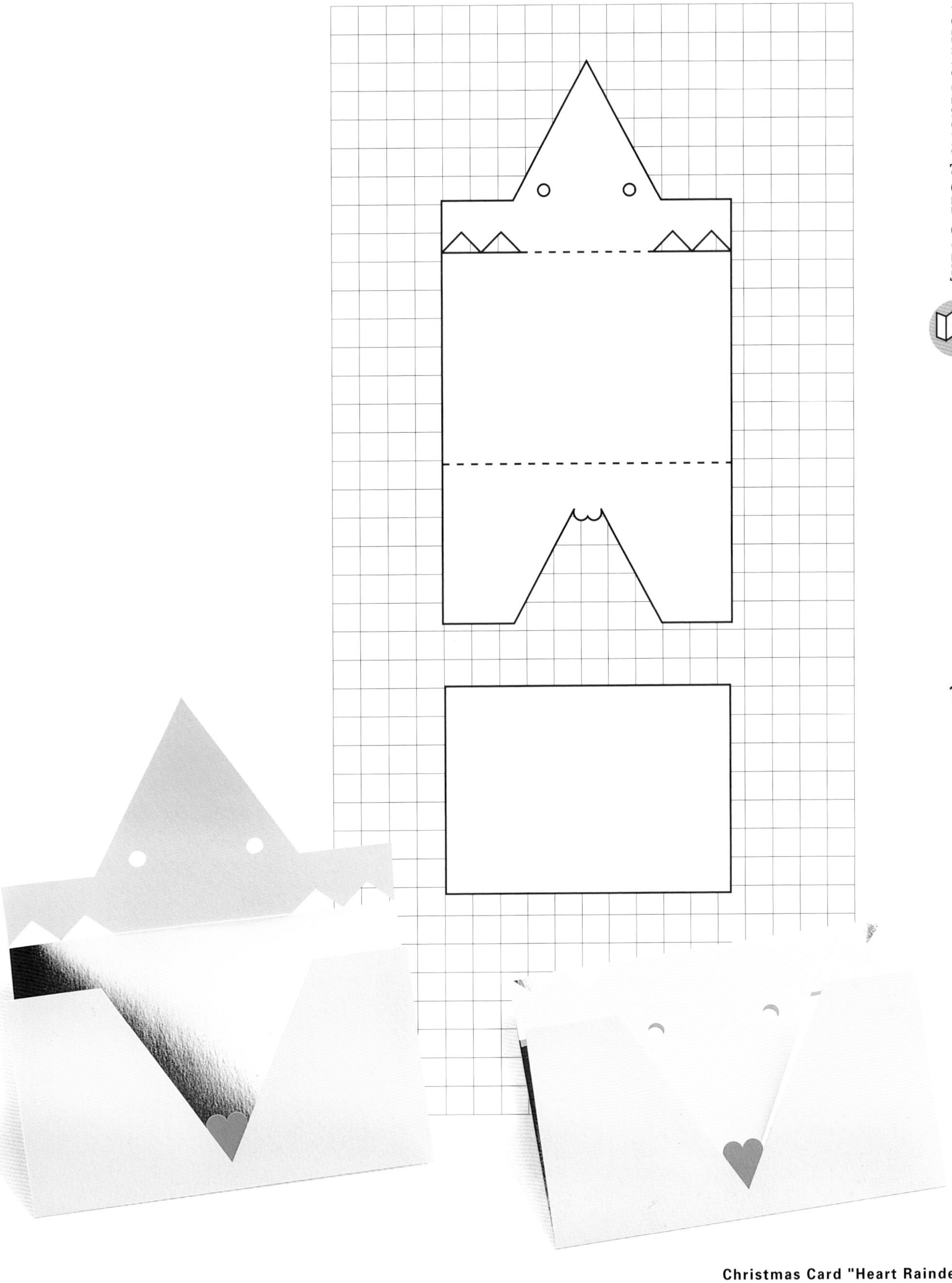

Christmas Card "Heart Raindeer"
クリスマス・カード・ハートトナカイ
Japan 2002
AD, D: Katsumi Komagata
DF, SB: One Stroke Co., Ltd.

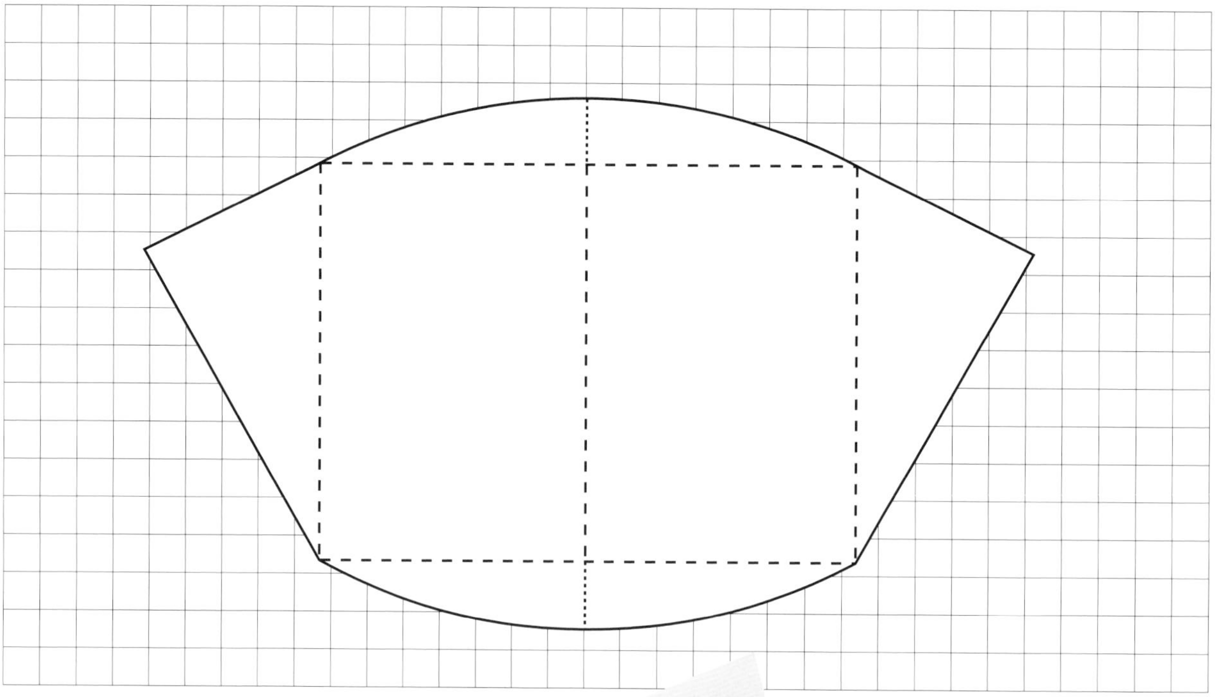

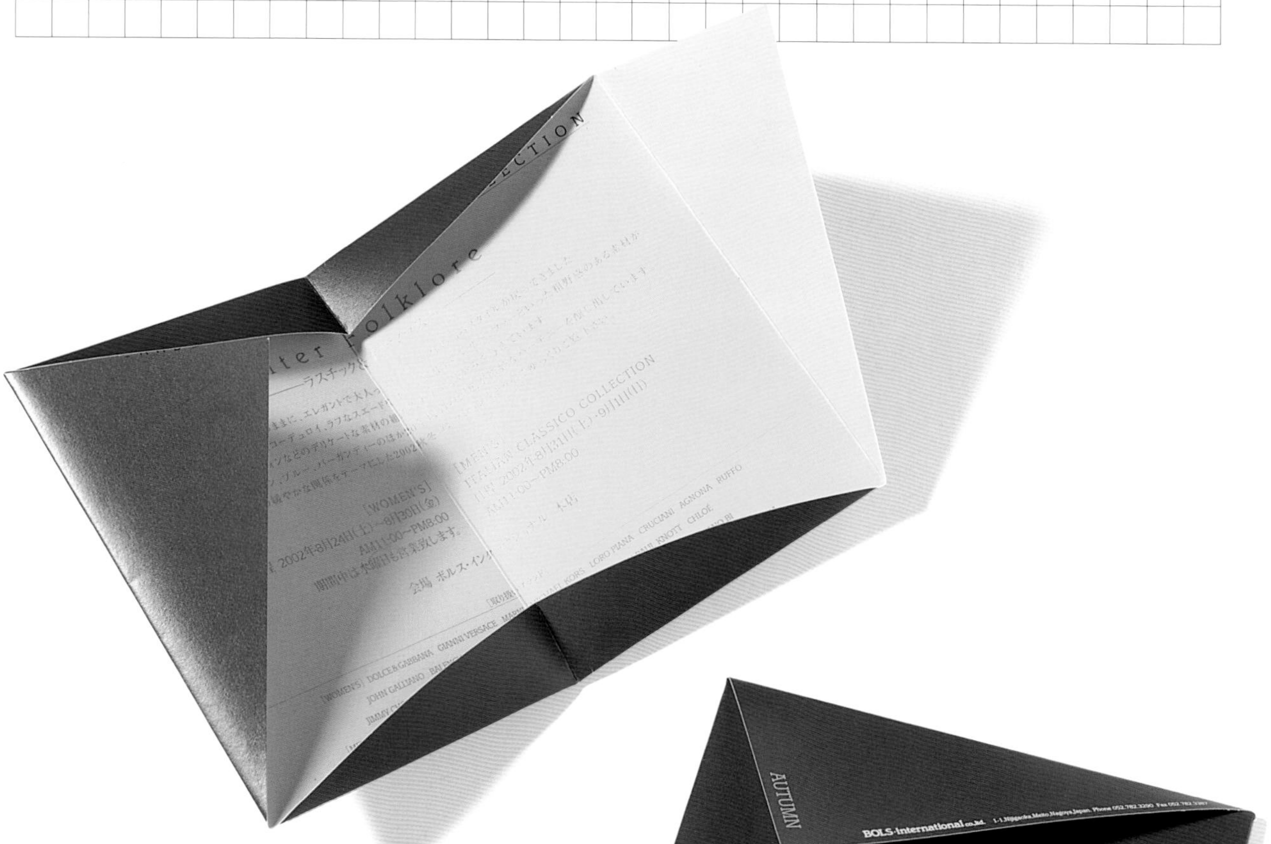

Collection Invitation Card

2002-2003年 秋・冬コレクション案内状
Japan 2001
CL: BOLS International Co., Ltd.
AD: Katsunori Watanabe
D: Hana Hosono
DF, SB: Bauhaus Inc.

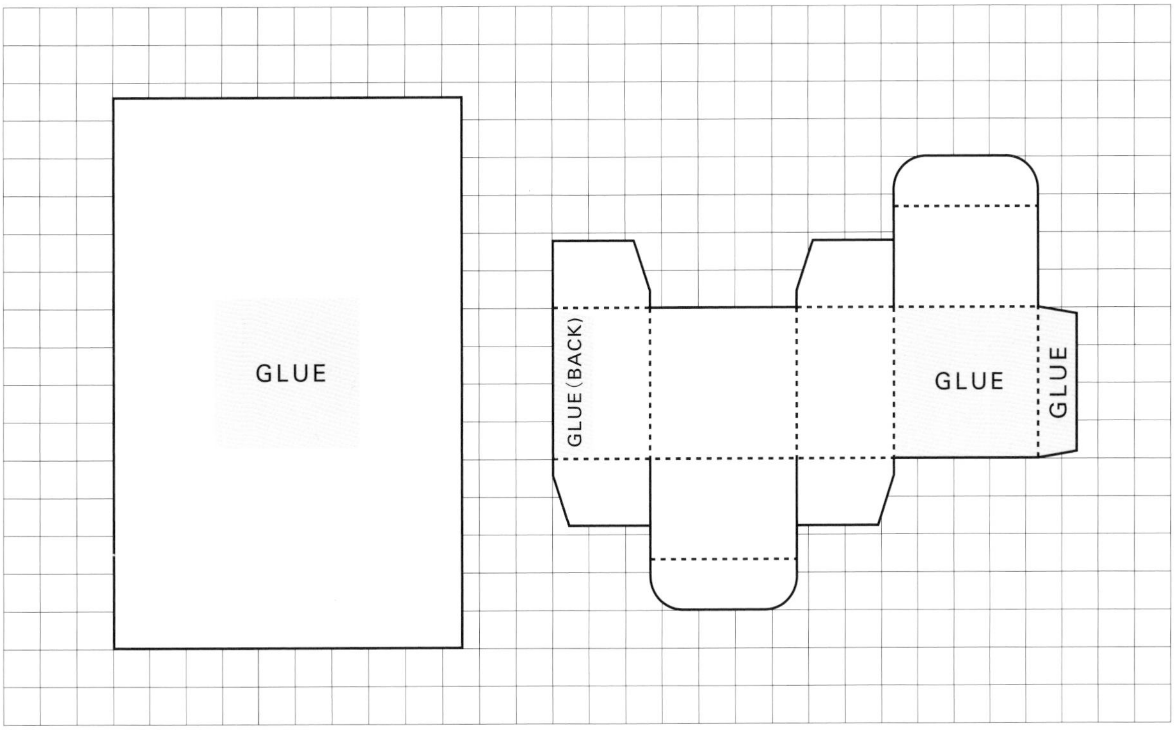

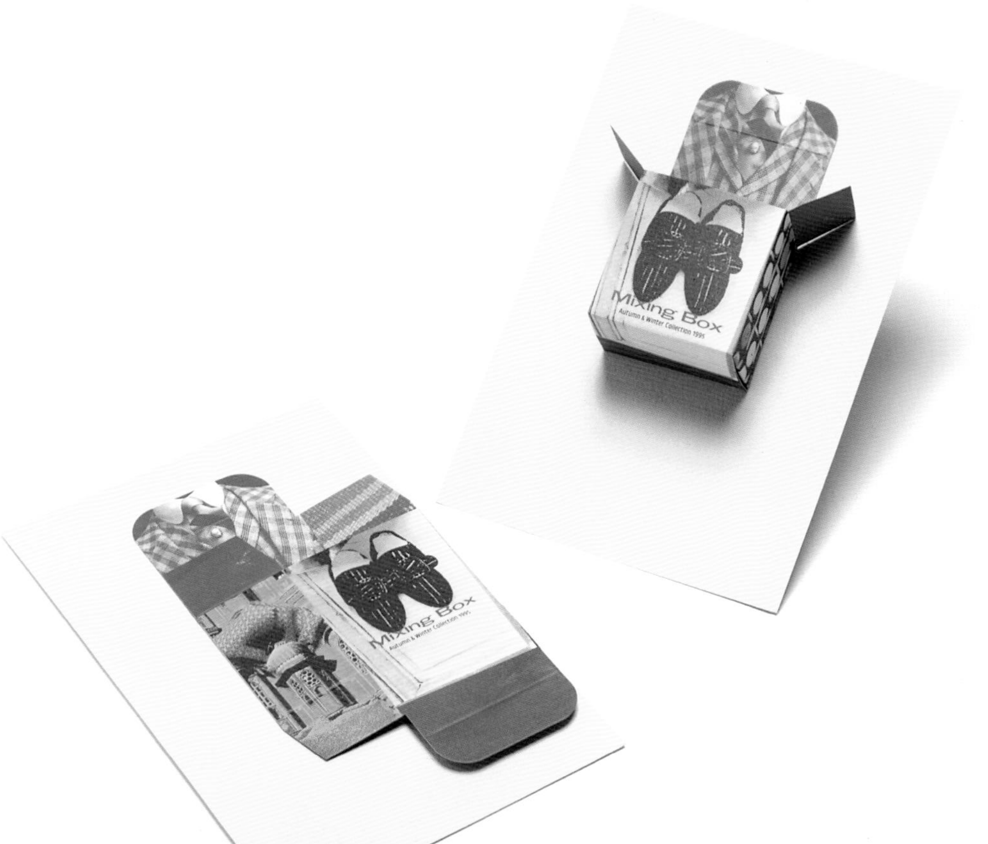

Autumn & Winter Collection Announcement DM

秋冬素材展示会告知DM

Japan 1995

CL: Sasaki Sellm Co., Ltd.
CD: Setsuko Matagi
AD, D: Akihiko Tsukamoto
DF, SB: Design Club

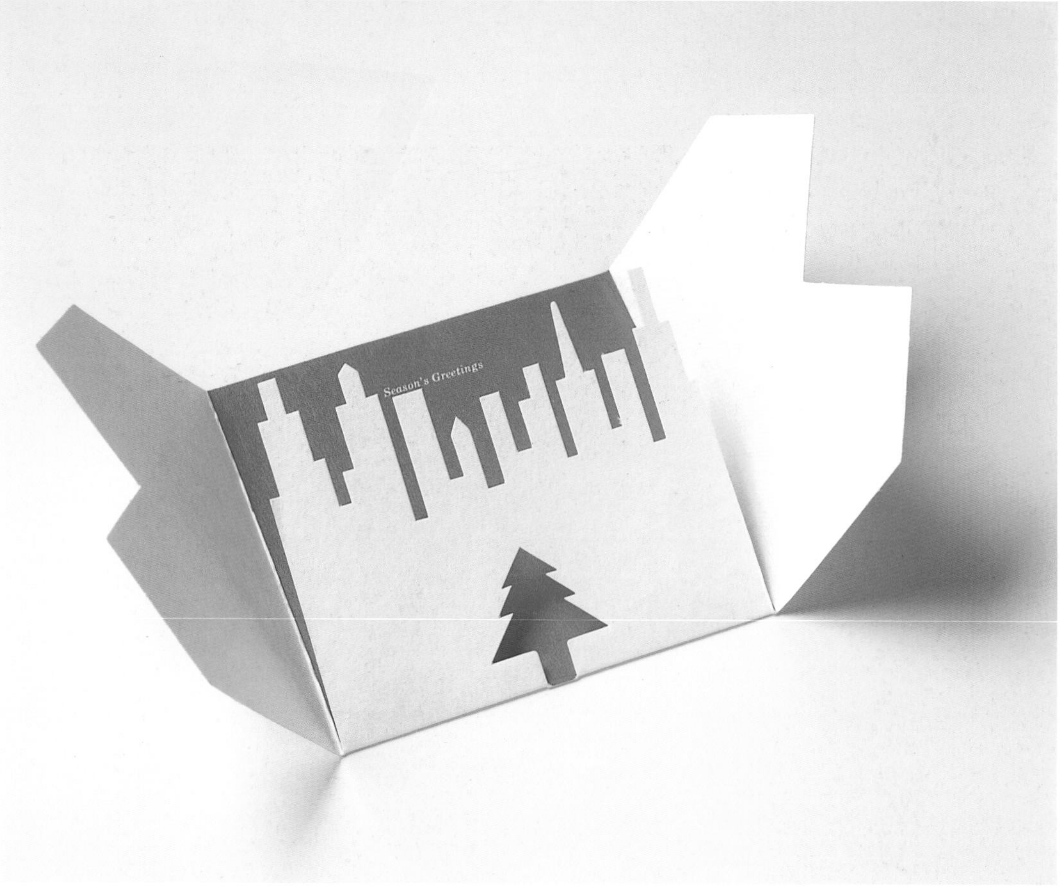

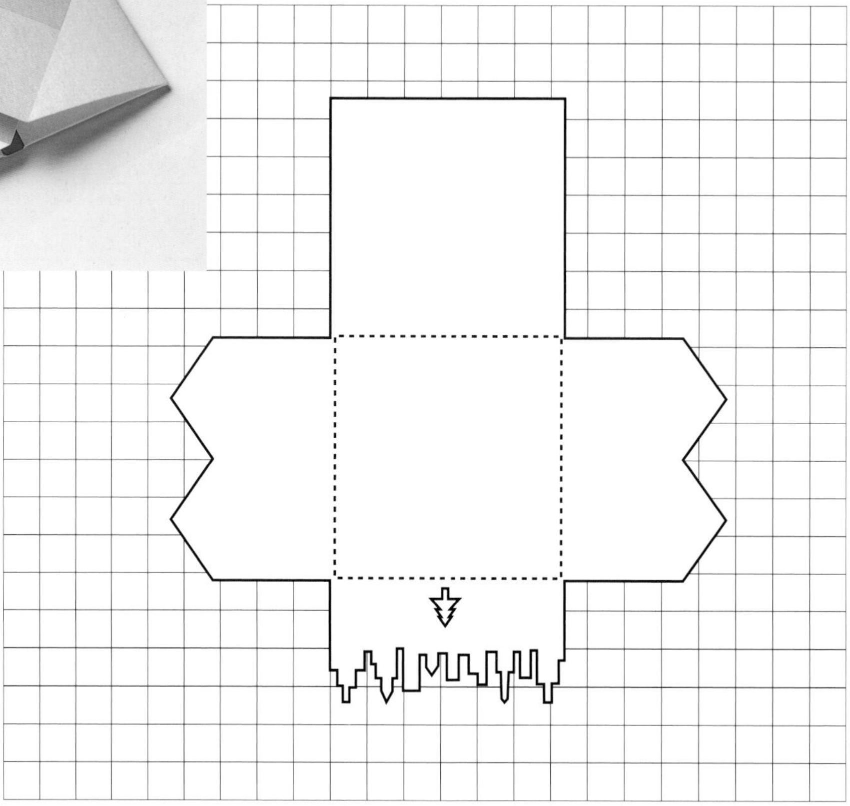

Christmas & New Year Card
クリスマス・新年挨拶状
Japan 1991
CL: Be International Corporation
D: Akihiko Tsukamoto
DF, SB: Design Club

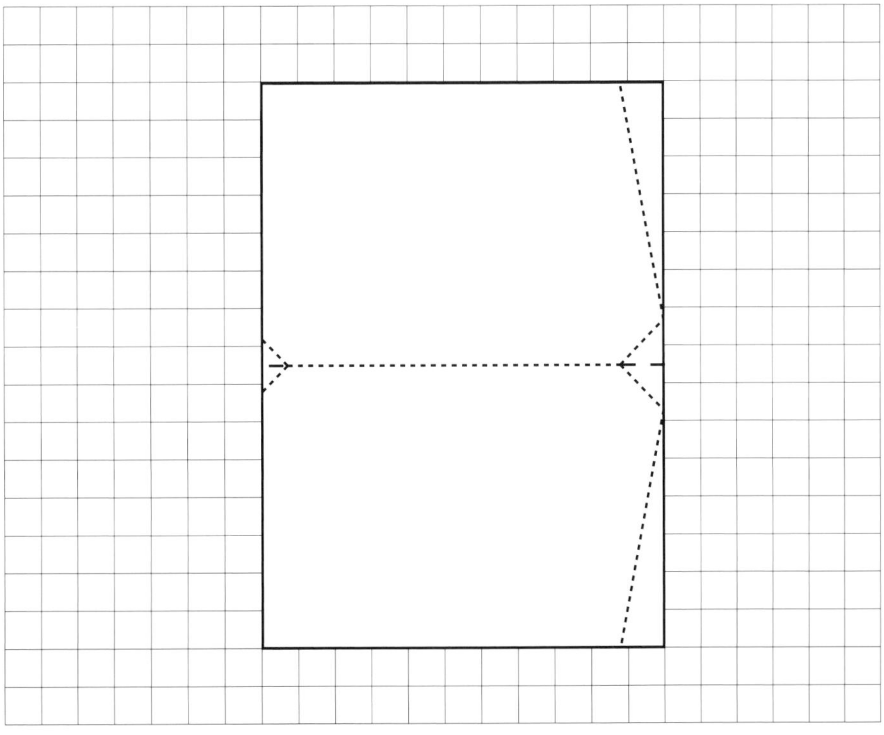

New Year's Card
年賀状
Japan 2003
CL:Akio Okumura
AD, D, SB: Akio Okumura

Greeting Card (Fossils)
グリーティング・カード（化石）
Japan 2001
CL: PLAN Y
AD, D, SB: Miyuki Yoshida

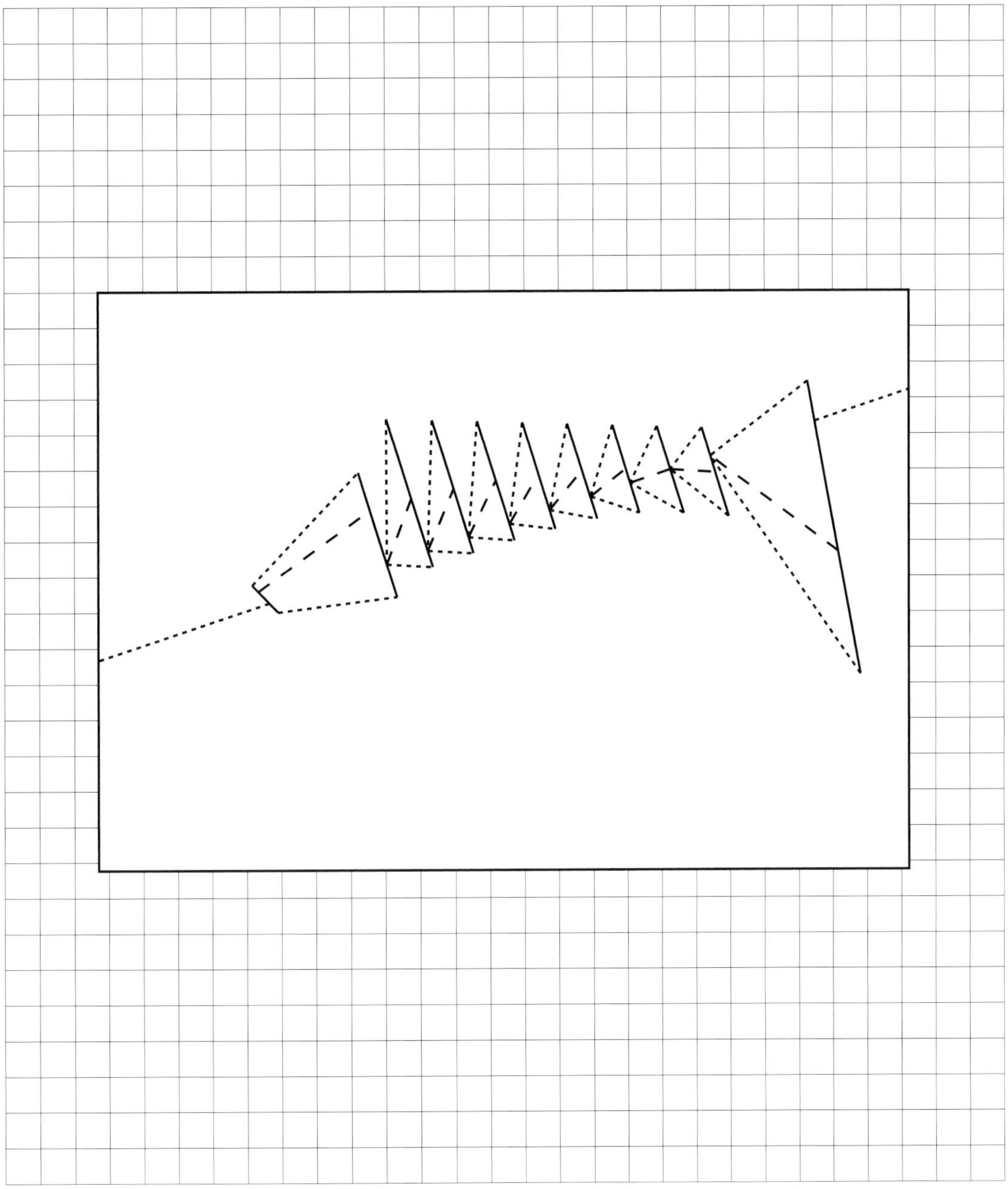

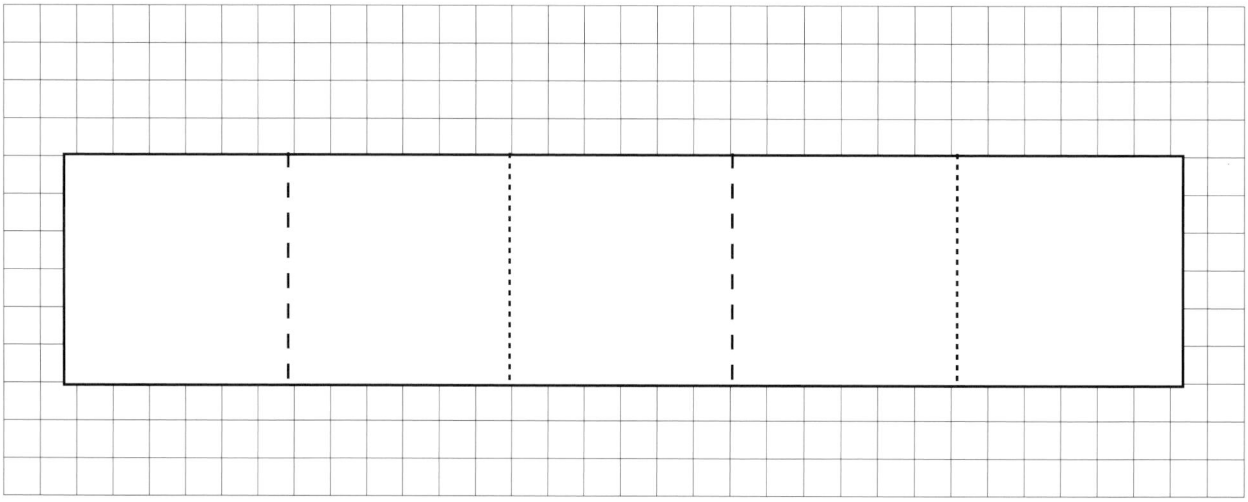

Mini Booklet
"Once Upon a Collins Street"
小型本「ワンス アポン コリンズ・ストリート」
Australia
CL: Hardie Grant Books
AD, D: Andrew Hoyne
P: Robyn Lea

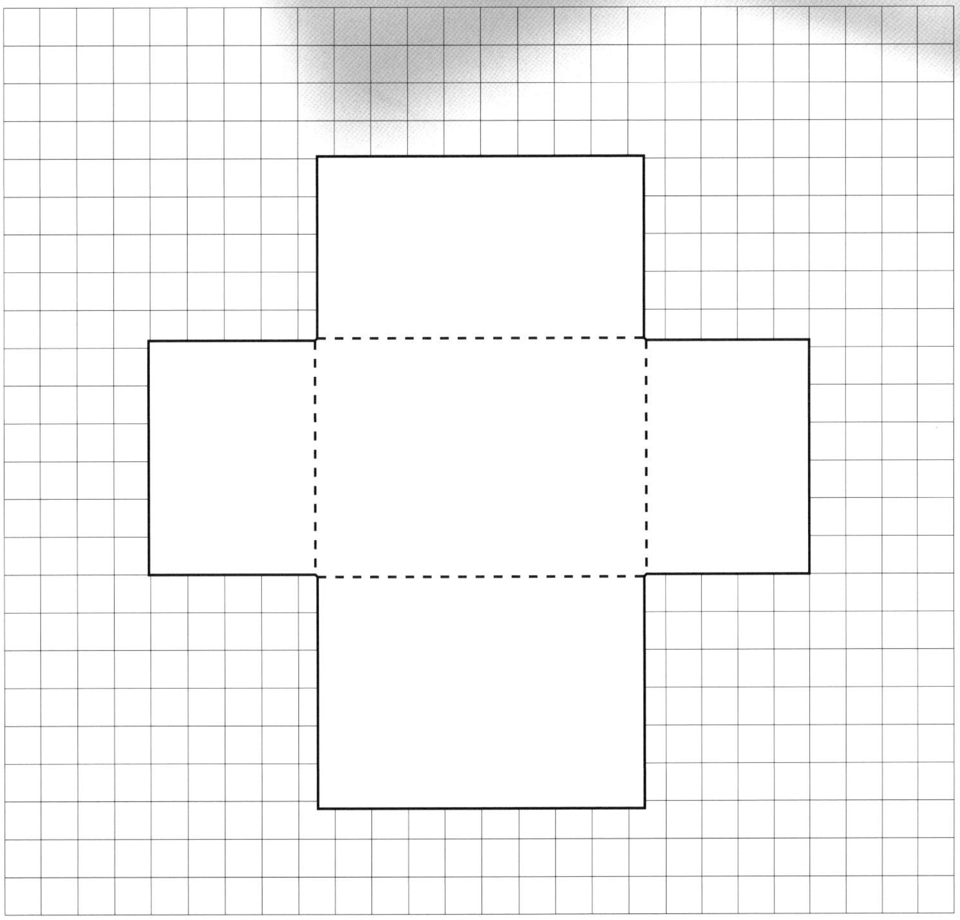

Collection Invitation Card

2002年 春・夏コレクション案内状

Japan 2002

CL: BOLS International Co., Ltd.

AD: Katsunori Watanabe

D: Hana Hosono

DF, SB: Bauhaus Inc.

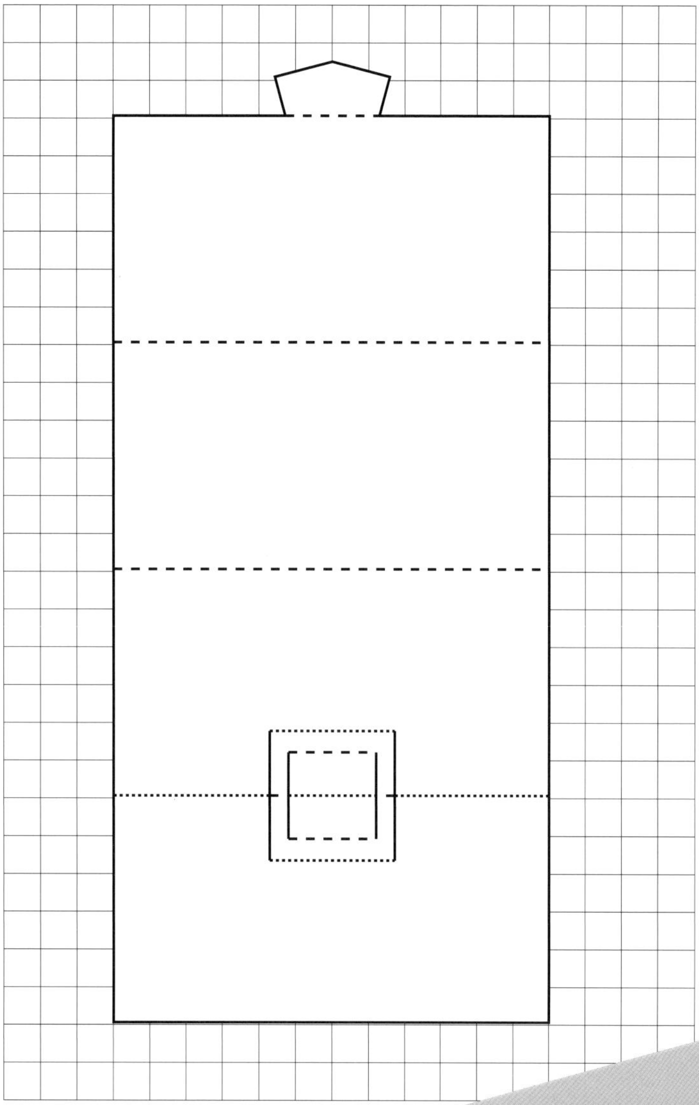

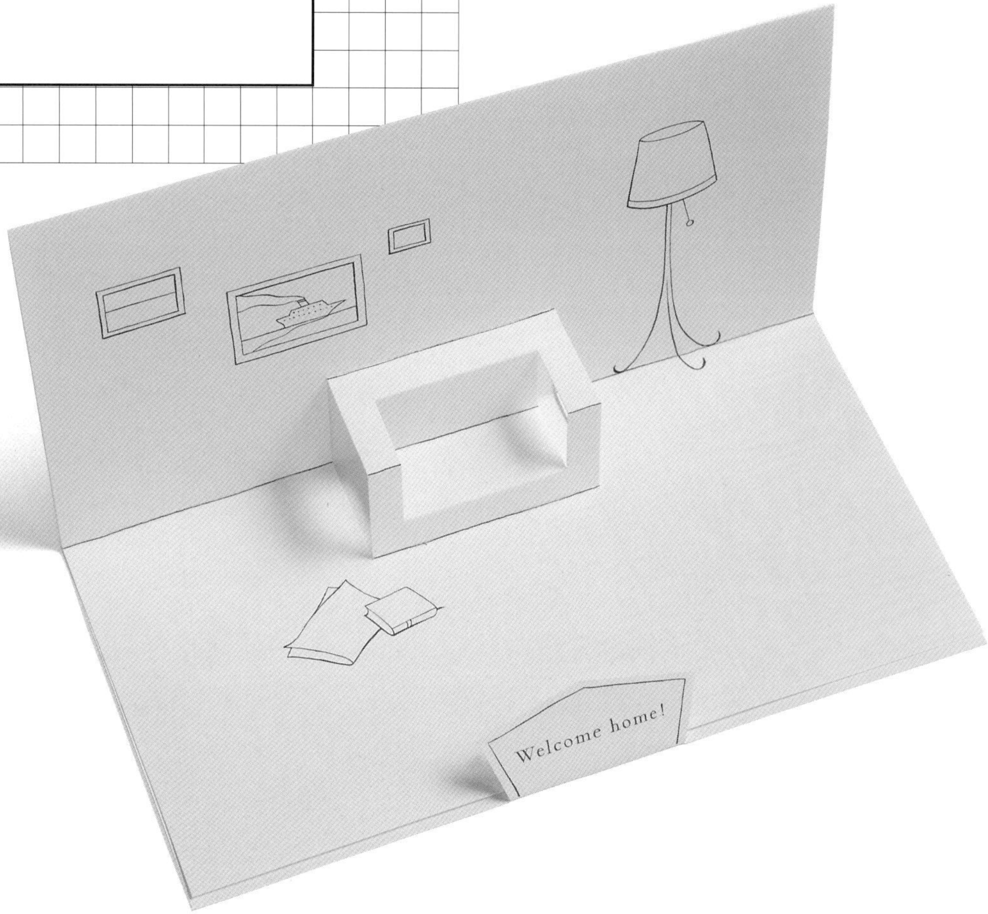

Greeting Card
祭日用カード
Switzerland 1999
CL: Buttenpapierfabrik Gmund
CD, AD, D, I: Lucia Frey, Heinz Wild
DF, SB: Wild & Frey, Agentur fur Design

Greeting Card
祭日用カード
Switzerland 1999
CL: Buttenpapierfabrik Gmund
CD, AD, D, I: Lucia Frey, Heinz Wild
DF, SB: Wild & Frey Agentur fur Design

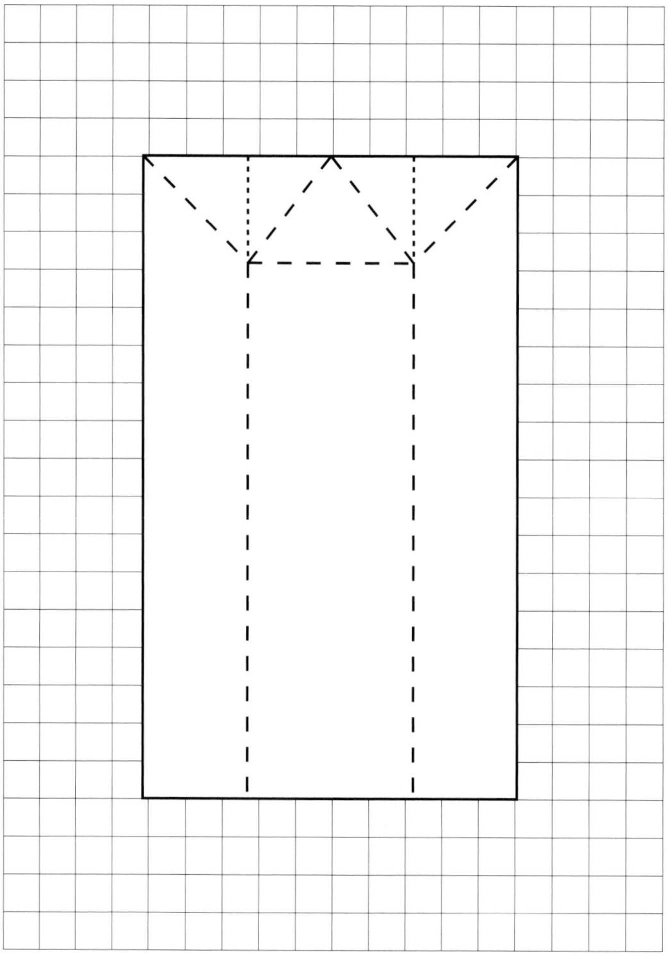

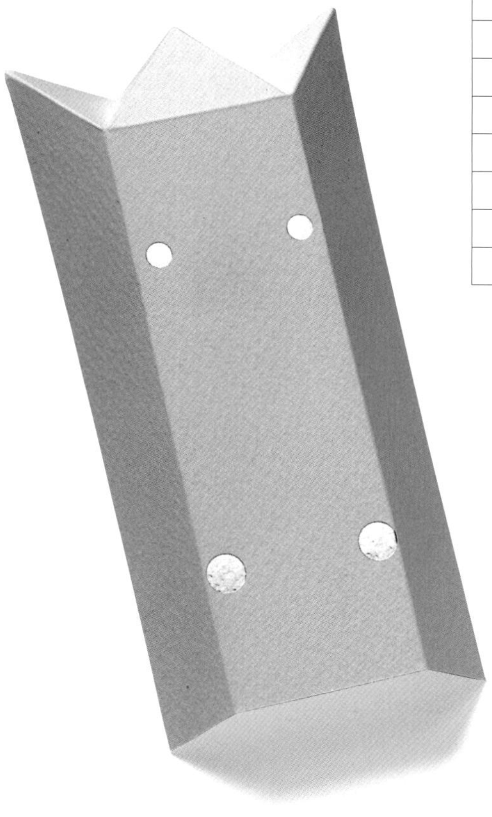

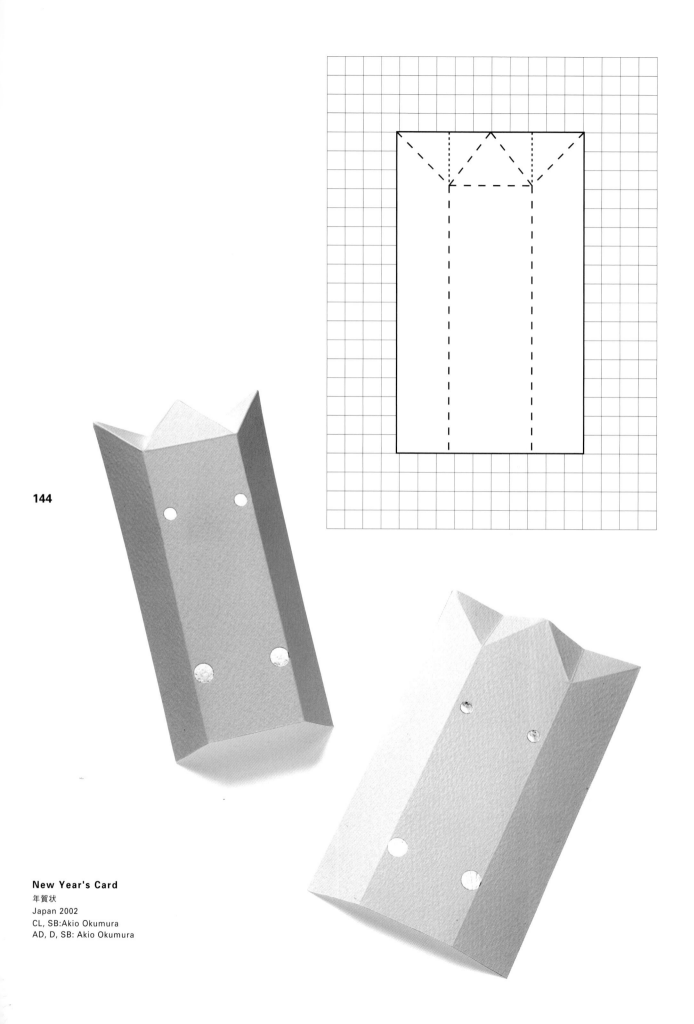

New Year's Card
年賀状
Japan 2002
CL, SB:Akio Okumura
AD, D, SB: Akio Okumura

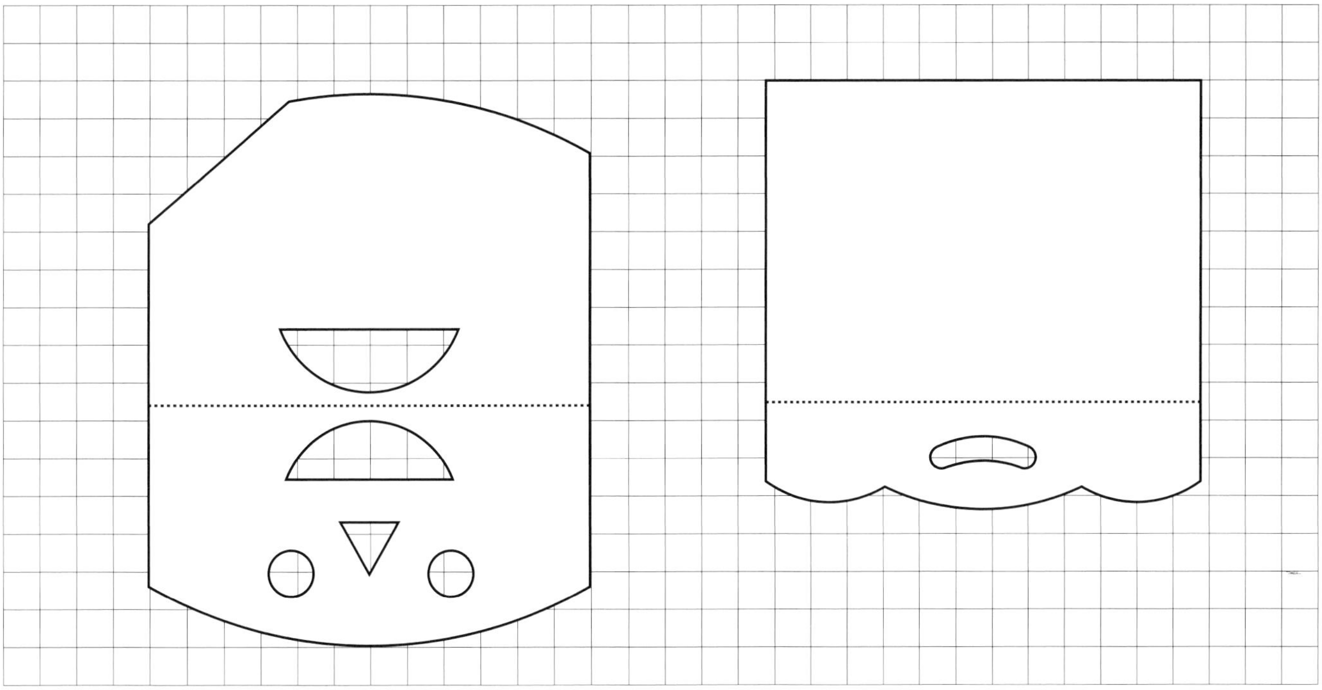

Christmas Crad "Santa"
クリスマス・カード・サンタ
Japan 2002
D: Katsumi Komagata
DF, SB: One Stroke Co., Ltd.

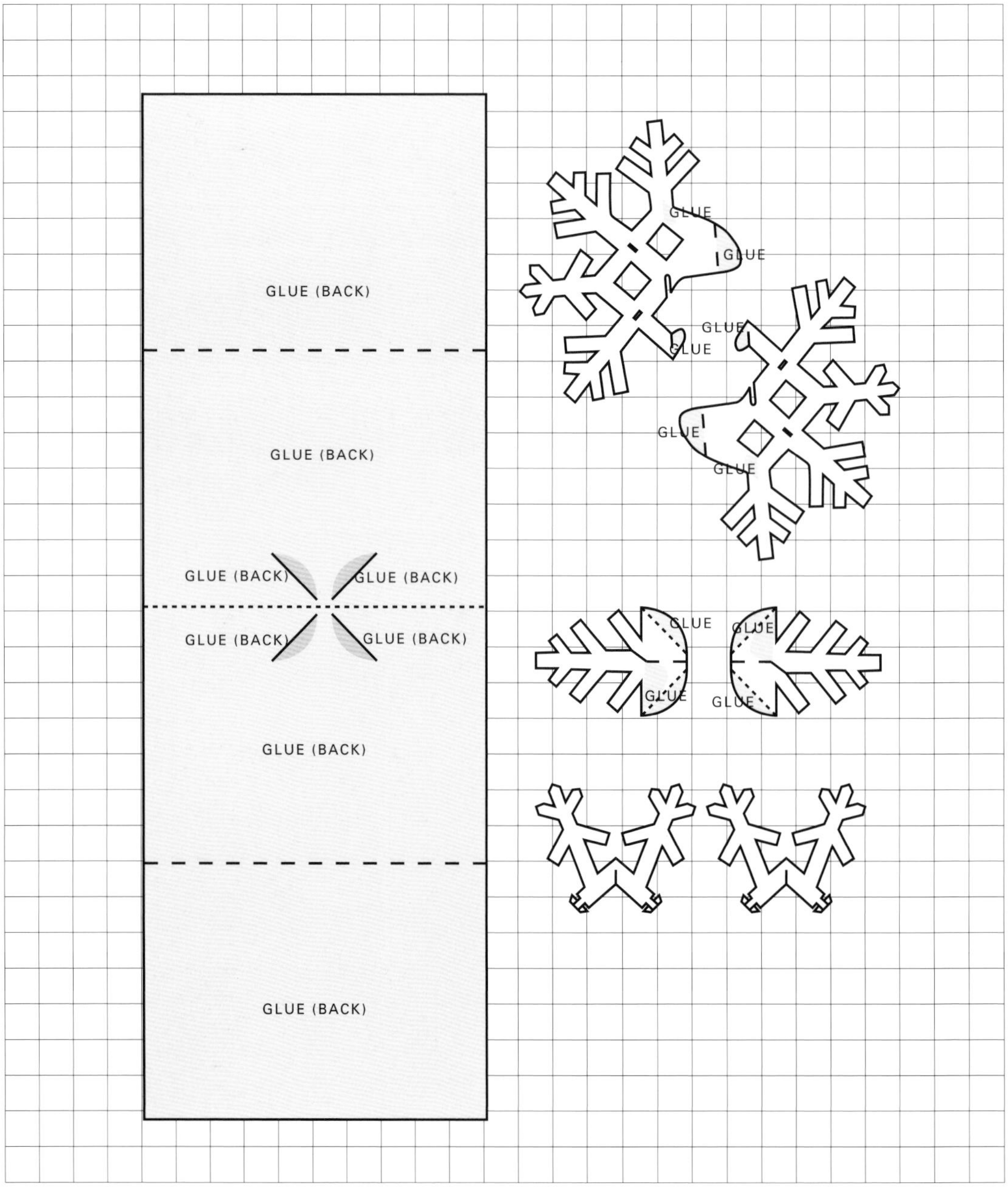

Pop-Up Snowflake
美術館ギフトカード
USA 2002
CL: Museum of Modern Art, New York City
CD: Ashley White
D, I, SB: Robert Sabuda

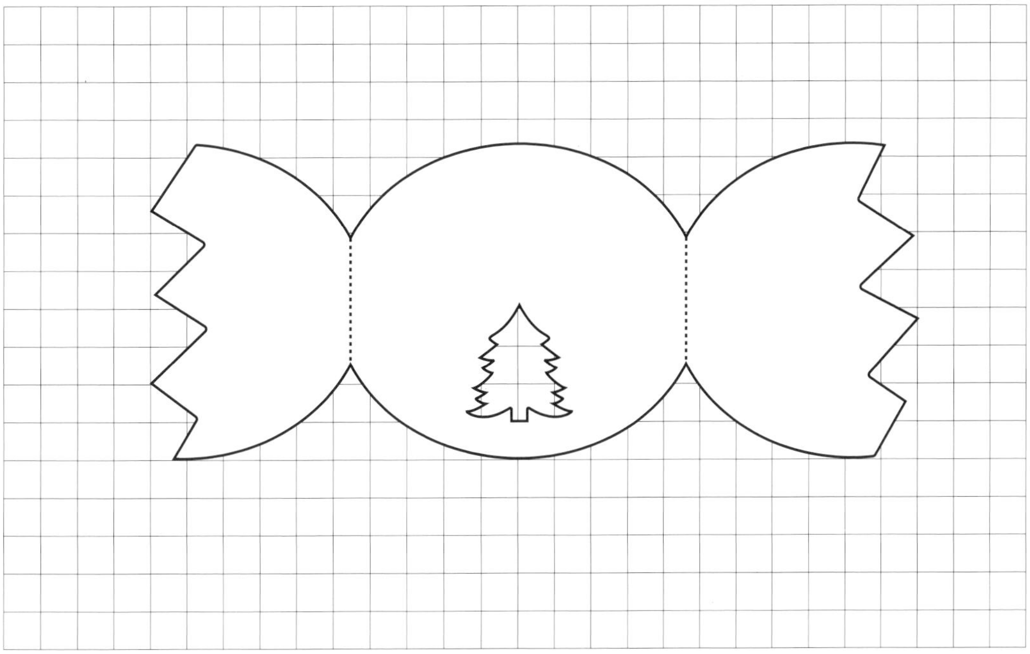

Christmas & New Year Card
クリスマス・新年挨拶状
Japan 1992
CL: Be International Corporation
D: Akihiko Tsukamoto
DF, SB: Design Club

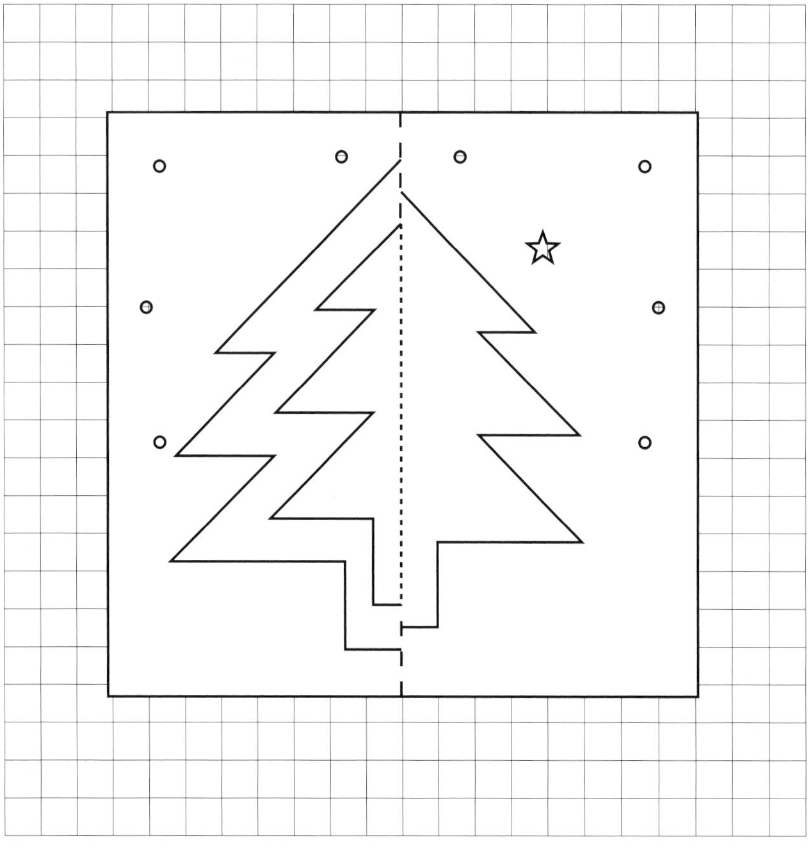

Christmas Card
"Three Dimensional Tree"
クリスマス・カード・立体ツリー
Japan 2002
AD, D: Katsumi Komagata
DF, SB: One Stroke Co., Ltd.

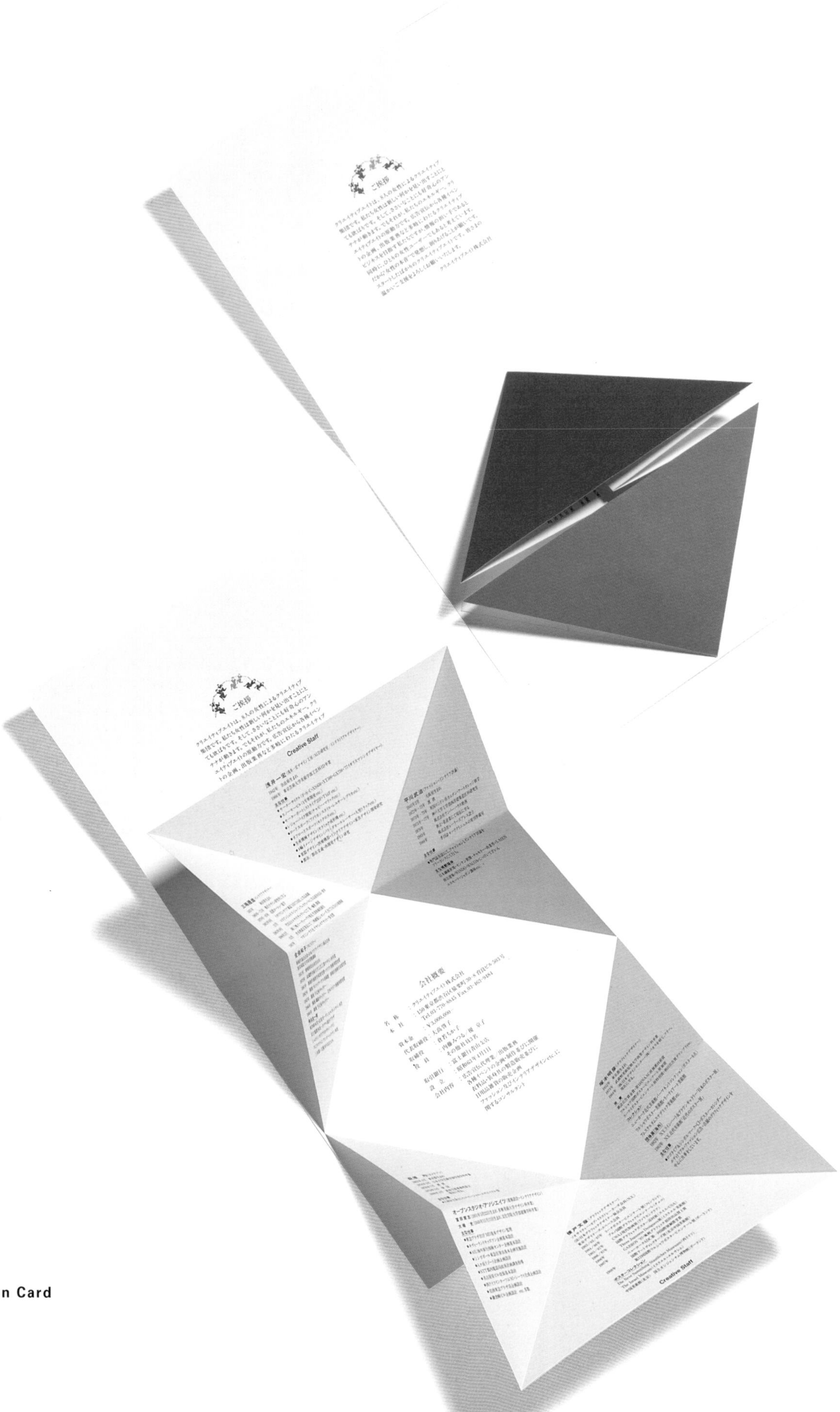

Invitation Card
招待状
Japan

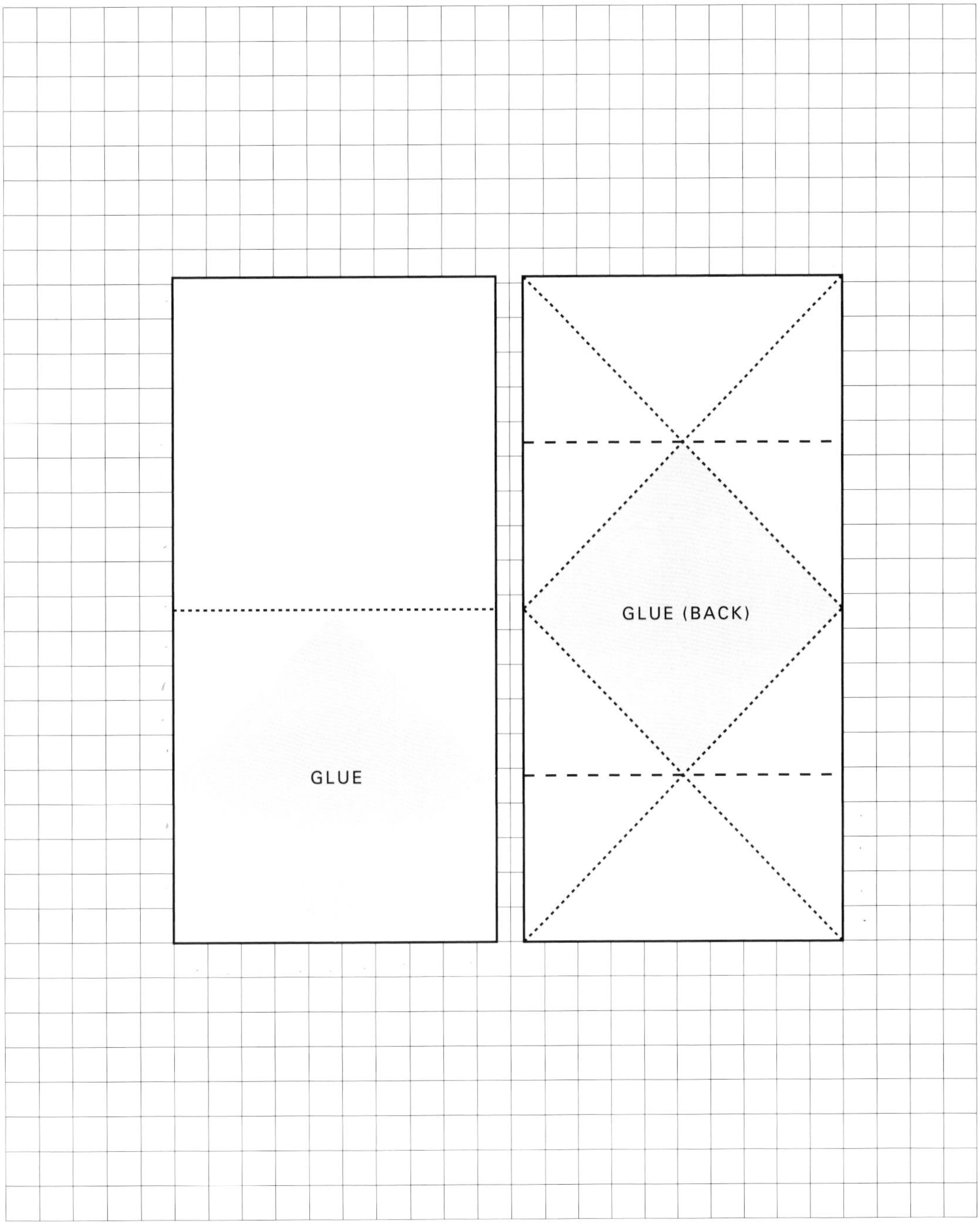
GLUE
GLUE (BACK)

Pop-Up Snowman
美術館ギフトカード
USA 2002
CL: Museum of Modern Art, New York City
CD: Ashley White
D, I, SB: Robert Sabuda

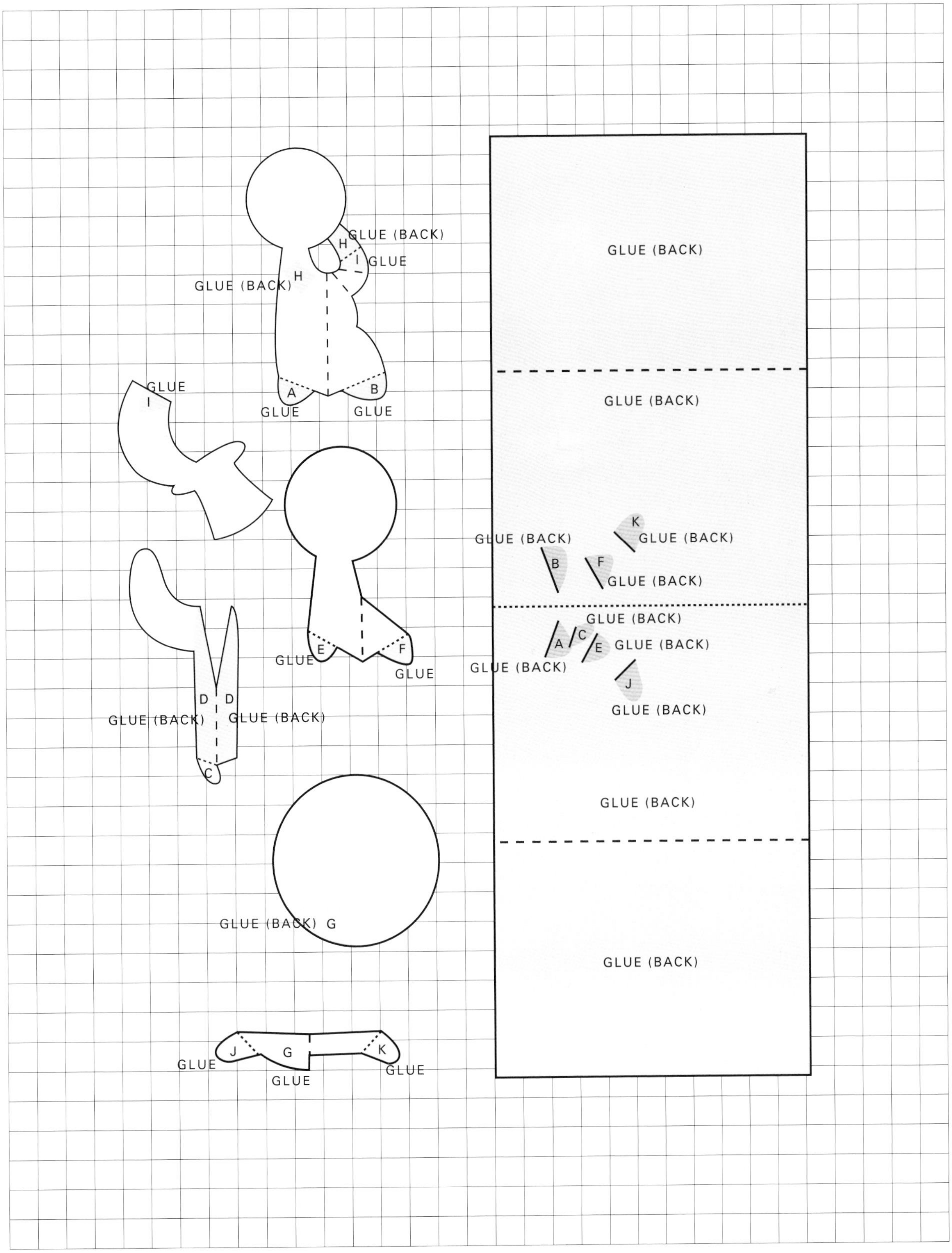
GLUE (BACK)
H
I
GLUE
GLUE (BACK)
H
A
B
GLUE
GLUE
GLUE
I
GLUE (BACK)
GLUE (BACK)
GLUE (BACK)
K
GLUE (BACK)
B
F
GLUE (BACK)
GLUE (BACK)
A
C
E
GLUE (BACK)
GLUE (BACK)
J
GLUE (BACK)
E
F
GLUE
GLUE
D
D
GLUE (BACK)
GLUE (BACK)
C
GLUE (BACK)
GLUE (BACK) G
GLUE (BACK)
J
G
K
GLUE
GLUE
GLUE

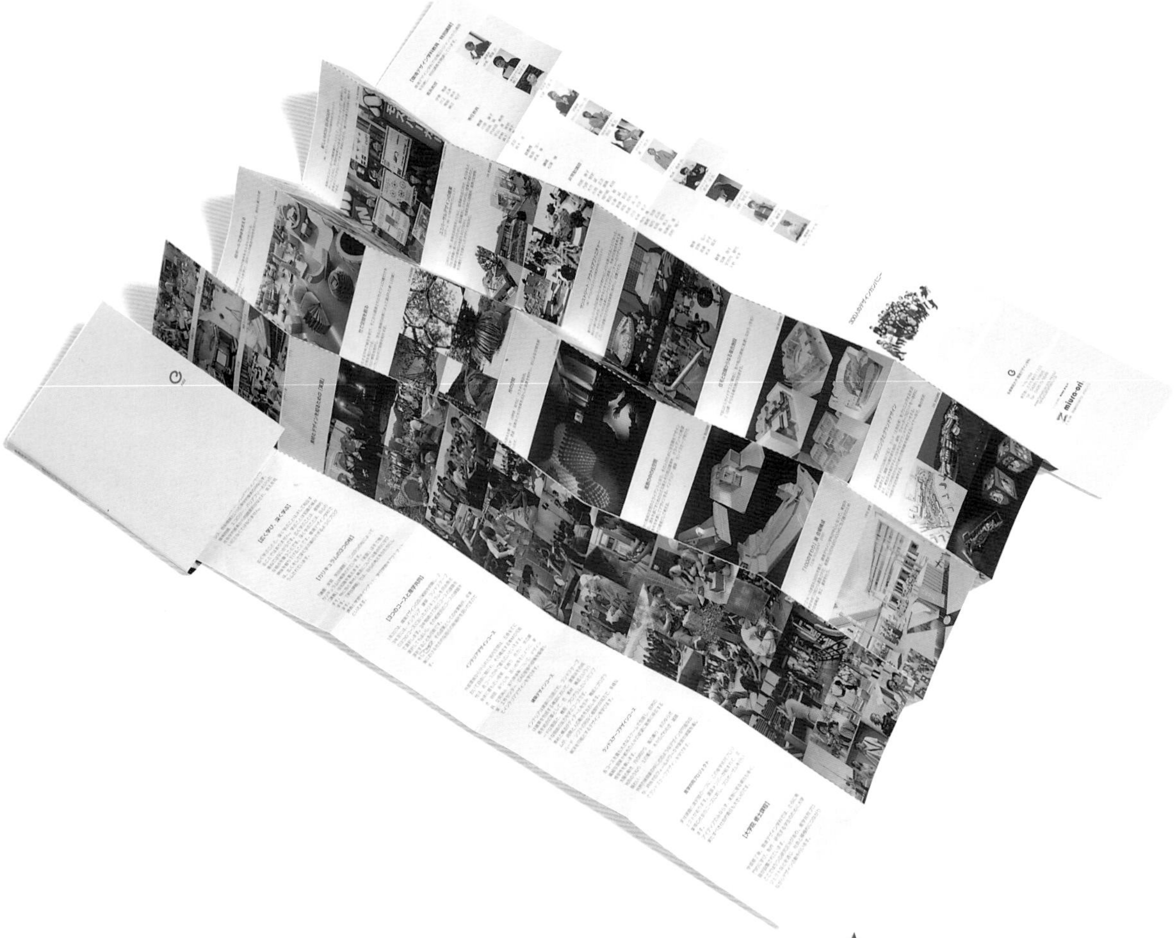

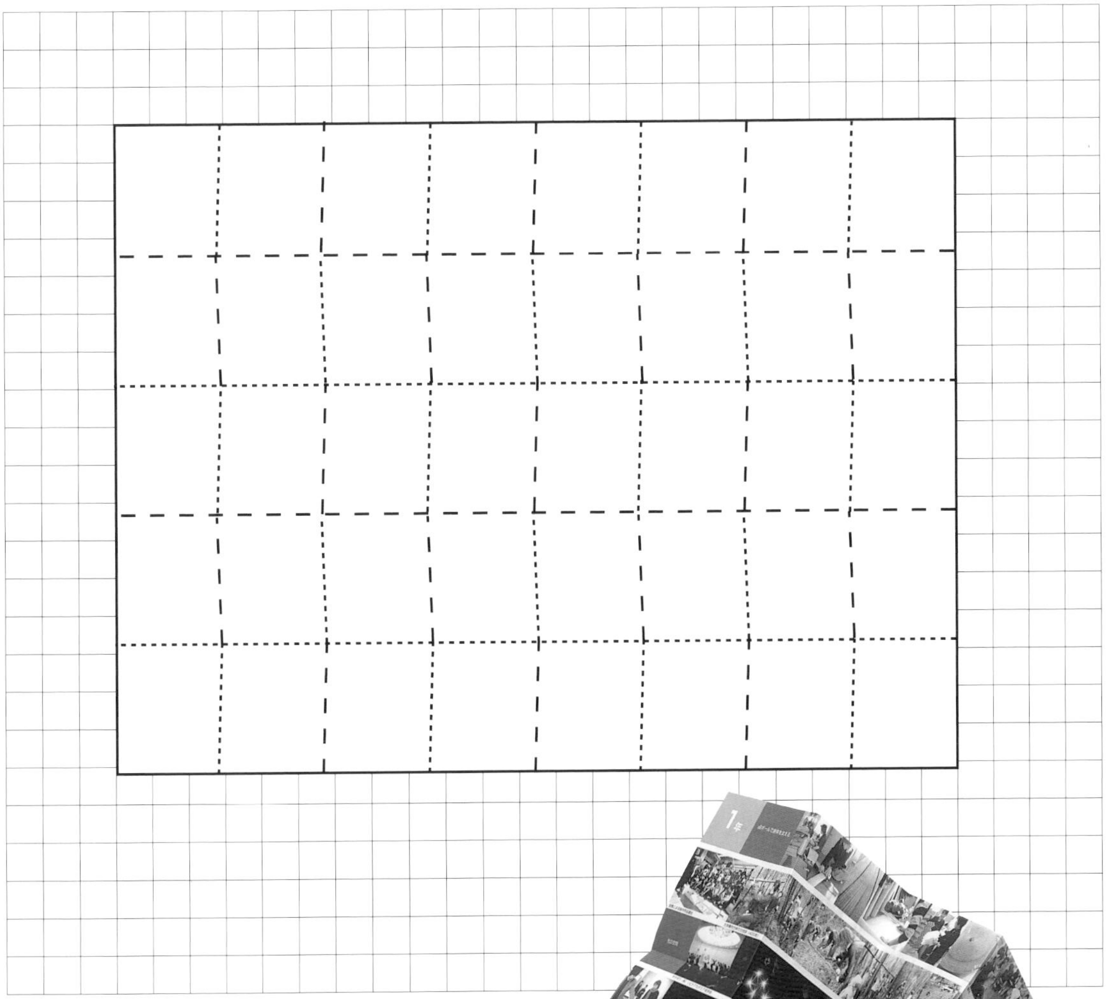

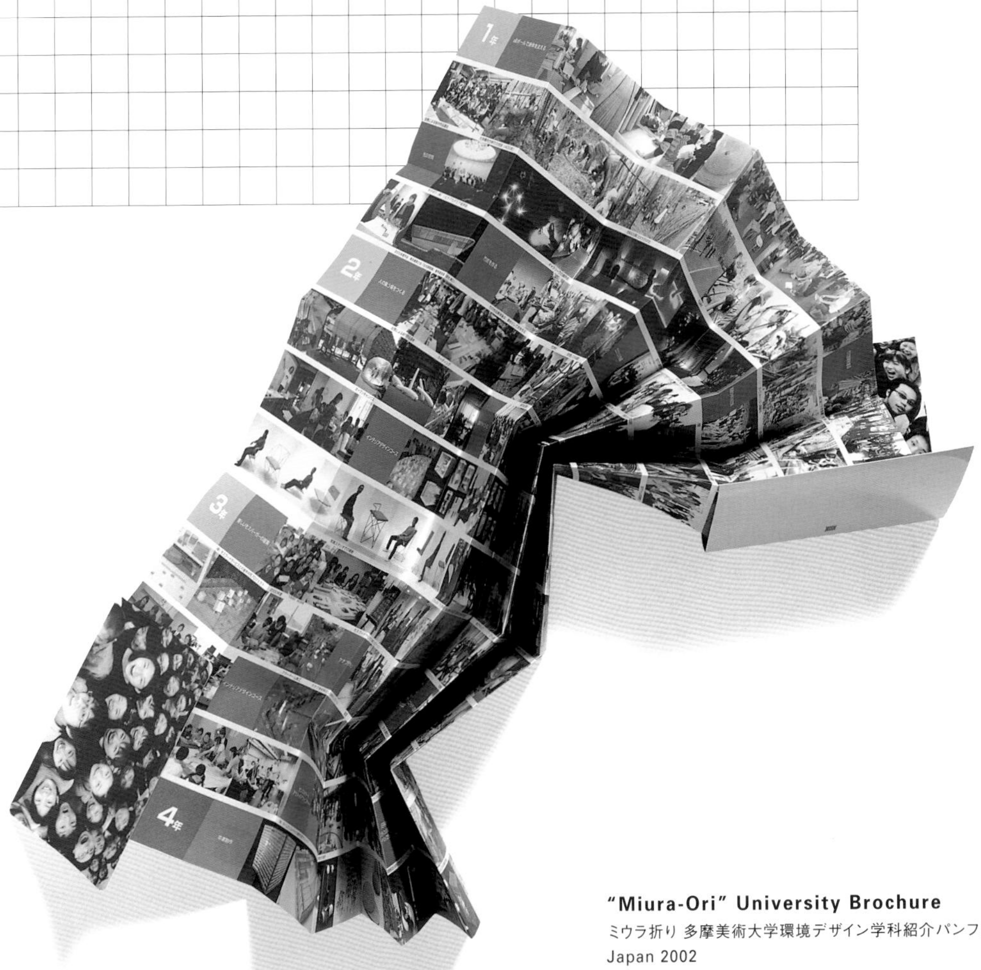

"Miura-Ori" University Brochure
ミウラ折り 多摩美術大学環境デザイン学科紹介パンフレット
Japan 2002
CL, DF:Tama Art University Enviromental Design Department
D: Kyono Koichi
SB: ORUPA Co., Ltd.

Miura-Ori is designed by Prof. Koryo Miura
ミウラ折りは三浦公亮東京大学名誉教授によって発明された折りである。

The Great Pyramids of Giza
デザインコンテスト最優秀作品
USA 2002
CL: Robert Sabuda pop-up contest
D, SB: Kyle Olmon

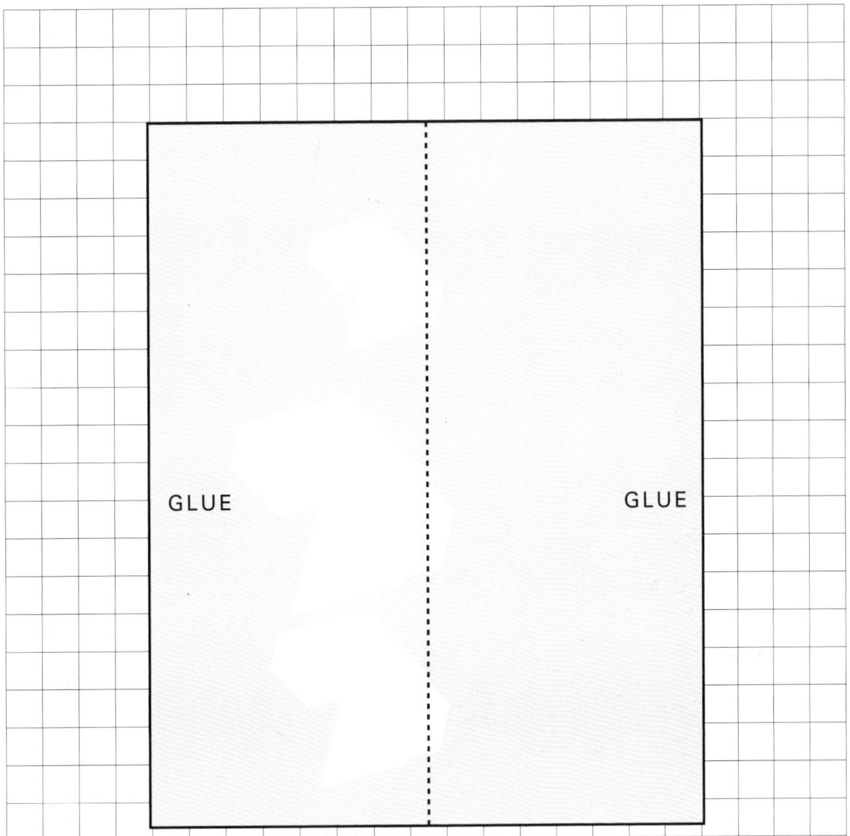
GLUE
GLUE

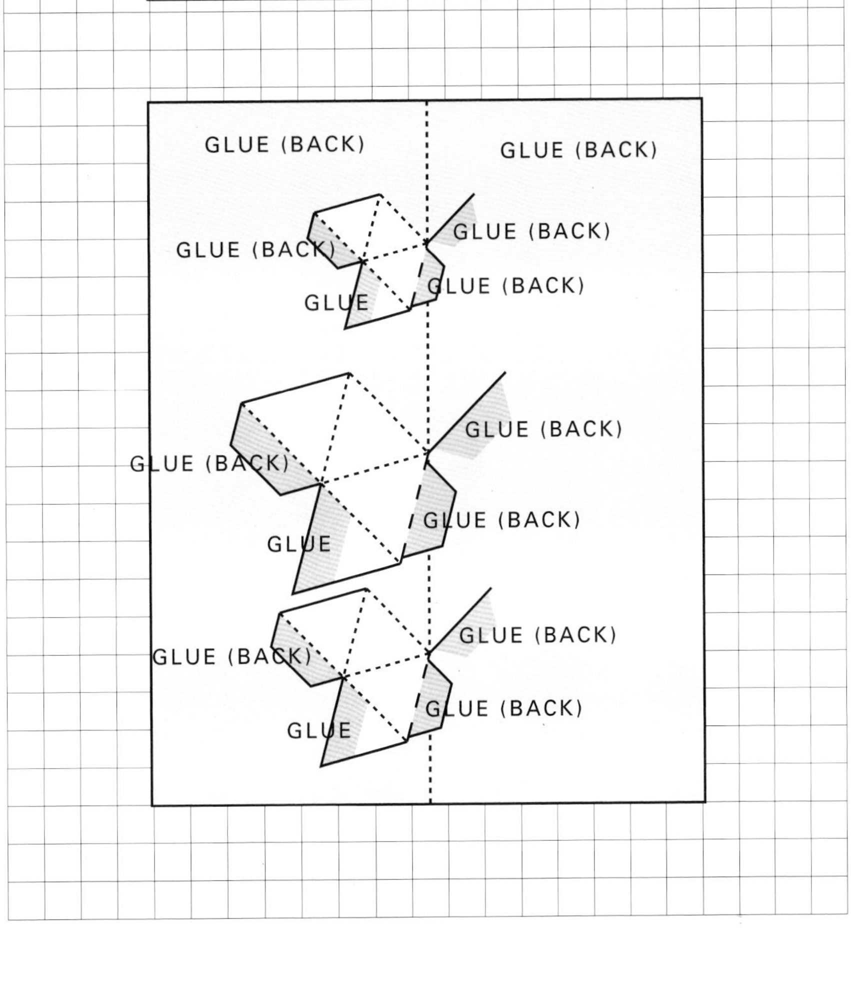
GLUE (BACK)
GLUE (BACK)
GLUE (BACK)
GLUE (BACK)
GLUE (BACK)
GLUE
GLUE (BACK)
GLUE (BACK)
GLUE (BACK)
GLUE
GLUE (BACK)
GLUE (BACK)
GLUE (BACK)
GLUE

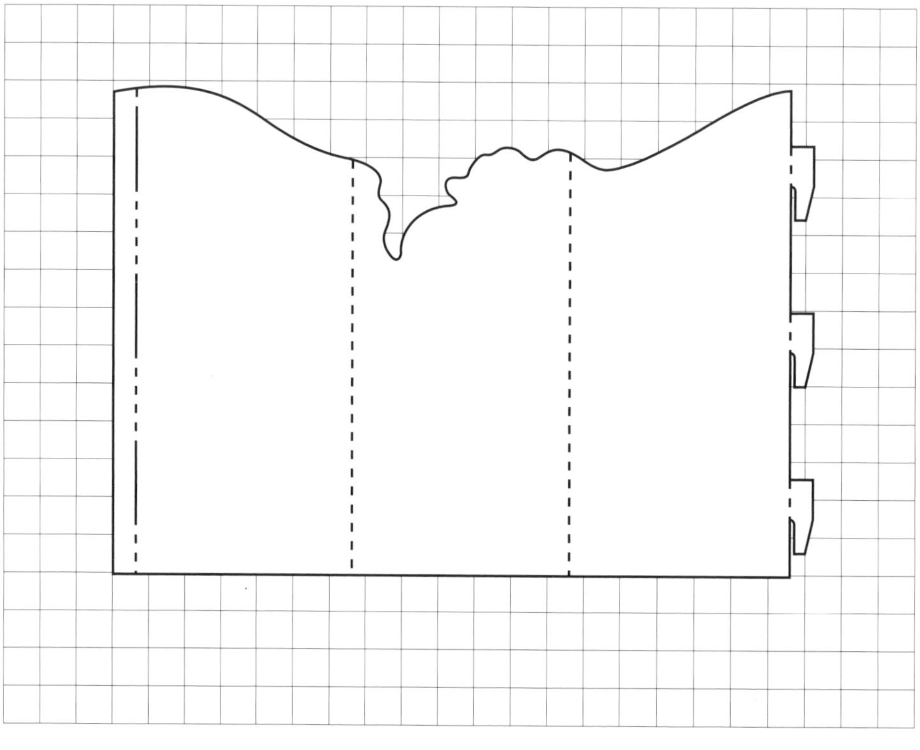

Retail POP
"Year of the Dragon"
食品 店頭POP
USA 2000
CL: Leeann Chin
AD, D: Alan Tse
DF, SB: Yamamoto Moss

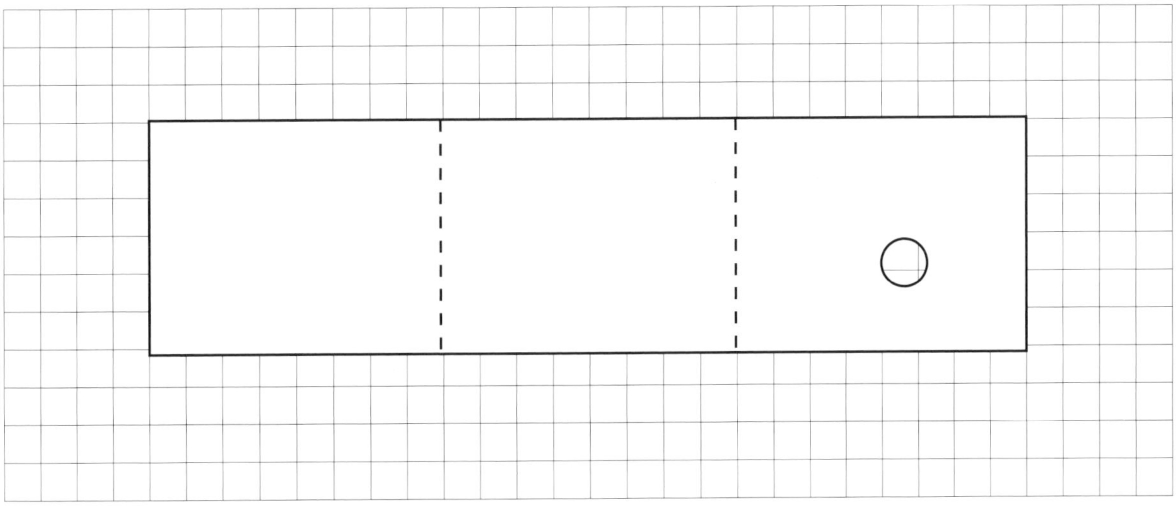

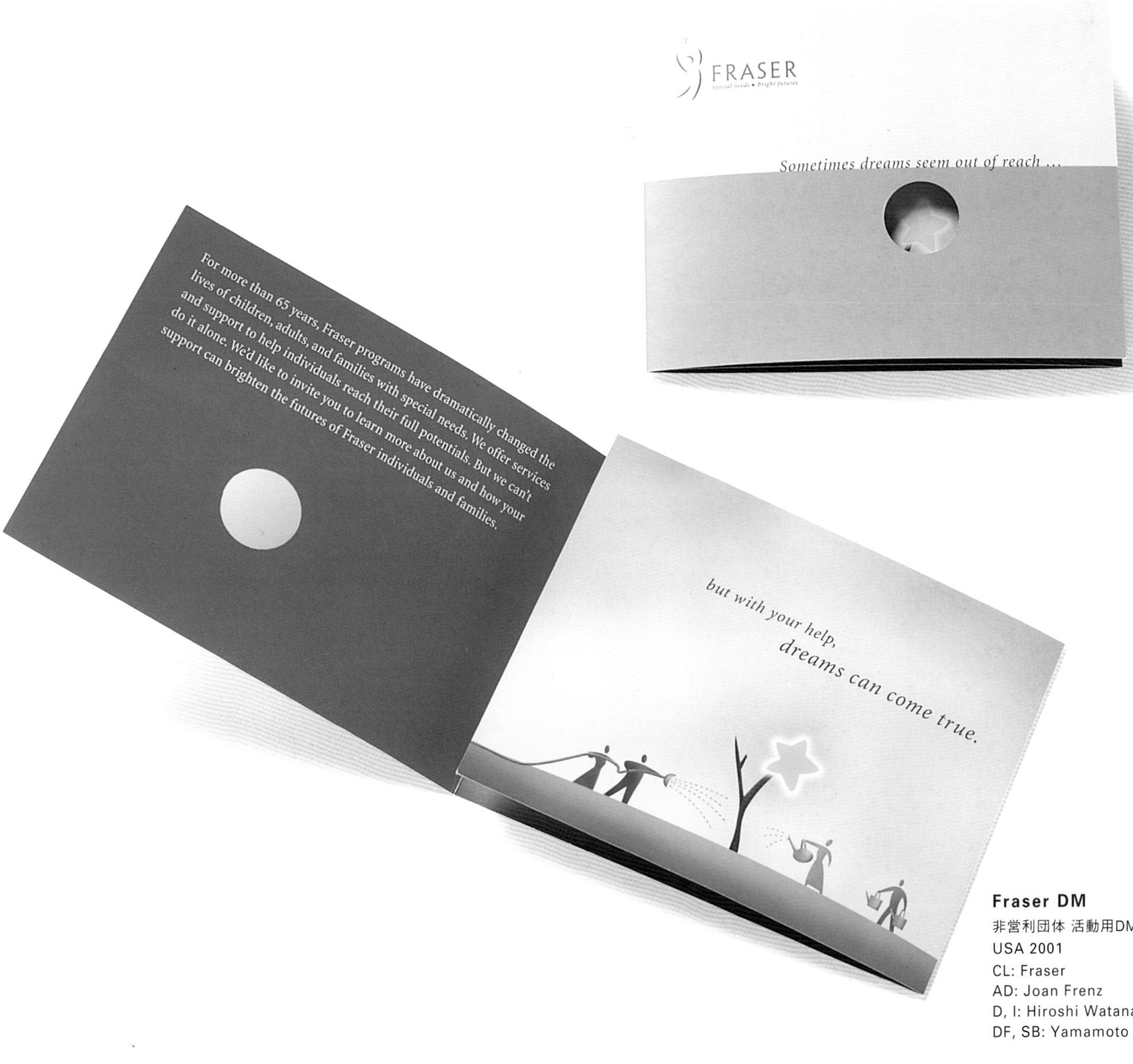

Fraser DM

非営利団体 活動用DM
USA 2001
CL: Fraser
AD: Joan Frenz
D, I: Hiroshi Watanabe
DF, SB: Yamamoto Moss

160

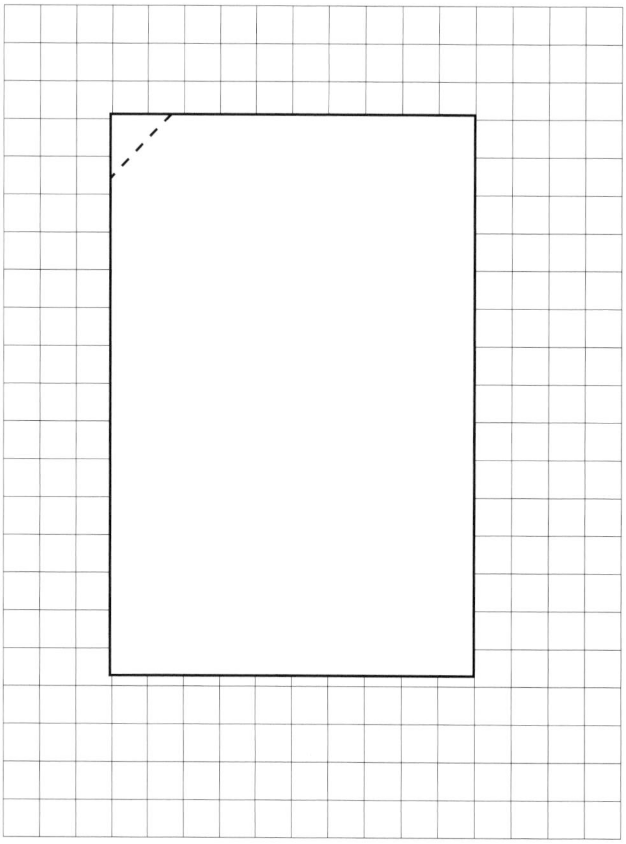

New Year's Card
年賀状
Japan 2001
CL: Gallery Interfom
AD, D, SB: Akio Okumura

Happy Birthday to You
Happy Birthday to You
May joy and happiness fill every minute
of your day. And may life's
most fantastic things always come your way!
Happy Birthday to You
May joy and happiness fill every minute
of your day. And may life's
most fantastic things always come your way!

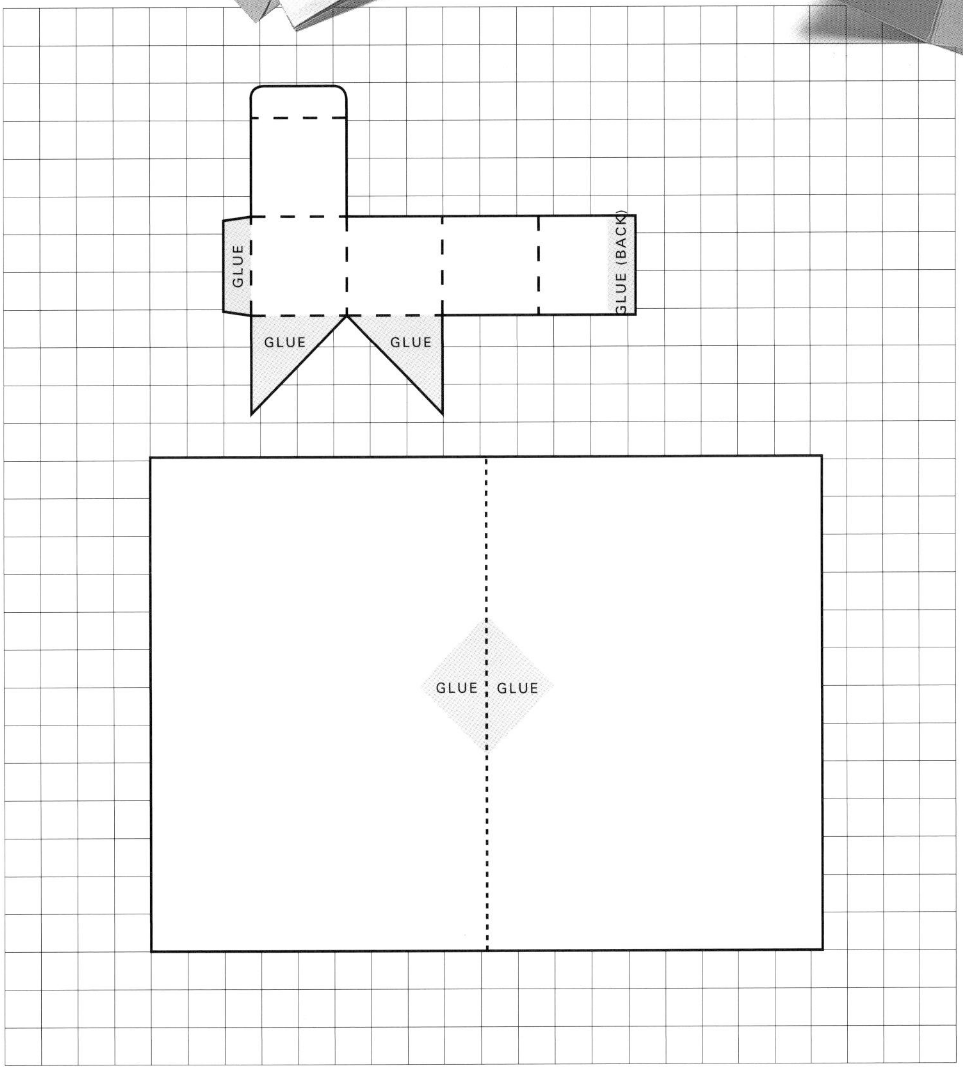

Birthday Gift Card
バースディ・ギフトカード
Japan 2000
CL, SB:Tsutsumu Co., Ltd.
CD, AD, D: Yuki Fujii

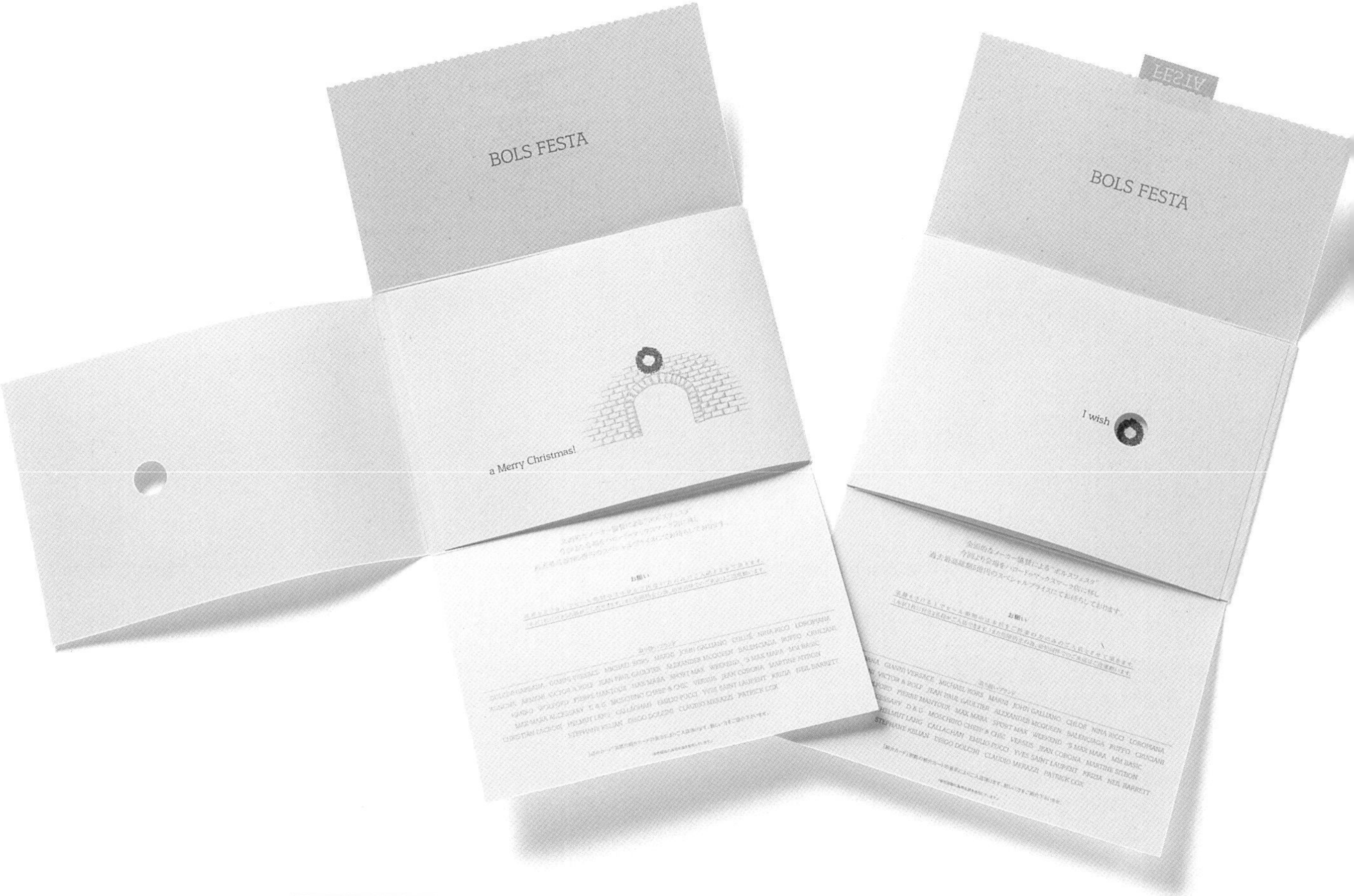

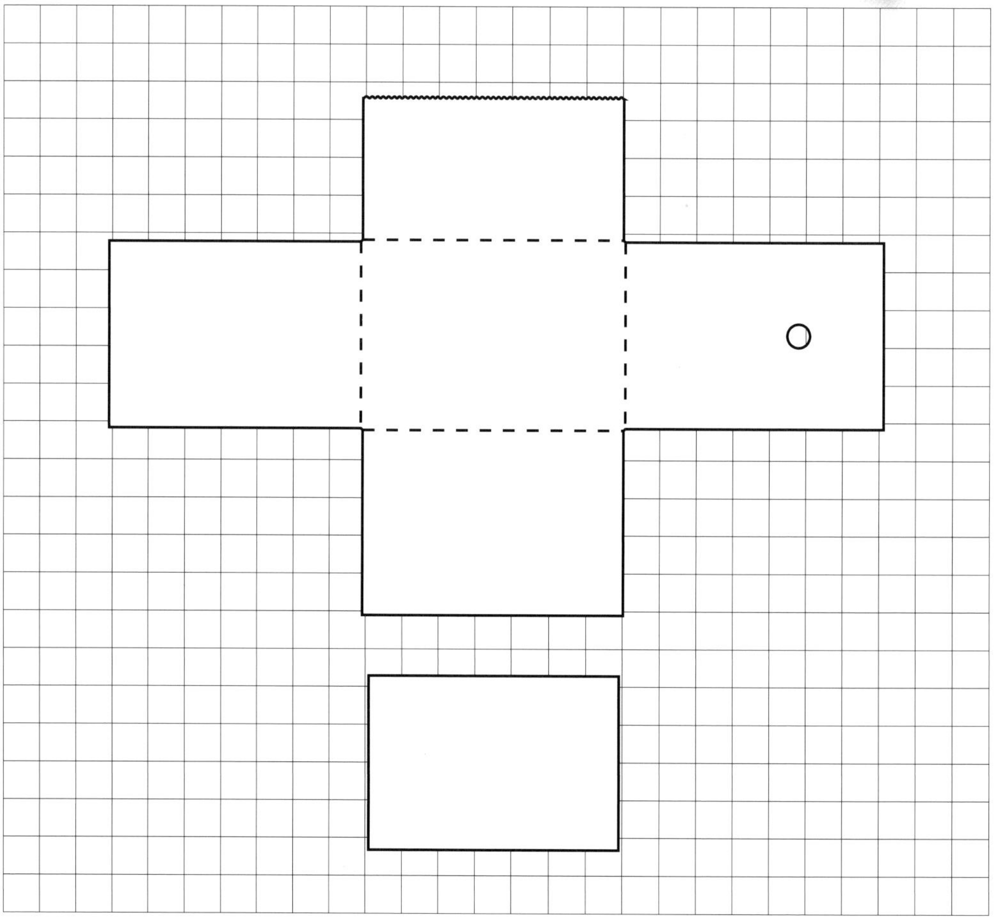

"BOLS FESTA" Invitation Card

ボルス・フェスタ案内状

Japan 2001

CL: BOLS International Co., Ltd.

AD: Katsunori Watanabe

D: Hana Hosono

DF, SB: Bauhaus Inc.

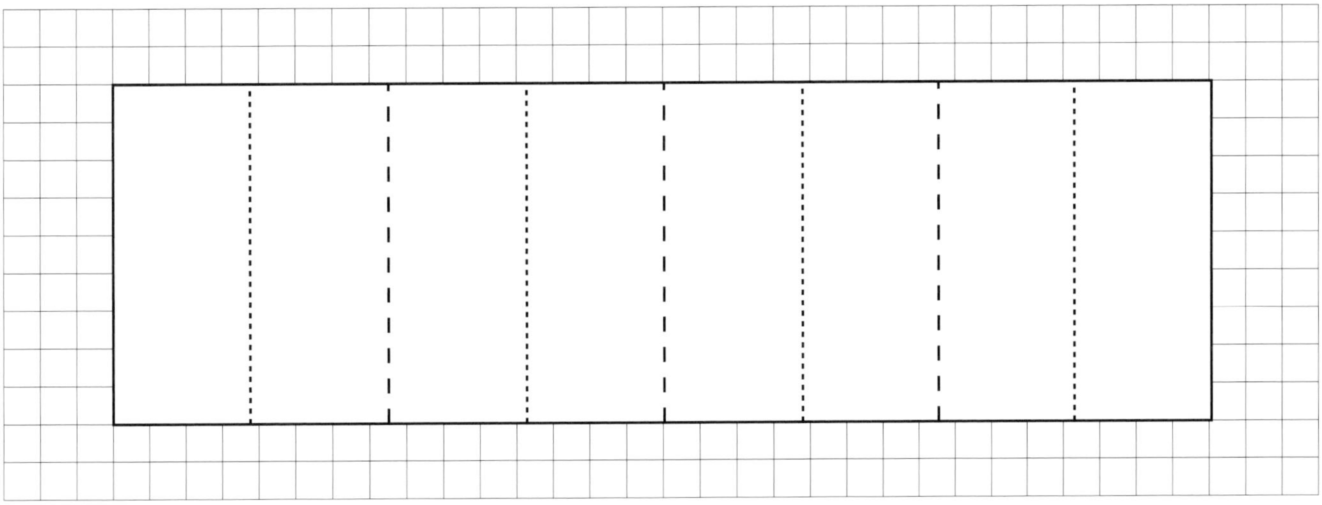

Birth Announcement DM "Nicolai"

出産告知DM

The Netherlands 1996

CL: Joanna v/o Zanden

AD, D: Erik Kessels

I: Various

DF, SB: Kessels Kramer

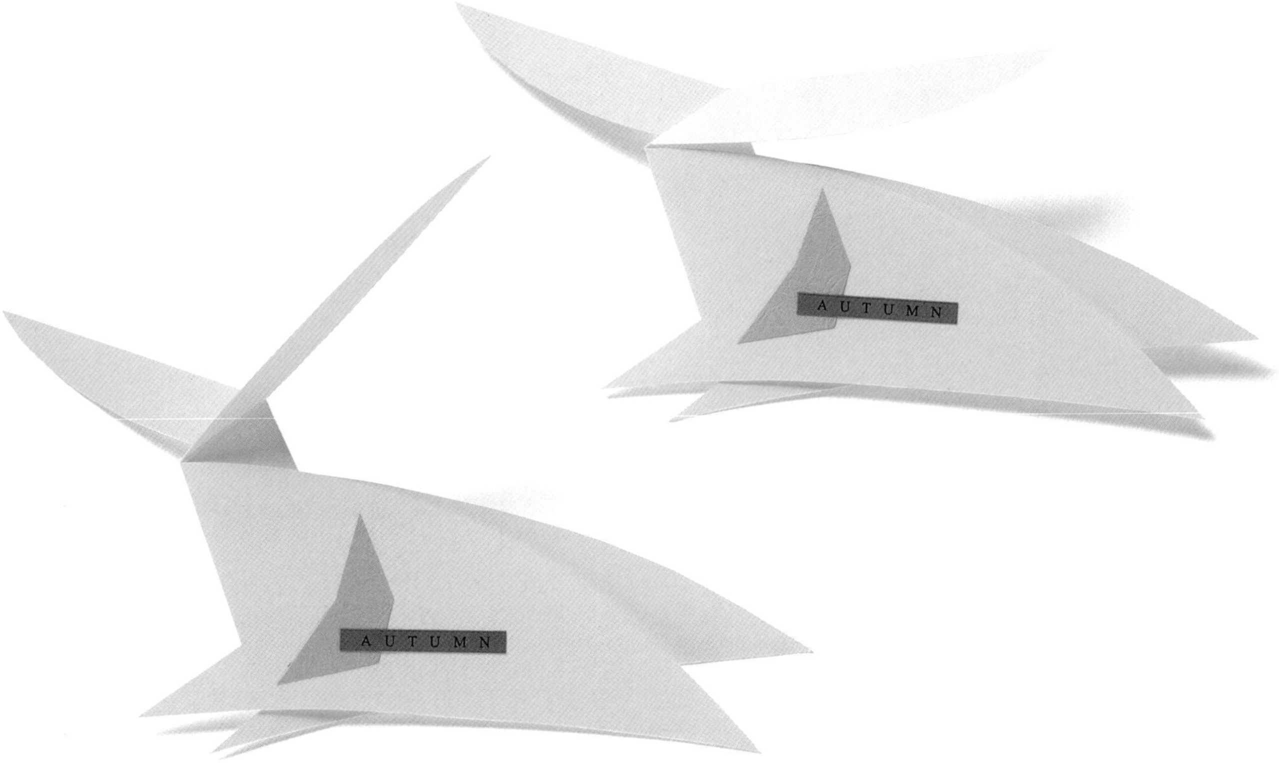

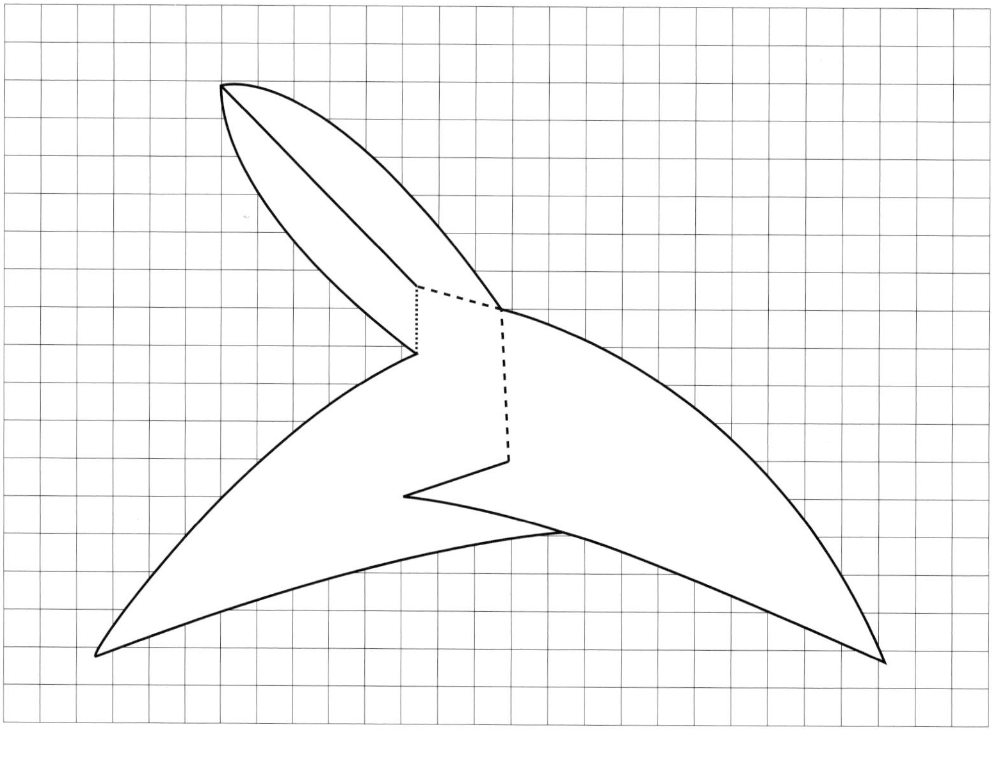

Greeting Card (Moon Rabit)
グリーティング・カード（月兎）
Japan 1997
CL: PLAN Y
AD, D, SB: Miyuki Yoshida

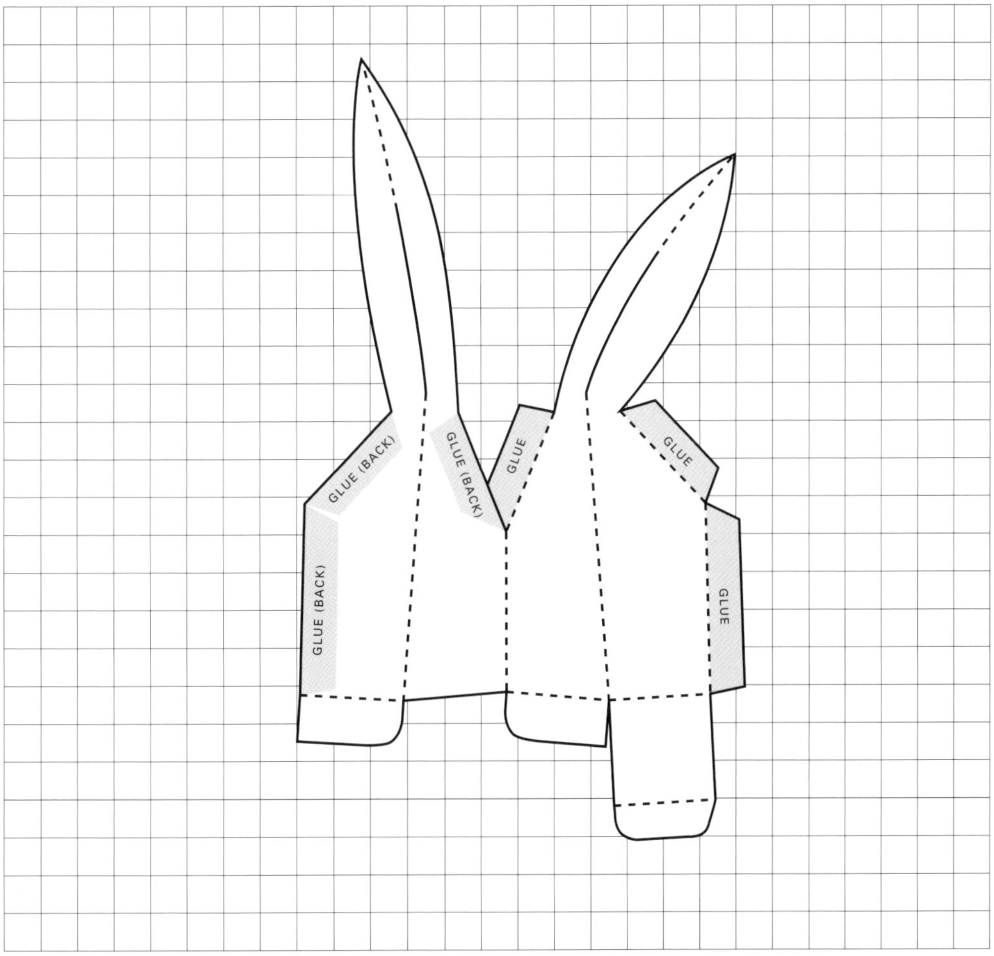

New Year Card (Rabit)
年賀状(はこうさぎ)
Japan 1998
CL: PLAN Y
AD, D, SB: Miyuki Yoshida

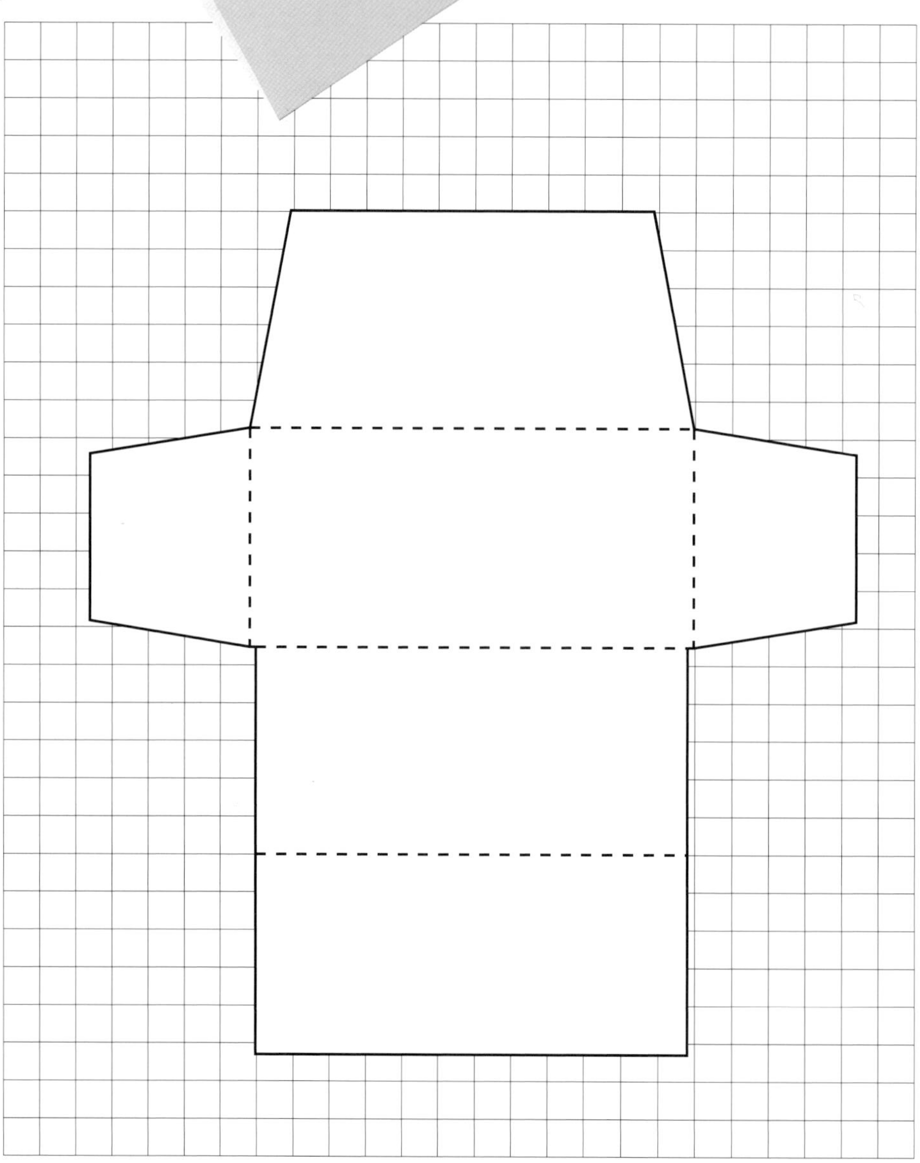

New Producut "POP SET" Announcemnt

新商品「POP SET」案内DM
Japan 2000
CL: Arjo Wiggins Canson KK
AD, D: Akihiko Tsukamoto
CW: Haruki Nagumo
DF, SB: Design Club

POP SET

ここから開けてください

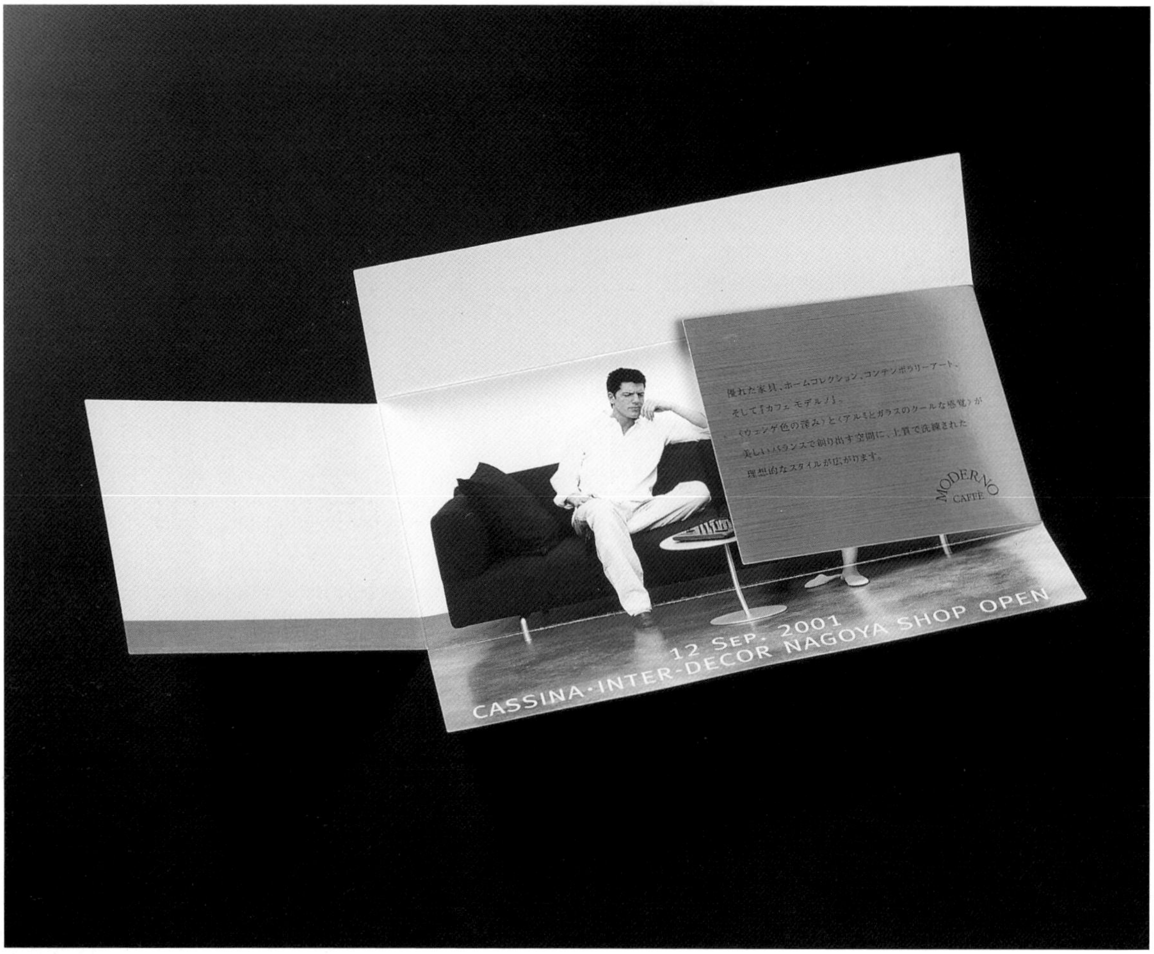

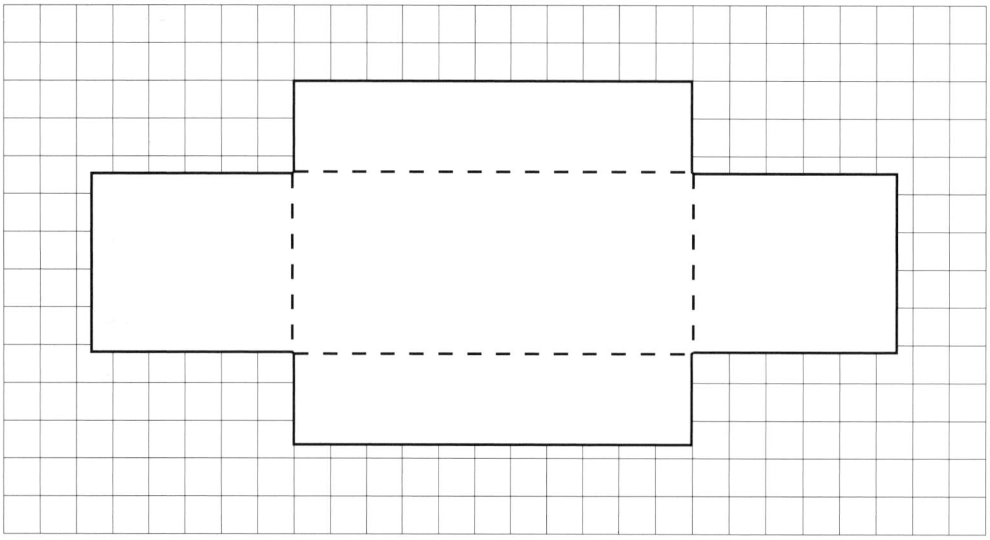

Openning Announcemnt DM

名古屋店オープン告知DM

Japan 2001

CL: Cassina IXC. Ltd.

AD, SB: H.D.O , Sho Sawada

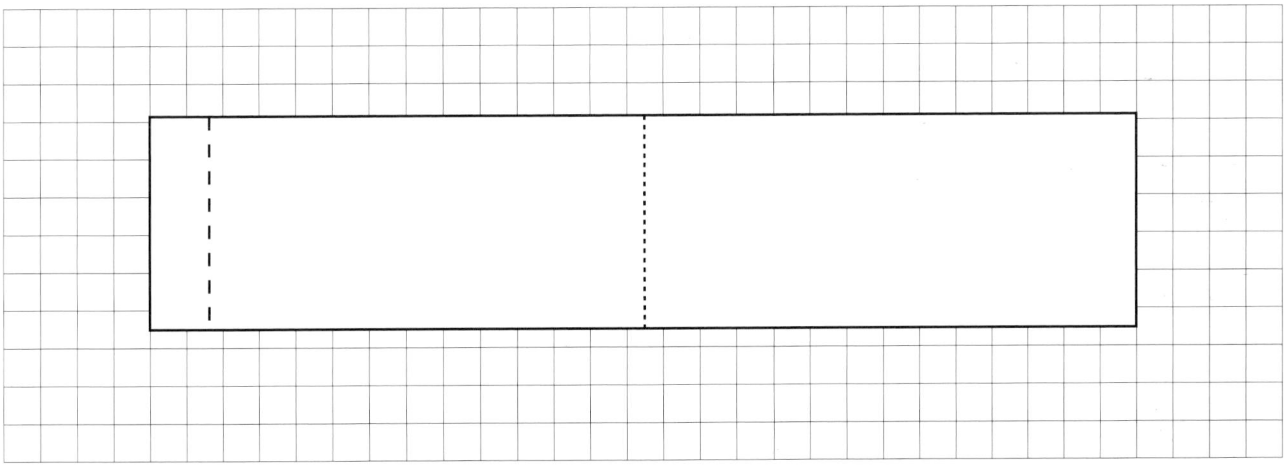

Design Firm New Year's Card
デザイン事務所年賀状
USA 2002
CL, SB:Sherff Dorman Purins
CD: Uldis Purins
D: Karen White
DF, SB: Sherff Dorman Purins

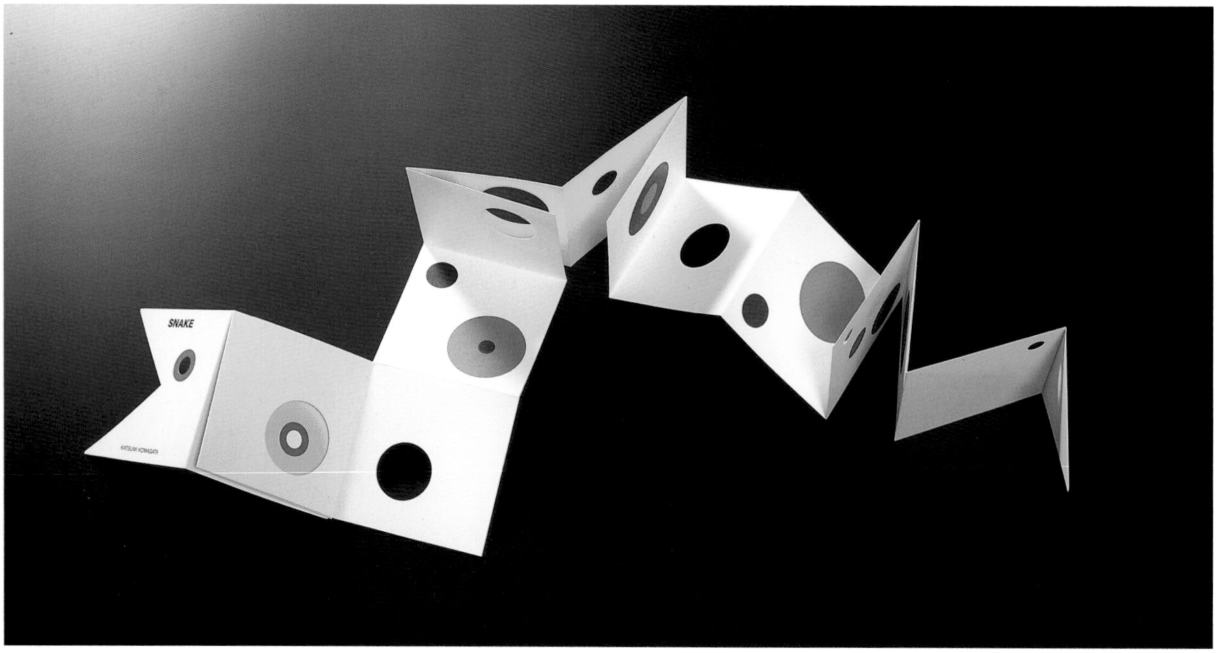

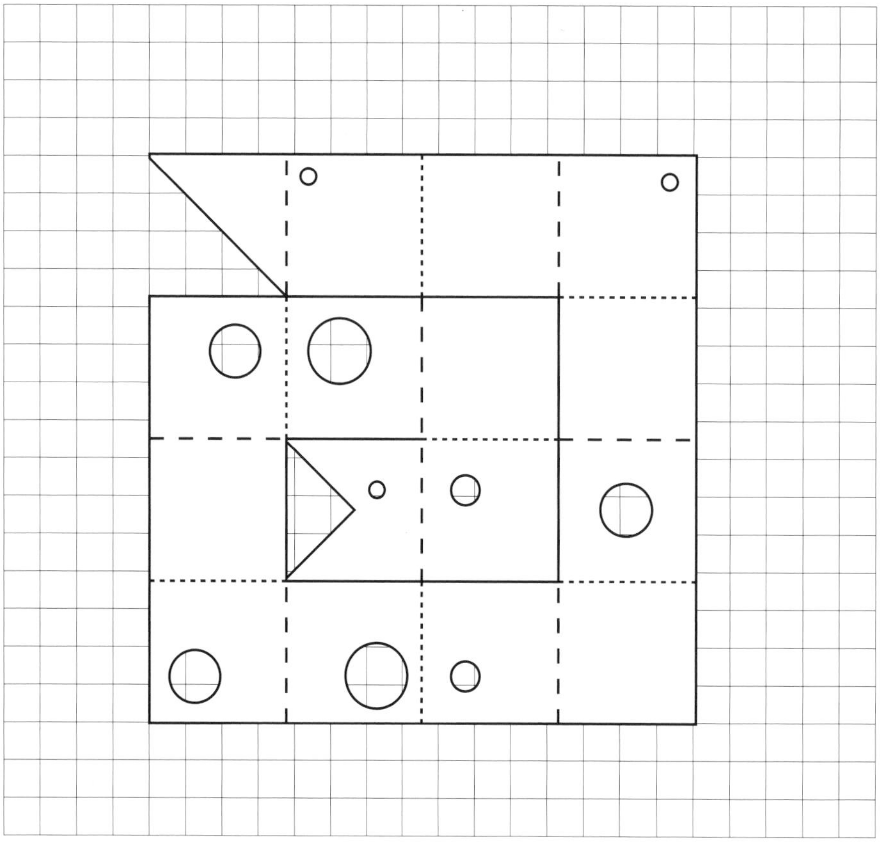

Design Farm Work
デザイン事務所作品
Japan 1995
CL, SB:One Stroke Co., Ltd.
D: Katsumi Komagata
DF, SB: One Stroke Co., Ltd.

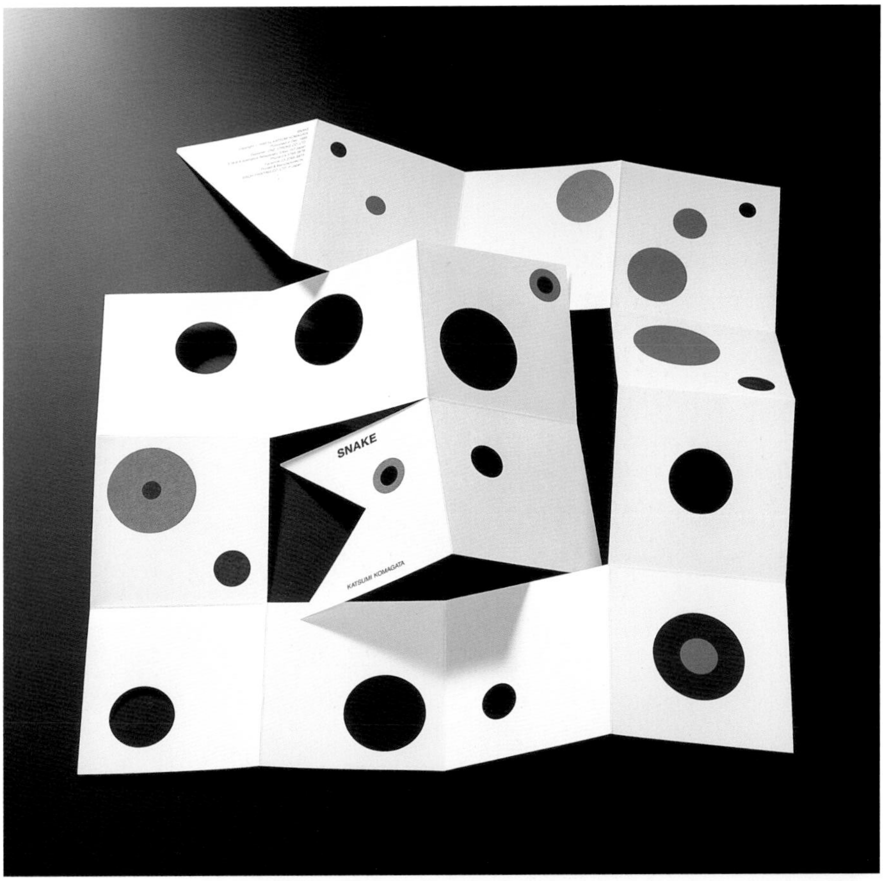
SNAKE
KATSUMI KOMAGATA

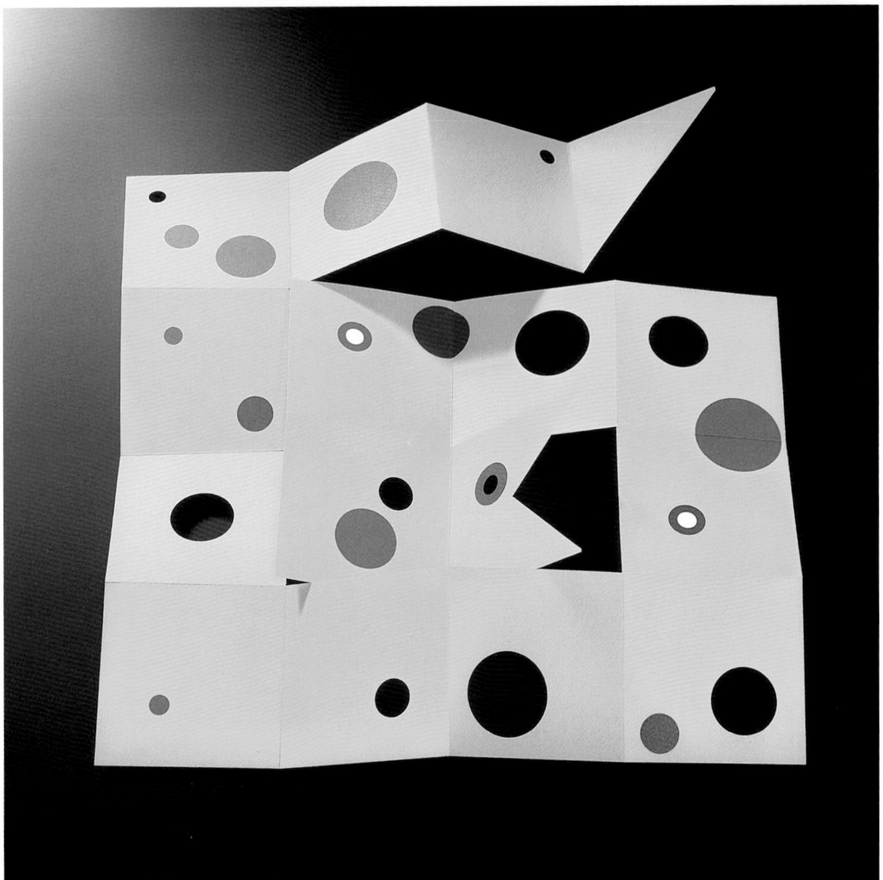

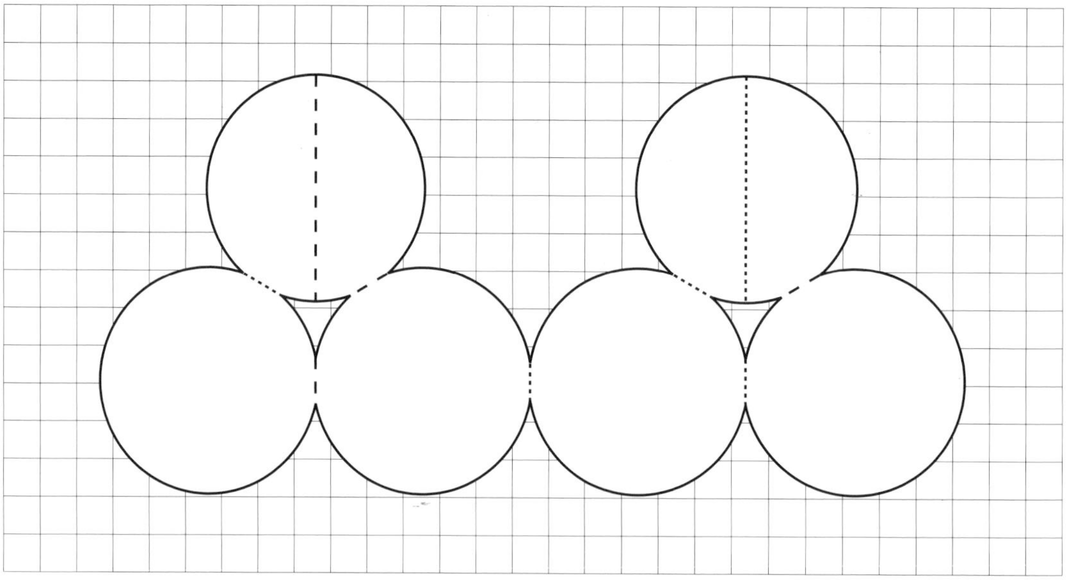

School Guide Pamphlet
スクールガイド・地図
Japan 2003
CL, SB:Vantan Career School

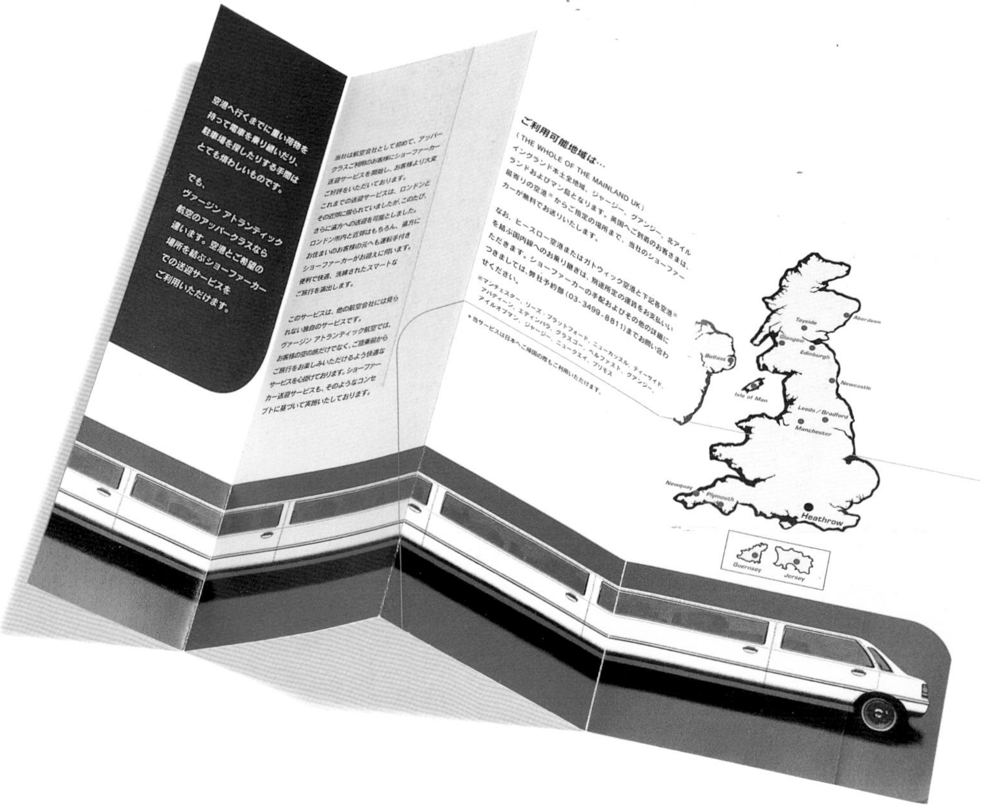

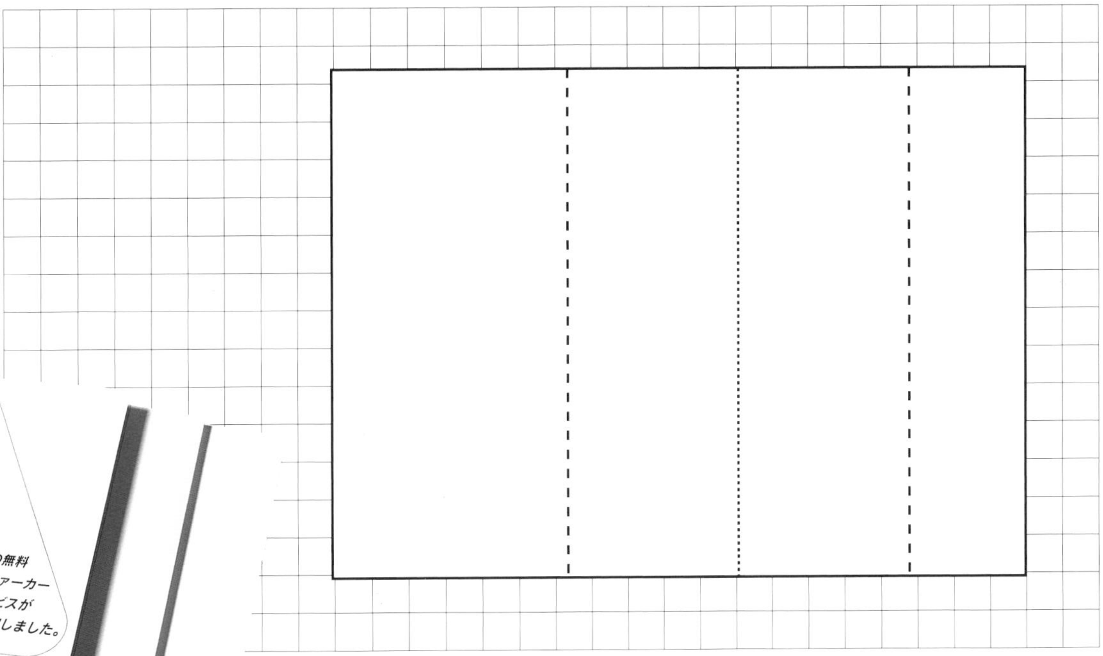

Service Information Pamphlet

空港送迎サービス案内パンフレット

Japan 2002

CL, SB: Virgin Atlantic Airlines

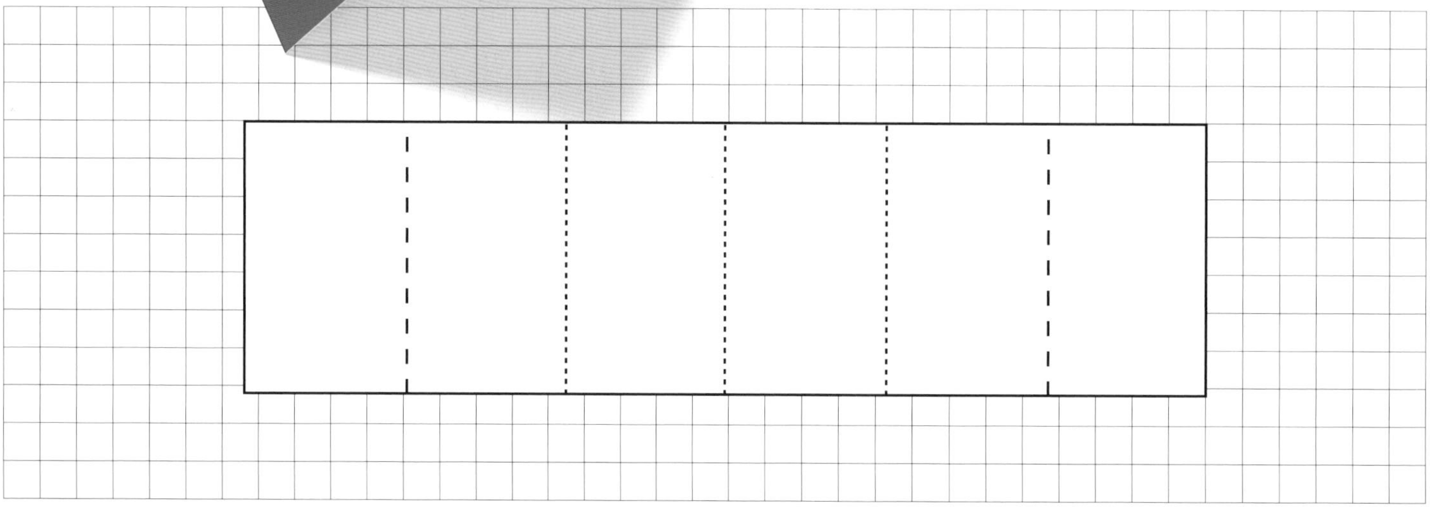

Promotional Brochure

デザイン事務所プロモーション用

Switzerland 2000

CL, SB:Walhalla

CD, AD, D, I: Walter Stahli, Marco Simoneth, Ibrahim Zbat

DF, SB: Walhalla

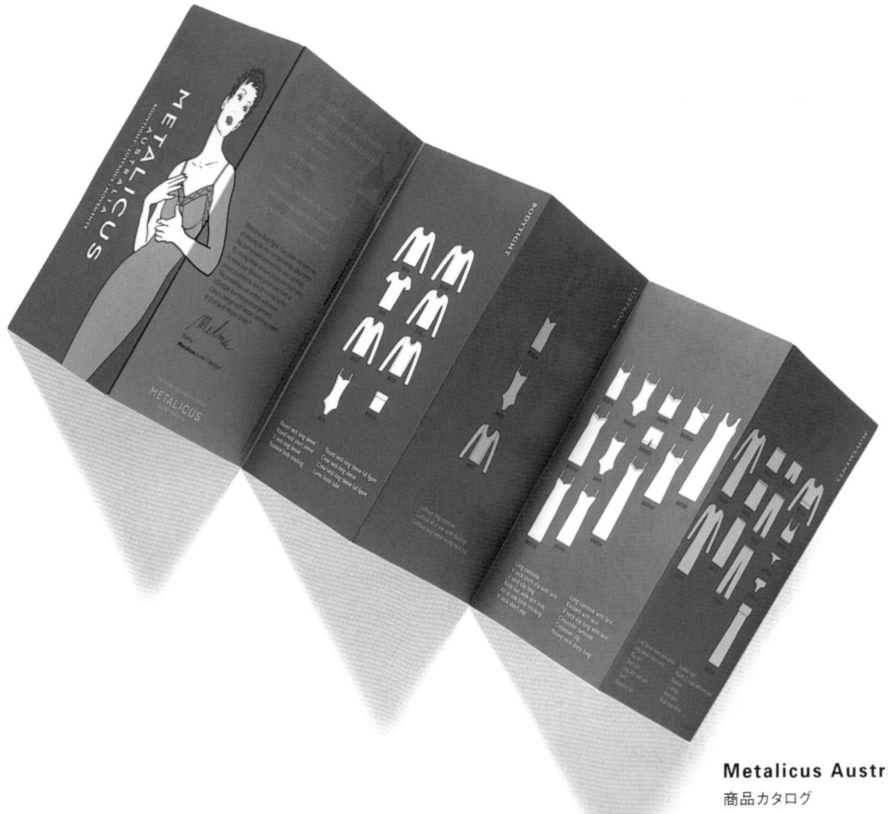

Metalicus Australia Catalog
商品カタログ
Australia
CL: Metalicus Australia
AD, D: Andrew Hoyne
DF, SB: Hoyne Design

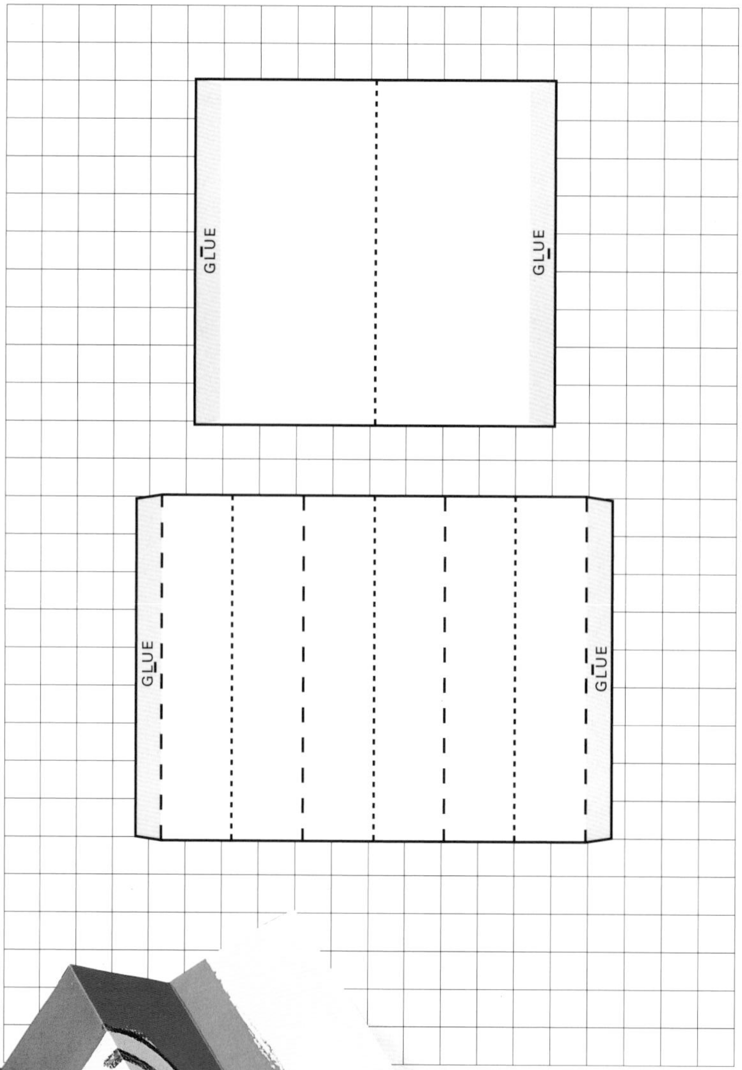

"Bing Bang Bongo" Opening Invitation DM

オープニング招待DM

Japan 1988

CL: A-project, Inc.

CD: Nobuo Inoue

AD, D: Akihiko Tsukamoto

Artist: Bluce Mclean

DF, SB: Design Club, NID Inc.

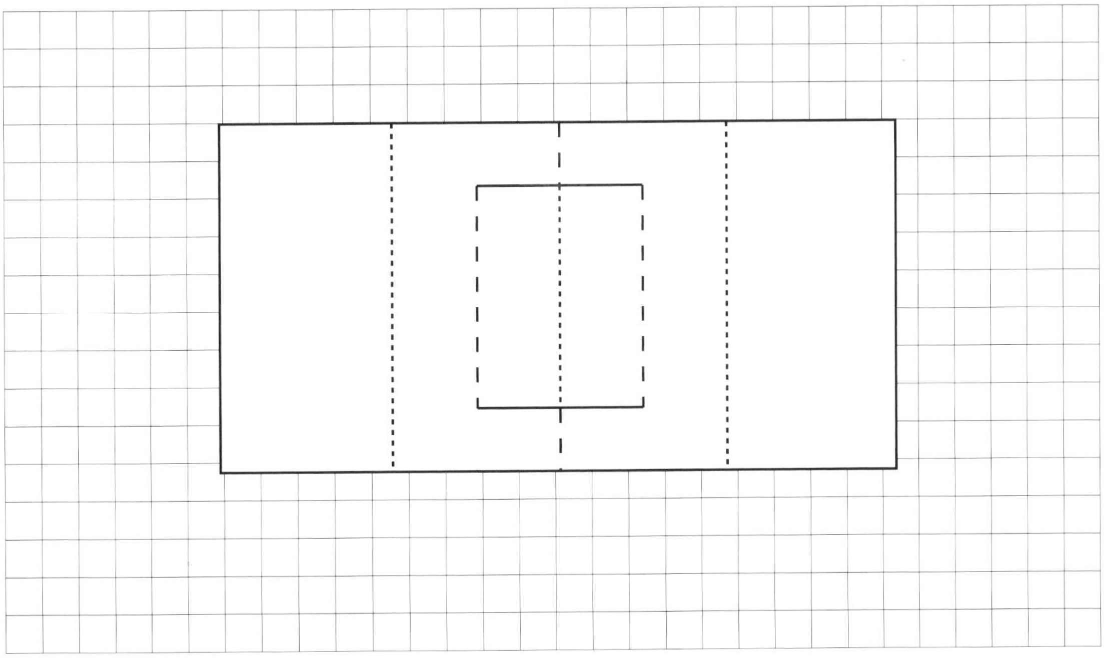

Ammusement Information Pamphlet

遊戯施設案内

Japan

CL, SB:Karnak

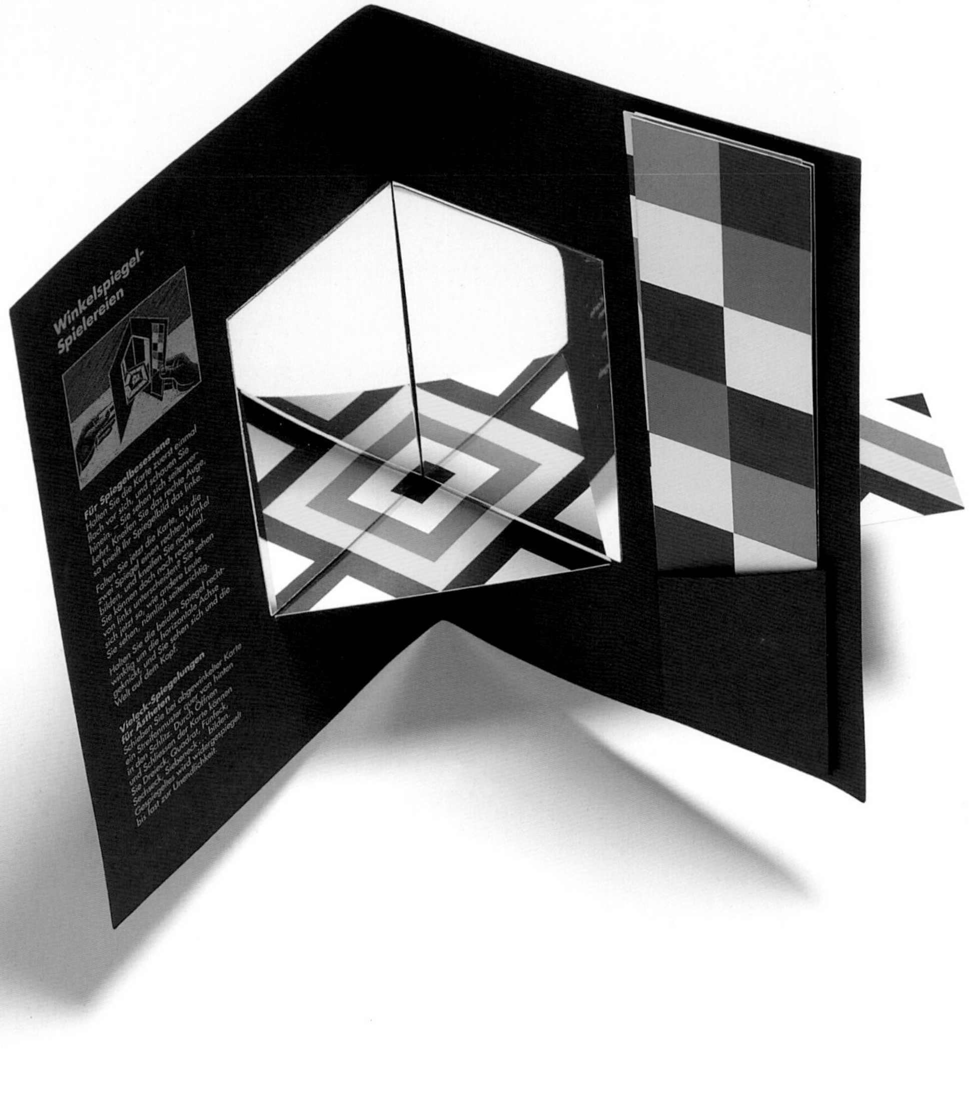

Mirror Card with Ernst Jandl Poem
鏡のカード
Switzerland 1996
D, SB:Casper Schwabe

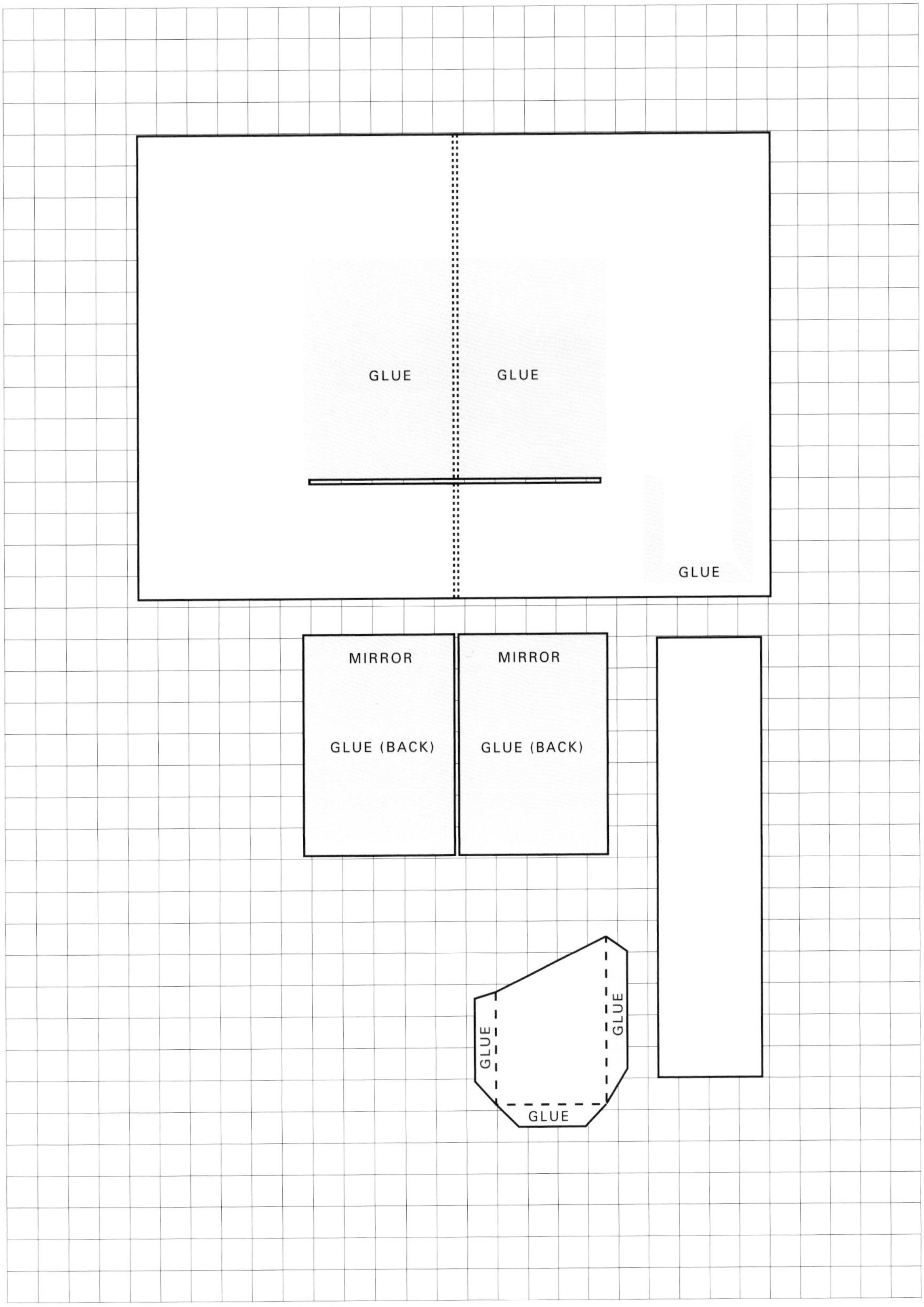
GLUE
GLUE
GLUE
MIRROR
MIRROR
GLUE (BACK)
GLUE (BACK)
GLUE
GLUE
GLUE

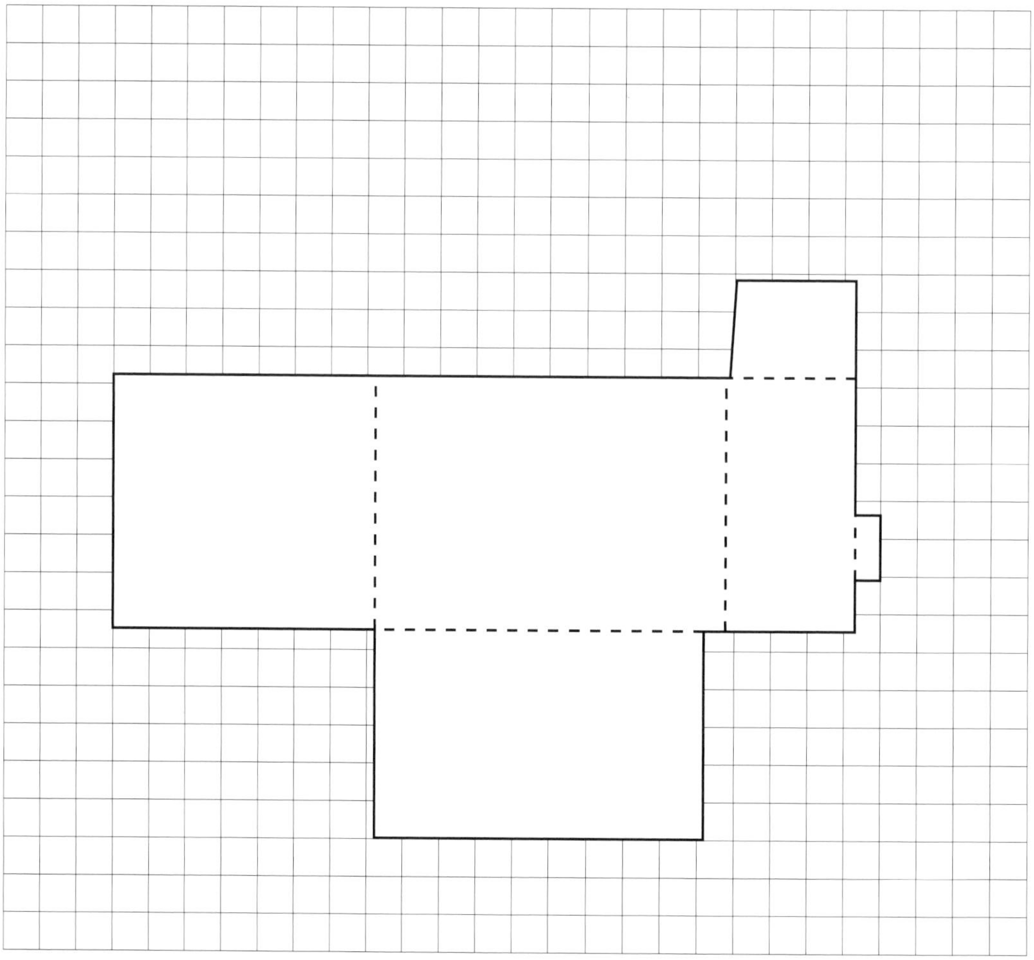

Campaign Announcement
"6,000 reasons to celebrate"
航空会社キャンペーン案内
Japan 2002
CL: Virgin Atlantic Airways
CD, CW: Yukiko Numaguchi
CD, AD, D, SB: Keisuke Unosawa

Highly
recommended
ご紹介キャンペーン 2002年11月1日–2003年2月28日
世界最新鋭のエアバス、A340-600新型機のヴァージン アトランティック航空日本路線就航を記念し、
フライング クラブの皆様がボーナスマイルを獲得できるビッグチャンスをご用意しました。
ぜひお友達や会社の同僚の方にヴァージン アトランティック航空をお勧めください。ご紹介いただいたお友達が
フライング クラブにご入会され、初めてフライトをご利用されると、以下のボーナスマイルを獲得いただけます。
Highly recommended 1 November 2002 – 28 February 2003
Celebrating Virgin Atlantic being the first airline in the world to fly the fantastic new Airbus A340-600 we've come up with a great idea to give you bonus flying club miles.
Simply introduce a friend or colleague to all the great benefits of our generous frequent flyer scheme and if they decide to sign up, you'll get:
8,500 miles (normally, 7,500 miles)
If they take their first round trip in Premium Economy during the campaign period (1 November 2002 – 28 February 2003).
25,000 miles (normally 20,000 miles)
If they take their first round trip in Upper Class during the campaign period (1 November 2002 – 28 February 2003).
So that means, if you introduce just one friend to Upper Class you could:
Receive a dining voucher worth ¥15,000 for use at selected restaurants (22,000 miles) OR
Take a breathtakingly romantic Helicopter Night Flight (24,000 miles)
Introduce two friends and enjoy:
A 2 night stay at Club Med Sahoro, Hokkaido world-class ski resort in winter (50,000 miles) OR
JR Shinkansen train & a 1 night stay at Hotel Granvia, Kyoto (45,000 miles)
Three friends for:
A Virgin Atlantic Economy ticket to London (60,000 miles) OR
A one night stay at Kikuya Ryokan, Izu Shuzen-ji for two (60,000 miles)
join flying club here...
membership number
00 614 856 097
Virgin's new Upper Class cabin offers the comfort of a stylish bar and a dedicated area for inflight beauty therapy.
The newly designed Economy and Premium Economy seats offer the widest seatback screens in the sky.

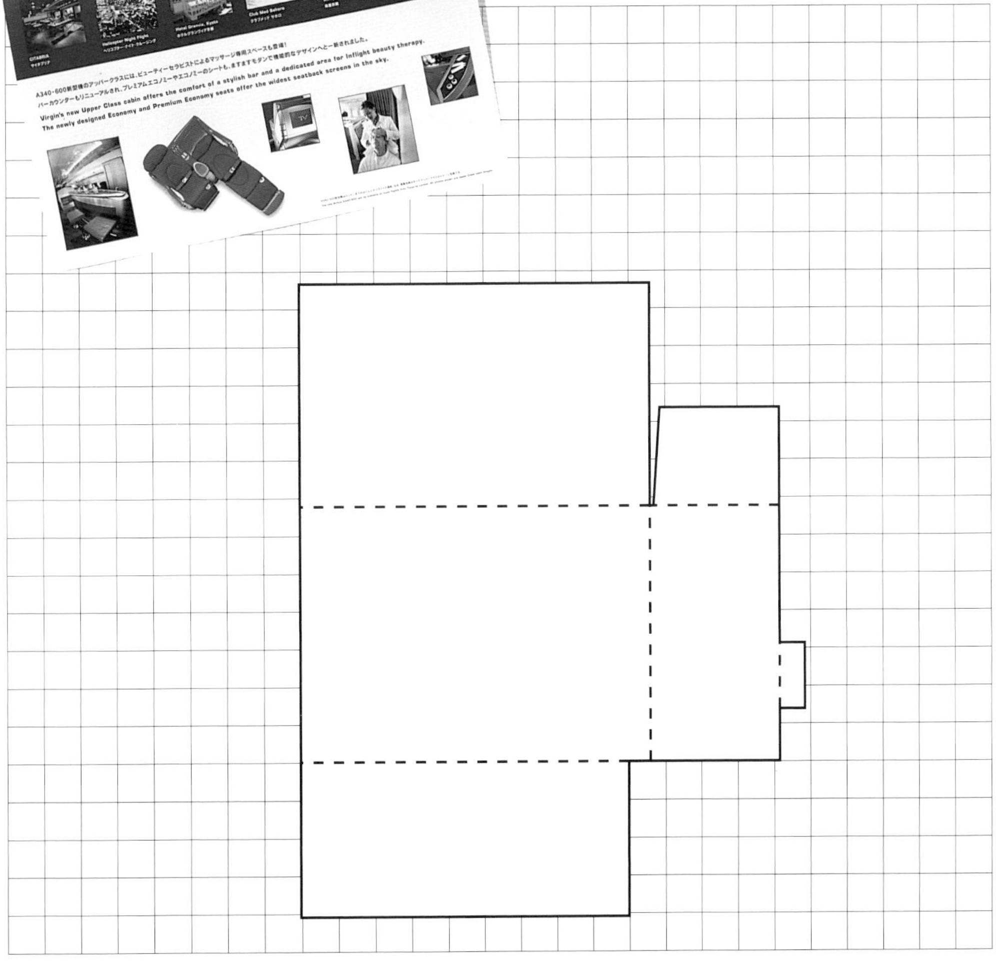

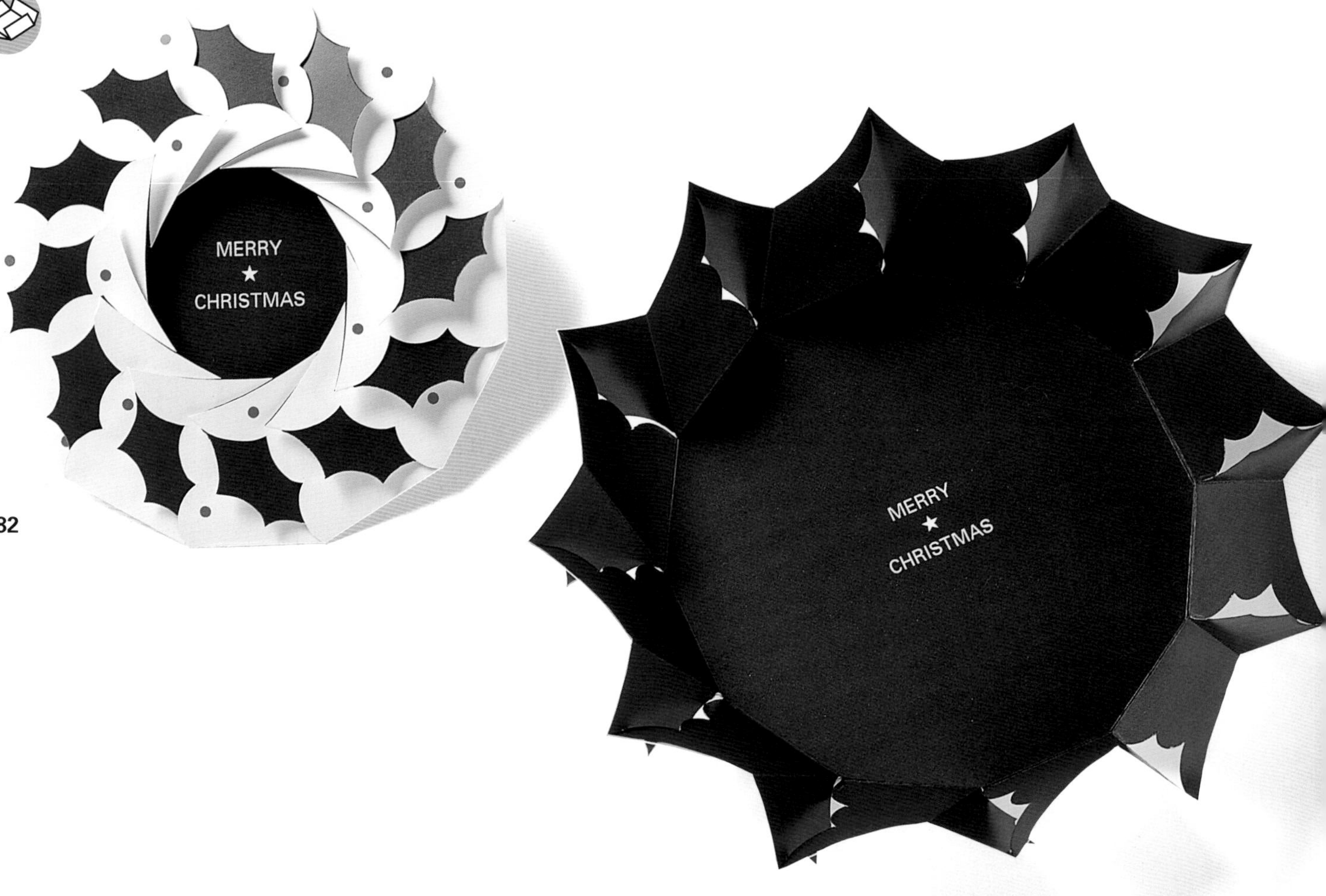

Greeting Card (Christmas)
グリーティング・カード（クリスマス）
Japan 1996
CL: PLAN Y
AD, D, SB: Miyuki Yoshida

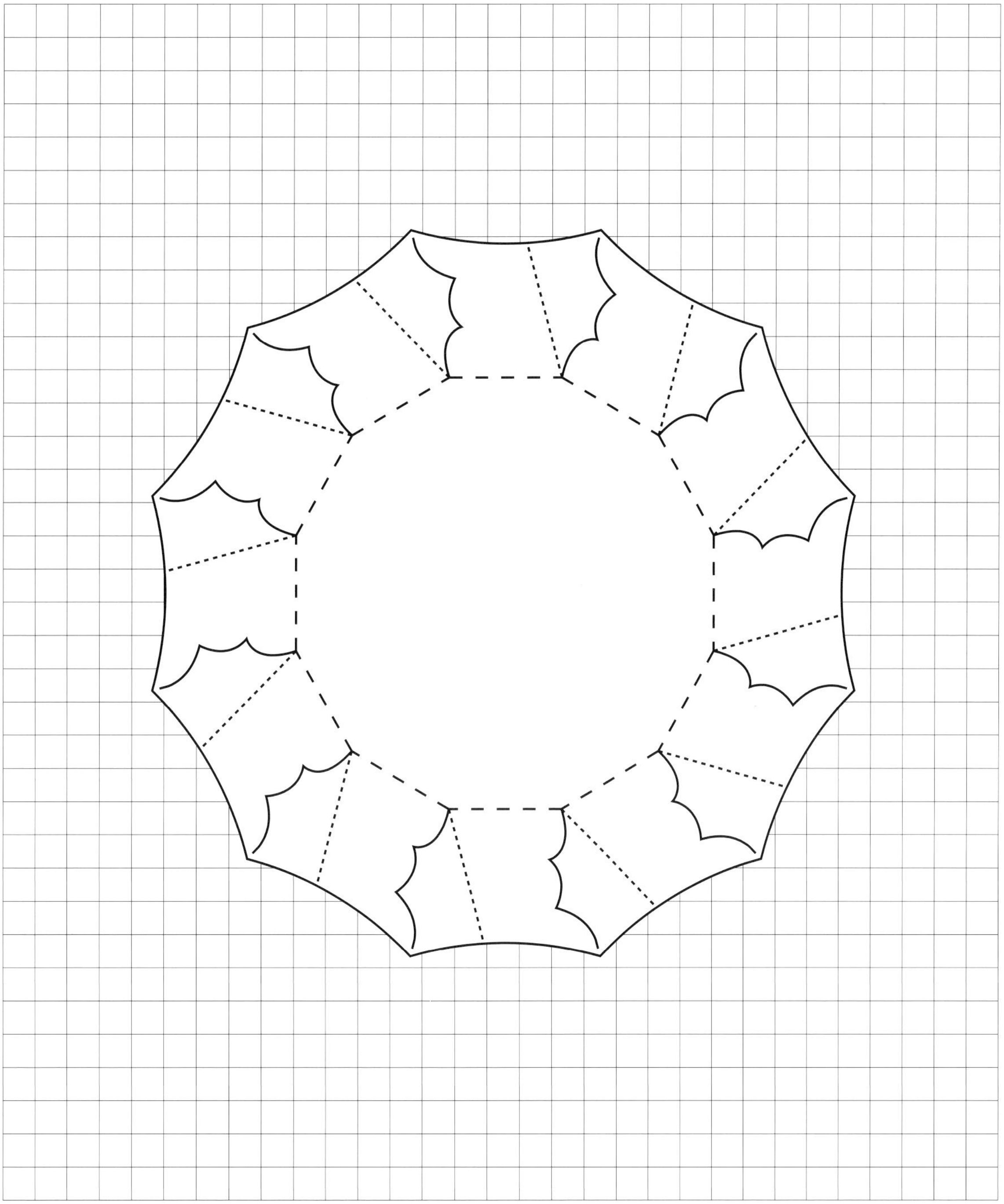

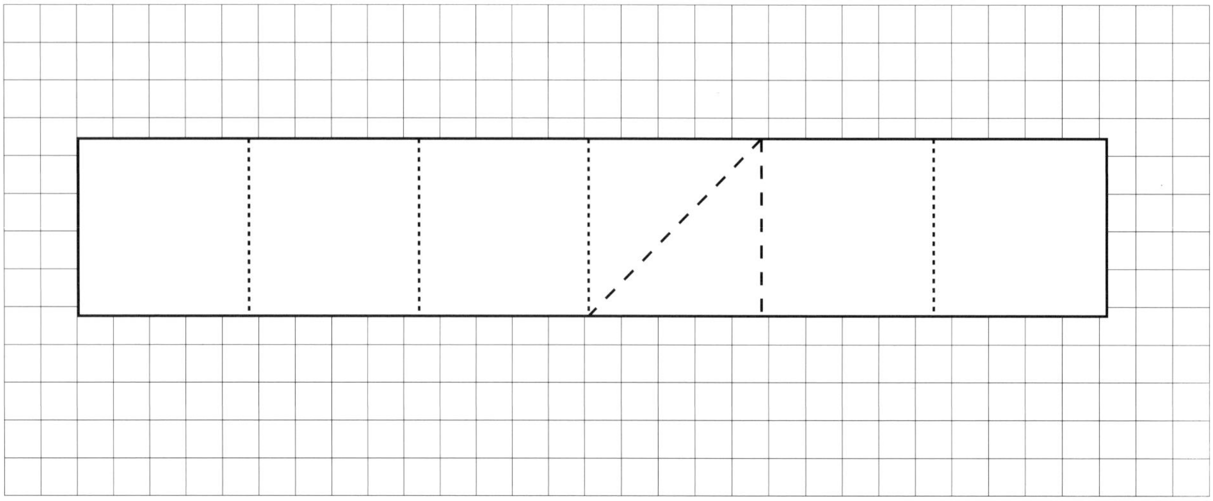

Cultural Institution Guide
"Dann eben Gewalt"

文化施設案内
Austria 1997
CL: Altes Kino Rankweil
AD, D: Peter Felder
P: Dietmar Mathis
DF, SB: Peter Felder Grafikdesign

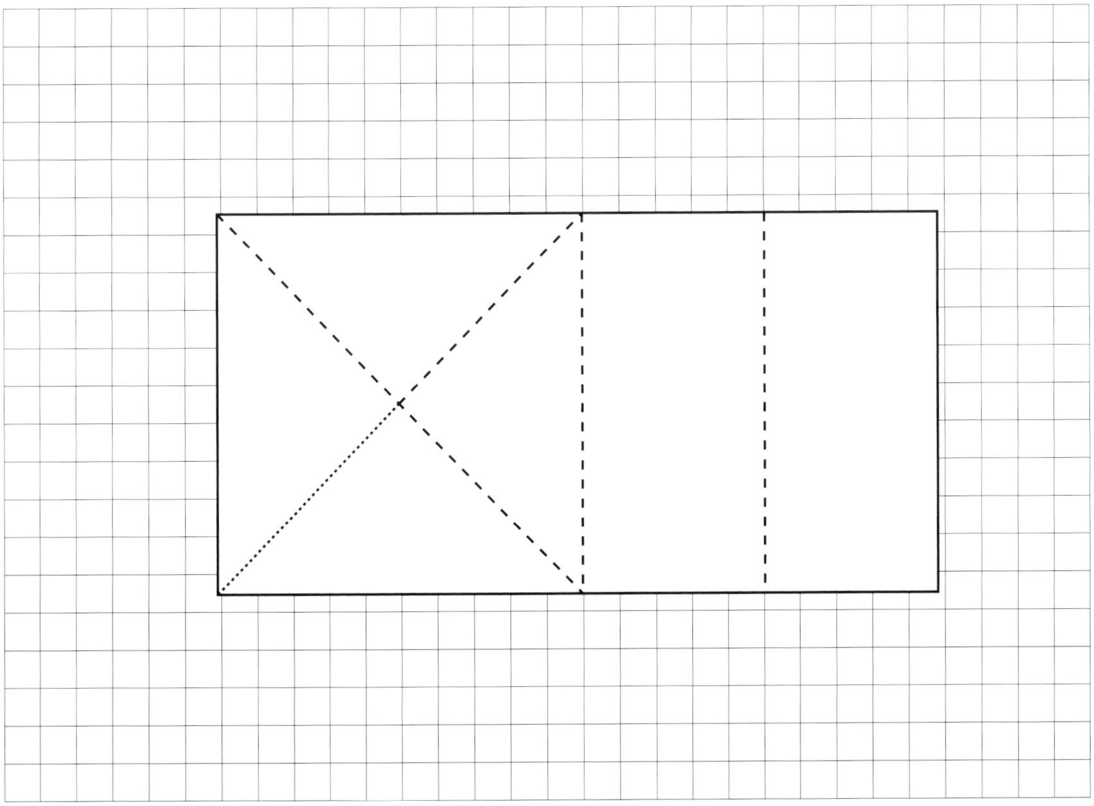

Exhibition Announcemnt DM

「秋の柳美展」展示会案内DM

Japan

CL, SB:Aki no Exhibition Committee

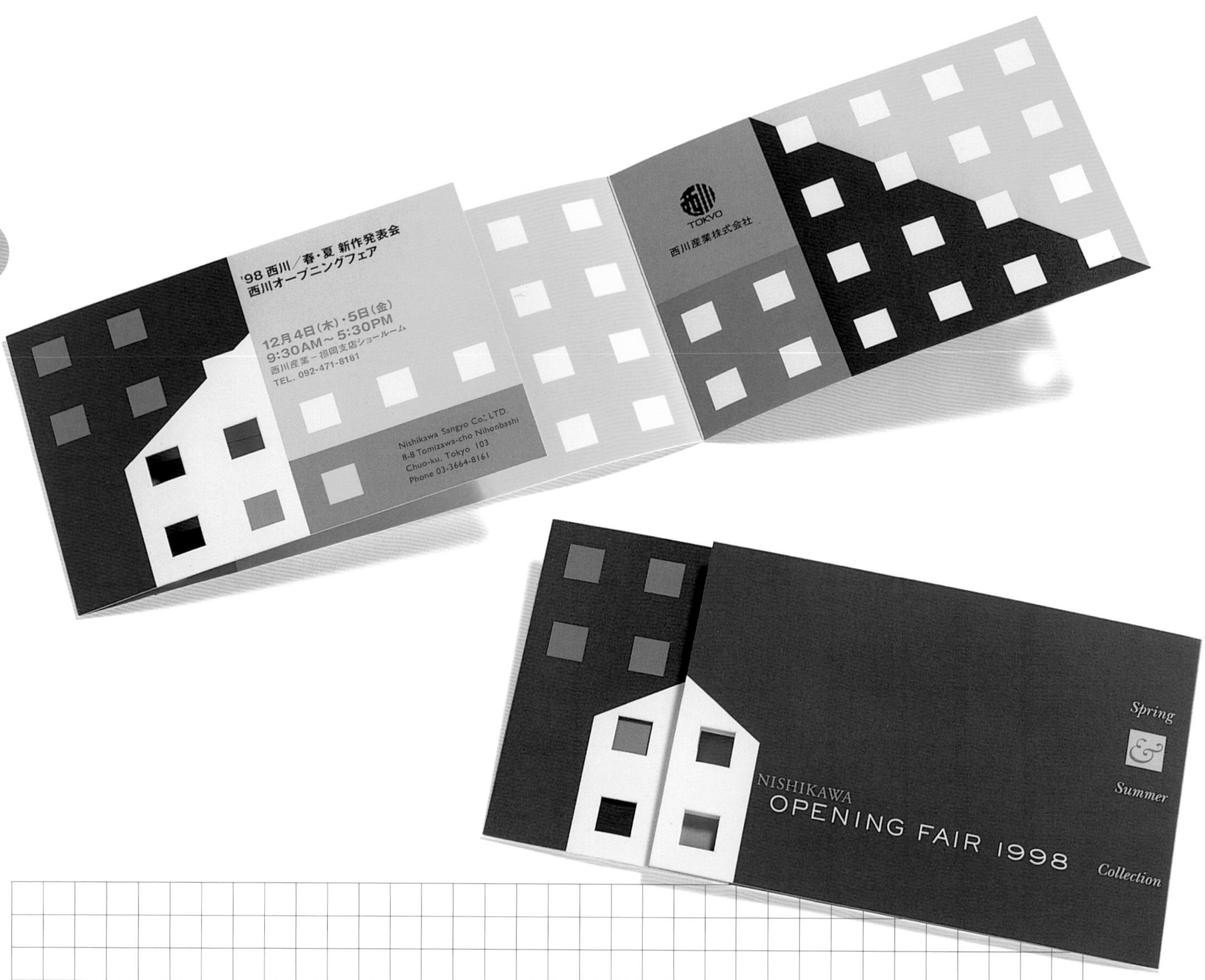

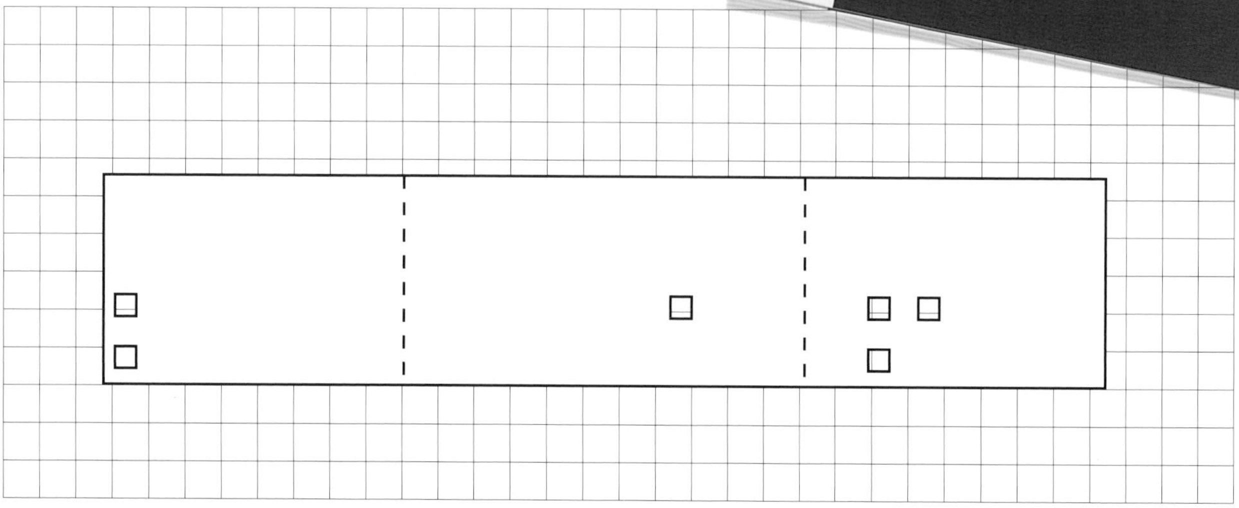

Event Announcemnt DM

イベント告知DM

Japan 1998

CL: Nishikawa Sangyo Co., Ltd.

AD, D: Katsunori Hironaka

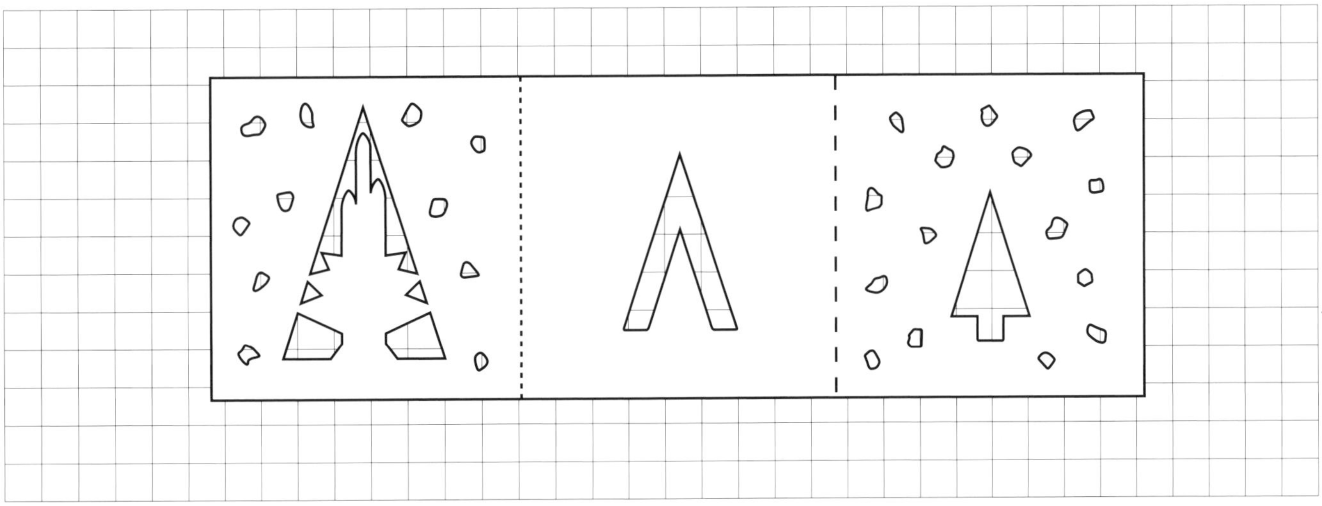

Christmas & New Year Card

クリスマス・新年挨拶状

Japan 1998

CL: Arjo Wiggins Canson KK

CD: Hiromi Ouchi

AD, D: Akihiko Tsukamoto

DF, SB: Design Club

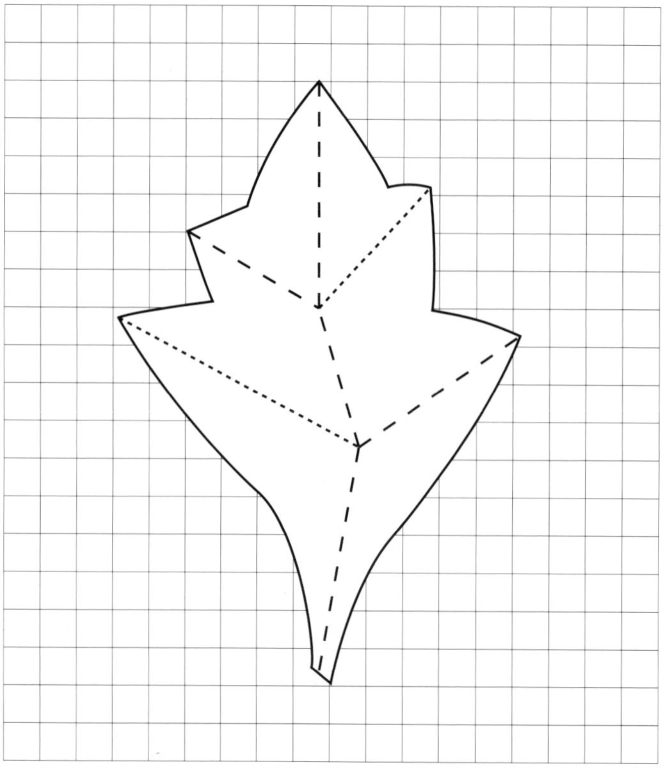

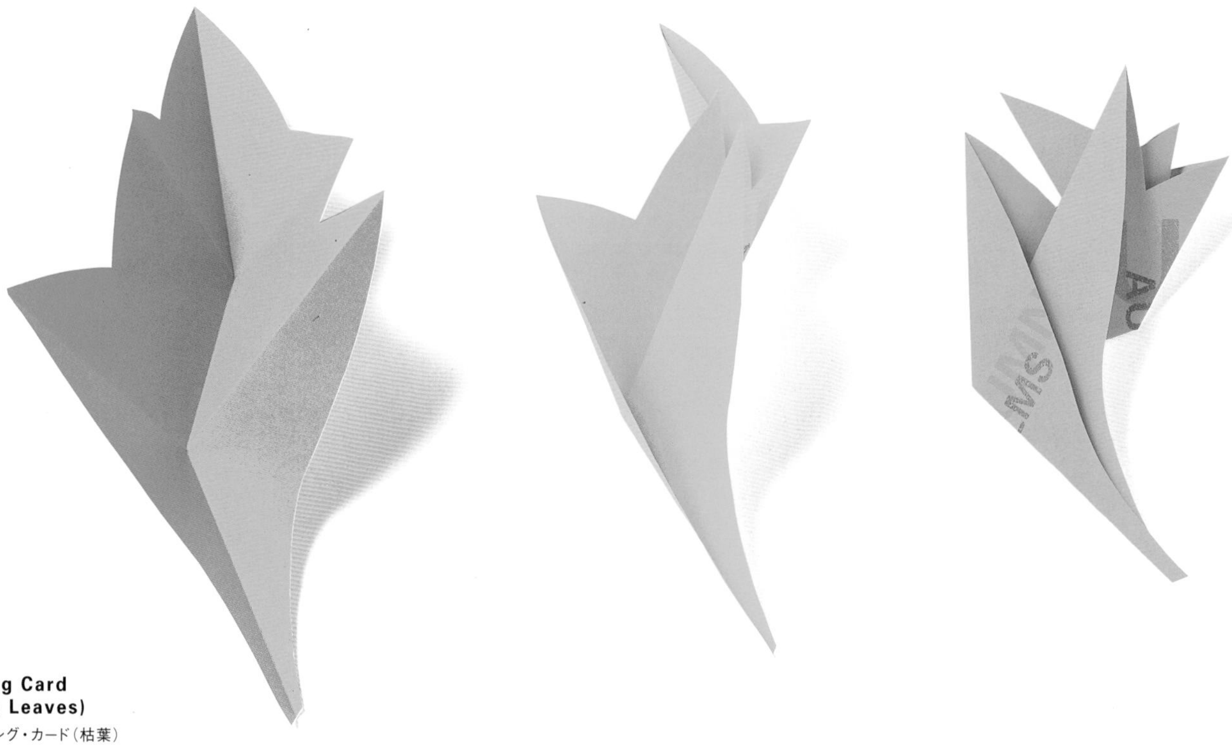

Greeting Card (Falling Leaves)

グリーティング・カード（枯葉）

Japan 1999

CL: PLAN Y

AD, D, SB: Miyuki Yoshida

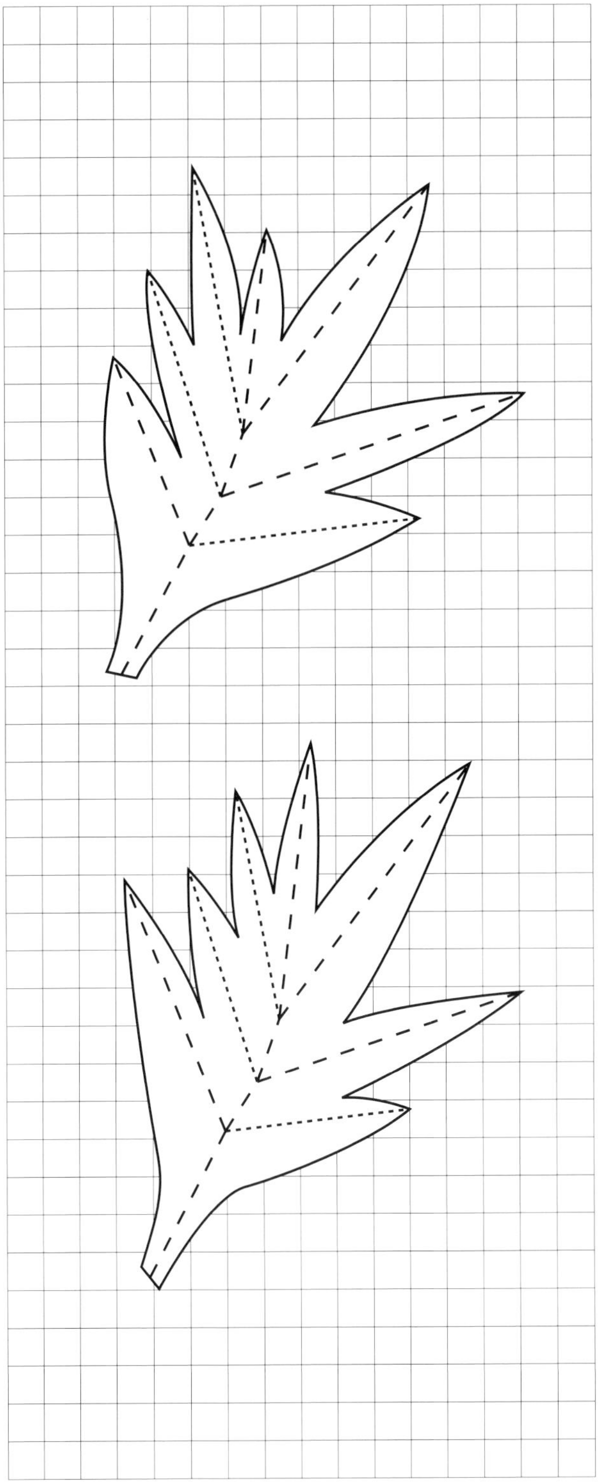

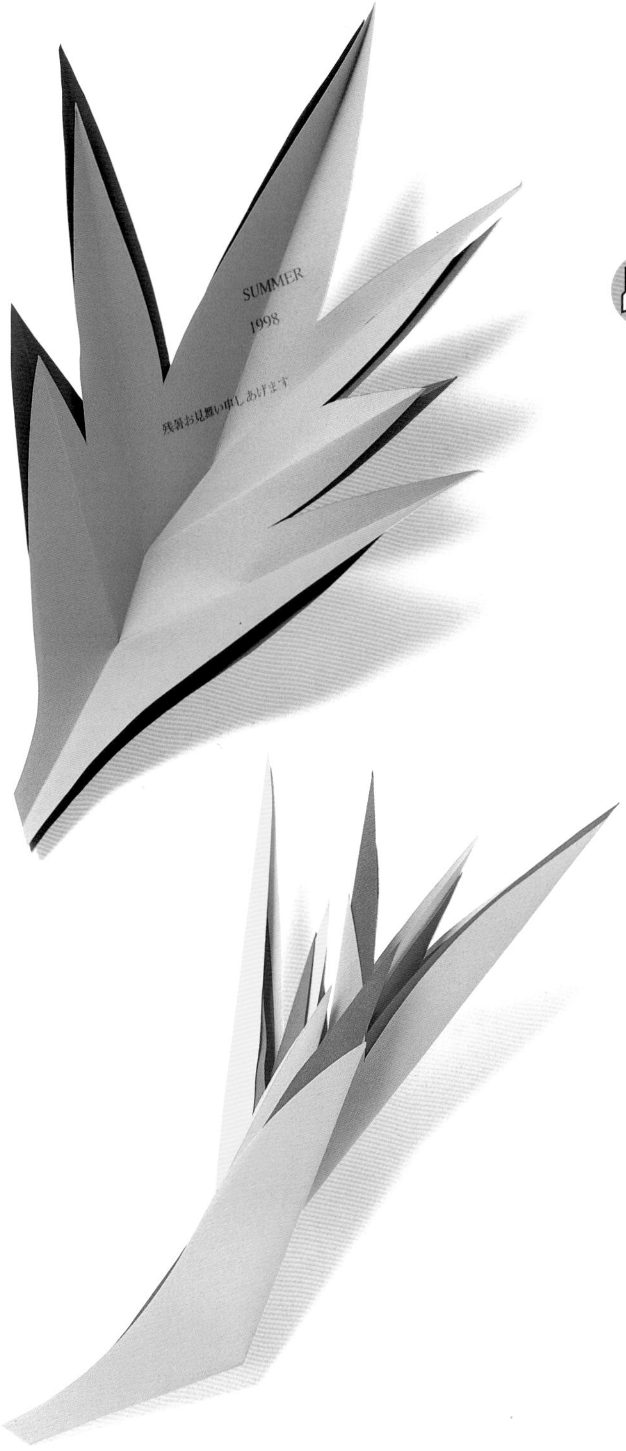

Summer Greeting Card (Bird)
暑中見舞(極楽鳥)
Japan 1998
CL: PLAN Y
AD, D, SB: Miyuki Yoshida

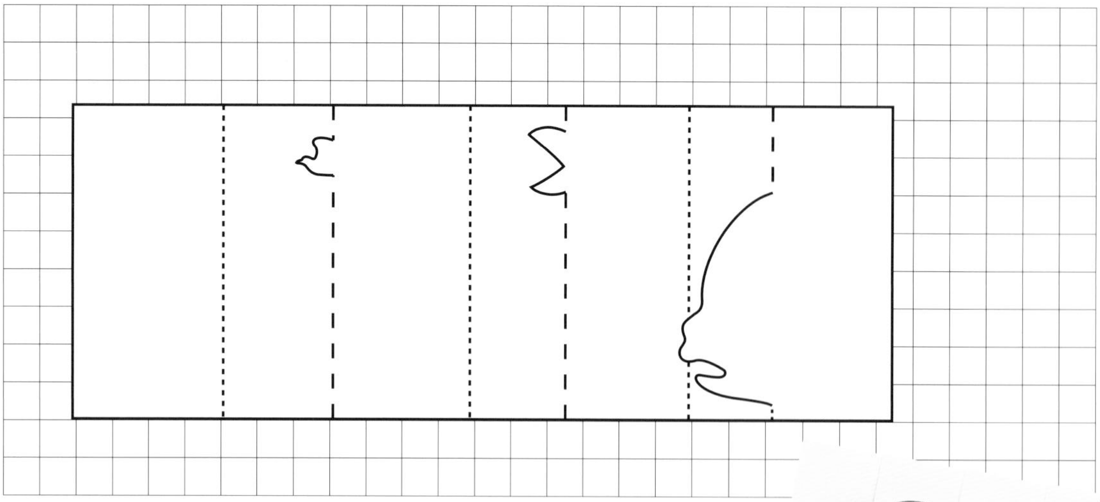

Fold Over Book "Are you OK?"
出版社商品「アーユーオッケー？」
Japan 2002
CL: Heibon-sha
AD, D: Katsumi Komagata
DF, SB: One Stroke Co., Ltd.

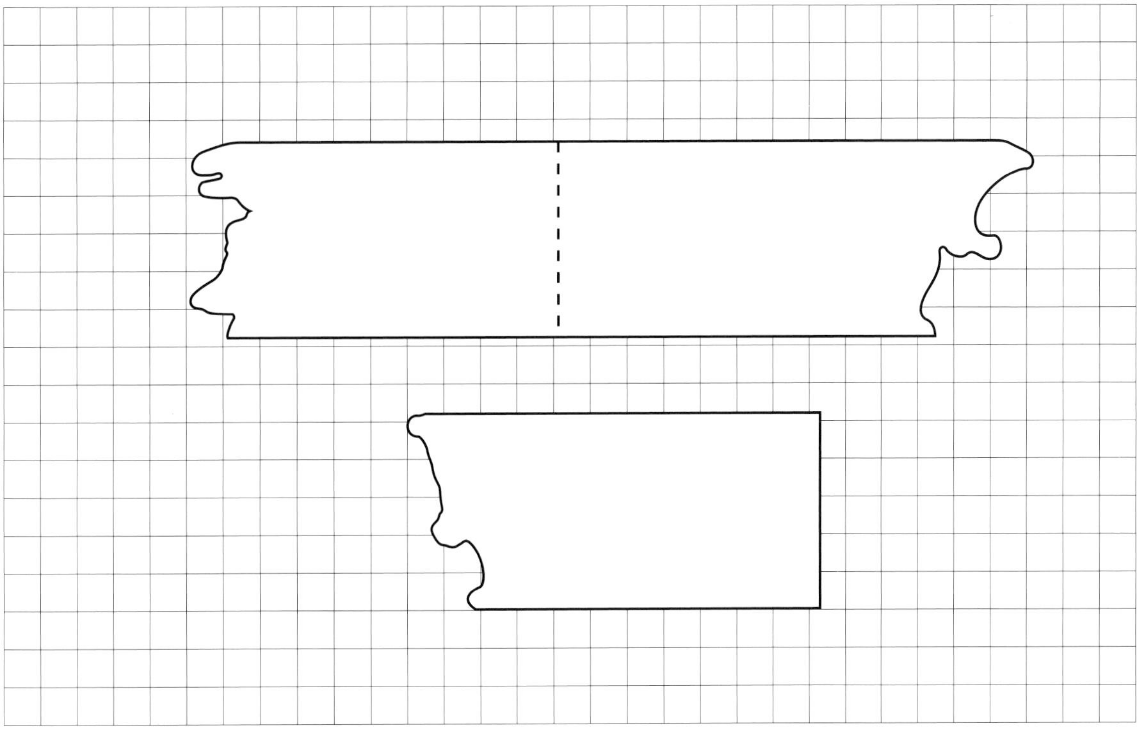

Opening Party Announcement DM
オープニング案内DM
Japan 1990
CL: Zegno Inc.
CD: Nobuo Inoue
AD, D: Akihiko Tsukamoto
DF, SB: Design Club, NID Inc.

Arjo Wiggins Curius Card
新紙シリーズ紹介DM／カード
Japan 2002
CL: Arjo Wiggins Canson KK
CD: Hiromi Ouchi
AD, D: Akihiko Tsukamoto
I: Frank Viva
CW: Masayuki MInoda
DF, SB: Design Club

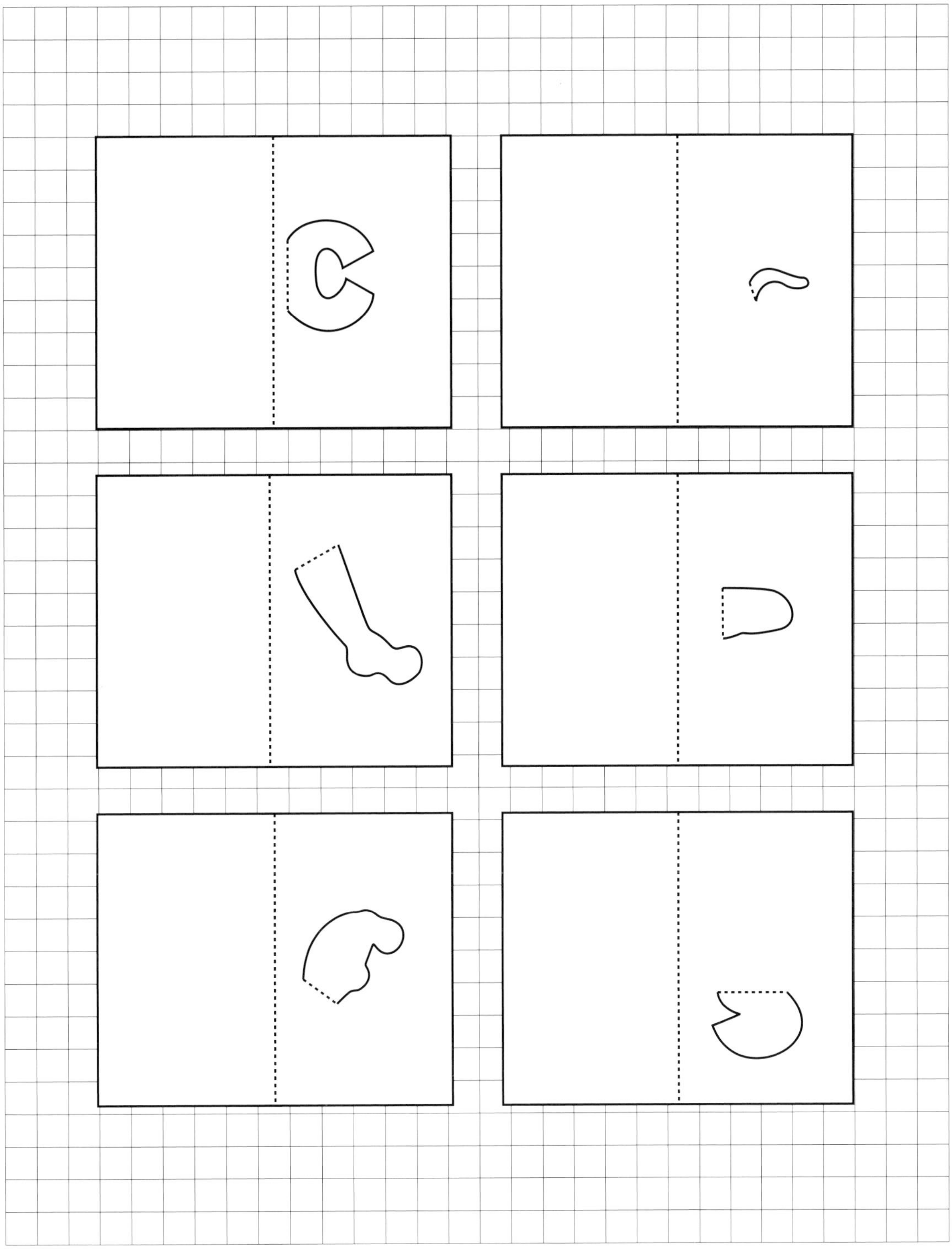

Montag, 24. Februar 1997
20.00 Uhr · Altes Kino Rankweil
Vortrag mit Filmbeispielen
Horror u. Gewalt im Fernsehen
Der Einfluß von Gewalt und angstmachenden Filminhalten auf Kinder, Möglichkeiten der Bewältigung, Filmtechnik und Sendeinhalte, Formen filmischer Gewaltdarstellung, Folgen filmischen Gewaltkonsums. Diskussionsmöglichkeit. Referent: Helmar Oberlechner, Medienpädagoge/Innsbruck
Dienstag, 11. März 1997
20.00 Uhr · Altes Kino Rankweil
Film
Fun - Mordsspaß
USA 1994 · R: Rafal Zielinski · L: 106 min.
mit: Alicia Witt, Renee Humphrey. Ab 16 Jahren.
Beim Autostoppen in einer amerikanischen Kleinstadt lernen sich zwei junge Mädchen kennen. Rasch schließen sie Freundschaft und verbringen fast wie in einem Liebesrausch - einen Nachmittag miteinander, der mit dem blutigen Mord an einer alten Frau endet.
Diskussionsmöglichkeit nach diesem Film.
Donnerstag, 13. März 1997
20.00 Uhr · Altes Kino Rankweil
Film
Benny´s Video
Ö 1992 · R: Michael Haneke · L: 105 min
mit: Arno Frisch, Angela Winkler, Ulrich Mühe.
Benny steht am Beginn der Pubertät. Er stammt aus bürgerlichem Haus. Seine Eltern sorgen sich kaum um ihn. In der Welt der Videofilme findet er emotionalen Ersatz. Allmählich - von den ihm am nächsten stehenden Menschen unbemerkt - verändern sich seine Wertmaßstäbe und sein Gefühl für Realität. Er lernt ein etwa gleichaltriges Mädchen kennen. Was wie eine scheue Liebesgeschichte anfängt, endet in einer Katastrophe.
Diskussionsmöglichkeit nach diesem Film.
Dienstag, 18. März 1997
20.00 Uhr · Altes Kino Rankweil
Film
21/2 Minuten
D 1996 · R: Rolf Schübel · L: 100 min
mit: Wandja Mues, Julia Brendler, Cem Sultan Ungan.
16. November 1990. Am späten Abend kommt es in Berlin zwischen jungen Türken und Deutschen zu einem Streit in der S-Bahn. Es dauert nur 21/2 Minuten von Haltestelle zu Haltestelle, dann liegen drei Deutsche zum Teil schwer verletzt am Boden. Dem Türken wird der Prozeß gemacht. Die Biografien von Täter und Opfer weisen eine erstaunliche Parallelität auf. Aber wie soll man versöhnliche Schritte tun, wenn man die Dynamik von Haß und Gewalt nicht begreift?
Diskussionsmöglichkeit nach diesem Film.
Mittwoch, 19. März 1997
Film · Schulvorstellung + 20.00 Uhr
Altes Kino Rankweil
D
Dann eben Gewalt

Cultural Institution Guide
"Dann eben Gewalt"
文化施設案内
Austria 1997
CL: Altes Kino Rankweil
AD, D: Peter Felder
P: Dietmar Mathis
DF, SB: Peter Felder Grafikdesign

Government Information "Gluren Bij De Buren"

行政施設案内

Belgium

CL: Provincie Vlaams - Brabant

CD, AD, D: Jo Klaps

DF, SB: Brussels Lof

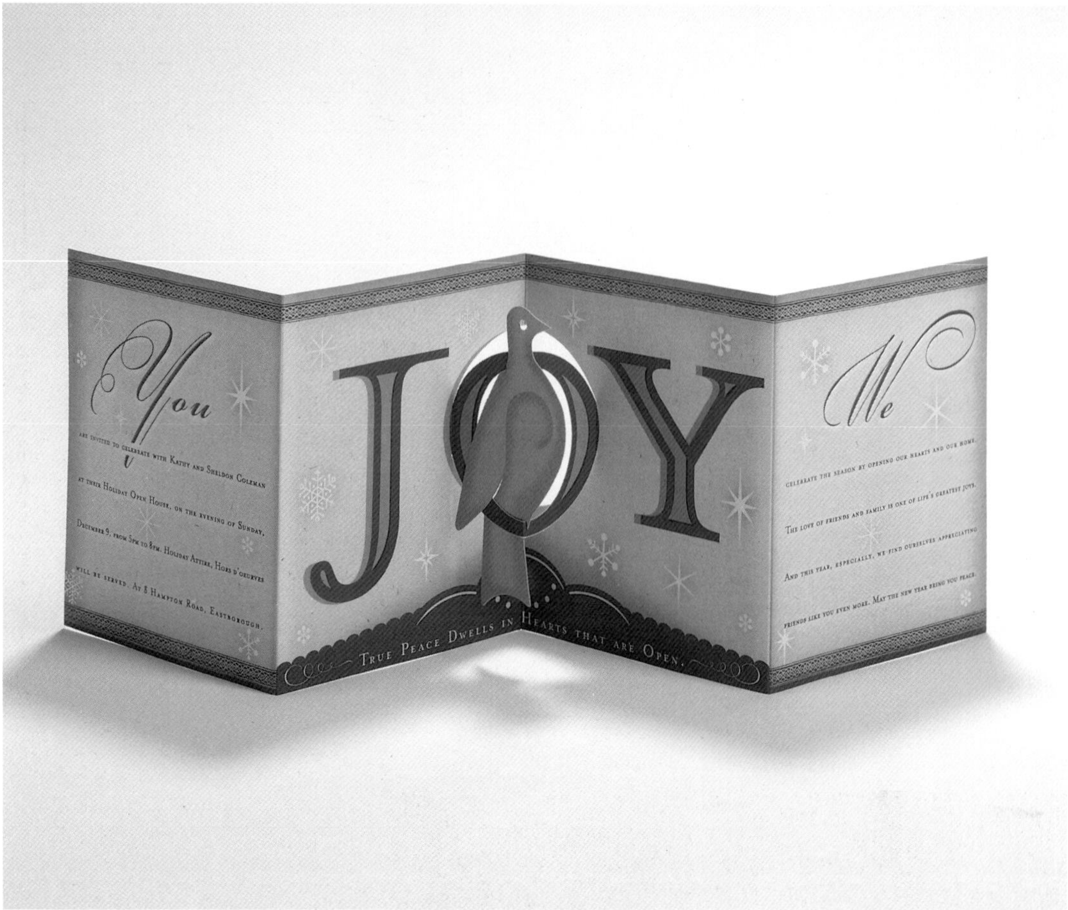

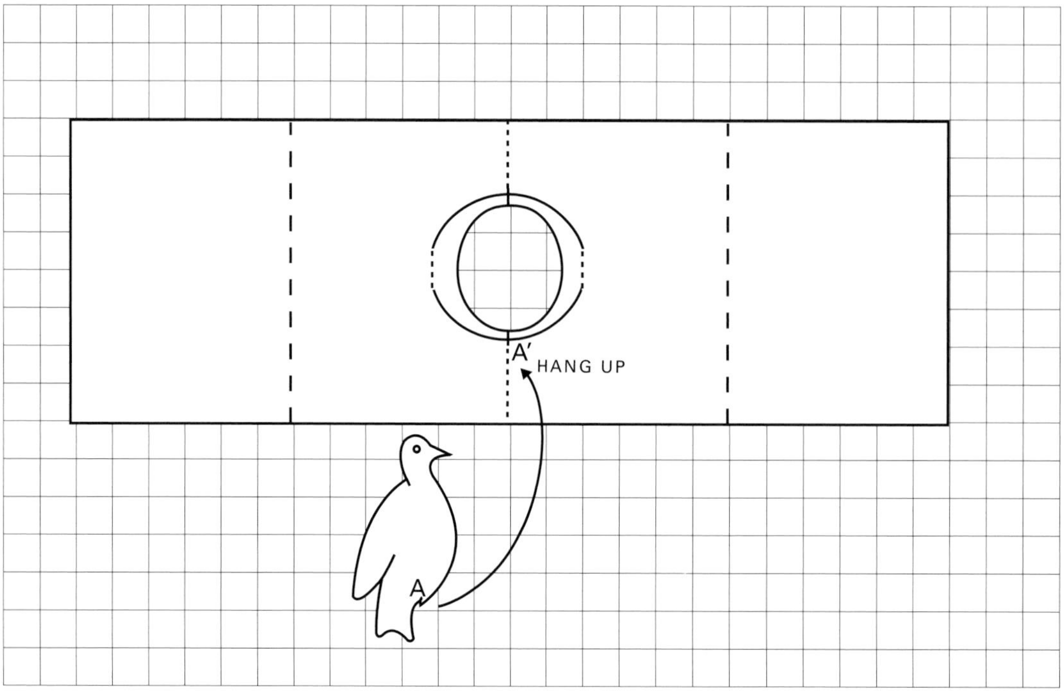

Holiday Invititation
宿泊施設 招待状
USA 2001
CL: Kathy & Sheldon Coleman
CD, D: Bill Gardner
AD, D: Brian Miller
DF, SB: Gardner Design

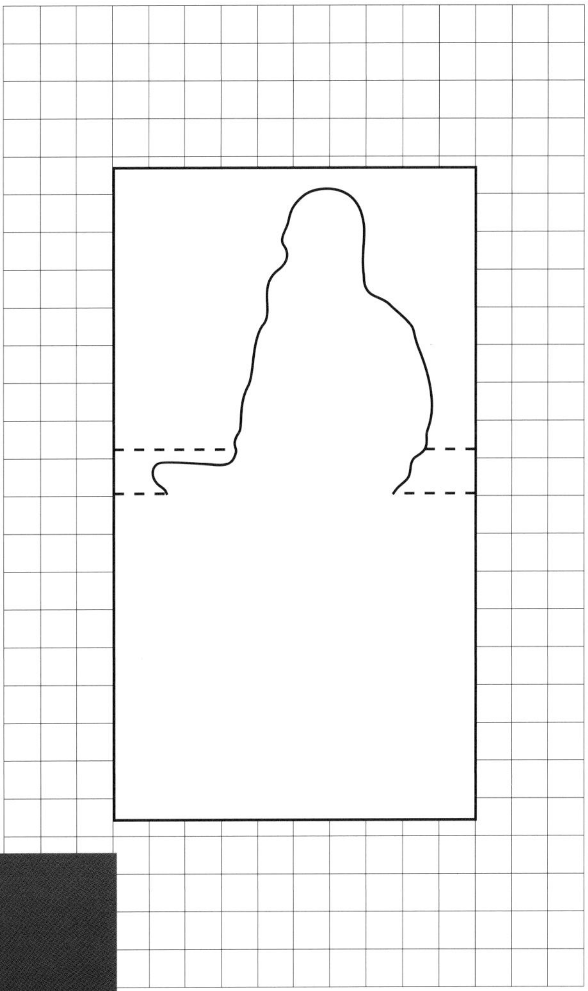

one's music library " Christmas Classics"
ワンズミュージックライブラリー「クリスマス クラシックス」
Japan 2002
CL: JTEX Co., Ltd.
AD, D: Masami Takahashi
DF, SB: Masami Design

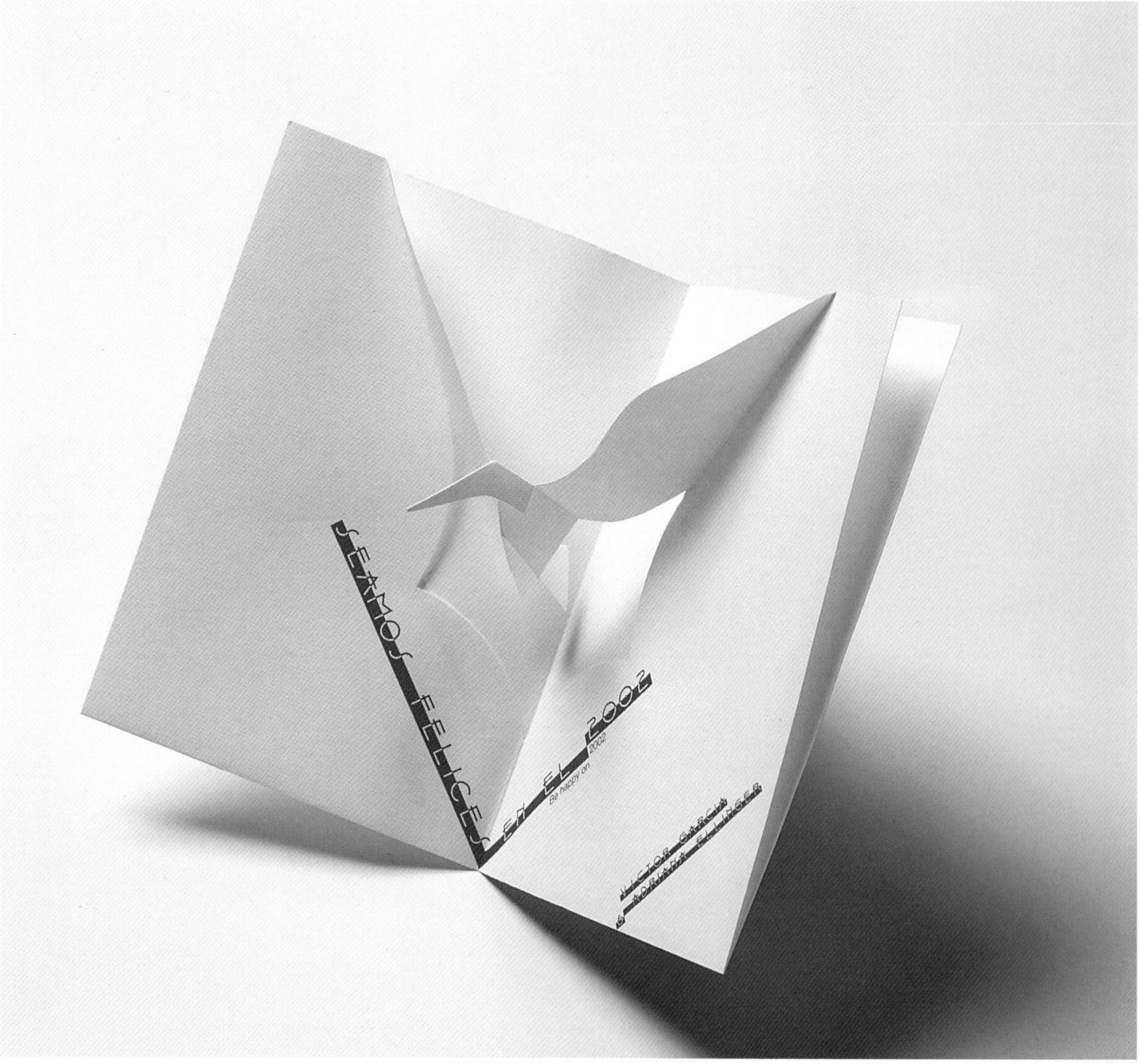

Design Firm New Year Greeting Card "Hummingbird"

デザイン事務所年賀状

Argentina 2001

CL: Victor Garcia & Adriana Ellinger

CD, AD, D, SB: Victor Garcia

DF: Victor Garcia & Adriana Ellinger

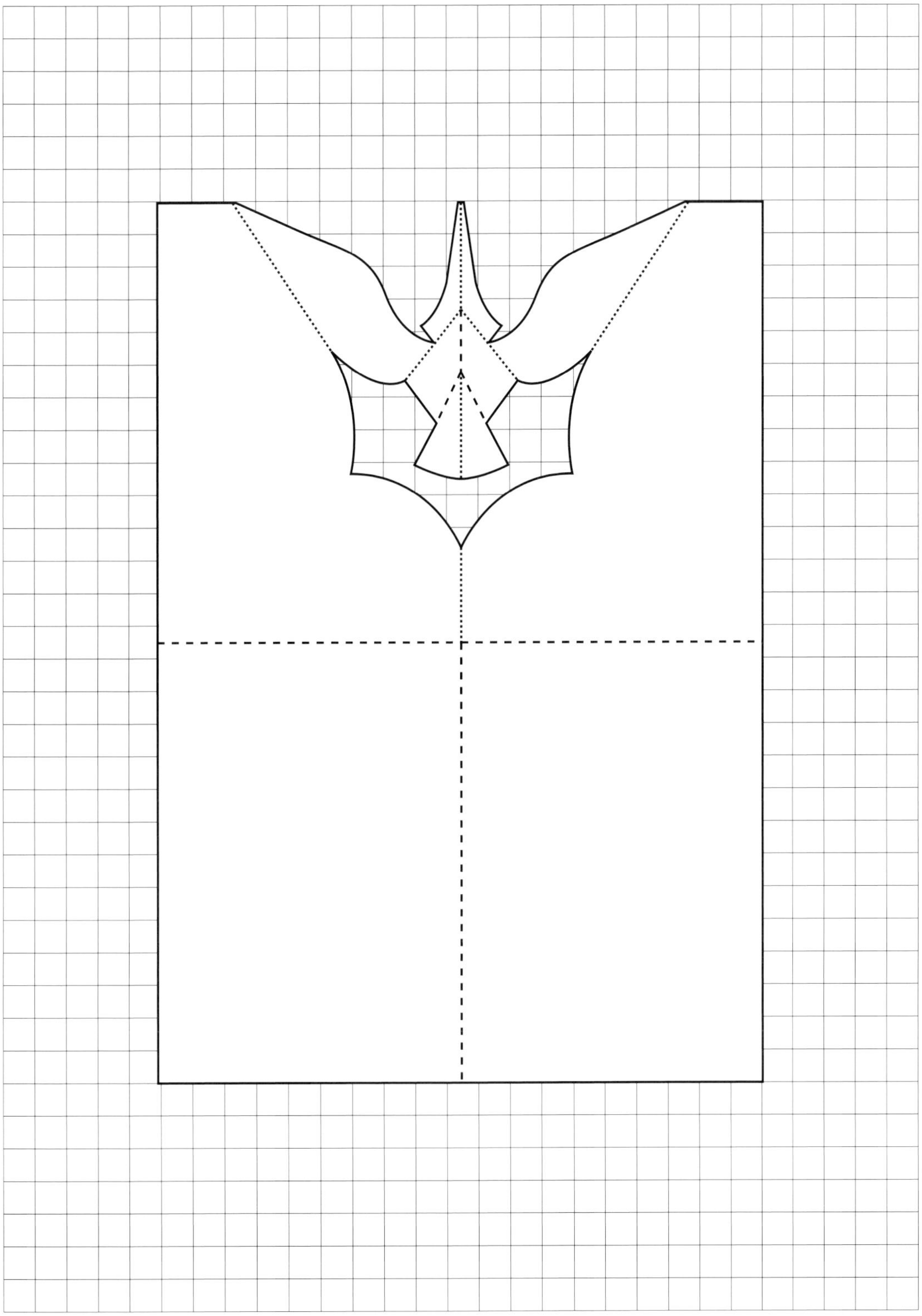

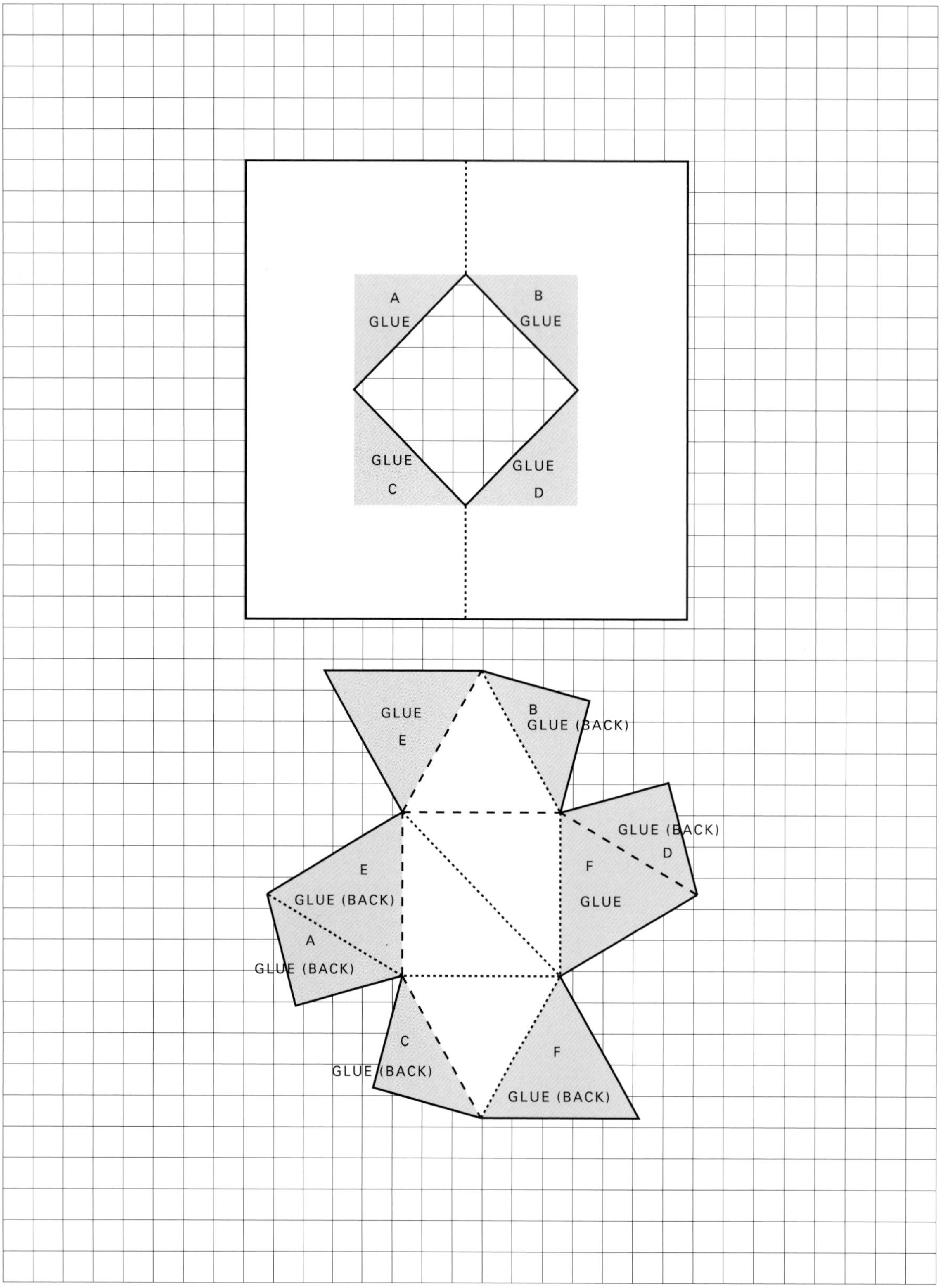
A
GLUE
B
GLUE
GLUE
C
GLUE
D
GLUE
E
B
GLUE (BACK)
GLUE (BACK)
D
E
F
GLUE (BACK)
GLUE
A
GLUE (BACK)
C
GLUE (BACK)
F
GLUE (BACK)

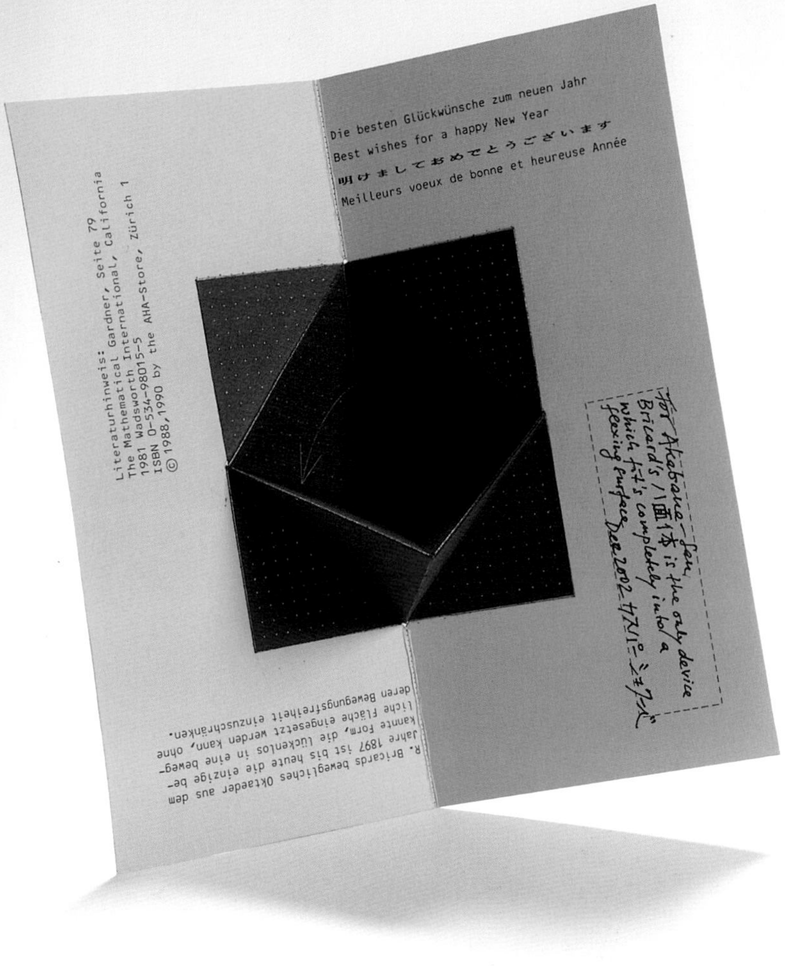

Bricard's Card
正八面体のカード
Switzerland 1990
D, SB:Casper Schwabe

Mail Order Postcards"Change The Game"
通販用カード
Austria 1999
CL: Hammerer + Partner
CD, D, I: Kurt Dornig
P: Klaus Andorfer
DF, SB: Kurt Dornig Grafik Design

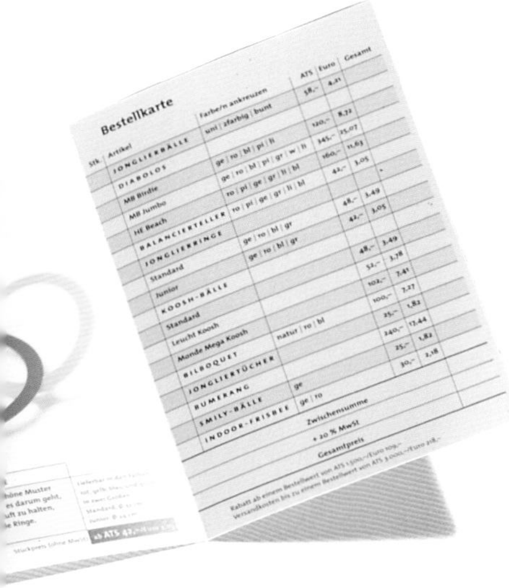

Moving Announcement & Holiday Card

事務所転居告知DM

USA 2000

CL, SB:Sorrell Company, Inc.

CD, AD, P: William Sorrell

AD, D: Lizette Gecel

I: Clip Art from "Ultimate Symbol"

DF, SB: Sorrell Company, Inc.

CONSTELLATION CARD©2001 SPIRAL / WACOAL ART CENTER & MASAMI TAKAHASHI
点と点の集合体によって形成される星座をデザインしたカード。
カードの空く穴は12星座共通の、1個として無駄な穴はない仕組み。

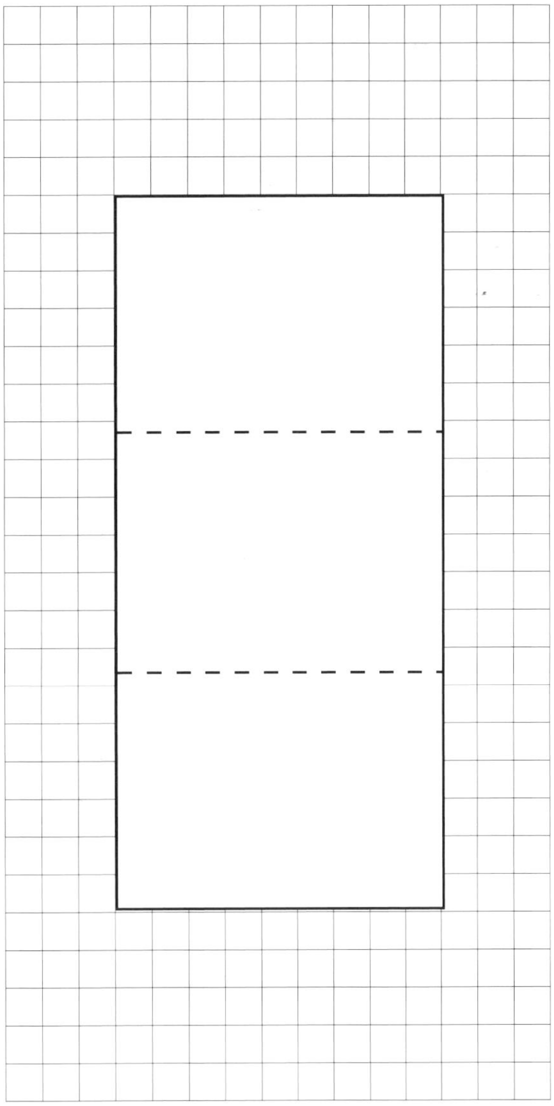

Constellation Card
コンステレーション・カード
Japan 2001
AD, D: Masami Takahashi
DF, SB: Masami Design

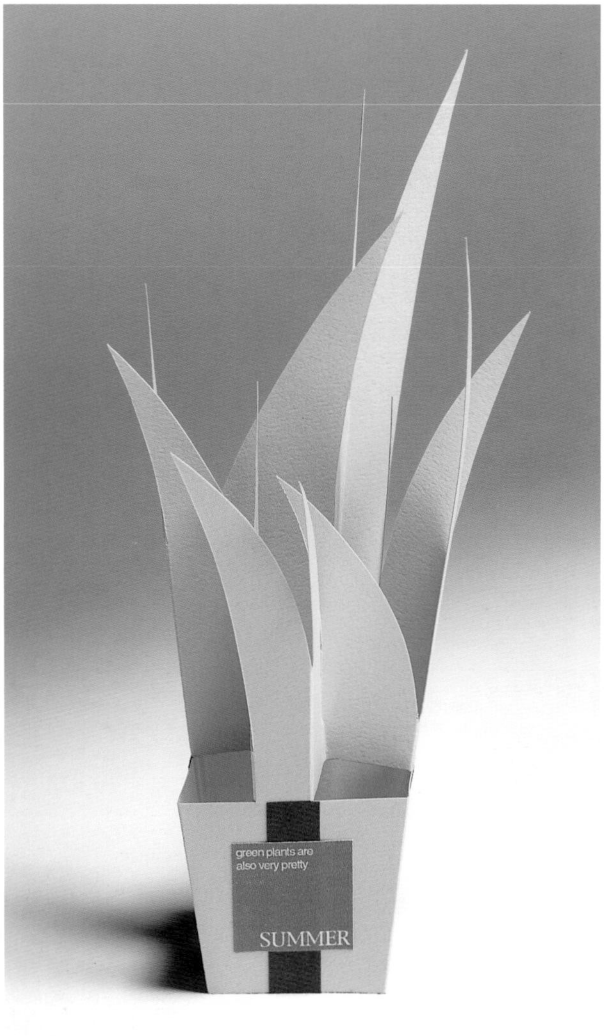

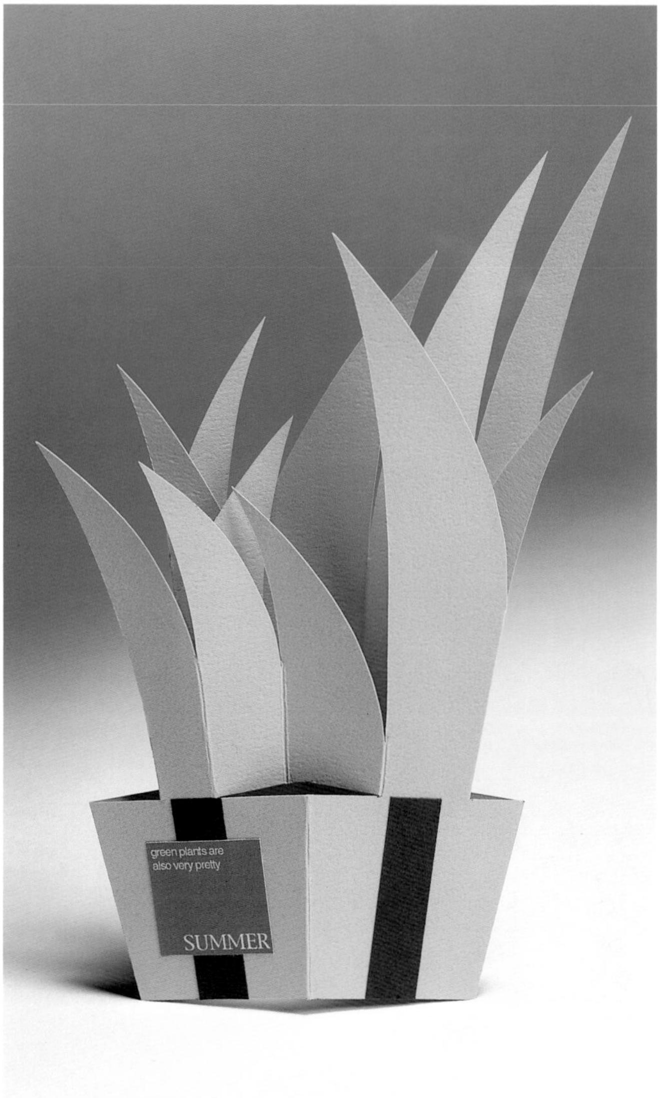

Summer Greeting Card (Green)
暑中見舞（グリーン）
Japan 1997
CL: PLAN Y
AD, D, SB: Miyuki Yoshida

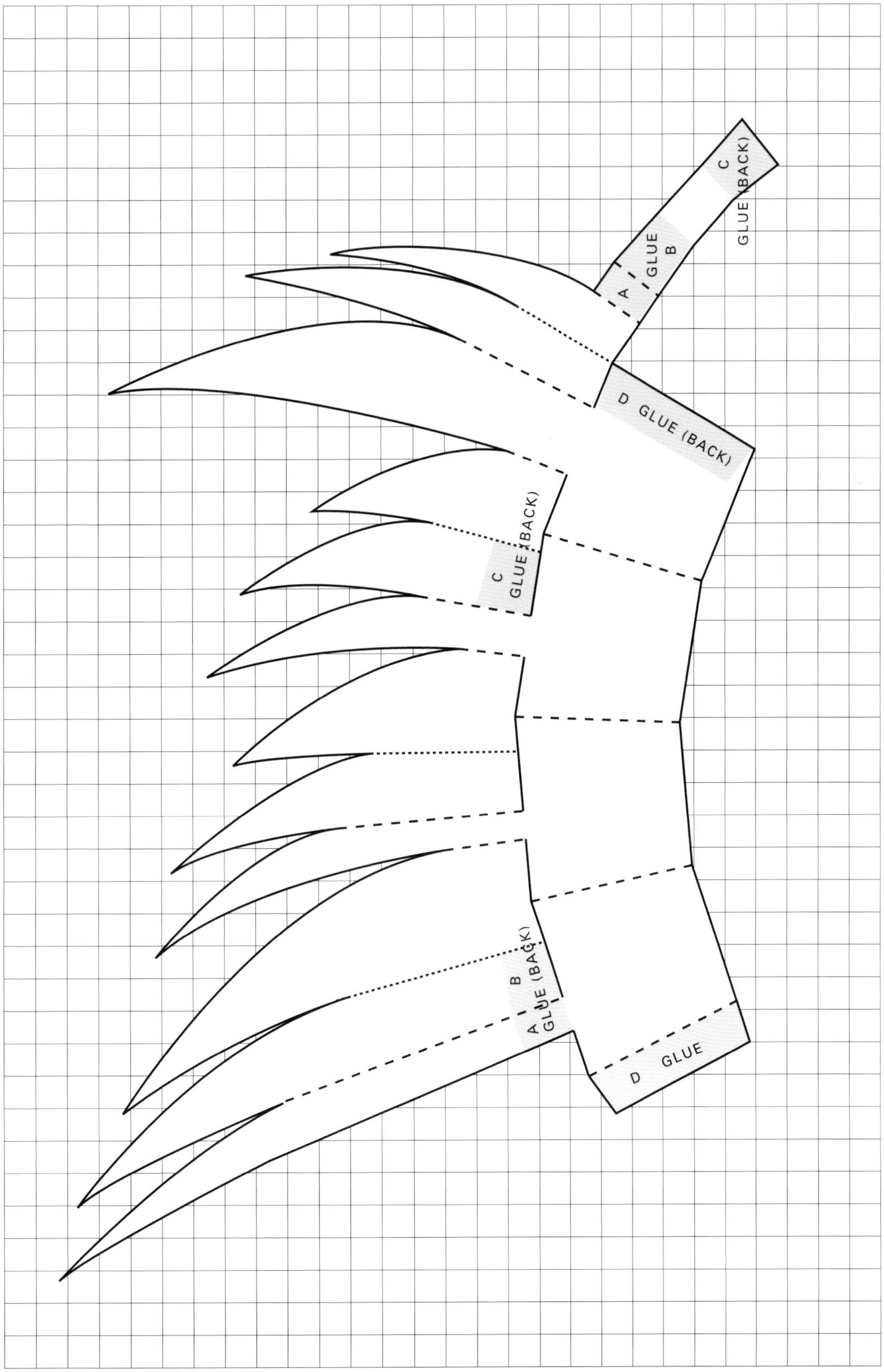
C
GLUE (BACK)
GLUE
B
A
D GLUE (BACK)
C
GLUE (BACK)
B
GLUE (BACK)
A
D GLUE

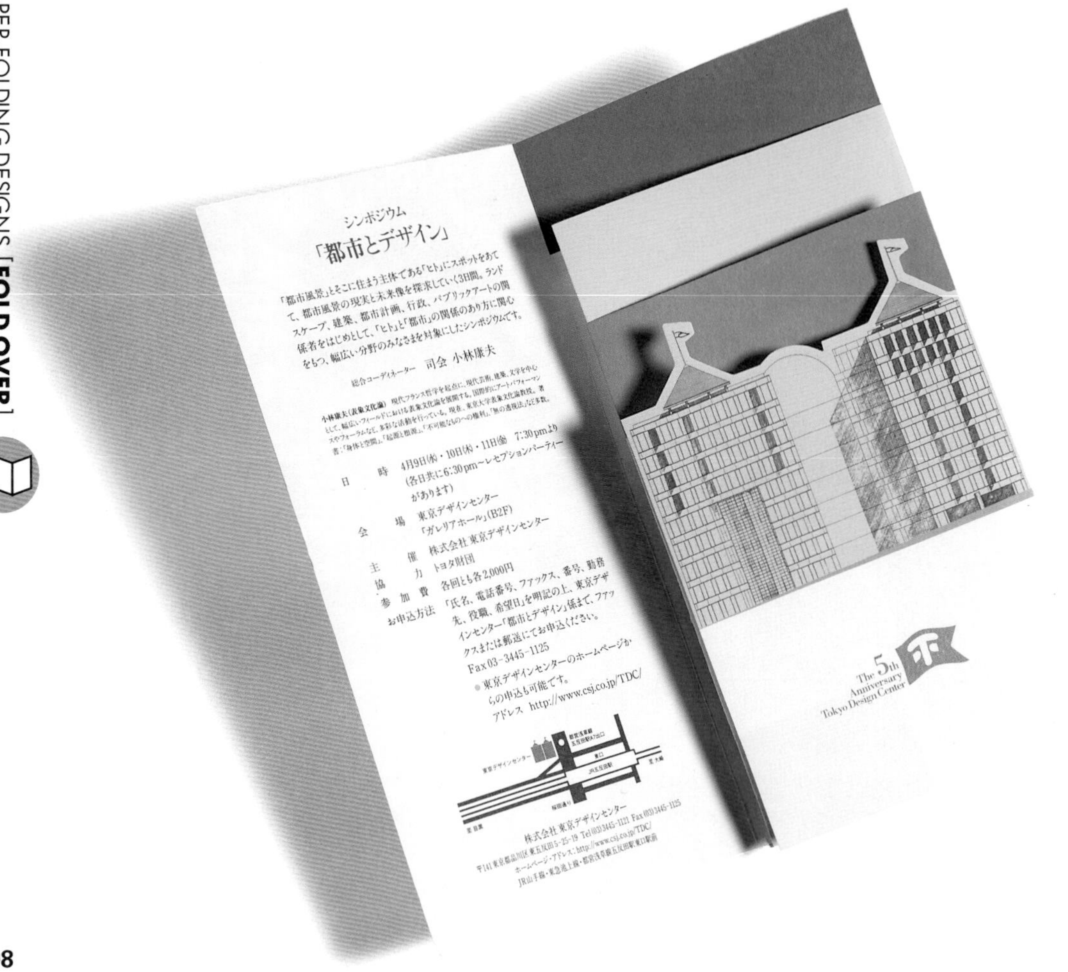

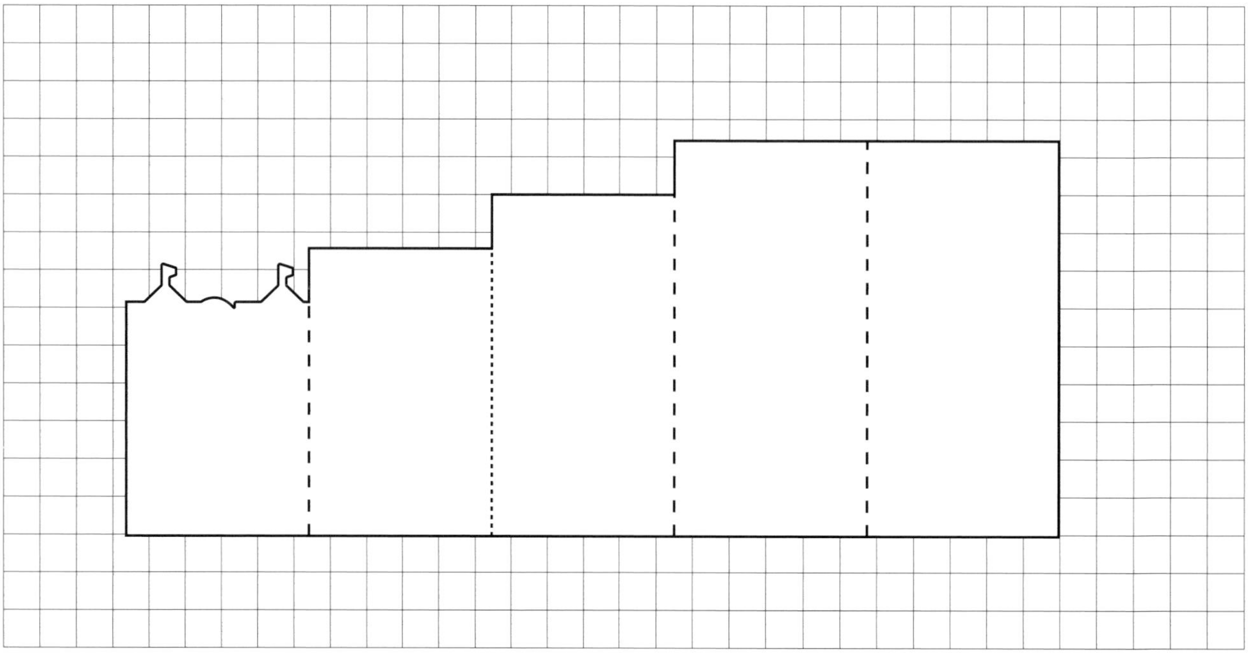

Event Announcement DM

シンポジウム案内DM

Japan 1997

CL: Tokyo Design Center

CD: Takako Terunuma

AD, D, SB: Akihiko Tsukamoto

DF: Accompany Co., Ltd.

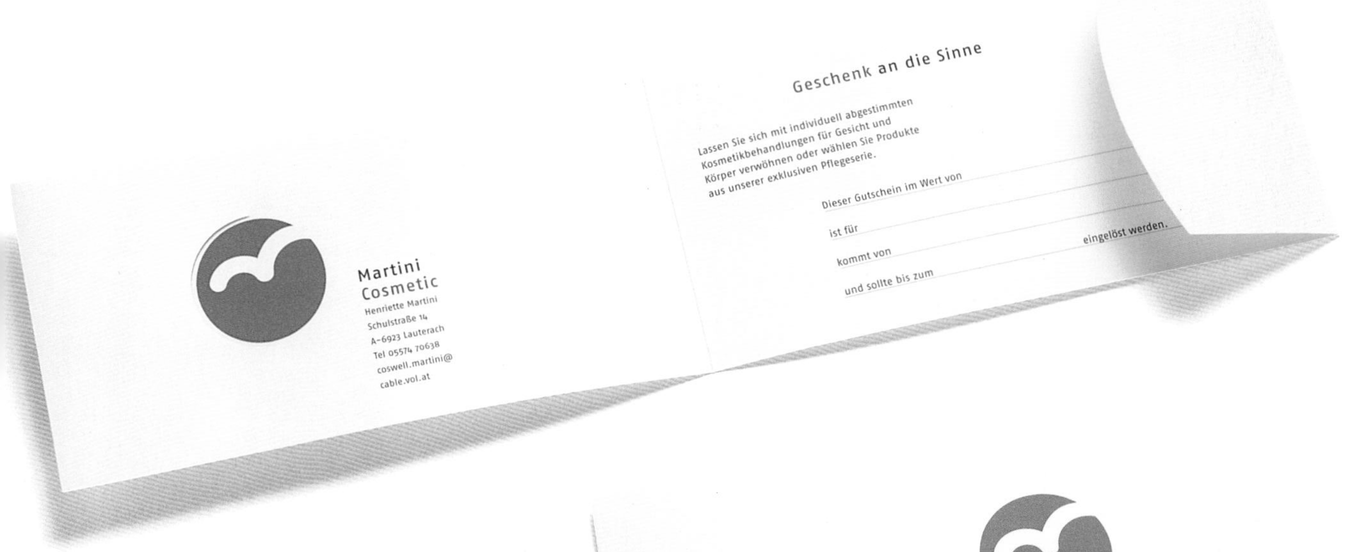

Martini
Cosmetic
Henriette Martini
Schulstraße 14
A-6923 Lauterach
Tel 05574 70638
coswell.martini@
cable.vol.at
Geschenk an die Sinne
Lassen Sie sich mit individuell abgestimmten
Kosmetikbehandlungen für Gesicht und
Körper verwöhnen oder wählen Sie Produkte
aus unserer exklusiven Pflegeserie.
Dieser Gutschein im Wert von
ist für
kommt von
und sollte bis zum
eingelöst werden.

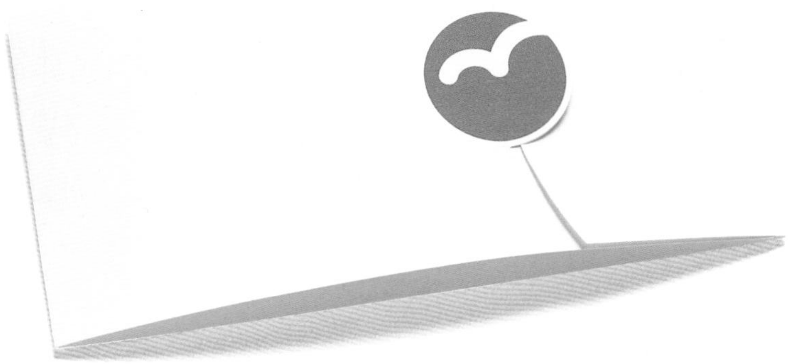

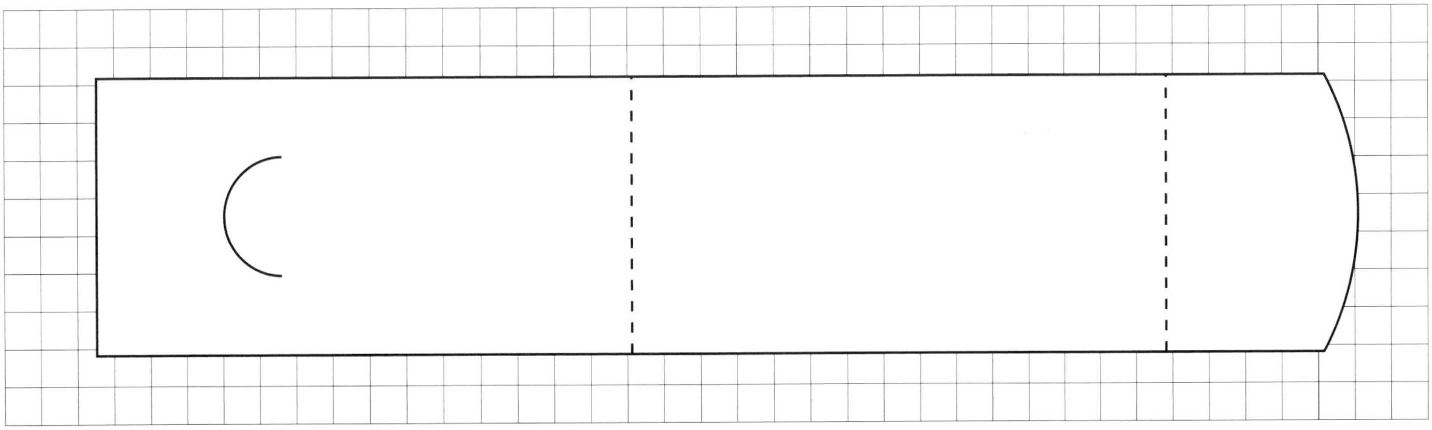

Martini Cosmetic Card
美容院顧客カード
Austria 2002
CL: Martini Cosmetic
CD, D: Kurt Dornig
DF, SB: Kurt Dornig Graphic

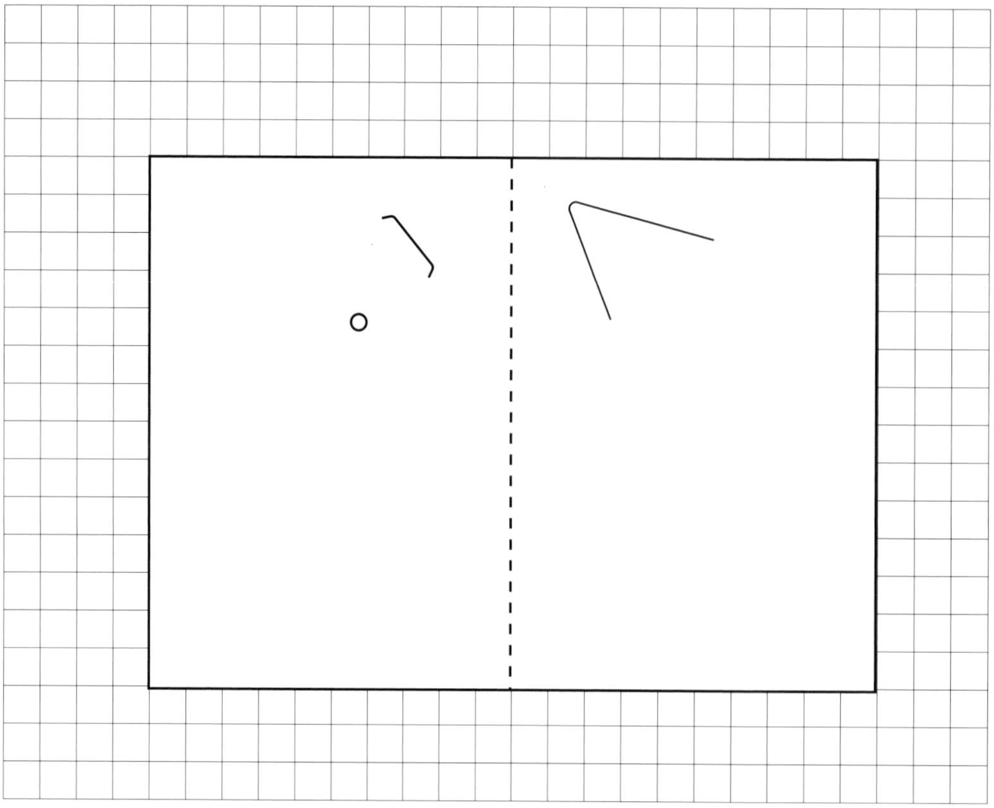

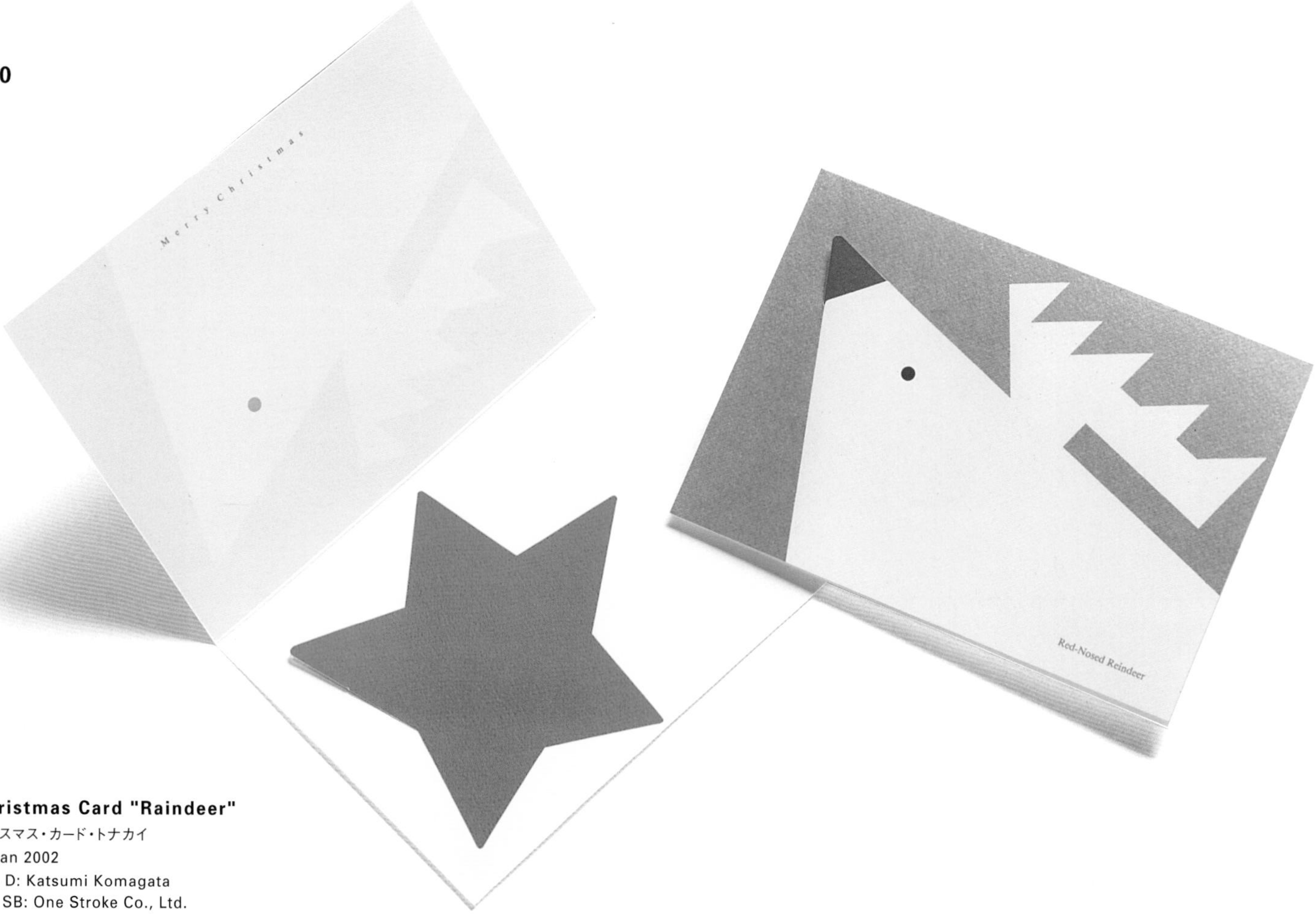

Christmas Card "Raindeer"
クリスマス・カード・トナカイ
Japan 2002
AD, D: Katsumi Komagata
DF, SB: One Stroke Co., Ltd.

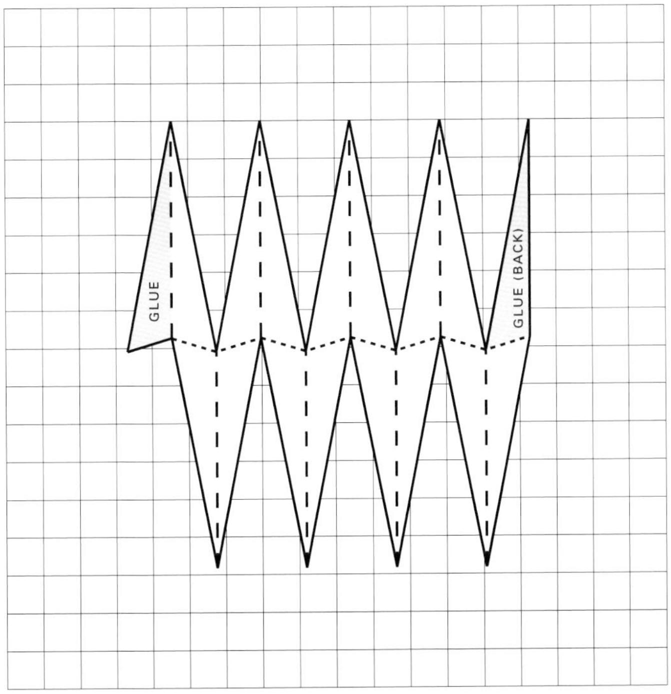

Christmas Card (Golden Star)
クリスマス・カード（金の星）
Japan 2000
CL: PLAN Y
AD, D, SB: Miyuki Yoshida

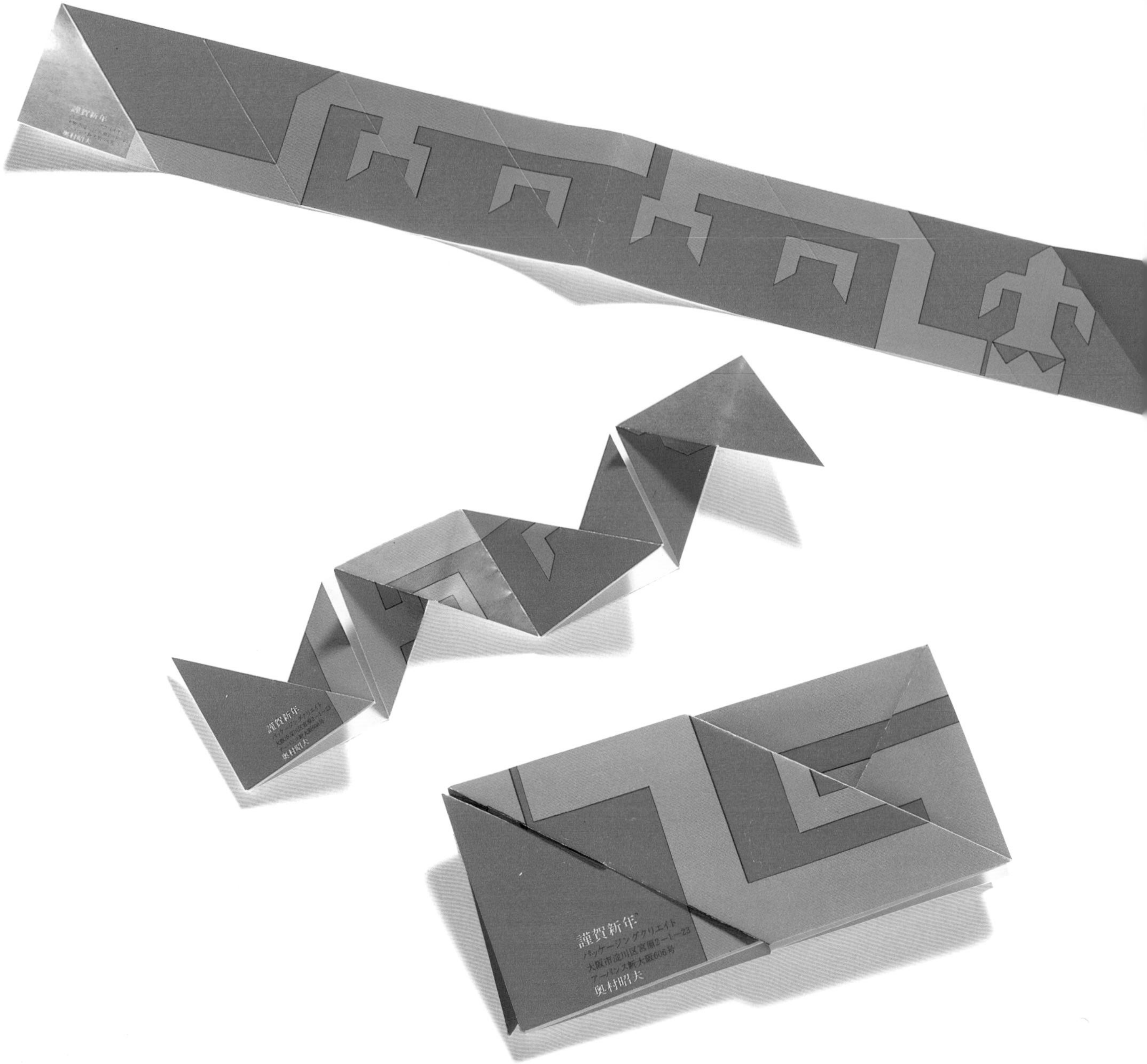

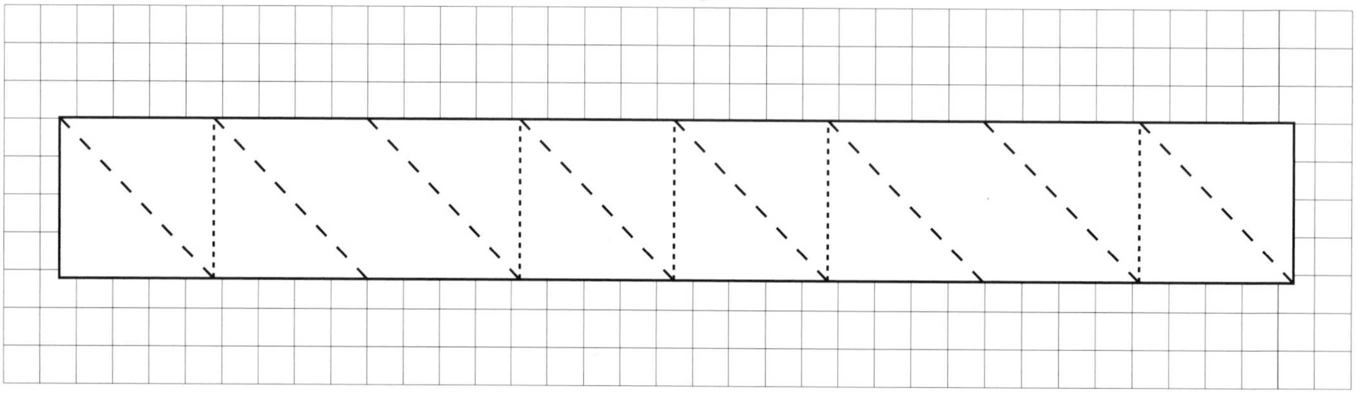

New Year's Card

年賀状

Japan 1976

CL: Packaging Create

AD, D, SB: Akio Okumura

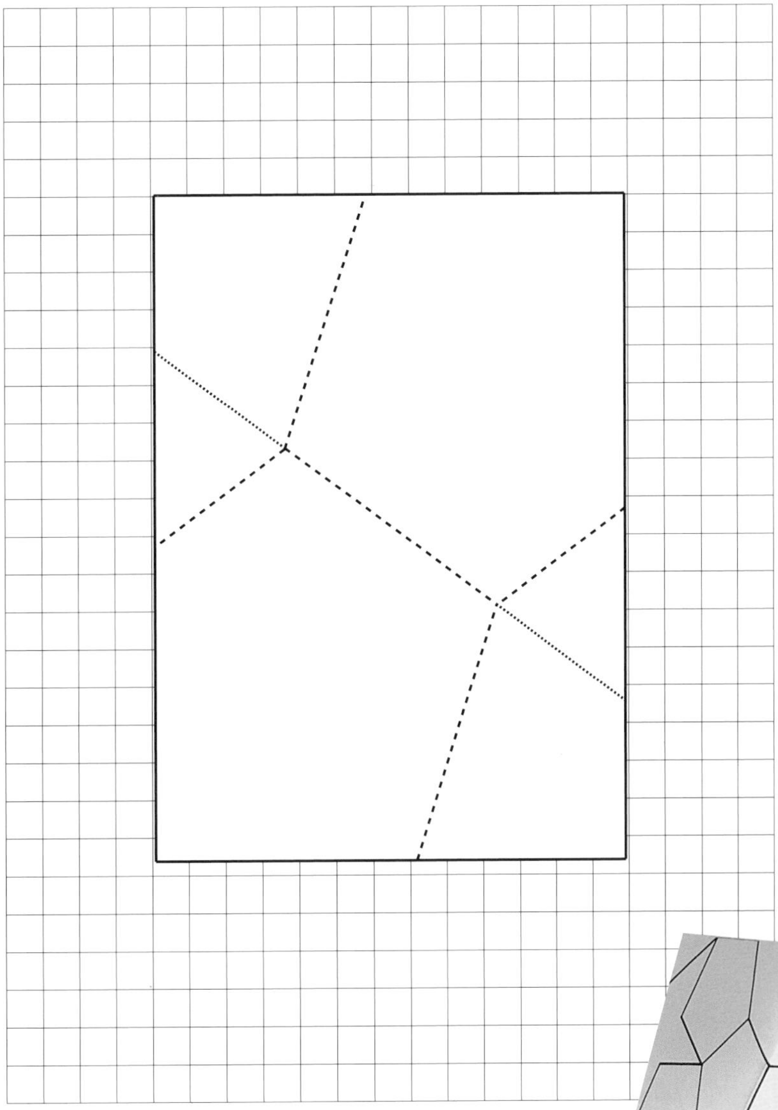

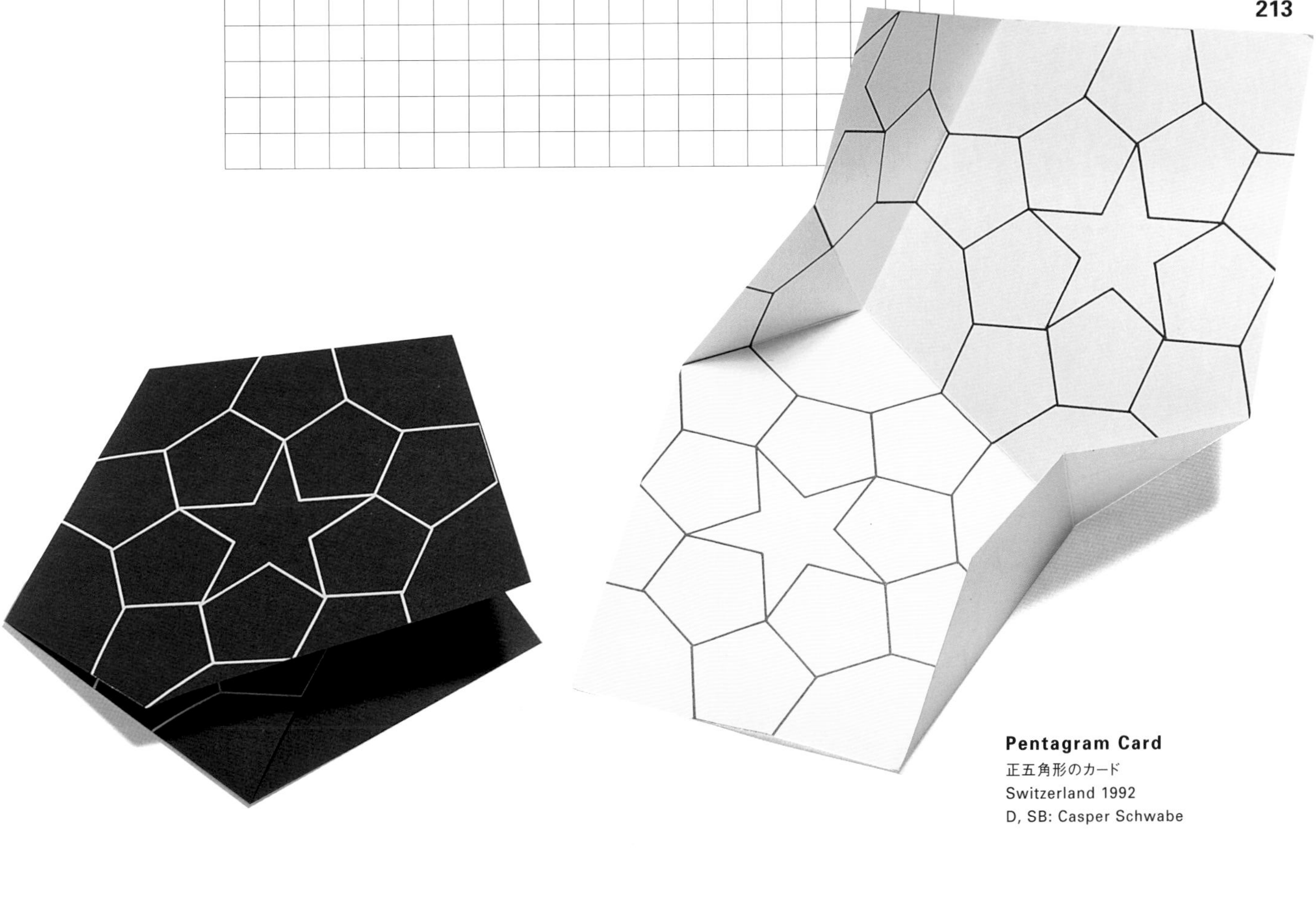

Pentagram Card
正五角形のカード
Switzerland 1992
D, SB: Casper Schwabe

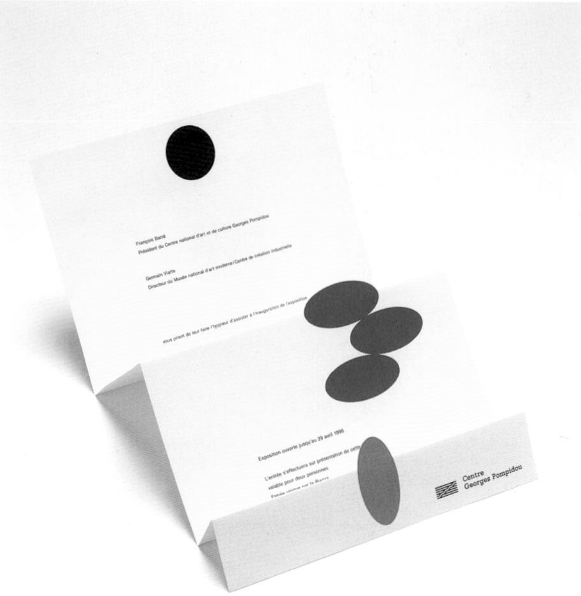

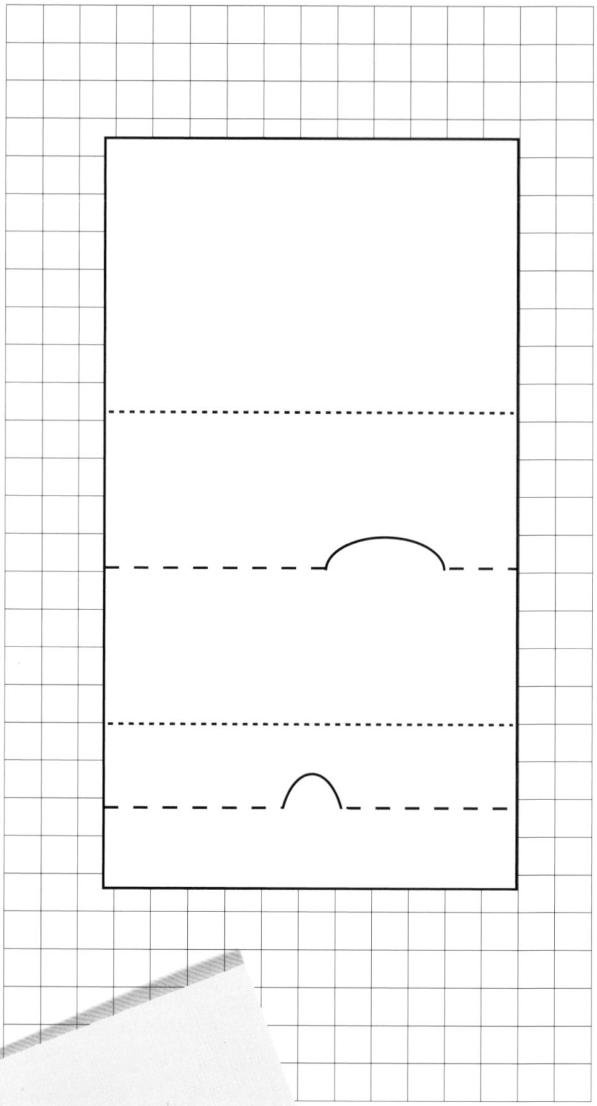

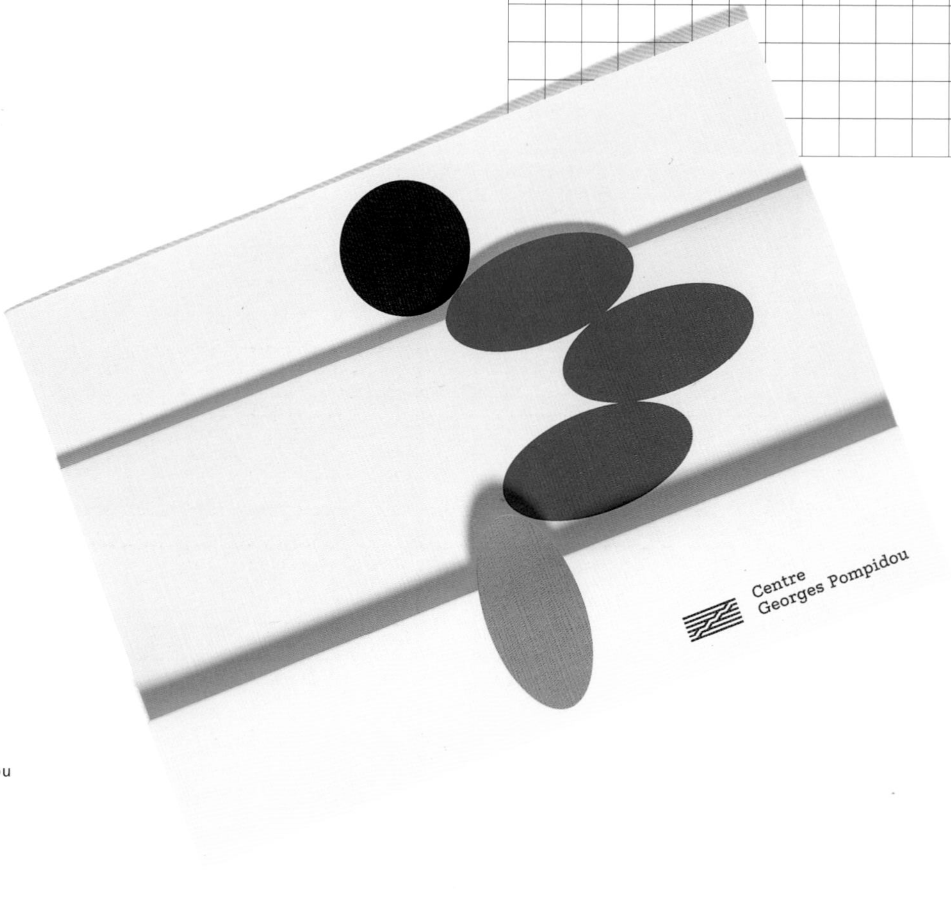

Design Japonais Invitation Card

Design Japonais展 案内状
Japan 1996
CL: Centre Georges Pompidou
AD, D: Katsumi Komagata
DF, SB: One Stroke Co., Ltd.

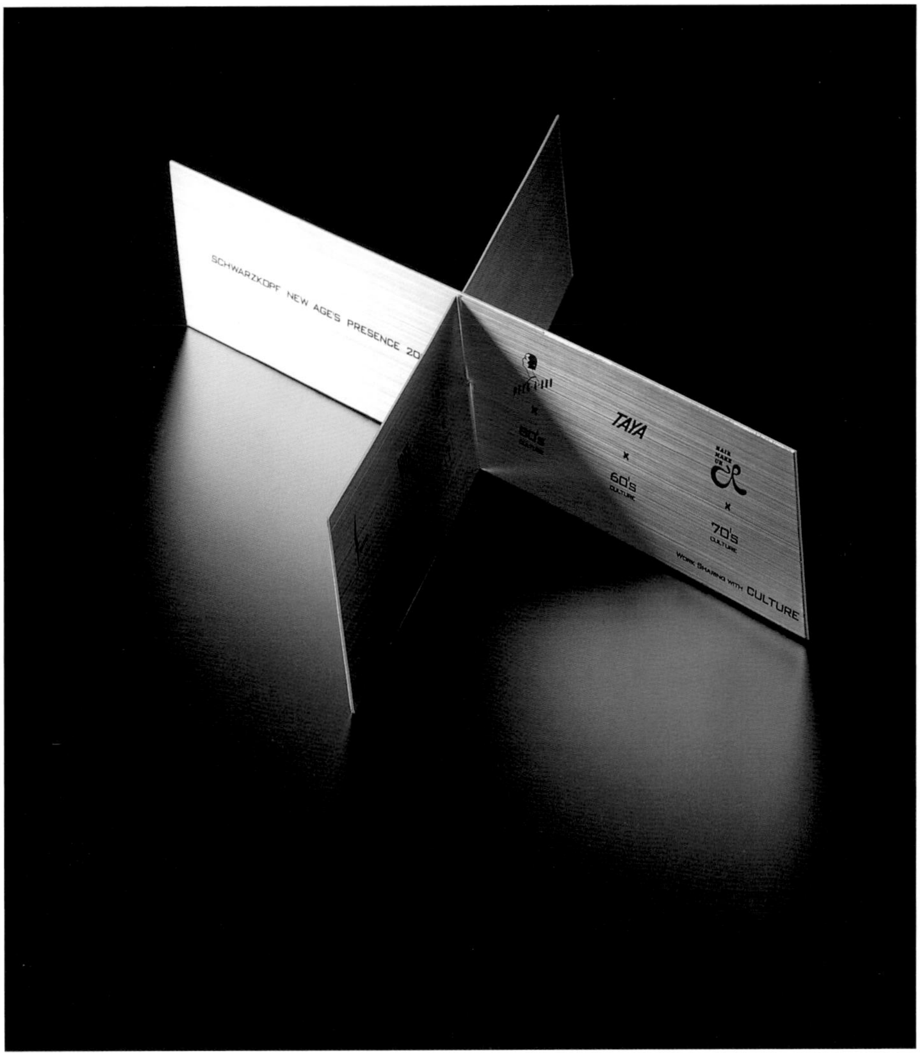

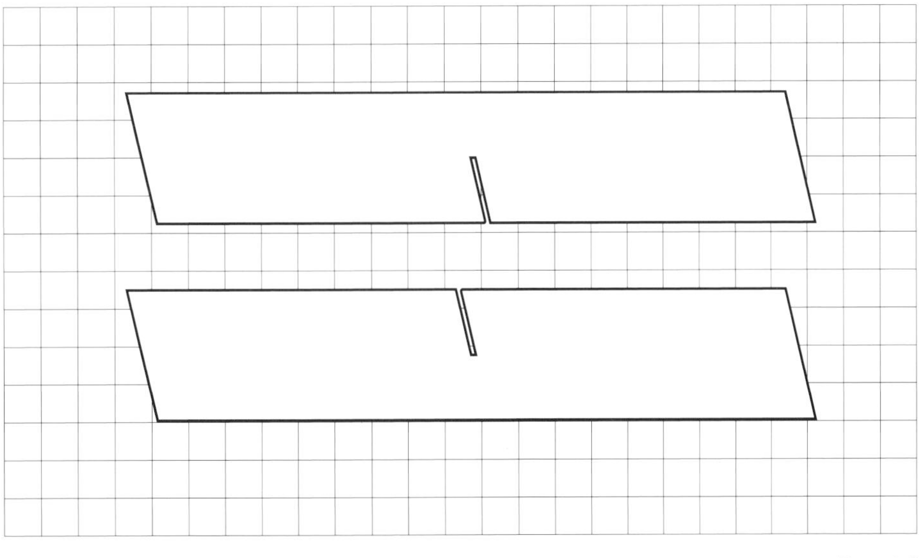

Event Announcement

イベント案内

Japan 2001

CL: Schwarzkopf K.K

AD: Michihiro Ishizaki

D: Ryo Sakamoto

P: Yoshitomo Tanaka

DF, SB: DRAFT Co., Ltd.

Flapper Promotion Tool

フラッパー プロモーションツール

Japan 2002

U.S.Patent #5759328 & Foreign Patents.

Licensed to BISOH PRINTING

CL: Kumon Educational Japan

CD, AD, D, DF: Kyodo Advertising

P: Wieden + Kennedy Tokyo

エンドレスにクルクルと紙面が変化していき、絵が変わっていく仕組みの折り。(P216-219)

The fold endlessly continues to show different pictures. (P216-219)

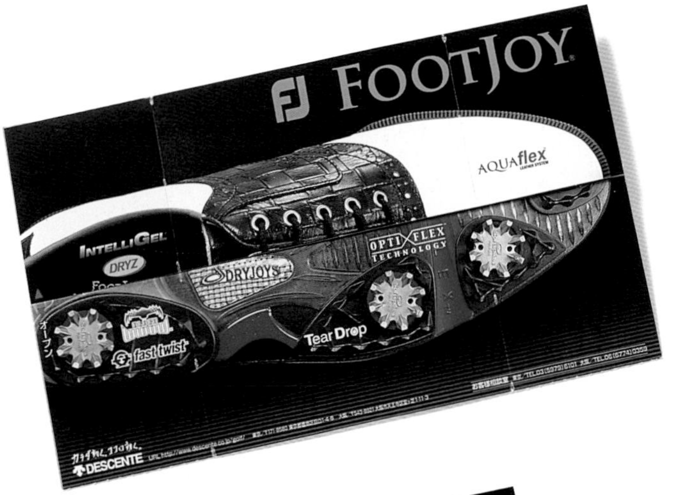

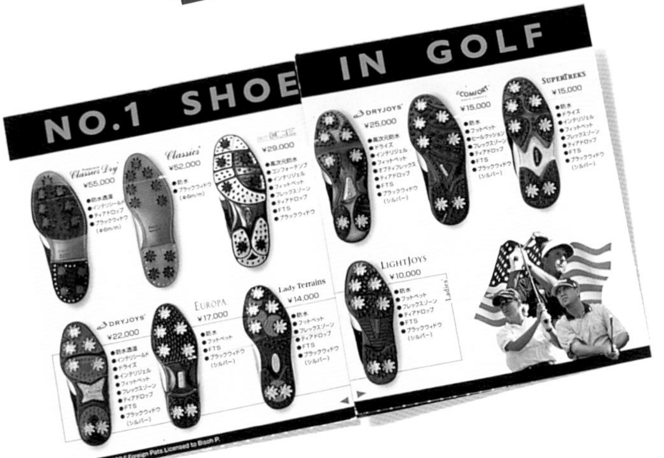

Flapper Promotion Tool
フラッパー プロモーションツール
Japan 2002
U.S.Patent #5759328 & Foreign Patents.
Licensed to BISOH PRINTING
CL: Foot Joy

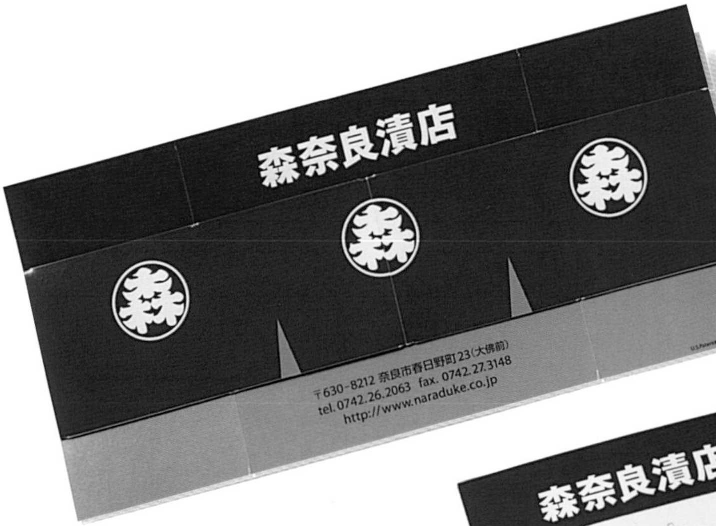

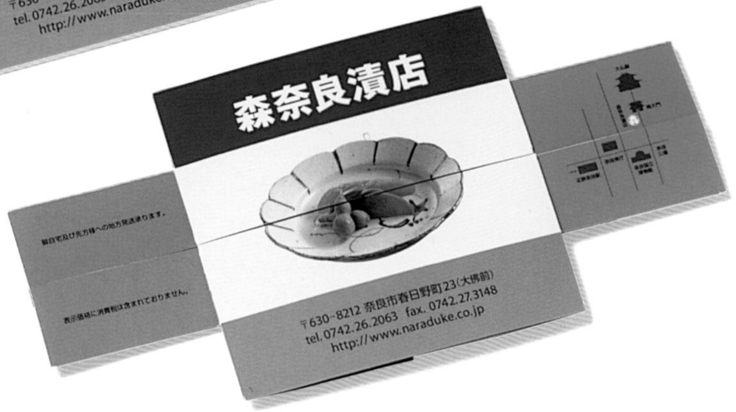

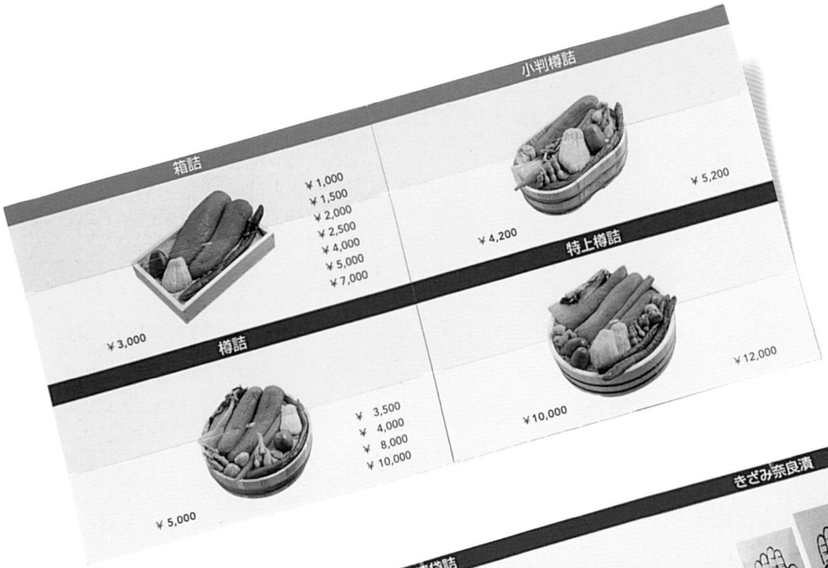

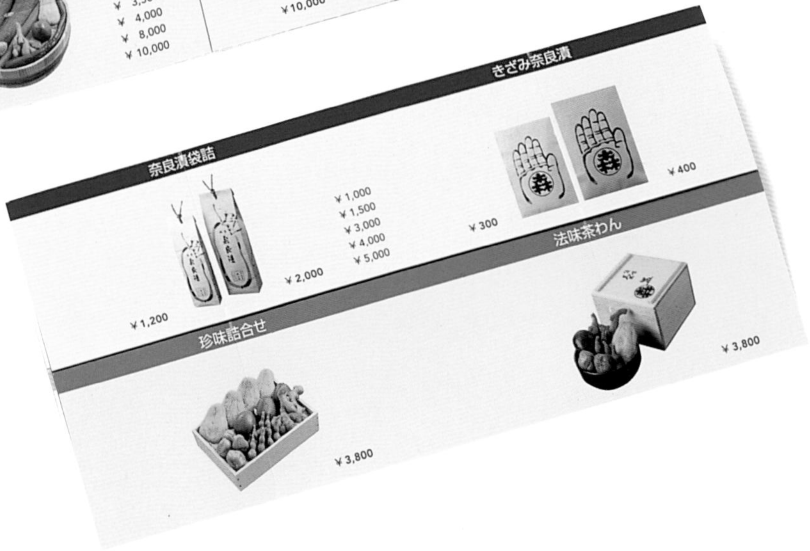

Flapper Promotion Tool

フラッパー プロモーションツール

Japan 2002

U.S.Patent #5759328 & Foreign Patents.

Licensed to BISOH PRINTING

CL: Mori Nara-Zuke

D: Masashi Katayama

DF: Tanaka Design Room

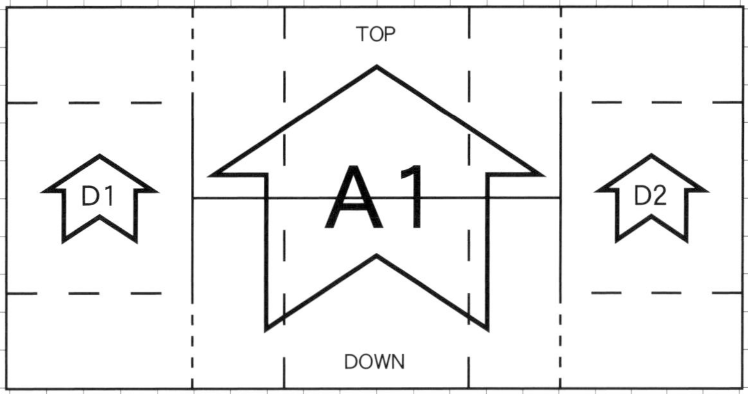
TOP
A1
D1
D2
DOWN

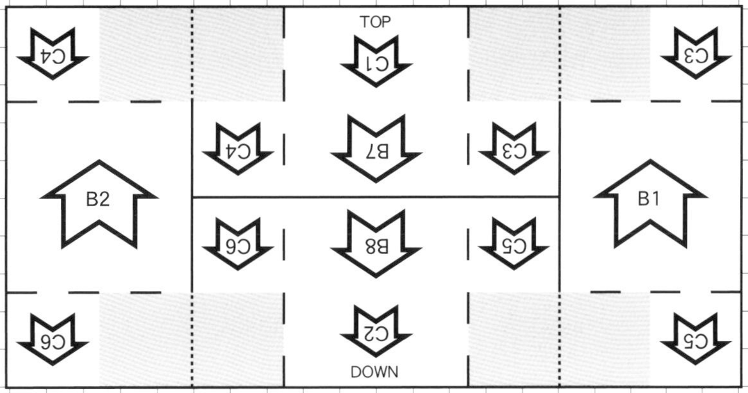
TOP
C4
C1
C3
C4
B7
C3
B2
B1
C6
B8
C5
C6
C2
C5
DOWN

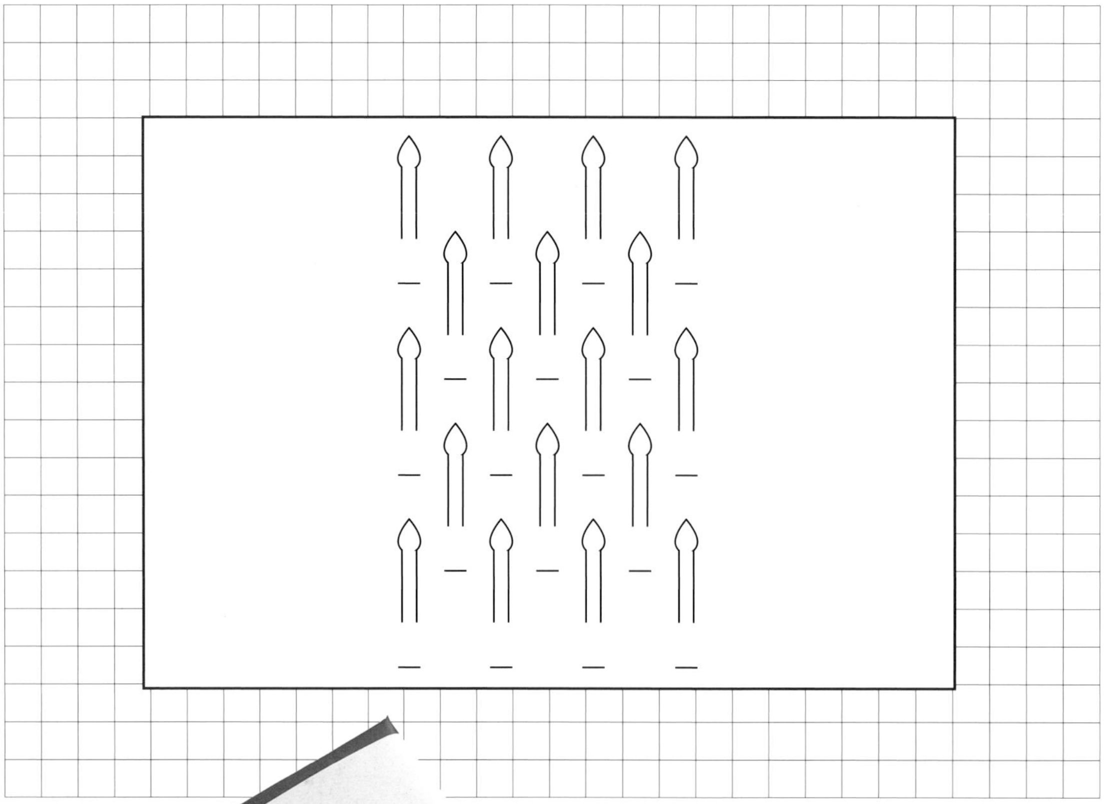

220

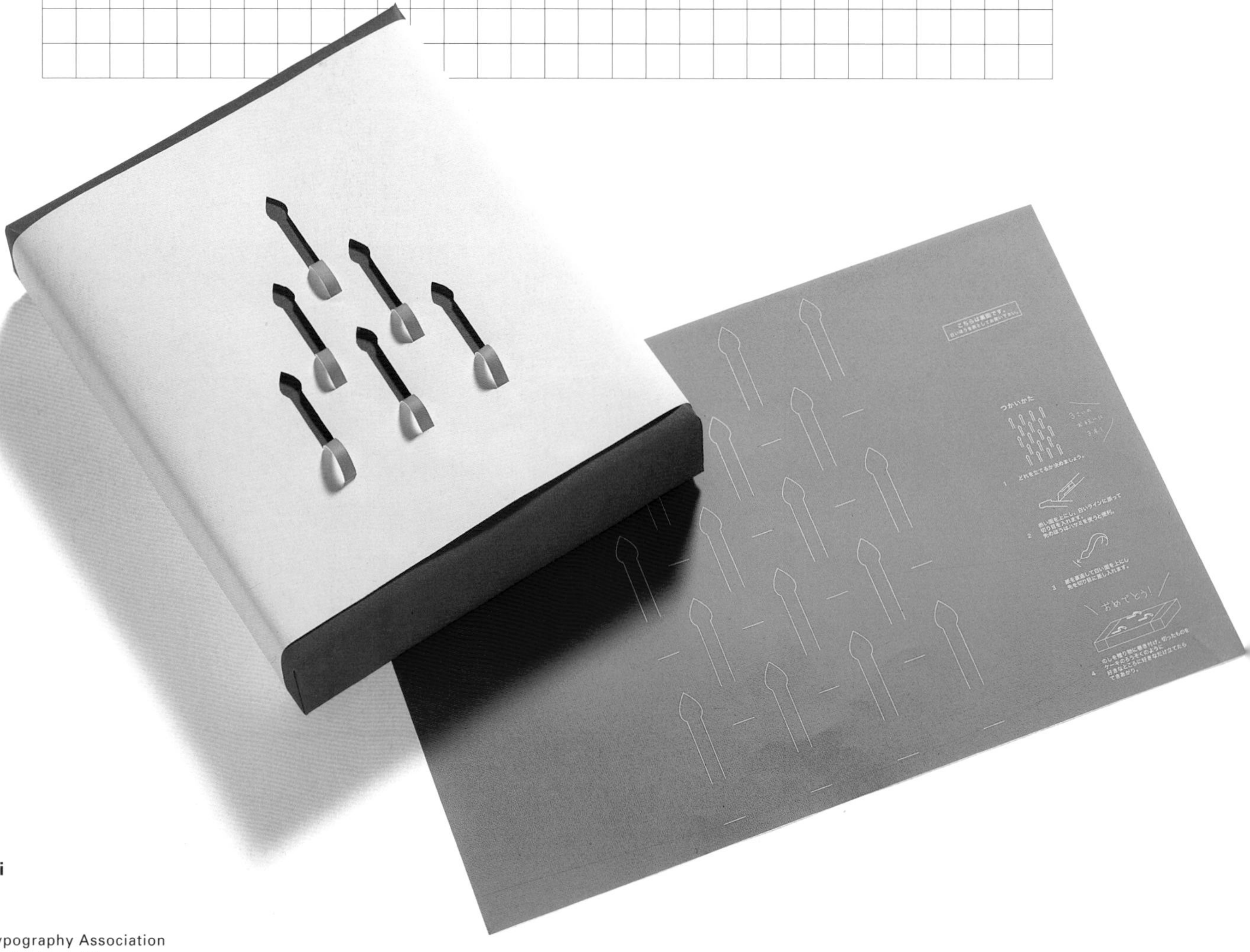

noshigami
のしがみ
Japan 2002
CL: Japan Typography Association
AD, D: Masami Takahashi
DF, SB: Masami Design

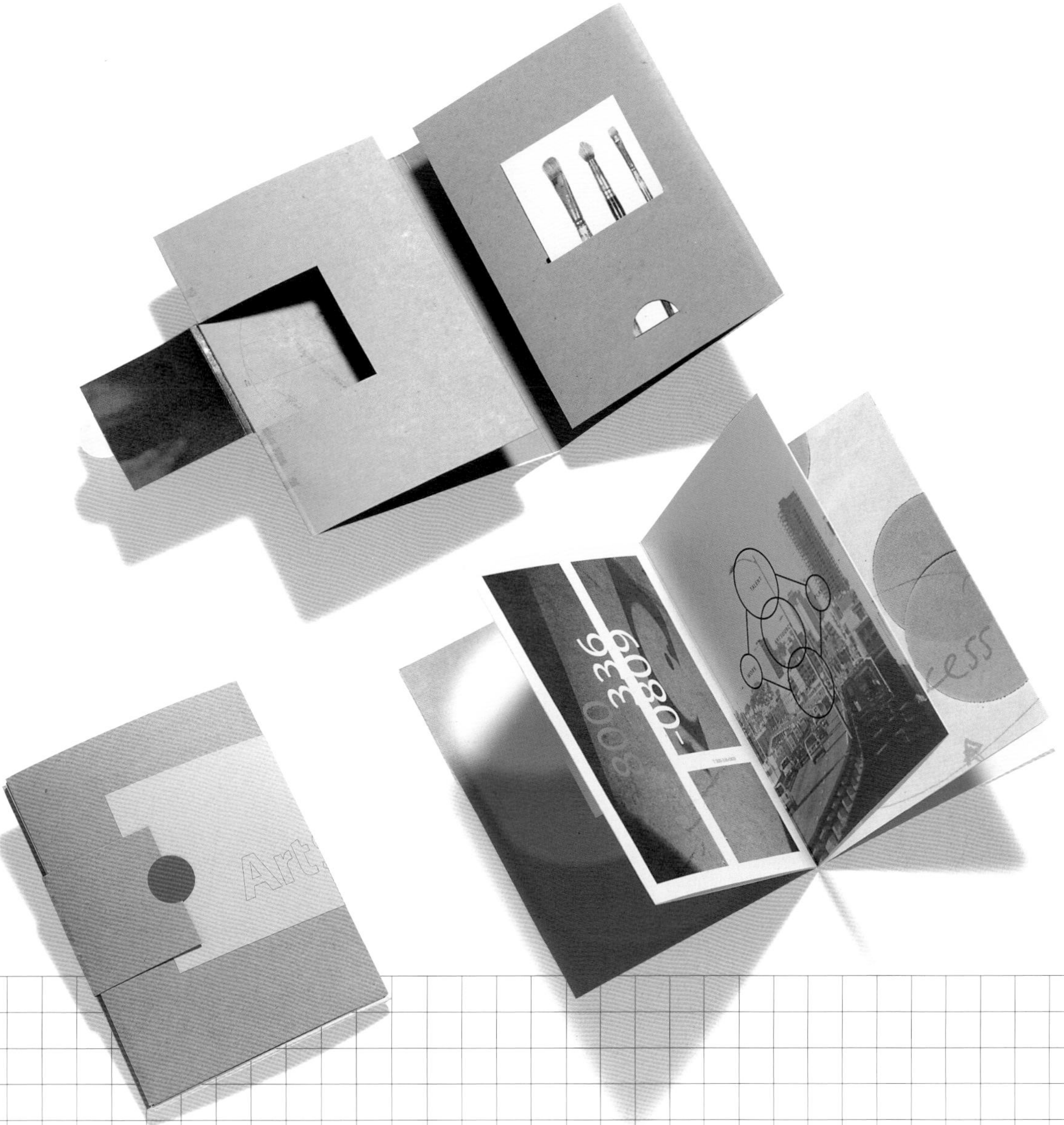

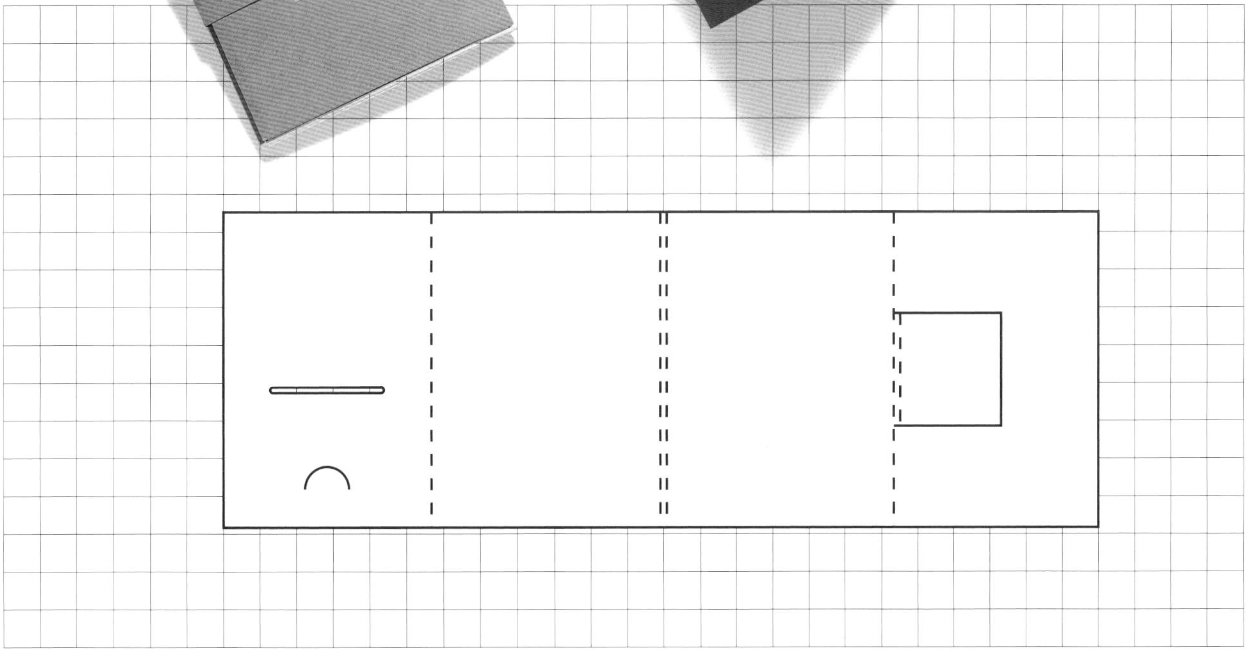

Promo DM
"Artsource Client & Talent Brochures"

人材派遣会社プロモーション用DM
USA 2001
CL: Artsource
CD, AD: Steve Barretto
D: Vanessa Dina Barlow
P: Daren Ferriera
DF, SB: Flux

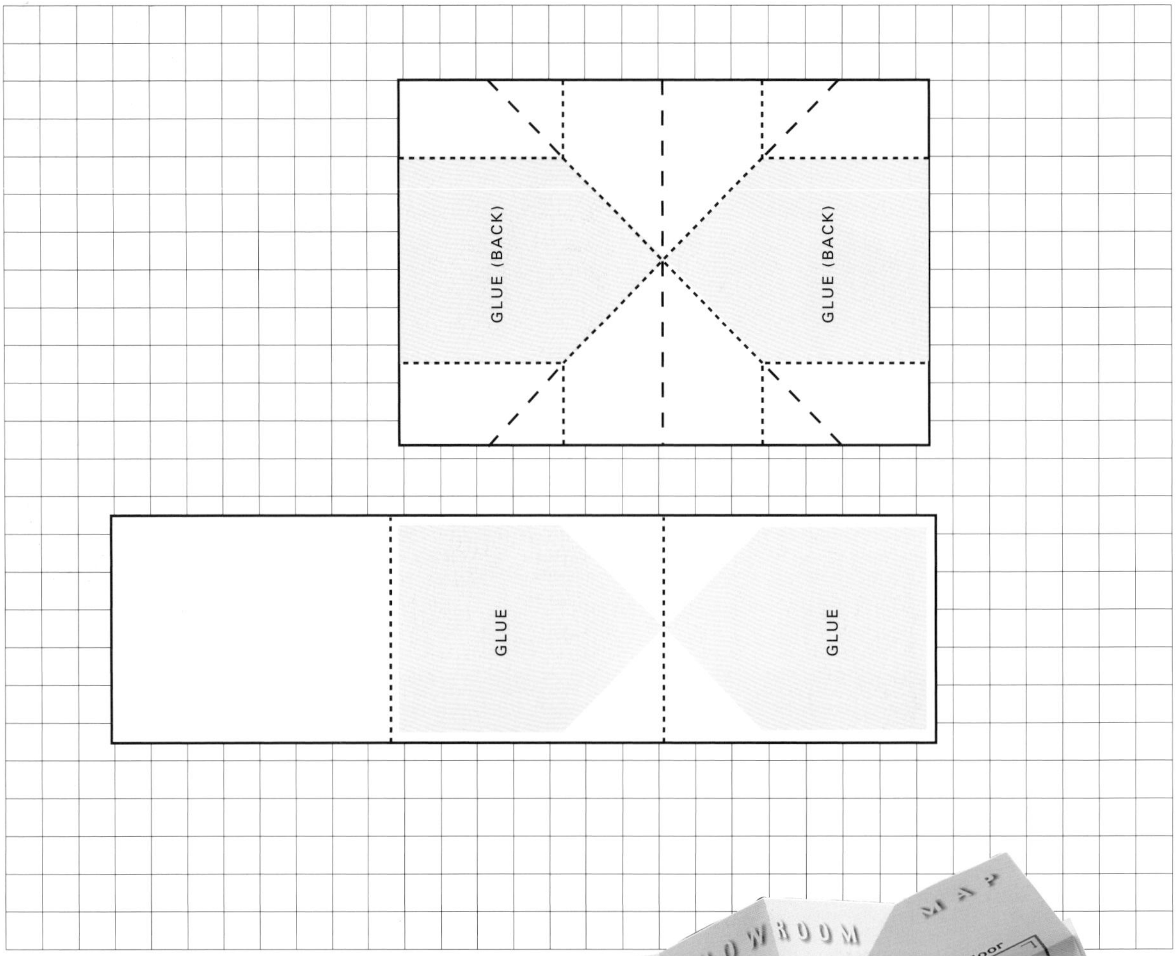

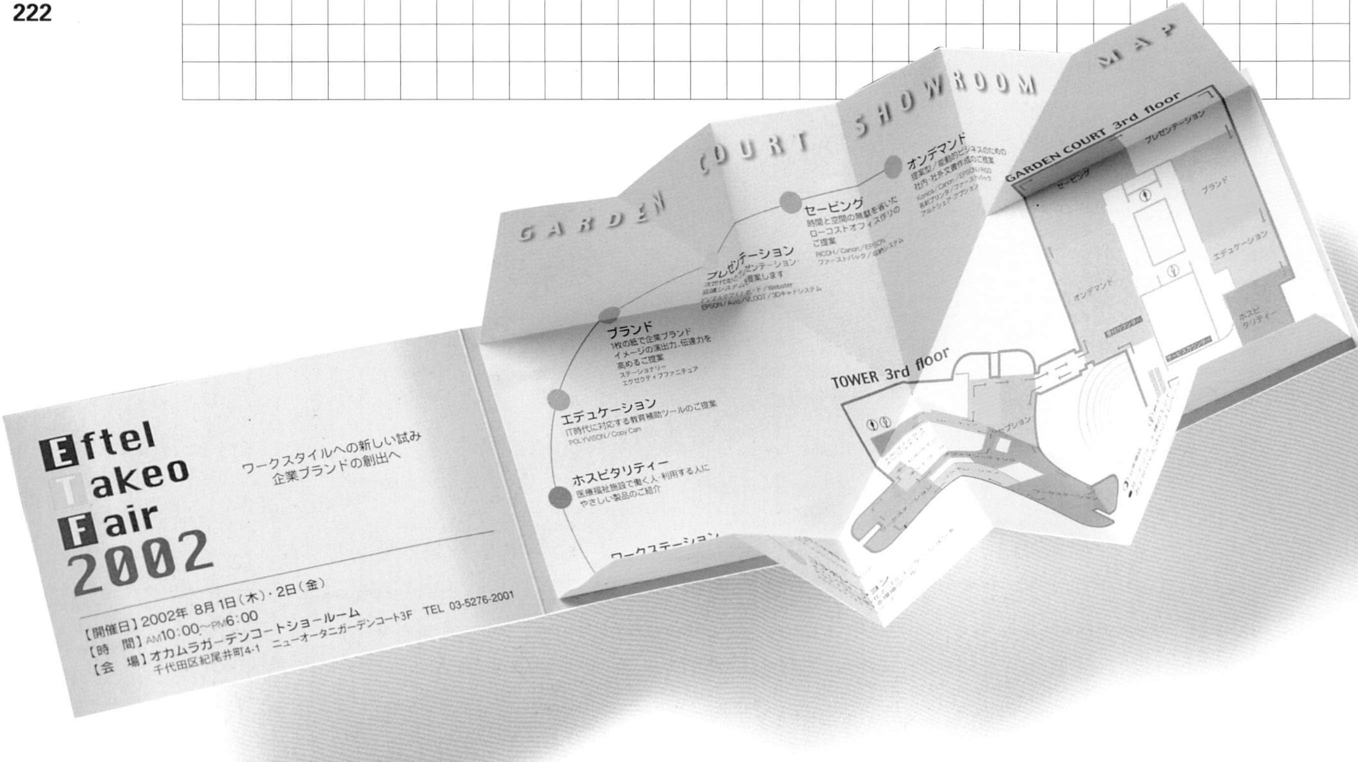

Folding Map "Takeo Fair 2002"
フォールディング マップ「エフテル竹尾フェア2002」
Japan 2002
実用新案登録3073982号
CL: Takeo
CD, AD, D: Taiga Kurihara
DF, SB: Bisoh Printing

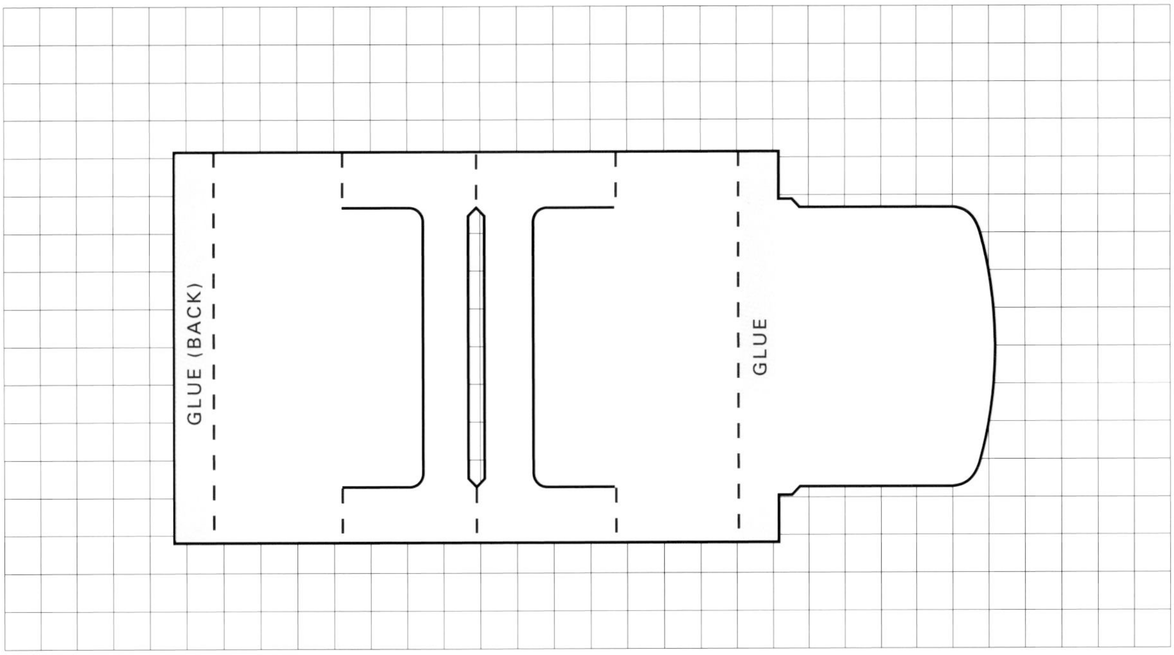

Pop Up Stand Calendar
ポップ アップ スタンド カレンダー
Japan 2002
U.S.Patent #5479732 & Foreign Patents.
Licensed to BISOH PRINTING
CL: Sanrio Co., Ltd.
CD, AD, D, DF: Sanrio Greeting Card Division

Promotional Tool - Pop Up Stand
ポップ アップ スタンド
Japan 2002
U.S.Patent #5479732 & Foreign Patents. Licensed to BISOH PRINTING
CL: Kumon Educational Japan Co., Ltd.
CD, AD, D, DF: Kyodo Advertising

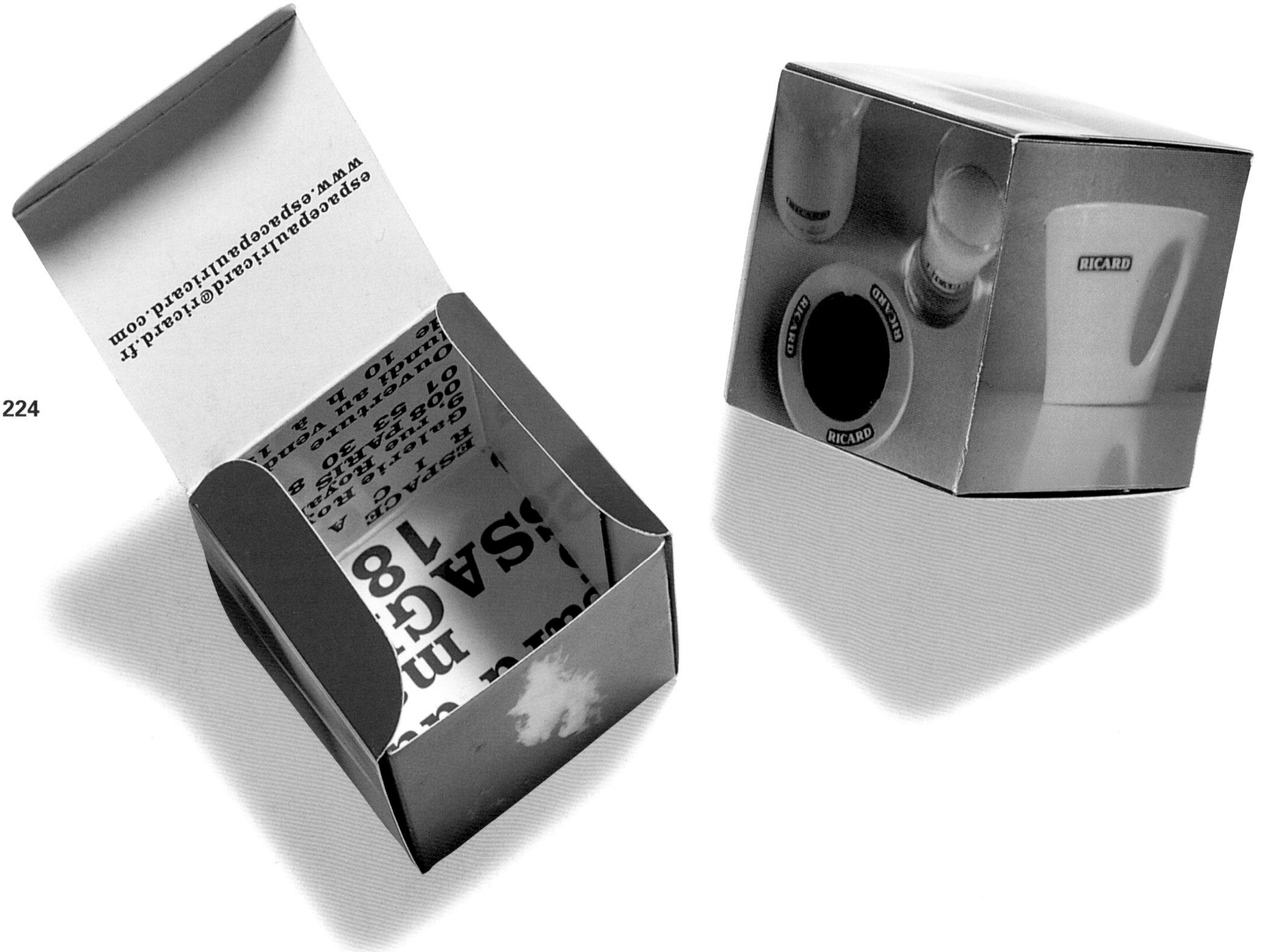

Exhibition Invitation
作品展覧会案内状
UK 2001
CL: Ricard Paris
CD, AD, D, P: Fabian Monheim
CD, AD, D: Sophia Wood

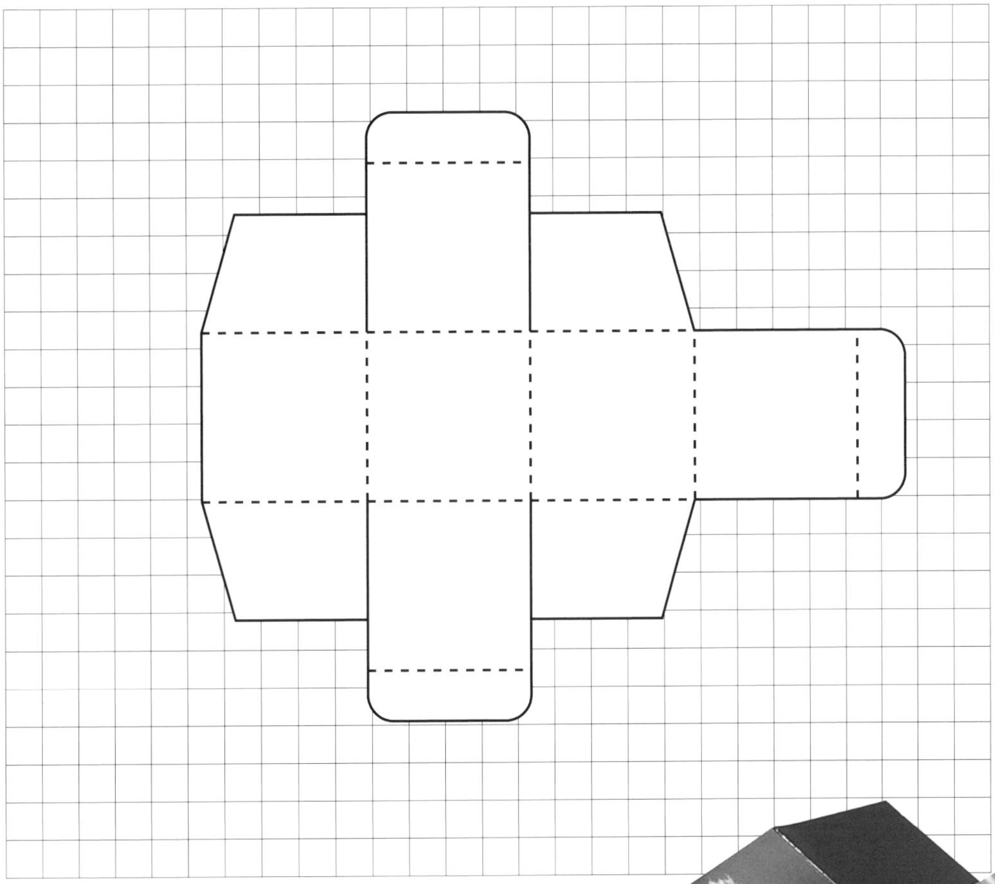

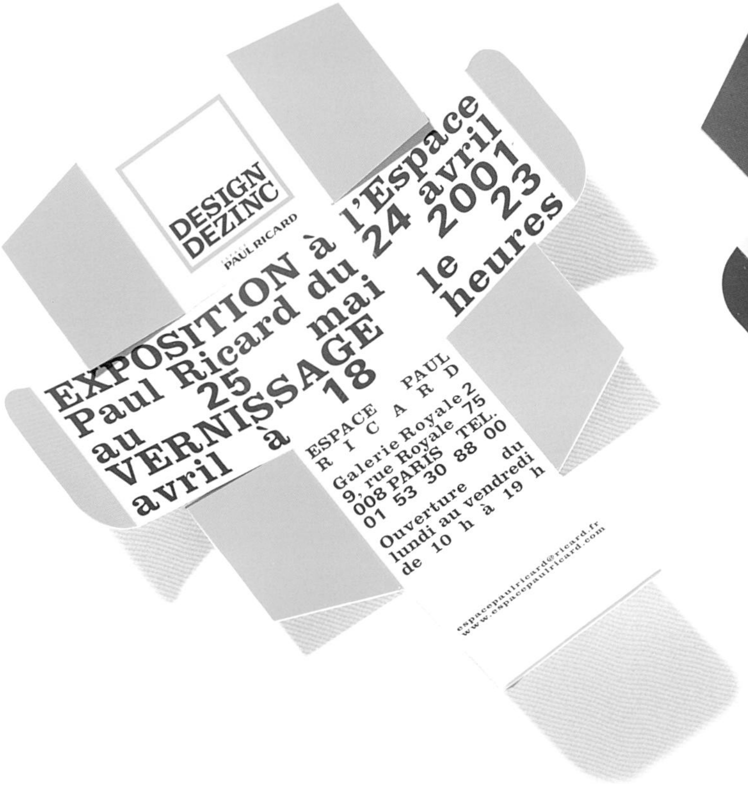
DESIGN
DEZINC
PAUL RICARD
EXPOSITION à l'Espace
Paul Ricard du 24 avril
au 25 mai 2001
VERNISSAGE le 23
avril à 18 heures
ESPACE PAUL
R I C A R D
Galerie Royale 2
9, rue Royale 75
008 PARIS TEL.
01 53 30 88 00
Ouverture du
lundi au vendredi
de 10 h à 19 h
espacepaulricard@ricard.fr
www.espacepaulricard.com

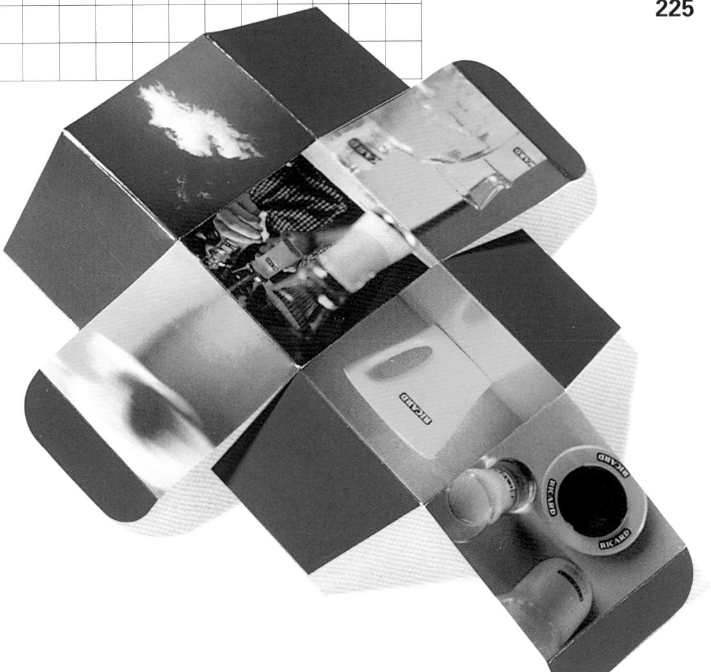
RICARD

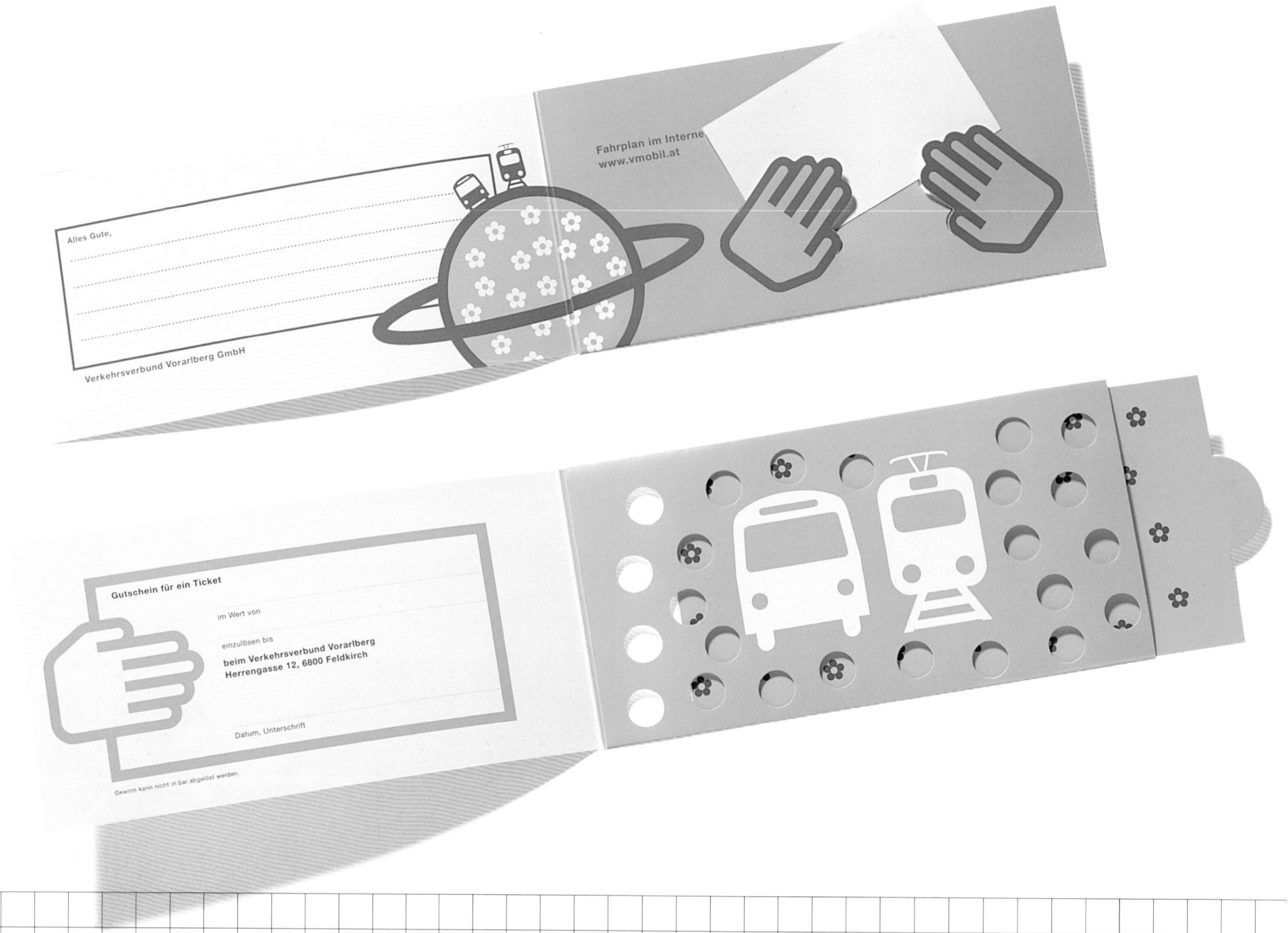

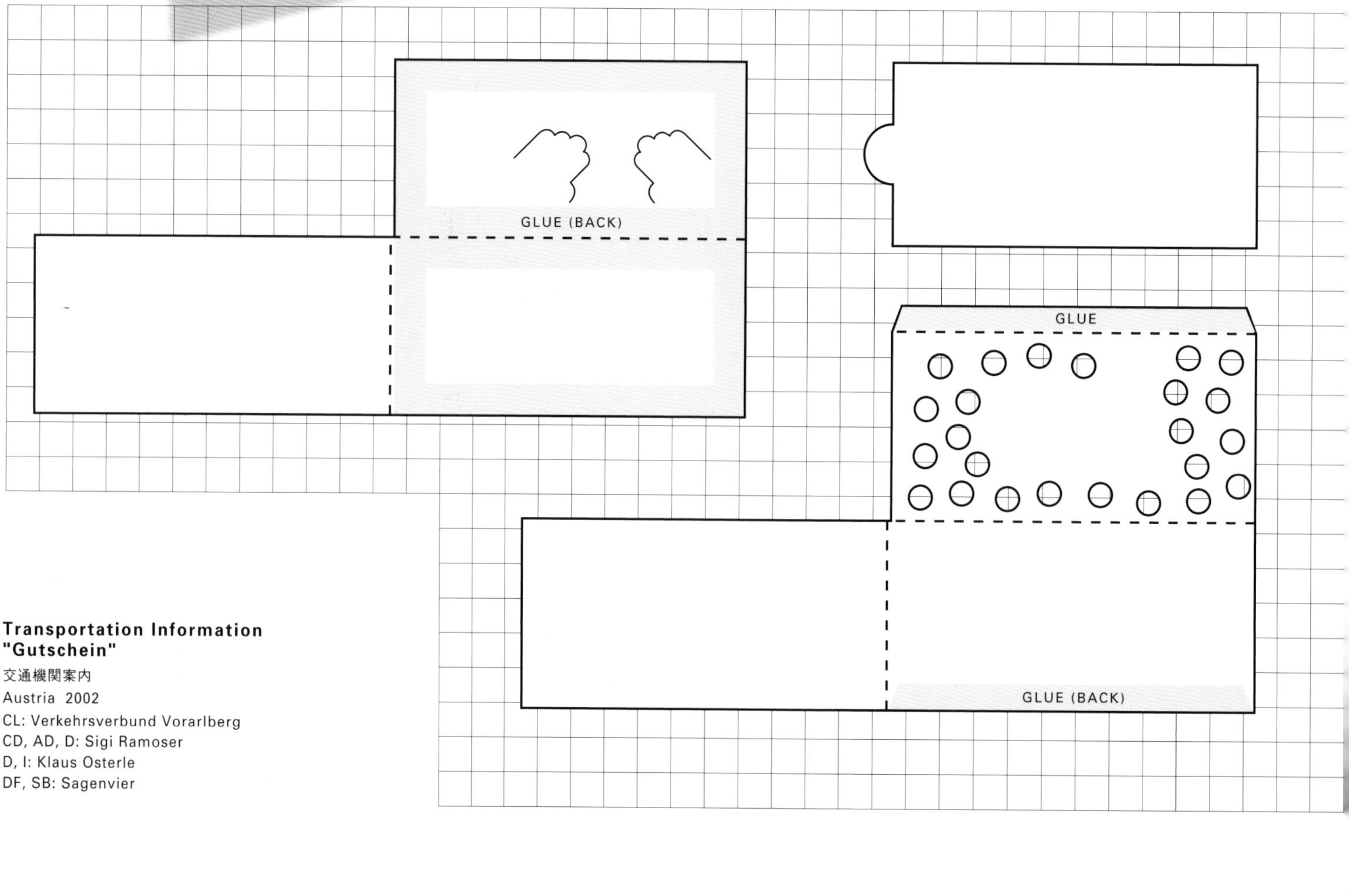

Transportation Information "Gutschein"

交通機関案内

Austria 2002

CL: Verkehrsverbund Vorarlberg

CD, AD, D: Sigi Ramoser

D, I: Klaus Osterle

DF, SB: Sagenvier

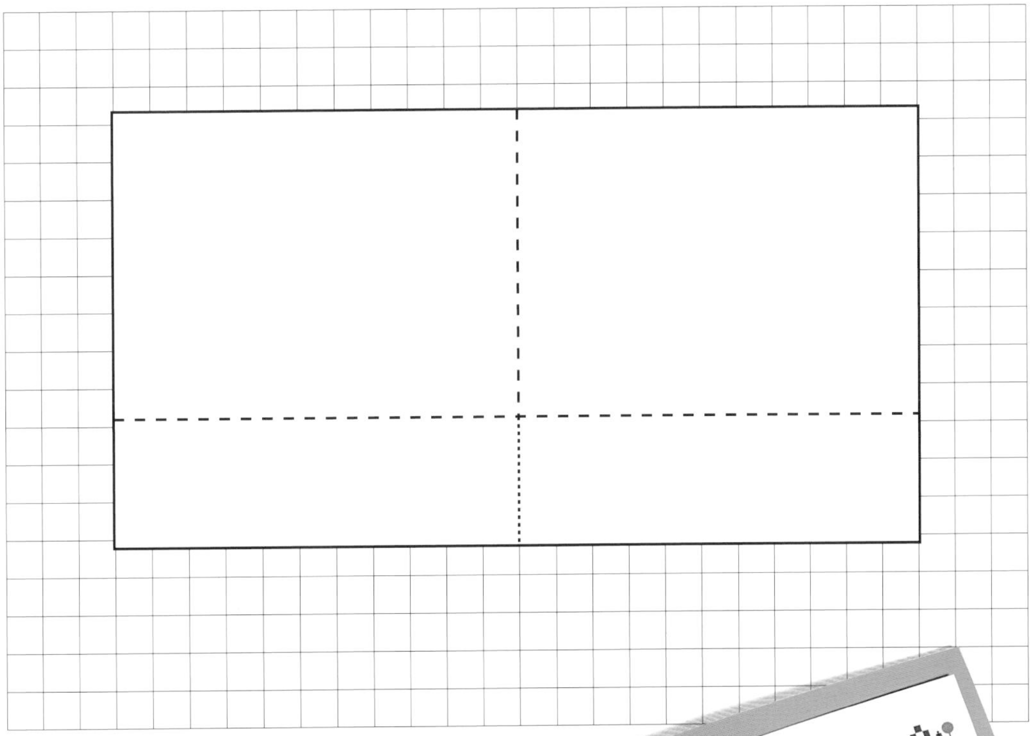

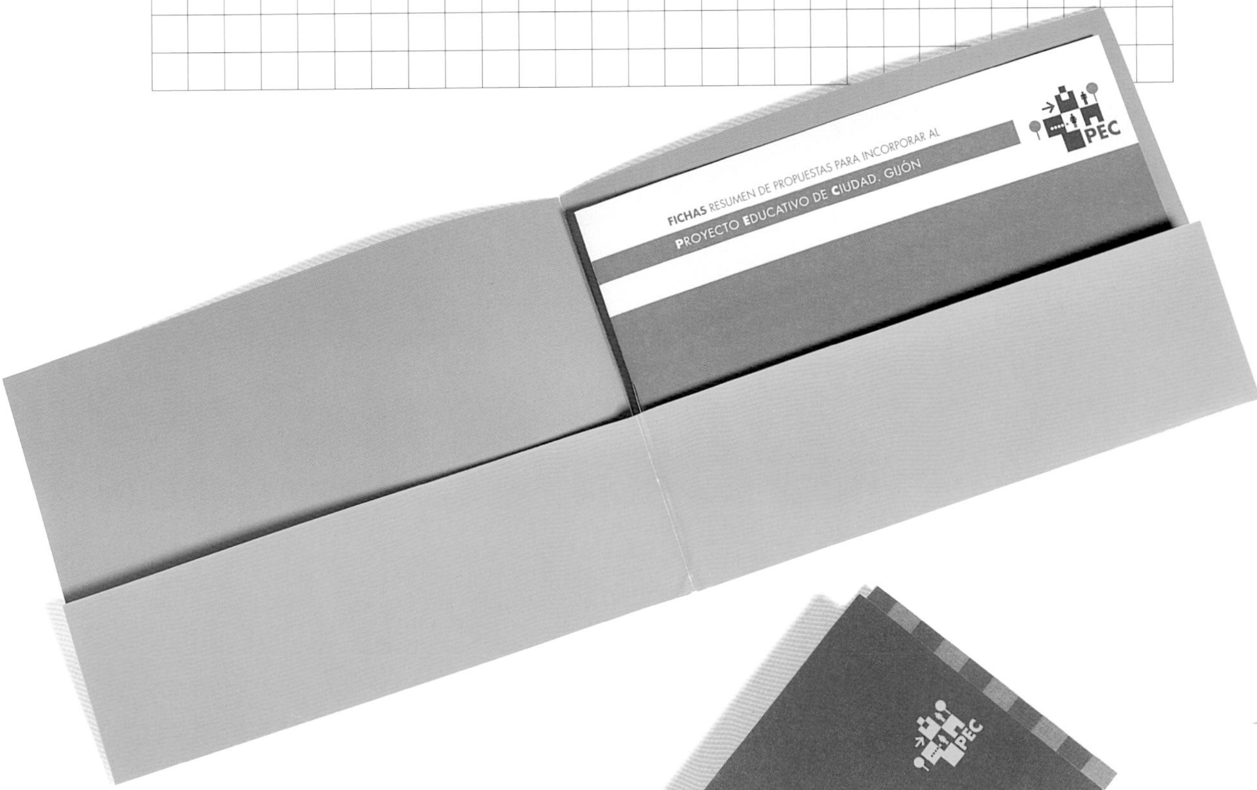

FICHAS RESUMEN DE PROPUESTAS PARA INCORPORAR AL
PROYECTO EDUCATIVO DE CIUDAD. GIJÓN
PEC

Organization Promotion Kit
慈善団体プロモーション用キット
Brazil
DF, SB: Santamarina Disenadores

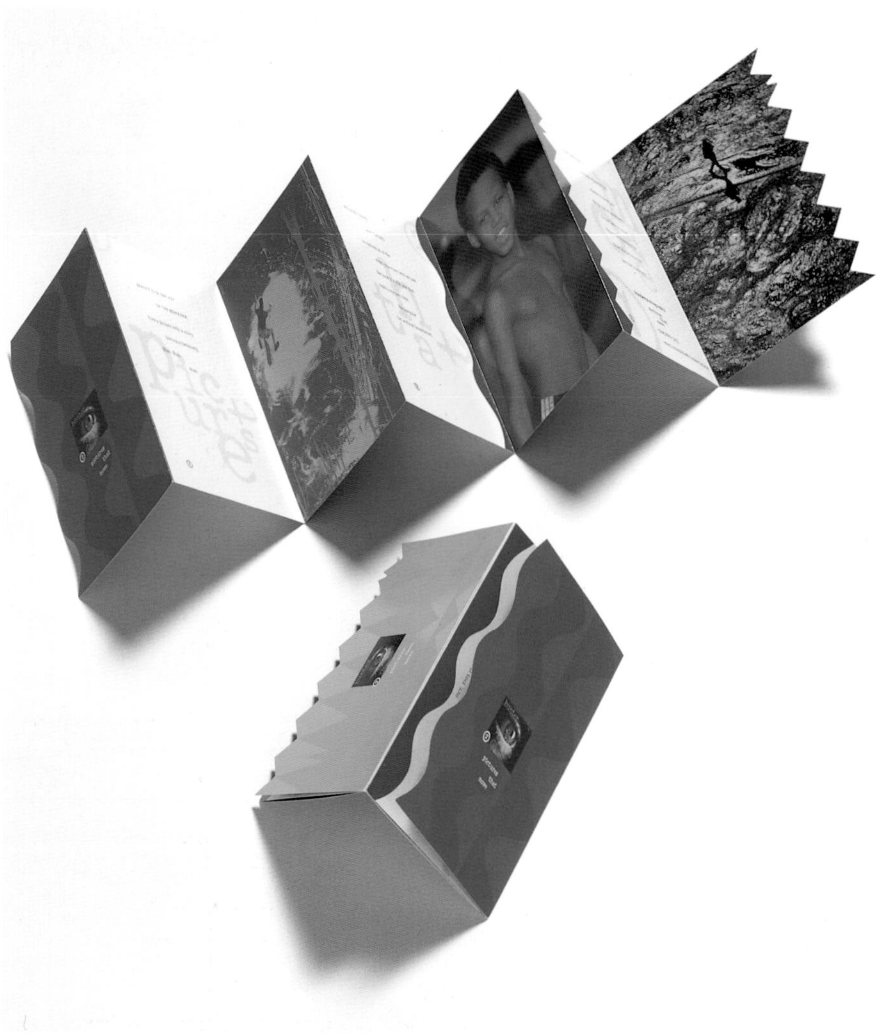

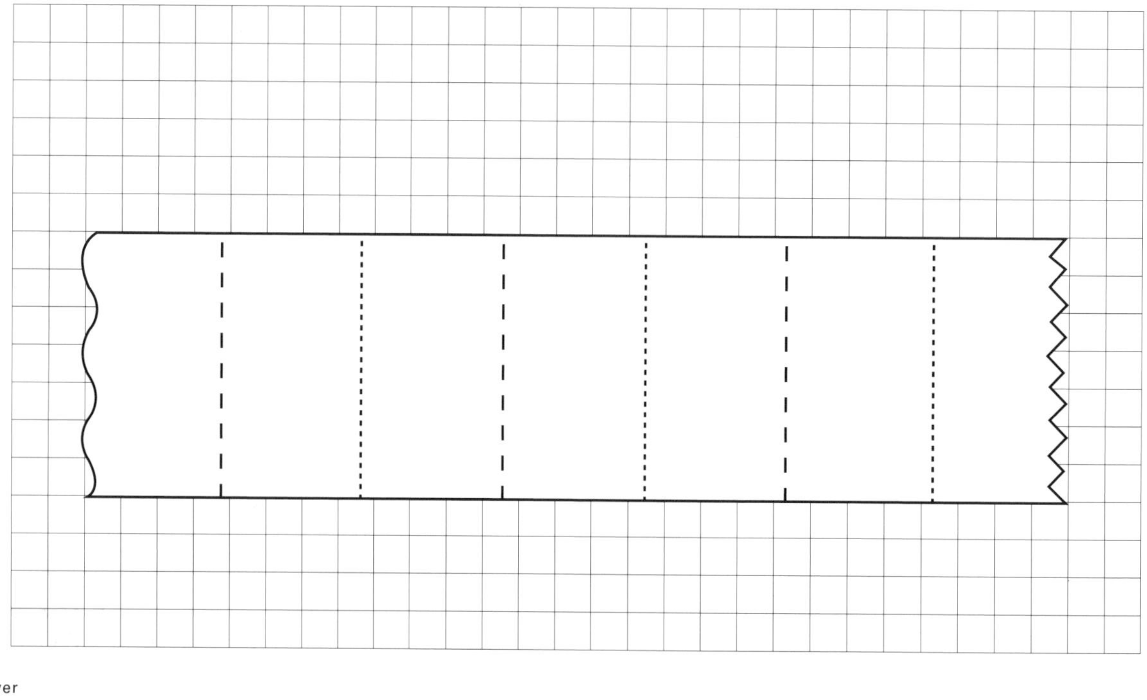

Invitation
展示会案内状
USA
AD, D: Marie Weaver
DF, SB: Weaver Design

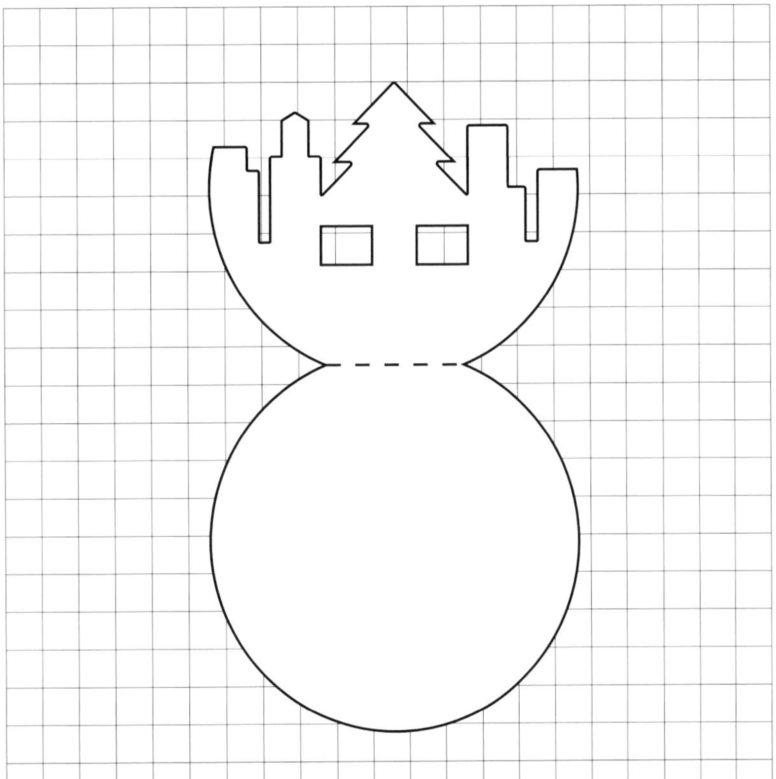

Christmas & New Year Card

クリスマス・新年挨拶状

Japan 1997

CL: Be International Corporation

D: Akihiko Tsukamoto

DF, SB: Design Club

Pop-Up Tree

美術館ギフトカード

USA 2002

CL: Museum of Modern Art, New York City

CD: Ashley White

D, I, SB: Robert Sabuda

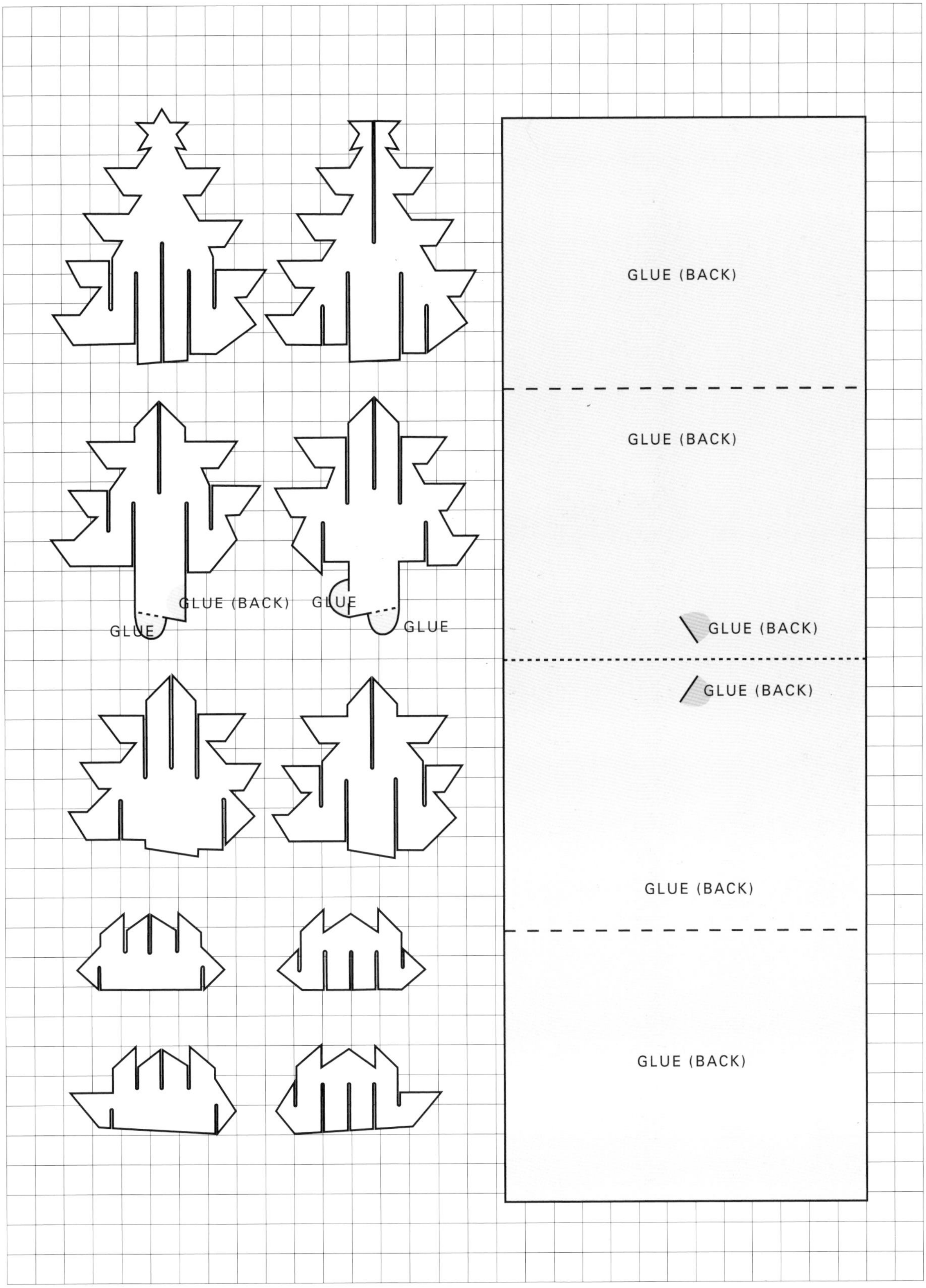
GLUE (BACK)
GLUE (BACK)
GLUE (BACK)
GLUE
GLUE
GLUE
GLUE (BACK)
GLUE (BACK)
GLUE (BACK)
GLUE (BACK)

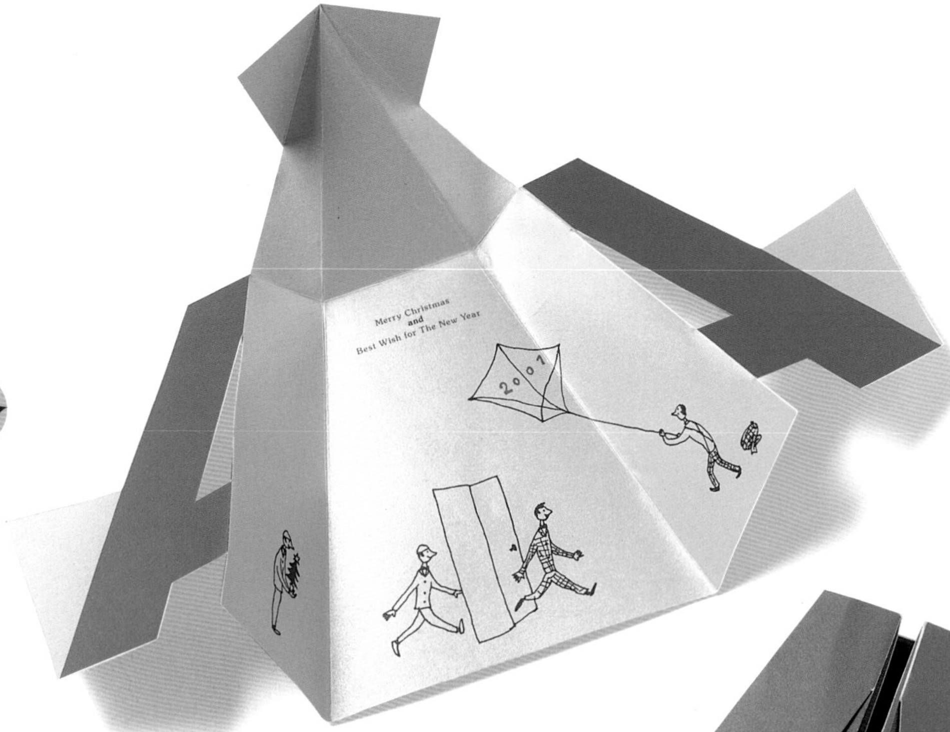

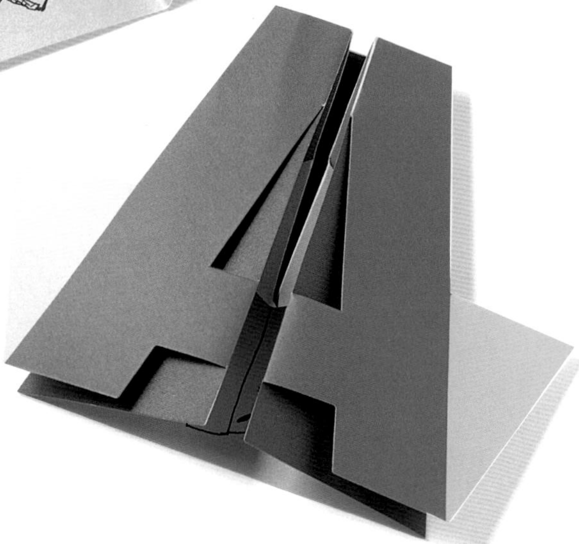

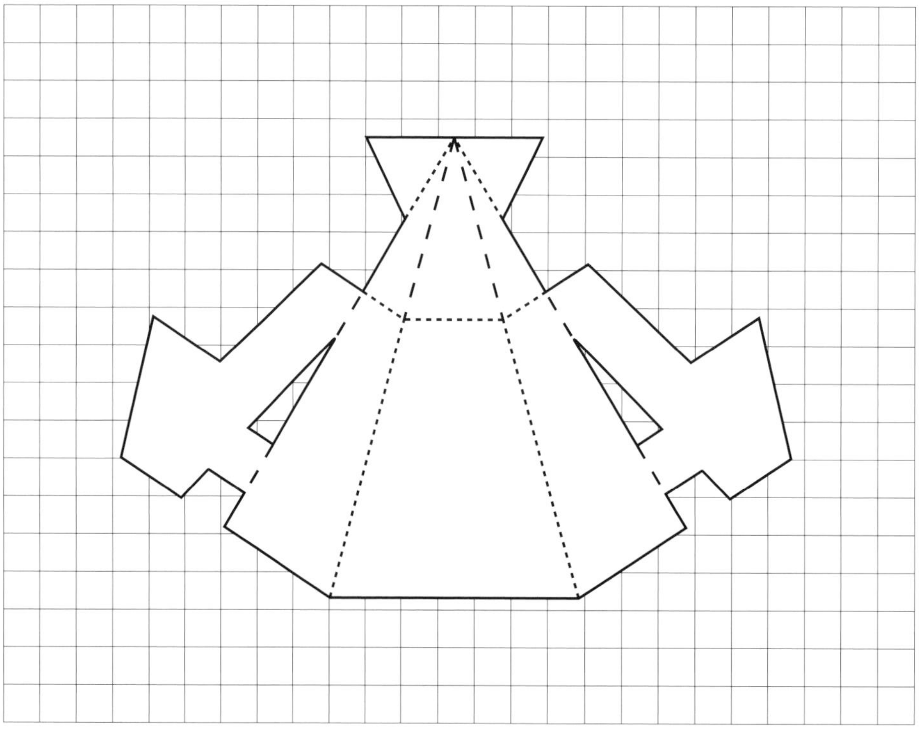

Christmas & New Year Card
クリスマス・新年挨拶状
Japan 2000
CL: Arjo Wiggins Canson KK
CD: Hiromi Ouchi
AD, D: Akihiko Tsukamoto
I: Yukari Miyagi
DF, SB: Design Club

SUBMITTORS' INDEX

Special thanks to the following submittor for submitting
their wonderful works in producing this book.

今回、本書の作成にあたり、以下の方々のご協力をいただきました。
本当にありがとうございました。

FOLDING

NEW ENCYCLOPEDIA OF **PAPER-FOLDING DESIGNS**
折り方大全集

Art Direction & Design
Natsumi Akabane
赤羽なつみ

Classification of the folds
Miyuki Yoshida
吉田美幸

Photographer
Kuniharu Fujimoto
藤本邦治

Classification Coordinator
Maya Kishida
岸田麻矢

Design Cooperation
Mika Ozawa
小澤美香

Editor
Ken Ozawa
小澤研太郎

Publisher
Shingo Miyoshi
三芳伸吾

2003年6月18日 初版第1刷発行

印刷・製本 (株)サンニチ印刷

定価 本体7,800円+税

発行所 ピエ・ブックス
〒170-0005 東京都豊島区南大塚2-32-4
編集 TEL：03-5395-4820 FAX：03-5395-4821 e-mail：editor@piebooks.com
営業 TEL：03-5395-4811 FAX：03-5395-4812 e-mail：sales@piebooks.com
HP：http://www.piebooks.com

ISBN4-89444-271-X

Printed in Japan

THE PIE COLLECTION

ADVERTISING PHOTOGRAPHY IN JAPAN 2002
年鑑 日本の広告写真2002

Pages: 240 (Full Color) ¥14,500+Tax

気鋭の広告写真をそろえた（社）日本広告写真家協会（APA）の監修による本年鑑は、日本の広告界における最新のトレンドと、その証言者たる作品を一堂に見られる貴重な資料として、国内外の広告に携わる方にとって欠かせない存在です。

A spirited collection of works compiled under the editorial supervision of the Japan Advertising Photographers' Association (APA) representing the freshest talent in the Japanese advertising world. An indispensable reference for anyone concerned with advertising in or outside Japan.

THE TOKYO TYPE DIRECTORS CLUB ANNUAL 2002
TDC年鑑 '02

Pages: 252 (Full Color) ¥15,000+Tax

温故知新の精神を大切にしながら、更に新しい次世代のタイポグラフィー＆タイポディレクション作品を探究する国際グラフィックデザイン・コンペティション「TDC」。インタラクティブ作品も拡充、より幅広いメディアの優れた作品を紹介しています。

JTDC—the international graphic design competition that investigates new generations of typography and type direction in light of masterpieces from the past. With the inclusion of interactive pieces in recent years, the 2002 annual presents outstanding works from an extensive range of media.

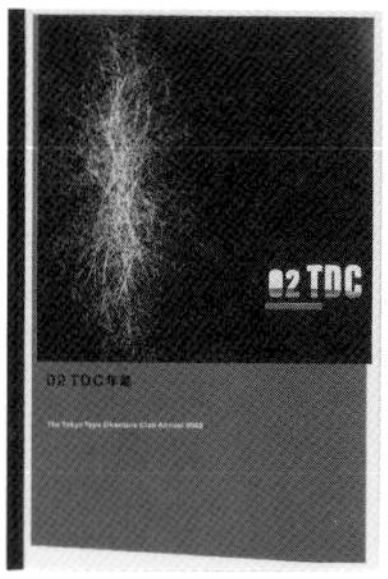

DIRECT MAIL ON TARGET
PR効果の高いDMデザイン

Pages: 224 (Full Color) ¥14,000+Tax

「送り手の思いを届ける」をコンセプトに、素材感を生かした作品、また封を切ったときの驚きや喜びを味わう作品など、イメージを消費者に訴えるダイレクトメールの数々を特集！新しく柔軟な発想が求められるDM制作にかかせない一冊です。

600 direct mail pieces designed to "deliver the intended message." This collection presents a wide variety of impression-making direct mailers that exploit the qualities of the materials they are made of, and surprise and delight their recipients upon opening. A must for anyone interested in creating new and uniquely conceived direct mail.

PRESENTATION GRAPHICS 2
プレゼンテーション グラフィックス 2

Pages: 224 (Full Color) ¥15,000+Tax

好評の前作をより充実させた続編。世界12カ国40名以上のクリエイターによるデザイン制作の発想からプレゼンテーション、完成までの特集。話題作品のアイデアスケッチをはじめ、今まで見ることのできなかった制作の裏側を紹介した貴重な1冊。

The sequel of our popular first edition. More than 40 creators from 12 countries illustrate the complete presentation process, from initial idea sketches and to polished comps. This unique, invaluable book shows aspects of the design world that rarely reach public domain.

CHARACTER WORLD
キャラクター ワールド

Pages: 232 (Full Color) ¥14,000+Tax

企業、団体、商品、イベントなどのPRに使用されたイメージキャラクターとシンボルマークを特集。基本的に収録作品は広告、ノベルティグッズ、パッケージなどの使用例と、キャラクター・プロフィール、制作コンセプトもあわせて紹介しています。

A special collection of image characters and symbol marks designed for use as PR tools for companies, organizations, products, and events. In addition to advertisements, novelties, packaging, and other actual examples of their applications, the works showcased are accompanied by design objective descriptions and character profiles.

TRAVEL & LEISURE GRAPHICS 2
トラベル＆レジャー グラフィックス 2

Pages: 224 (Full Color) ¥15,000+Tax

ホテル、旅館、観光地、交通機関からアミューズメント施設までのグラフィックス約350点を一挙掲載！！パンフレットを中心にポスター、DM、カードなど…現地へ行かなければ入手困難な作品も含め紹介。資料としてそろえておきたい１冊です！

A richly varied selection of 350 samples of travel and leisure guide graphics. The collection conveniently presents tour information, sightseeing guides, posters, promotional pamphlets from airline, railroad companies, hotels, inns, facilities, and more. Pick up this one-volume reference, and have it all at your fingertrips without having to leave your seat, let alone leave town!

TYPOGRAPHIC COMPOSITION IN JAPAN
日本の文字組・表組 デザイン

Pages: 224 (Full Color) ¥14,000+Tax

日本語はタテ組もヨコ組も可能であり、使用される文字も多様性に富んでいます。本書は会社案内、PR誌、カタログ、雑誌…などの媒体から優れた日本語の文字組・表組のレイアウトを目次、本文レイアウト、表組のカテゴリー別に紹介します。

Japanese can be composed horizontally or vertically, using a variety of characters and syllabaries. This book presents outstanding examples of Japanese typography and tabulated data from media such as company profiles, PR brochures, catalogs, and magazines, categorized as: Table of Contents, Main Text, and Tables.

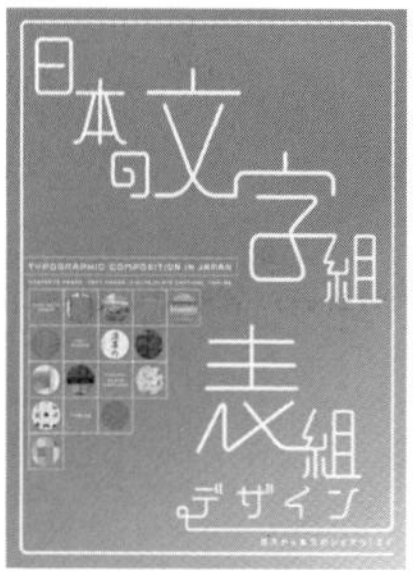

PAPER IN DESIGN
ペーパー イン デザイン

Pages: 192 (Full Color) + Special reference material (paper samples) ¥16,000+Tax

DM、カタログをはじめ書籍の装丁、商品パッケージなど、紙素材を利用し個性的な効果を上げている数多くの作品をアイテムにこだわらず紹介。掲載作品で使われている紙見本も添付、紙のテクスチャーを実際に確かめることができる仕様です。

A special collection of graphic applications that exploit the role paper plays in design. This collection presents a wide range of applications—DM, catalogs, books, and product packaging, etc.—in which paper is used to achieve unique visual statements. Actual paper samples accompany each work to demonstrate their texture and tactile qualities.

PICTOGRAM AND ICON GRAPHICS
ピクトグラム & アイコン グラフィックス

Pages: 200 (160 in Color) ¥13,000+Tax

ミュージアムや空港の施設案内表示から雑誌やWEBサイトのアイコンまで、業種別に分類し、実用例とともに紹介しています。ピクトグラムの意味や使用用途などもあわせて紹介した、他に類をみないまさに永久保存版の１冊です。

The world's most outstanding pictograms and applications. From pictographs seen in museums, airports and other facility signage to icons used in magazines and on the web, the examples are shown isolated and in application with captions identifying their meanings and uses. Categorized by industry for easy reference, no other book of its kind is as comprehensive—it is indeed a permanent archives in one volume!

MAIL ORDER GRAPHICS: Catalog + Web
通販カタログ+WEB グラフィックス

Pages: 304 (Full Color) ¥15,000+Tax

世界各国の通販カタログと通販Webサイトの中からデザイン、機能性に優れた作品を厳選。カタログとWebサイトの両方を駆使し、大きな反響を得ている数々の通販デザインを紹介しています。デザイナーからの声も載せた貴重な一冊です。

Mail-order design that moves consumers and sells products! This collection presents functionally and visually outstanding examples of catalog and website design, which working in tandem have created sensations in the world of mail order. With commentary by the designers, this volume forms a valuable resource of catalog design—both in-print and on-line.

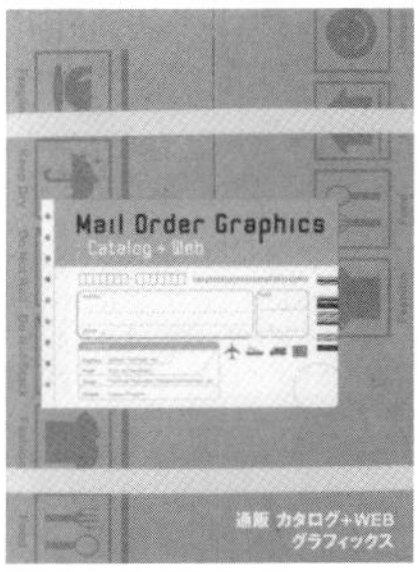

BUSINESS PUBLICATION STYLE
PR誌企画&デザイン 年間ケーススタディ

Pages: 224 (Full Color) ¥15,000+Tax

PR誌の年間企画スケジュールとビジュアル展開を１年分まとめて紹介します。特集はどういう内容で構成しているのか？エッセイの内容と執筆人は？など、創刊・リニューアル時の企画段階から役立つ待望の１冊です。

Year-long case studies of 40 critically selected PR magazines.What should the content of the feature stories composed ? What should the subject of the essays be and who should write them? This eagerly awaited collection promises to assist in the planning stages for the inauguration or renewal of business periodicals.

NEW COMPANY BROCHURE DESIGN 2
ニュー カンパニー ブローシャー デザイン 2

Pages: 272 (Full Color) ¥15,000+Tax

デザインの優れた案内カタログ約150点とWEB約50点を厳選。WEBサイトはカタログと連動した作品を中心に紹介しています。また各作品の企画・構成内容がわかるように制作コンセプト・コンテンツのキャッチコピーを具体的に掲載しています。

A selection of over 150 superbly designed brochures and 50 corresponding websites. All works are accompanied by descriptions of their design objectives and catch copy, to provide added insight into their planning and compositional structures.

SMALL PAMPHLET GRAPHICS
スモール パンフレット グラフィックス

Pages: 224 (Full Color) ¥14,000+Tax

街や店頭で見かける様々な企業、ショップのパンフレットを衣・食・住・遊の業種別に紹介します。気軽に持ち帰ることができる数多くの小型パンフレットの中からデザイン性に優れた作品約300点を厳選しました。

A collection introducing a wide variety of company and shop pamphlets found in stores and around town, grouped under the categories "food, clothes, shelter, and entertainment." 300 small-scale pamphlets selected for their outstanding design qualities from the great many pieces available to customers for the taking.

ONE & TWO COLOR GRAPHICS IN JAPAN
日本の1&2色 グラフィックス

Pages: 224 (Full Color) ¥15,000+Tax

2色までの刷色で効果的にデザインされた日本のグラフィック作品を、使用された刷色の色見本とDICナンバーを紹介。グラデーションが効果的な作品やダブルトーンの作品には、色のかけ合わせと濃度変化がわかるカラー・チャートを併載しています。

A collection of Japanese graphics that are effectively reproduced using only one or two ink colors. Posters, flyers, direct mailers, packaging and more, that have no less impact than their four-color competition. Each work is presented together with color swatches and the DIC numbers of their ink colors used.

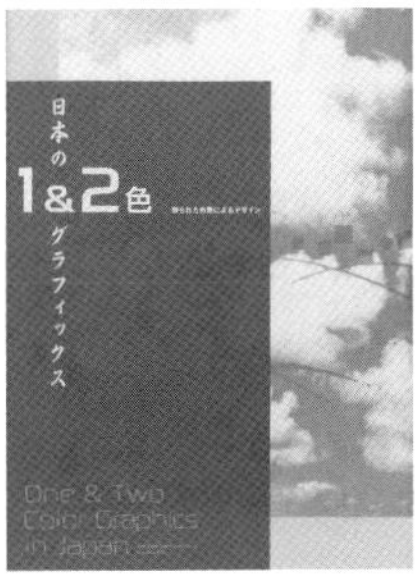

NEW SHOP IMAGE GRAPHICS
ニュー ショップ イメージ グラフィックス

Page: 224 (Full Color) ¥14,000+Tax

大好評！ショップの空間演出&グラフィック・デザインの特集、第2弾！日々新しくオープンする、雑貨店、飲食店、ブティックなどの様々なショップ。オリジナリティ溢れる魅力的な最新のショップを衣・食・住に分類して紹介します。

The unique graphics and dramatic architectural interiors of the most talked about new stores! This sequel to our popular collection on shop interiors and their supporting graphics, presents the most original and attractive recently opened variety stores, restaurants, and boutiques in aclassification that covers the three essential areas of living: food,clothes, and shelter.

ENVIRONMENT/WELFARE-RELATED GRAPHICS
環境・福祉 グラフィックス

Pages: 240 (Full Color) ¥15,000+Tax

環境保全への配慮が世界的な常識となりつつある今日、企業も積極的に環境・福祉など社会的テーマを中心にした広告キャンペーンを展開しています。国内外の優れた環境・福祉広告を紹介した本書は今後の広告を考えるために必携の1冊となるでしょう。

Environmental conservation is now a worldwide concern, and corporate advertising campaigns based on environmental and social themes are on the rise. This collection of noteworthy local and international environment/welfare-related publicity is an essential reference for anyone involved in the planning and development of future advertising.

THE PIE COLLECTION

NEW LOGO WORLD
ニュー ロゴ ワールド

Page: 416 (Full Color) ¥15,000+Tax

世界中から集めた最新ロゴマーク約3000点を収録。幅広いジャンル、世界40カ国以上のクリエイターを網羅した充実の一冊です。CIとして、商品やイベントのロゴとして、その「顔」となる個性的で洗練されたデザインの秀作を紹介します。

The third and most fantastic volume in our logo mark series features over 3000 of the world's newest logomarks. These top works, representing a comprehensive range of designers from more than 40 countries, act as the uniquely refined "face" in corporate identity, as well as product and event branding.

365 DAYS OF NEWSPAPER INSERTS 2
365日の折込チラシ大百科 2

Page: 256 (Full Color) ¥14,000+Tax

札幌から福岡まで国内の主要都市13カ所、365日を通して収集した折込チラシを業種別に約1000点掲載。年々グレードアップするチラシデザインのテクニックを余すところなく発揮した作品が満載の1冊です。

The sequel to our popular leaflet collection! 1000 superb newspaper inserts collected in 13 major Japanese cities oduring the course of one year, categorized by industry. This volume is packed with leaflets that give full play to ever-improving design techniques.

SMALL JAPANESE STYLE GRAPHICS
スモールジャパン スタイル グラフィックス

Page: 224 (Full Color) ¥15,000+Tax

日本伝統の文様・イラスト・色彩等、和のテイストが随所にちりばめられたグラフィック作品を1冊にまとめました。古き良き日本の美意識を取り入れ、現代のクリエイターが仕上げた作品は新しい和の感覚を呼びさまします。

Traditional Japanese motifs, illustrations, colors—collection of graphicworks studded with the essence of "wa" (Japanese-ness) on every page. See how contemporary Japanese designers incorporate time-honored Japanese aesthetics in finished works that redefine the sensibility known as "Japanese style."

EVERYDAY DIAGRAM GRAPHICS
エブリデイ ダイアグラム グラフィックス

Page: 224 (Full Color) ¥14,000+Tax

本書はわかりやすいということにポイントを置き、私たちの身の回りや街で見かける身近なダイアグラムを特集しました。マップ・フロアガイド・チャート・グラフ・仕様説明など、わかりやすいだけでなく、見ていて楽しいものを紹介しています。

This collection features diagrams of the sort we constantly meet in our daily lives, selected with their ready 'digestibility' in mind. The maps, charts, graphs, floor guides and specifications introduced here are not just easy to understand, they' re fun to look at, too.

NEW CALENDAR GRAPHICS
ニュー カレンダー グラフィックス

Pages: 224 (Full Color) ¥13,000+Tax

国内外のクリエイターから集めた個性豊かなカレンダー約200点を、企業プロモーション用、市販用と目的別に収録した、世界の最新カレンダーを特集!! カレンダーの制作現場に、欠かすことの出来ない実用性の高い一冊です。

Over 200 of the newest and most original calendars from designers around the world! Categorized by objective, this collection includes calendars for the retail market as well as those designed as corporate publicity pieces.

カタログ・新刊のご案内について

総合カタログ、新刊案内をご希望の方は、はさみ込みのアンケートはがきをご返送いただくか、90円切手同封の上、ピエ・ブックス宛お申し込みください。

CATALOGS and INFORMATION ON NEW PUBLICATIONS

If you would like to receive a free copy of our general catalog or details of our new publications, please fill out the enclosed postcard and return it to us by mail or fax.

CATALOGUES ET INFORMATIONS SUR LES NOUVELLES PUBLICATIONS

Si vous désirez recevoir un exemplaire qratuit de notre catalogue généralou des détails sur nos nouvelles publication. veuillez compléter la carte réponse incluse et nous la retourner par courrierou par fax.

CATALOGE und INFORMATIONEN ÜBER NEUE TITLE

Wenn Sie unseren Gesamtkatalog oder Detailinformationen über unsere neuen Titel wünschen.fullen Sie bitte die beigefügte Postkarte aus und schicken Sie sie uns per Post oder Fax.

ピエ・ブックス

〒170-0005 東京都豊島区南大塚2-32-4
TEL: 03-5395-4811 FAX: 03-5395-4812
www.piebooks.com

PIE BOOKS

2-32-4 Minami-Otsuka Toshima-ku Tokyo 170-0005 JAPAN
TEL：+81-3-5395-4811 FAX：+81-3-5395-4812
www.piebooks.com